Forensic Ecogenomics

Forensic Ecogenomics

The Application of Microbial Ecology Analyses in Forensic Contexts

Edited by

T. KOMANG RALEBITSO-SENIOR

School of Science and Engineering, Teesside University, Tees Valley, United Kingdom

ELSEVIER

ACADEMIC PRESS

An imprint of Elsevier

Academic Press is an imprint of Elsevier
125 London Wall, London EC2Y 5AS, United Kingdom
525 B Street, Suite 1800, San Diego, CA 92101-4495, United States
50 Hampshire Street, 5th Floor, Cambridge, MA 02139, United States
The Boulevard, Langford Lane, Kidlington, Oxford OX5 1GB, United Kingdom

Library of Congress Cataloging-in-Publication Data
A catalog record for this book is available from the Library of Congress

British Library Cataloguing-in-Publication Data
A catalogue record for this book is available from the British Library

ISBN: 978-0-12-809360-3

For information on all Academic Press publications visit our website at https://www.elsevier.com/books-and-journals

Publisher: Sara Tenney
Acquisition Editor: Elizabeth Brown
Editorial Project Manager: Joslyn Chaiprasert-Paguio & Kathy Padilla
Production Project Manager: Priya Kumaraguruparan
Cover Designer: Mark Rogers

Typeset by TNQ Books and Journals

To my three Senior men

CONTENTS

LIST OF CONTRIBUTORS

Chawki Bisker
Teesside University, Tees Valley, United Kingdom

Jifeng Cai
Central South University, Changsha, PR China

Lorna Dawson
The James Hutton Institute, Aberdeen, United Kingdom

Sheree J. Finley
Alabama State University, Montgomery, AL, United States

Juanjuan Guo
Central South University, Changsha, PR China

Yadong Guo
Central South University, Changsha, PR China

Gulnaz T. Javan
Alabama State University, Montgomery, AL, United States

Ayodeji O. Olakanye
Teesside University, Tees Valley, United Kingdom

Sait Özsoy
University of Health Sciences, Ankara, Turkey

Michael K.P. Pyle
London, United Kingdom

Frederike C.A. Quaak
Netherlands Forensic Institute, The Hague, The Netherlands

T. Komang Ralebitso-Senior
Teesside University, Tees Valley, United Kingdom

Amy E. Rattenbury
Wrexham Glyndŵr University, Wrexham, United Kingdom

Lagabaiyila Zha
Central South University, Changsha, PR China

PREFACE

According to the *Oxford English Dictionary* (https://en.oxforddictionaries.com/), the following terms are defined: cross-disciplinary—"relating to or representing more than one branch of knowledge; interdisciplinary"; multidisciplinary—"combining or involving several academic disciplines or professional specializations in an approach to a topic or problem"; and transdisciplinary—"relating to more than one branch of knowledge; interdisciplinary." While not a volume on semantics, the definition of terms, their intended meanings, and envisaged applications have become increasingly important within the forensic sciences. The term "forensic ecogenomics" was developed in 2014 in response to a peer-review comment, which stipulated that "microbial forensics" had a specific definition and intended context/application. In its widest sense, the interdisciplinary science that is forensic ecogenomics was defined in the literature as "the application of molecular microbial ecology techniques at the interface of (environmental) forensics, microbiology and archaeology." Specifically, it is expansive toward macrobial community dynamics analyses in different environments for comprehensive all-inclusive forensic diagnostics. Therefore it encapsulates application of the full range of culture-dependent and molecular microbial/macrobial ecology techniques within forensic sciences and contexts. It is interchangeable with: (1) "microbioforensics" where molecular analyses of "microbiological (spores, pollen, algae) and macrobiological (skeletal remains) materials" provide links between samples from a crime scene and a suspect or victim; (2) "forensic microbiology" where the microbiomes of living and deceased human beings, the surrounding ecosystems (soil, water, sediment), and plants/insects in the vicinity of a crime scene are characterized as part of intelligence gathering or to estimate the postmortem/postmortem submersion/time-since-burial intervals; and (3) "microbial forensics" where microbial strains and/or communities that have been used in crimes are traced and identified.

Overall, forensic ecogenomics has recognized potential in the field of forensic science where its attendant techniques should be applied as part of a new crime scene investigative toolkit. As a result, its utility is linked inherently with other established and novel forensic subdisciplines including bio-/geotaphonomy, environmental forensics, forensic botany, forensic chemistry, forensic entomology, forensic geoscience, and geoforensics. Although most studies to date have focused on bacterial communities, which is a long-standing dilemma within microbial ecology from where forensic ecogenomic techniques have been adopted, it is apparent that "mycoforensics" is encapsulated within forensic ecogenomics. Also, and despite the high volume of literature on cadaver (proxy)- and decomposition-based studies, forensic ecogenomics has other contextual applications, including, but not limited to, antemortem "microbial fingerprinting," tracing/checking counterfeit micro-based products, and identifying sources of deliberate environmental degradation, with relevant microbial ecology techniques such as stable isotope probing, fluorescent in situ hybridization, and genechips still to be explored.

In summary, this book aims to: highlight the current trends and achievements within forensic ecogenomics; identify and propose new areas for future exploration; and reflect on the ethical (and legislative) frameworks that guide this exciting cross-, multi-, and transdisciplinary area. It is envisaged that every reader will recognize the explicit and implicit diversities of the discipline, which highlight its inherent tremendous opportunities for all researchers and practitioners to engage and advance the requisite knowledge development towards validated application in crime scenes and ultimately court proceedings.

T. Komang Ralebitso-Senior BA BSc(Hons) PhD

ACKNOWLEDGMENTS

This is with grateful acknowledgment to:

Elsevier for another opportunity following closely behind the *Biochar Application: Essential Soil Microbial Ecology* book, Joslyn Chaiprasert-Paguio for her friendly and patient professionalism, and Liz Brown for her support in the "background";

The reviewers who endorsed my book proposal and at times identified oversights, the authors of chapters for helping to translate my concept into an actual book, and the researchers who could not contribute to the manuscript for various reasons but still shared some of their perspectives with me;

My research students who contributed to realizing this ambition through their thoughts, scientific inquisitiveness, and dedicated work. They include Aristeidis Aristeidou, Baz Armstrong, Ronja Bergmann, Susan Bowes, Sophie Browne, Monica Chimutsa, Victoria Clarke, Henny Folorunso, Patrick Gilhooley, Chloe Jones, Tom Lennon, Ryan Martin, Shaun Prior, Lyndsey Smith, and Anthony Stead;

My colleagues for their listening and supportive ears;

My Family by Birth and Love for being my champions always but especially in moments of self-doubt; and

My First Family—Eric, Kamy, and Karabo—for making me complete, believing in me, and being my constant and loving strength.

CHAPTER 1

General Introduction: Method Applications at the Interface of Microbial Ecology and Forensic Investigation

T. Komang Ralebitso-Senior, Ayodeji O. Olakanye
Teesside University, Tees Valley, United Kingdom

THE CONTEXT AND RATIONALE

Microbial ecology, or "microbiome science and technology," has a newfound role in forensic and crime scene science. Thus an inherently multidisciplinary topic where soil scientists, soil ecologists, microbiologists, molecular microbial ecologists (microbiome scientists), computer scientists, and environmental engineers have exchanged knowledge during the past few decades has a real opportunity to initiate a second molecular revolution in forensic analyses. This is evidenced by the emergence and use of several terms and disciplines that have explicit and/or inferred meanings. The applications of these novel disciplines can be specific, precise, or interchangeable, sometimes depending on who is using them and the context. It is essential therefore to provide the background and provenance for each of these terms and disciplines by reflecting on their origins as understood from published literature, what their original intended meanings were, and their uniqueness and/or overlaps. The discussion is presented within the context of the other established or well-recognized forensic subdisciplines. Also since most of the subsequent deliberations are underpinned by "forensic taphonomy" (e.g., Stokes et al., 2009), the discipline is discussed in a dedicated section herein and then in Chapters 2 and 3.

According to Coyle (2004), "forensic botany" "*is a marriage of many disciplines ...* [that includes] *plant anatomy, plant growth and behavior, plant reproductive cycles and population dynamics, and plant classification schemes (morphological and genetic) for species identification.*" Bock and Norris (1997) included plant ecology in this list within their historical overview that also reflected the application of the discipline in real criminal investigations. This particular reference justifies therefore the study of plant–microbe interactions within forensic contexts, which is yet to be explored. Parallel to molecular analyses in other forensic subdisciplines, Ferri et al. (2009) targeted two DNA regions, psbA-trnH and trnL-trnF, of the chloroplast to create a species identification system, which subsequently differentiated plants at family, genus, and species levels. Similarly, Ward et al. (2005)

Forensic Ecogenomics
ISBN 978-0-12-809360-3
http://dx.doi.org/10.1016/B978-0-12-809360-3.00001-1

developed polymerase chain reaction assays for the mitochondrial genome and tested these successfully using 25 different species of grass. Uitdehaag et al. (2016) used trace soil samples for parallel terminal restriction fragment length polymorphism (T-RFLP) bacterial community profiling and palynology in a rape case.

As reflected by many researchers (Chen et al., 2009; Dekeisshieter et al., 2009; Donaldson and Lamont, 2013; Forbes, 2008; Forbes and Perrault, 2014; Kasper et al., 2012; Statheropoulos et al., 2005, 2007; Vass et al., 2004; Vass et al., 2008; Vass, 2012), "forensic chemistry," the use of chemical science in forensic contexts, is probably one of the more established forensic subdisciplines for postmortem interval (PMI) estimation. It is underpinned typically by the use of spectroscopy, spectrometry, chromatography, magnetic resonance, and mass spectroscopy, among other techniques, to measure the concentrations of a range of decompositional and metabolic products including, but not limited to, volatile organic compounds, fatty acids, lipids, and proteins (see also Chapter 3, Table 3.1).

The biochemical products that are characteristic of specific decomposition stages are also responsible for attracting certain insect species to the decomposing carrion (Arnaldos et al., 2005; Carvalho et al., 2000; Dillon, 1995; LeBlanc and Logan, 2010; Ma et al., 2012; Paczkowski et al., 2012; Tomberlin and Benbow, 2015). This establishes a direct link to "forensic entomology" where the successional entomological clades that colonize the carrion/cadaver and contribute to its rate of decomposition have been used widely in aiding PMI calculations, including in real crime scenarios (see also Chapters 4 and 8). The colonization trends are determined further by environmental conditions and associated materials such as temperature, sunlight, and clothing (Denier, 1940; Hobischak et al., 2006; Sharanowski et al., 2008). New areas of forensic entomology research will most likely include microbe–insect interactions (e.g., Schmidtmann and Martin, 1992; Tomberlin et al., 2012) both in aboveground and subsurface analyses.

A state-of-the-art perspective on the use of fungi in criminal investigations in the subdiscipline of "forensic mycology" (or mycoforensics) was presented in a critical review by Hawksworth and Wiltshire (2011) to reflect the amount of research and case work that was developed prior to the year of publication. The authors then presented a renewed perspective in 2015 with additional discourse on the importance of also analyzing the gut contents of cadavers to aid PMI estimations. The importance of the human mycobiome has been deliberated within the context of human health and disease (Ghannoum, 2016), and by highlighting how studies of this important clade lag significantly behind those on bacteria. Therefore efforts are being made in forensic mycology with studies of specific fungal species on the decomposing cadaver (Sidrim et al., 2010), functional groups during specific decomposition stages (e.g., ammonia and postputrefaction fungi; Carter and Tibbett, 2003; Tibbett and Carter, 2003), and communities in the surrounding decompositional ecosystem/gravesoil (Chimutsa et al., 2015; Tranchida et al., 2014) (see also Chapter 7). As for any emergent science, justified debates on the applicability and limitations of mycoforensics (e.g., Ishii et al., 2007; Menezes et al., 2008; Bellini et al., 2016) are essential to inform robust experimental questions and designs to then establish the discipline as a reliable forensic tool.

A paraphrased definition of "forensic geoscience" by Ruffell and McKinley (2005) is the scientific study of all Earth surface materials for application to legal investigation. The authors provided different methods or categories of techniques that are applied in forensic geoscience on the basis of scale. These included, but were not limited to, resistivity, electromagnetics, ground-penetrating radar (e.g., Schultz, and Martin, 2012), remote sensing and geographic information systems at the large scale, electron microscopy, and soil color at the microscopic level (e.g., Petraco et al., 2008). Although not proposed by the authors, the use of some of these techniques may be useful in validating forensic ecogenomic analyses of soils impacted by cadaver decomposition as in the case of clandestine burial and grave location. In a subsequent review, Ruffell (2010) expanded the discourse on the importance of, and requirement for, appropriate use of terminology in forensic science and proposed "microbioforensics" for "*the study of microbiological (spores, pollen, algae) and macrobiological (skeletal remains) materials.*" Ruffell (2010) also defined "environmental chemistry" as the use of any of the methods in forensic pedology, forensic geology, forensic geoscience, geoforensics and soil forensics "*as well as chemistry, biology, physics and the environmental sciences in the assessment of environmental impact.*" Therefore the effects of a decomposing material (cadaver/proxy) on the surrounding ecosystem can be extrapolated as a form of "environmental impact," as explored in Chapter 9.

Potentially synonymous and probably used interchangeably with "microbioforensics" is "microbial forensics." This subdiscipline was first defined by Budowle (2004) as "*a scientific discipline dedicated to analysing evidence from a bioterrorism act, biocrime, or inadvertent microorganism/toxin release for attribution purposes.*" The term was used subsequently in a self-titled book (Budowle et al., 2005) as "*the science that will help bring to justice criminals and terrorists who use biological material to cause harm. ... it* [the book] *covers a variety of areas from forensic science, to microbiology, to epidemiology, to bioinformatics, and to legal issues.*" The term and discipline have since been applied by multiple researchers largely within the biocrime and bioterrorism contexts, although Petrisor et al. (2006) provided a scientific discipline-based description as "*the focusing of microbiology, virology, biochemistry and molecular biology for use in environmental forensic investigations.*"

Coined in 2014 in response to a peer-review comment, which stipulated that "microbial forensics" had a specific definition and intended context/application, the term "forensic ecogenomics" was defined subsequently in the literature as "*the application of molecular microbial ecology techniques at the interface of (environmental) forensics, microbiology and archaeology*" to "*expand on initial applications of microbiological analyses of soil*" (Ralebitso-Senior et al., 2016). Furthermore, we proposed that "forensic ecogenomics" encompassed "microbial forensics" and "environmental forensics" (Chimutsa et al., 2015). Overall, forensic ecogenomics is the study of micro-/macrobial community dynamics in

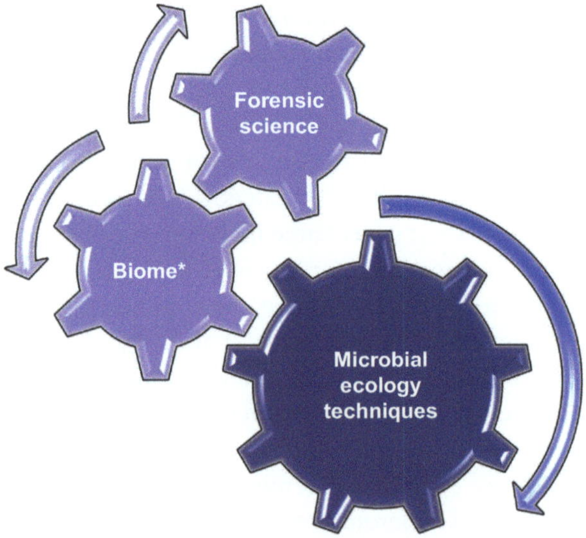

Figure 1.1 An illustrative definition of forensic ecogenomics. *Biome encapsulates the micro- and macrobiota of the human body or mammalian taphonomic proxy, pre- and postmortem, and the surrounding ecosystem, e.g., cadaver decomposition island.

different environments for forensic diagnostics and is probably interchangeable with "forensic microbiology" as used, for example, by Singh and Crippen (2015) and Carter et al. (2017). Therefore its intended applications and contexts, as depicted in Fig. 1.1, include characterization of:

1. The human microbiome premortem for human-related forensic analysis such as "microbial fingerprinting" in crime scenes (e.g., Benschop et al., 2012) and postmortem;
2. The "thanatomicrobiome," which was coined by Dr. J. Gulnaz to mean "*a diverse assortment of microorganisms located in internal organs (brain, heart, liver, and spleen) and blood samples collected after a human dies*" (see also Chapter 6) or, more generally, "*the microorganisms of the human host after death*" (Can et al., 2014); and "*the study of the microbes colonizing the internal organs and orifices after death*" (Javan et al., 2016);
3. Above- and belowground profiling of the "necrobiome," which was defined by Benbow et al. (2013) as "*the community of species (e.g., prokaryotic and eukaryotic) associated with decomposing remains of heterotrophic biomass, including animal carrion and human corpses*";
4. "Epinecrotic" microorganisms, which were defined by Pechal et al. (2013) as "*microbial communities associated with external surfaces of carrion*" and reinterpreted by Javan et al. (2016) as the "*microbial communities residing in and/or moving on the surface of decomposing remains*";

5. Microbial communities of decomposition-impacted ecosystems including soil and water; and
6. The epinecrobiome and thanatomicrobiome profiling parallel to ecosystem necrobiome analyses following subsurface burials, which are comparisons that are yet to be explored robustly.

In general, there are many contexts where forensic ecogenomics is potentially applicable, as recognized by Parkinson et al. (2009) and Lerner et al. (2006), for example, or has already been applied, even if this particular term/designation was not used. These forensic contexts were explored comprehensively (Ralebitso-Senior et al., 2016) with supporting considerations for the use of microbial ecology techniques in terrestrial, aquatic, and human ecosystems. A further and updated critique is provided in Chapter 9, particularly with deliberations on method development and/or validation. As evidenced in the literature, research interest in applying forensic ecogenomic methods has increased albeit with a particular focus on determinations of PMI and postburial interval (PBI) or time since burial (TSB) interval aboveground and, to a lesser extent, postmortem submersion interval (PMSI) estimations and belowground scenarios (Table 1.1). Finally, the potential of forensic ecogenomics/microbiology in research, case studies, and real crime scenes will be realized fully when considered and applied with due cognizance of the related forensic subdisciplines (forensic botany, forensic chemistry, forensic mycology, bio-/geotaphonomy, forensic entomology) individually and in combinations, as relevant.

Although most of this book focuses on decomposition-related forensic ecogenomics, to reflect the current trend the other equally important contexts are considered further in Chapter 9. Briefly, these include profiling of the "microbial fingerprint" and its potential use in scenes of crime parallel to conventional fingerprinting, overlaps with environmental forensics, additional techniques that can expand the current forensic ecogenomic toolkit, and novel contexts where forensic ecogenomics is not yet applied. For example, can microbial community characterization be used in forensic investigations to link: objects to the person who touched them (Aaspõllu et al., 2011; Fierer et al., 2010; Nishi et al., 2015); shoes to their users (Goga, 2012); and soils from similar geographical regions (Habtom et al., 2017)?

FORENSIC TAPHONOMY

Taphonomy originates from the Greek words *taphos* and *nomos*, which mean burial and a system of law. It was defined by Haglund and Sorg (1997) as the study of the various processes associated with cadaver decomposition in relation to PMI, causes and mode of death, location of clandestine graves, and identification of the dead. These researchers added that forensic taphonomy is an aspect of forensic anthropology that is used to recreate events that occurred during and after death by gathering and analyzing

Table 1.1 A temporal overview (2006–17) of the application of bio/physicochemical, culture-based, and molecular microbial ecology analyses in body/mammalian analog decomposition studies in a forensic context

Microbial ecology technique	Study location	Study context	Animal model	Biochemical or physicochemical analysis	Key study findings	References
N/A	Underground	Microbial activity	Sheep (*Ovis aries*)	Temperature, CO_2, soil pH, C_{mis}, C, and N content	Temperature had an effect on rate of tissue mass loss; correlation between CO_2 evolution and tissue mass loss	Carter and Tibbett (2006)
T-RFLP and PLFA	In situ aboveground	Soil bacteria and fungi	Human cadaver	Not determined	Successional changes in the bacterial and fungal community	Parkison et al. (2009)
N/A	Surface microcosm	Soil chemistry, microbial activity	Pig (*Sus scrofa domesticus*)	Tissue mass loss, CO_2, soil pH, nitrate, NH_4^+ concentration, phosphate, potassium, electroconductivity	Freezing had no effect on decomposition; changes in microbial activity and soil chemistry due to the presence of skeletal muscle tissue	Stokes et al. (2009)
N/A	Above and belowground	Ninhydrin reactive nitrogen (NRN)	Pig (*Sus scrofa domesticus*)	Not determined	Soil NRN analysis can be used within 2 months for belowground and 97 days for aboveground investigations	van Belle et al. (2009)
Culture based/ qPCR	In situ aboveground	Soil lipolytic and proteolytic bacteria	Pig (*Sus scrofa domesticus*)	Temperature	Increase in lipolytic bacteria during active decomposition; decrease in proteolytic bacteria from fresh to advanced decay	Howard et al. (2010)
LH-PCR	In situ aboveground	Soil bacteria	Human cadaver	Not determined	Recovered amplicons for anaerobic and nitrogen-fixing bacteria	Moreno et al. (2011)

454 Pyrosequencing (NGS)	In situ aboveground	Cadaver bacteria community	Human cadaver	Not determined	Shift from aerobic to anaerobic bacteria between the initial and end point of bloat stage	Hyde et al. (2013)
Illumina (NGS)	Surface microcosm	Soil and carcass epinecrotic community	Mouse	Soil pH	Use of bacterial and eukaryote clades as microbial clocks in PMI	Metcalf et al. (2013)
Illumina (NGS)	Surface microcosm	Soil bacteria, archaea, and fungi	Mice (*Mus musculus*)	Soil pH	Changes in *Mus musculus* necrobiome during active and advanced decay; shifts differed between sterile and nonsterile soils	Lauber et al. (2014)
454 Pyrosequencing (NGS)	In situ aboveground	Epinecrotic bacterial community	Pig (*Sus scrofa domesticus*)	Microbial metabolic community profiling with Biolog EcoPlates	Bacterial community succession at phylum and family taxonomic levels suggested that the shifts could be used to estimate and define unique minimum decomposition intervals	Pechal et al. (2014)
DNA-/RNA-based DGGE	Subsurface microcosm	Soil bacterial and fungal necrobiome	Pig (*Sus scrofa domesticus*)	Temperature, soil pH	Microbial diversity changed temporally with decomposition	Bergmann et al. (2014); Olakanye et al. (2014); Chimutsa et al. (2015)
			Pig (*Sus scrofa domesticus*)/plant litter (*Agrostis*/*Festuca* spp.)	Temperature, soil pH	Dominance of 16S rRNA gene for *Sus scrofa domesticus* soils; dominance of 18S rRNA gene for the *Agrostis*/*Festuca* spp. soils	Olakanye et al. (2015)

Continued

Table 1.1 A temporal overview (2006–17) of the application of bio/physicochemical, culture-based, and molecular microbial ecology analyses in body/mammalian analog decomposition studies in a forensic context—cont'd

Microbial ecology technique	Study location	Study context	Animal model	Biochemical or physicochemical analysis	Key study findings	References
454 Pyrosequencing (NGS)	In situ aquatic environment	Epinecrotic bacterial community	Pig (*Sus scrofa domesticus*)	pH, dissolve oxygen, temperature, salinity, oxidation-reduction potential	Successional changes in the bacterial communities between summer and winter in a freshwater habitat	Benbow et al. (2015)
Illumina (NGS)	Subsurface microcosms	Soil bacterial and fungal necrobiome	Pig (*Sus scrofa domesticus*)/ plant litter (*Agrostis*/ *Festuca* spp.)	Temperature, soil pH	*Micromonospora*, *Sphingobacterium*, *Pedobacter*, and *Tyroborus* identified as microbial clock and season indicators; *Sphingobacterium* differentiated between pig and plant litter soil necrobiomes	Olakanye and Ralebitso-Senior (2017)
Illumina (NGS)	In situ	Soil bacterial and fungal necrobiome	Pig (*Sus scrofa domesticus*)/ leaf litter (*Quercus robur*)	Temperature, soil pH	Methylophilaceae and Anaerolineaceae identified as potential microbial clocks for pig and leaf litter, respectively	Olakanye et al. (2017)
FAME	In situ aboveground	Soil microbial community	Pig (*Sus scrofa domesticus*)	Soil pH, soil moisture	Shift in FAME profiles aligned with the start of the active decay up to the dry period	Breton et al. (2016)
Illumina (NGS)	In situ aboveground	Soil microbial community	Pig (*Sus scrofa domesticus*)	Not determined	Seasonal changes associated with postmortem microbial communities; soil microbes are part of the postmortem microbial community	Carter et al. (2015)

Culture-based analysis	In situ aboveground	Culturable aerobic bacteria	Pig (*Sus scrofa domesticus*)	Soil temperature, soil pH, and oxidation-reduction potentials	Different locations on the taphonomic proxy tended to host different bacteria; the culturable aerobic bacterial communities changed over time	Chun et al. (2015)
N/A	In situ aboveground	Soil biochemical analysis	Pig (*Sus scrofa domesticus*)	Soil pH, moisture content, TC, TN, PO_4, lipid-phosphorus in soil	Increase in soil pH and concentration of TN, PO_4 and lipid-phosphorus	Benninger et al. (2008)
Illumina (NGS)	In situ aboveground	Soil bacterial necrobiome	Human cadaver	Soil pH, TOC, TN, PO_4, NO_3, NH_3	Increases in TOC, PO_4 and NH_3; changes in functional community composition	Cobaugh et al. (2015)
DNA-based	In situ aboveground	Soil biochemical analysis and DNA extract	N/A	Moisture content, pH, TOC, TC, TN, lipid-phosphorus in soil	Increases in TN, lipid-P, and water pH when compared to the control site	Damann et al. (2012)
454 Pyrosequencing (NGS)	In situ aboveground	Necrobiome	Human cadaver	Temperature	Bacteria members, *Ignatzschineria*, and *Wohlfahrtiimonas* spp., associated with flies recorded at bloat stage; actinobacter recorded after dehydration and skeletonization	Hyde et al. (2015)
Illumina (NGS)	Above and belowground	Soil bacteria	Human cadaver	Not determined	Decreases in diversity, taxa richness, and evenness in surface decomposition; increased taxa richness but decreased evenness in subsurface decomposition; proteobacteria dominant in both above- and belowground contexts	Finley et al. (2016)

Continued

Table 1.1 A temporal overview (2006–17) of the application of bio/physicochemical, culture-based, and molecular microbial ecology analyses in body/mammalian analog decomposition studies in a forensic context—cont'd

Microbial ecology technique	Study location	Study context	Animal model	Biochemical or physicochemical analysis	Key study findings	References
Illumina (NGS)	Sterile cardboard boxes; buccal cavity and rectum	Premortem microbiome; necrobiome	Adult female Sprague–Dawley rat carcasses	Not determined	Bacterial communities from two different body sites became more similar with decomposition; proteobacteria became more predominant temporally; sarcocaphagous insects increased mass loss but had no detectable impact on microbiome profiles	Guo et al. (2016)
Illumina (NGS)	In situ aboveground and microcosm	Soil epinecrotic community	Mouse and mammalian corpse	pH, total nitrogen, and ammonium concentration	Seasonal microbial changes with soil as primary sources of decomposers; soil type had little or no effect on epinecrotic community	Metcalf et al. (2016)
Illumina (NGS)	In situ aboveground	Soil epinecrotic community	Pig (*Sus scrofa domesticus*)	Temperature	Difference between necrobiome communities of the gravesoils and control site; carcass mass had no influence	Weiss et al. (2016)
N/A	In situ belowground	Soil biochemical analysis, microbial biomass, and activity	Pig (*Sus scrofa domesticus*)	TC, TN, pH, moisture content, NH_4^+, amino acids, microbial biomass, and activity	Increases in TC, TN, microbial biomass, activity, amino acid, and NH_4^+ of the gravesoil when compared to the control site	Hopkins et al. (2000)

Colony PCR	In situ aquatic environment	Marine bacterial	Pig (*Sus scrofa domesticus*)	Not determined	Involvement of saprophytic bacteria in marine decomposition; bacteria successional and seasonal differences recorded	Dickson et al. (2011)
N/A	In situ aboveground	Soil biochemical analysis	Human cadaver	DOC, DON, pH, EC, SO_4^{2-}, NH_4^+, NO_3^-, TDN	Increases in EC, DOC, and DON; increase in SO_4^{2-} of gravesoil suggested anaerobic respiration; decrease in pH values of gravesoil; increased nutrient movement of decomposition by-product off-site	Aitkenhead-Peterson et al. (2012)
454 Pyrosequencing (NGS)	In situ aboveground	Soil epinecrotic bacterial community	Pig (*Sus scrofa domesticus*)	Temperature	Changes in bacterial community with increased activity during spring, summer, and winter but decrease in autumn	Pechal et al. (2013)
PCR, PCR-DGGE, and cloning	In situ aboveground	Carcass of necrophagous insect and bacterial community	Pig (*Sus scrofa domesticus*)	Temperature, relative humidity	Shift in necrophagous insect and bacterial communities observed from the mouth and rectum attributed to seasonal effects and carcass depletion	Iancu et al. (2015)
qPCR, cloning, Sanger sequencing	In situ aboveground	Gut bacterial communities	Human cadaver	Not determined	Decrease in relative abundance of *Bacteroides* and *Lactobacillus*, as potential PMI indicator.	Hauther et al. (2015)

DGGE, Denaturing gradient gel electrophoresis; *DOC*, dissolved organic carbon; *DON*, dissolved organic nitrogen; *EC*, electron conductivity; *FAME*, fatty acid methyl ester; *LH-PCR*, length heterogeneity-polymerase chain reaction; *N/A*, not available; *NGS*, next-generation sequencing; *PFLA*, phospholipid fatty acid; *PMI*, postmortem interval; *qPCR*, quantitative polymerase chain reaction; *TC*, total carbon; *TDN*, total dissolved nitrogen; *TN*, total nitrogen; *TOC*, total organic carbon; *T-RFLP*, terminal restriction fragment length polymorphism.

decomposing cadaver data, differentiating between perimortem and postmortem changes in remains, and estimating the PMI.

According to Carter and Tibbett (2008), taphonomy, a branch of paleontology, was established to understand how the ecology of a site is affected by the presence of decomposing remains and in turn how the site ecology affects the decomposing remains. Aspects of these definitions collectively underpin and justify the novel approaches where microbial communities of the cadaver and the soil directly beneath and/or around it (gravesoil) are characterized using a range of what were largely (molecular) microbial ecology techniques. As a consequence, forensic taphonomy, which underpins all other forensic subdisciplines on human remains, also underscores forensic ecogenomics. Therefore bio- and geotaphonomy are discussed comprehensively in Chapters 2 and 3, with each chapter illustrating its applicability and limitations within specific example contexts. A degree of overlap is therefore inevitable.

CADAVER AND CADAVER DECOMPOSITION

The Decomposition Process

According to Damann and Carter (2013), death is the irreversible cessation of the brain and the circulatory and respiratory systems of the body. It is a dynamic process that can occur in seconds or be prolonged (Forbes and Carter, 2015). A cadaver is a dead human body consisting of lipids and proteins, a high water content, microorganisms, and a low carbon-to-nitrogen ratio (Carter and Tibbett, 2008). After death, a cadaver undergoes a series of complex biochemical and pathological breakdown processes ranging from depletion of tissue oxygen by internal microorganisms to autolysis of cells and tissues, and invasion by external microorganisms and scavengers (Carter and Tibbett, 2008; van Belle et al., 2009; Zhou and Byard, 2011). As reported by Janaway (1996), dropping of the lower mandible and loss of eyelid tension are two of the immediate effects that denote death.

Subsequent to this, cadaver decomposition, a destructive process, begins approximately after 4 min. This process manifests more microscopically than macroscopically and progresses through various stages of autolysis, putrefaction, and decay (Vass et al., 2002; Carter and Tibbett, 2008; Forbes and Carter, 2015). Also decomposition is a complex process mediated by enzymatic digestion and microbial activities coupled with pertinent environmental conditions, which eventually lead to nutrient migration from the cadaver to the surrounding ecosystem (Vass et al., 2002).

Determinants of the Decomposition Rate

Several factors such as temperature, moisture/water activity, trauma, body mass, and associated material including clothing are recognized as key determinants of cadaver decomposition rate. Typically, their individual and collective influences differ between aboveground and underground situations (Mann et al., 1990; Carter and Tibbett, 2008; Zhou and Byard, 2011) with cadaver decomposition rate often slower in underground environments. This, however, contrasts observations where increases in subsurface temperatures, up to 38°C, for example, can lead to higher decomposition rates (Carter and Tibbett, 2006). In general, increases in body temperature result in increased biological activity (Carter and Tibbett, 2008) such as that of putrefactive or anaerobic catabolic bacteria between 21 and 38°C (Zhou and Byard, 2011). In contrast, the activities of this microbial community were reduced or inhibited at temperatures below 4°C (Zhou and Byard, 2011), while both enzymatic and microbial activity were observed to stop at −5°C belowground (Carter and Tibbett, 2006). According to Vass et al. (2002), cadaver decomposition is affected more significantly by temperature than moisture. In contrast, Carter et al. (2010) stated that the relationship between decomposition and temperature can be modified by soil moisture, while soil microorganisms play an important role in cadaver decomposition.

The high (60–80% w/w; Carter et al., 2010) water content of a cadaver affects microbial activity where rapid desiccation can inhibit decomposition and lead to mummification (Carter and Tibbett, 2008), while extreme wet conditions promote water logging and adipocere formation. Both situations slow the decomposition rate or arrest the decomposition process altogether (Campobasso et al., 2001; Carter and Tibbett, 2008; Zhou and Byard, 2011). Therefore the applicability of forensic microbiology/ecogenomics might be considerably limited during such arrested decompositional conditions, although the role of polyextremophiles is yet to be investigated.

Several researchers (Campobasso et al., 2001; Carter and Tibbett, 2008; Mann et al., 1990) have posited that insects and external microorganisms can enter the cadaver through pre- and postmortem cuts and open wounds, colonize and use it as a source of nutrients, and consequently increase the rate of its decomposition. Finally, clothing, or associated materials, in combination with insect activity where maggots avoid sunlight by gathering under clothing, for example (Mann et al., 1990; Campobasso et al., 2001; Zhou and Byard, 2011), can increase the rate of decomposition. All these parameters are discussed in requisite detail within specific contexts in Chapters 2, 3, and 4.

Stages of Cadaver Decomposition

Texts such as *Human Body Decomposition* (Hayman and Oxenham, 2016) and Chapters 2 and 3 of this book chart the specific stages of body decomposition and the attendant methods that are commonly applied. We present here an appropriately succinct discourse on cadaver decomposition stages toward a focus on the role of biological processes. The associated (molecular) microbiological analyses and parallel biochemical metabolic pathways are considered with the as yet unexplored scope also highlighted.

As introduced earlier, cadaver decomposition is a complex phasic process before skeletonization and takes days, months, or years to complete. Within the first few hours of death, the body undergoes changes, which are of particular importance in PMI estimation. These changes are often called the "mortis triad" and they entail *algor mortis*, *livor mortis*, and *rigor mortis*:

1. *Algor mortis*: This is the process of body cooling after death when it loses temperature from the normal average of 37°C until it reaches ambience with the surrounding environment. It is used to estimate time after death but is dependent strongly on the surrounding environmental conditions (Forbes, 2008; Tibbett, 2008).
2. *Livor mortis*: This is also known as lividity and is the settling of blood in capillaries and veins as a result of gravitational pooling (Tibbett, 2008). *Livor mortis* becomes noticeable between 20 min and 10 h with the formation of purple-red skin discoloration, with maximum lividity occurring between 6 and 12 h after death. This has been used effectively by pathologists to estimate death time and establish body repositioning in postmortem analysis.
3. *Rigor mortis*: This stage has been attributed to chemically mediated muscle and joint stiffening due to a decline in cellular ATP and increase in cellular pH (Forbes and Carter, 2015). The conversion of ATP to ADP increases lactic acid production and results in high cellular pH (Janaway et al., 2009; Bristow et al., 2011). *Rigor mortis* becomes noticeable in 2 to 3 h after death by the stiffening of the facial muscles followed by the entire body within 12 h (Forbes, 2008; Gunn, 2009). After death, the intracellular calcium ion concentration increases due to cell membrane rupture and causes binding of the muscle filaments myosin and actin in the absence of the regulatory proteins tropomyosin and troponin. The result is stiffening of the dead muscles (Gunn, 2009). The reversibility of *rigor mortis* is thought to be initiated by muscle cell cathepsin proteolytic enzymes that initiate filament separation (Gill-King, 1997). As for *algor mortis*, the use of *rigor mortis* for PMI estimation also depends on the surrounding environmental conditions.

In general, cadaver decomposition is controlled by two catabolic processes: autolysis and putrefaction.

Autolysis

Autolysis is described as the enzymatic breakdown of soft tissues within a cadaver (Janaway et al., 2009; Forbes and Carter, 2015). Following death, the heart stops beating and the internal aerobic microorganisms deplete body oxygen. This leads to an increase in blood carbon dioxide and a concomitant decrease in pH and ultimately cell poisoning (Vass et al., 2002; Carter and Tibbett, 2008; Alaeddini et al., 2010), all of which mark the beginning of autolysis. According to Gunn (2009), the rate of cell death differs among tissue types. For example, the brain dies within 3 to 7 min while the skin can still be cultured after 24 h.

During autolysis, cells and organic compounds, such as lipids, proteins, and carbohydrates, are catabolized by internal cellular enzymes principally lipases, proteases, and amylases. Cell rupture then results with the release of nutrient-rich fluids (Vass et al., 2002; van Belle et al., 2009). According to Gill-King (1997), cadaver tissue breakdown occurs in the following sequence: (1) stomach, intestines, blood, heart, and digestive organs; (2) thoracic cavity and lungs; (3) bladder and kidneys; (4) nervous tissues and brain; (5) skeletal muscles; and (6) hair, connective tissues, and integument.

According to Damann and Carter (2013), the intestines, pancreas, and stomach are usually the first soft tissue organs to decompose because of the high concentrations of lytic enzymes, while the prostate and uterus are usually the last. Therefore the sequence described earlier, and these particular organs, can be followed and targeted, respectively, in thanatomicrobiome-based forensic ecogenomics with complementary thanatochemistry-based determinations of PMI. Autolysis becomes visible with the formation of fluid-filled swellings on the skin with subsequent sloughing off the body (Vass et al., 2002; Forbes, 2008). As reported by Forbes (2008), enteric anaerobic bacteria produce hydrogen sulfide, which reacts with deoxygenated blood to blacken the outer blood vessels.

Putrefaction

Putrefaction is soft tissue breakdown into gases, liquids, and small molecules by anaerobic microorganisms. It originates primarily from the gut following the generation of anaerobic conditions in the cadaver as initiated by autolysis (Vass et al., 2002; Bull et al., 2006; Forbes, 2008). The sequential transition from aerobic bacteria, mostly of the phyla Bacteroidetes and Firmicutes, to fermentative anaerobic bacteria, such as *Bacteroides* spp., *Clostridium* spp., *Staphylococcus* spp., *Streptococcus* spp., and Enterobacteriaceae, during putrefaction has been reported by many researchers (Damann and Carter, 2013; Forbes and Carter, 2015; Janaway et al., 2009). Also reported by Hyde et al. (2013), Metcalf et al. (2013), and Pechal et al. (2014) are putrefactive bacteria including *Escherichia* spp., *Lactobacillus* spp., and *Proteus* spp., which can proliferate on the skin due to the presence of catabolic products of carbohydrates, lipids, and proteins (Forbes and Carter, 2015). During the anaerobic state, carbohydrates, lipids, and proteins are catabolized to organic acids, such as butyric, lactic, and propionic, and gases, including ammonia, hydrogen sulfide, sulfur dioxide, and methane.

Some unique features of the putrefactive stage include cadaver swelling, color change, and foul smell (Campobasso et al., 2001; Forbes, 2008; Vass et al., 2002). According to Damann and Carter (2013), an example of the conversion of the amino acid arginine into ornithine by *Enterococcus feacalis* enzymes and the further conversion of ornithine into putrescine by *Escherichia coli* was reported by Wilson in 2008. The decarboxylation of ornithine and lysine into odorous putrescine (Eq. 1.1) and cadaverine (Eq. 1.2) was also reported by Gill-King (1997). Consequently, these two microbial metabolic products are often detected by cadaver-trained dogs.

$$\underset{\text{Ornithine}}{H_2NCH_2CH_2CH_2CH_2COOH} \xrightarrow{\text{ornithine decarboxylase}} \underset{\substack{\text{Putrescine} \\ (1,4\text{-butanediamine})}}{H_2NCH_2CH_2CH_2CH_2NH_2} \tag{1.1}$$

$$\underset{\text{Lysine}}{H_2NCH_2CH_2CH_2CH_2CH(NH_3)COOH} \rightarrow \underset{\substack{\text{Cadaverine} \\ (1,5\text{-pentanediamine})}}{H_2NCH_2CH_2CH_2CH_2CH_2NH_2} \tag{1.2}$$

An important aspect of putrefaction is cadaver color change. According to Gill-King (1997), this is due to two decompositional phenomena: (1) hemoglobin breakdown and subsequent conversion of heme to bile pigments; and (2) formation of sulfide precipitates within tissues and blood vessels.

The first obvious sign of color change is a greenish-purple skin discoloration resulting from the formation of sulfhemoglobin in settled blood. This reaction occurs as sulfur-containing amino acids such as cysteine are catabolized by cysteine desulfydrase to ammonia, hydrogen sulfide and pyruvic acid (Eq. 1.3) (Gill-King, 1997).

$$\underset{\text{Cysteine}}{HSCH_2CH(NH_2)COOH} \xrightarrow{\text{cysteine desulphydrase}} H_2S + NH_3 + \underset{\text{Pyruvic acid}}{CH_3COCOOH} \tag{1.3}$$

The subsequent reaction of hydrogen sulfide with hemoglobin results in the formation of sulfhemoglobin (Clark et al., 1997). Also, as reported by Gill-King (1997), the reaction between phenylpyruvic acid and ferric ion in soil causes the formation of a green precipitate on the decomposing cadaver (Eq. 1.4).

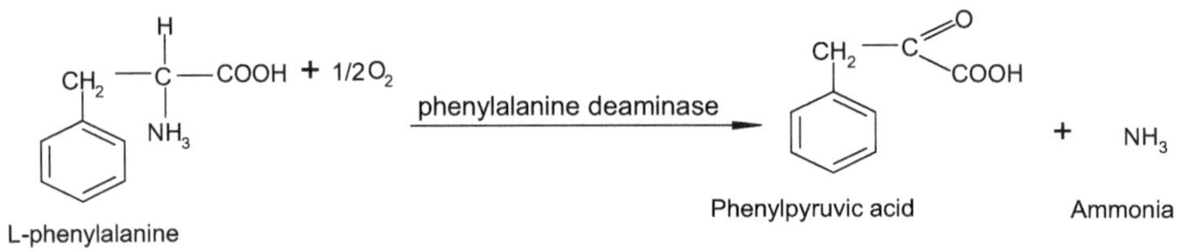

$$\text{Phenylpyruvic acid} + \text{Ferric ion } (Fe^{3+}) \longrightarrow \text{Green complex} \tag{1.4}$$

Sulfate-reducing bacteria of the order Desulfarcales were identified in gravesoils and are known to produce green precipitates that appear early at the right anterior abdominal wall (Damann and Carter, 2013). The breakdown of hemoglobin and other hemoproteins in the liver into different bile pigments also produces color. For example, biliverdin, a green color bile pigment, may be reduced to a bilirubin red-color pigment, which is further reduced to urobilin with a brown color, while reaction of hydrogen sulfide with iron produces a black precipitate of ferrous sulfide on the cadaver (Eq. 1.5) (Gill-King, 1997). Damann and Carter (2013) posited that the first appearance of the black precipitate is observed around the ears and nose.

$$\underset{\text{Hydrogen sulfide}}{H_2S} + Fe \longrightarrow \underset{\substack{\text{Ferrous sulfide} \\ \text{(black precipitate)}}}{FeS} + H_2 \tag{1.5}$$

As a result of high microbial activity during putrefaction, volatile gases and carbon dioxide are trapped within the cadaver, which causes bloating and swelling (Vass et al., 1992). Both propionic acid and butyric acid have been identified during this bloat stage. Also bloating can be so marked that it results in the displacement of grave earth through abdominal cavity gas expansion (Gill-King, 1997). The subsequent loss of gases then results in soil and body well collapse (Gill-King, 1997; Vass et al., 2002), and it is probably at this stage that differentiation between decomposition processes that are driven by cadaver-derived necrobiome, when compared to ecosystem (soil)-derived biota, becomes a challenge. Prior to this, the presence of gases and fluid accumulation lead to skin rupture and the reestablishment of aerobic conditions (Carter and Tibbett, 2008).

Generally, a temperature range of 21–38°C is required for putrefaction to occur, while considerable reductions in the putrefactive process result at temperatures below 10°C and above 40°C (Forbes, 2008). As a consequence, decomposition-related forensic ecogenomic/microbiology studies and analyses are required to determine further the impacts of temperature on PMI and TSB estimations as a result of aboveground versus subsurface depositions.

Decay

The reestablishment of aerobiosis signifies the beginning of decay (Carter and Tibbett, 2008). Proteins and fats decompose to phenolic compounds and glycerol, respectively. Some of the catabolism products identified include putrescine, indole, cadaverine, 3-methyl indole (skatole), and fatty acids (Vass et al., 2002). Overall, decay is a period of rapid catabolism due to the activities of microorganisms, insects, and scavengers (Vass et al., 2002; Carter and Tibbett, 2008; Tibbett, 2008). Therefore proteolytic and lipolytic microbial communities and strains in particular can be profiled and targeted as microbial clocks to infer the decay phase. Temporal forensic entomological analysis can then be used parallel to ecogenomic/microbiological characterization. According to Damann and Carter (2013), the face and head are usually the first points of skeletal exposure, although areas of injury or wound may also affect this (Mann et al., 1990).

Although cadaver decomposition is a natural process that starts with autolysis and putrefaction, major breakdown results from the actions of insects and scavengers (Carter and Tibbett, 2008). Many insect species have been identified including blow flies (*Diptera calliphoridae*), flesh flies (*Diptera sarcophagidae*), and beetles (*Coleoptera* spp.) (Carter and Tibbett, 2008; Forbes and Carter, 2015; Ururahy-Rodrigues et al., 2008). According to Mann et al.

(1990), during the decomposition of a cadaver placed outside in a warm or hot environment, it only takes a few seconds for flies to colonize. Fly arrival, coupled with egg laying and eventual larvae formation, increases the rate of decomposition with the bulk of the soft tissue breakdown caused by larvae (Mann et al., 1990; Carter and Tibbett, 2008). In a terrestrial environment, scavengers can consume 35%–75% of the cadaver volume, although this may rise during winter when insect and microbial activities slow (Carter and Tibbett, 2008).

MICROBIOLOGY OF DECOMPOSITION

Several researchers (Forbes, 2008; Forbes and Carter, 2015; Janaway et al., 2009) have suggested that microbial catabolism starts after the cessation of autolysis, which results in a predominantly anaerobic environment that favors gastrointestinal tract and respiratory system bacteria proliferation. According to Janaway et al. (2009), "*autolysis occurs independently from any bacterial action, while putrefaction, the reduction and liquefaction of tissue, is a microbiologically dominated process.*" Anaerobic organisms, such as *Bifidobacterium*, *Streptococcus*, *Clostridium*, *Enterobacter*, and *Bacteroides* species, enter the tissues and the rest of the body, including bone, via the lymphatic and vascular systems (Gill-King, 1997; Forbes, 2008; Forbes and Carter, 2015). With anaerobic microorganism proliferation, the only viable obligate aerobic microorganisms found on decomposing tissues are *Micrococcus*, *Enterococcus*, *Pseudomonas*, and *Acinetobacter* species (Gill-King, 1997; Janaway et al., 2009).

Approximately 90% of the culturable microorganisms isolated from decomposing tissues are strict anaerobes, with Gram-positive nonsporulating strains (such as *Bifidobacterium* spp.) giving the highest counts (Janaway et al., 2009). Enterobacteriaceae, including *Lactobacillus* and *Streptococcus* spp., have also been observed but in lower numbers. Metcalf et al. (2013) and Pechal et al. (2014) reported shifts from aerobic bacteria of the Actinobacteria and Firmicutes phyla to dominance of facultative anaerobic bacteria including *Lactobacillus*, *Streptococcus*, and *Staphylococcus* spp. in the mouth and skin of a carcass. Nonetheless, other bacteria, such as *Bacillus* spp. and *Pseudomonas* spp., have been reported (Janaway et al., 2009) but in lower numbers. Other documented organisms include: *Proteus* spp.; *Salmonella* spp.; *Klebsiella* spp.; *Serratia* spp.; *Flavobacterium* spp.; and *Pseudomonas* spp. (Janaway et al., 2009). As reported by Sidrim et al. (2010), fungi, such as *Aspergillus* spp., *Penicillium* spp., and *Candida* spp., were isolated and identified from human cadavers during the bloat and putrefaction stages. Likewise, Carter and Tibbett (2008) reported several strains of the fungal taxa Ascomycetes and Basidiomycetes in gravesoil.

CHEMISTRY OF DECOMPOSITION

Cadaver decomposition is a complex process that begins with the initial postmortem mortis triad and is followed by the soft tissue decomposition processes, which are characterized by the catabolism of proteins, carbohydrates, and lipids.

Protein Decomposition

Proteins undergo enzymatic degradation at a nonuniform rate by proteolysis (Sabucedo and Furton, 2003; Forbes, 2008). The rate of cadaver proteolysis is dependent on moisture content, temperature, and microbial activity (Vass et al., 2002). Specifically, the rate is reduced by cooling but enhanced by warming (Janaway et al., 2009). The epithelial cells and neurons are usually the first soft tissue proteins to putrefy (Dent et al., 2004), although brain, kidney, and liver decomposition also occur (Gill-King, 1997). In contrast, proteins such as the epidermis reticulum and muscles are more resistant to proteolysis, while connective tissues and cartilage are the most resistant (Gill-King, 1997; Forbes, 2008). Collagen and keratin in particular exhibit resilience to biological and chemical agents and consequently remain intact among skeletal remains (Forbes, 2008; Janaway et al., 2009). Proteolytic bacteria include *Bacillus*, *Micrococcus*, and *Pseudomonas* species (Janaway et al., 2009). Together with these species, gastrointestinal tract sulfate-reducing bacteria also play important roles.

Key metabolites of proteolysis include amino acids, peptones, proteoses, and polypeptides. Other metabolites are phenolics and gases such as hydrogen sulfide, carbon dioxide, methane, and ammonia (Forbes, 2008). The sulfur-containing amino acids are catabolized by desulfhydralation to yield ammonia, hydrogen sulfide, sulfides, pyruvic acid, and thiols (Gill-King, 1997; Knight and Presnell, 2005).

According to Forbes (2008), the sulfide metabolites do not metabolize, although they are oxidized to sulfates under aerobic conditions by bacteria such as *Thiobacillus* spp. to produce sulfurous acid in soil. Subsequently, the amine components of the amino acids are liberated as ammonia, which then may be converted to ammonium (Eq. 1.6) at low soil pH (Gill-King, 1997; Forbes, 2008).

$$\underset{\text{Ammonia}}{NH_3} + H^+ \rightarrow \underset{\text{Ammonium}}{NH_4^+} \tag{1.6}$$

Ammonium compounds promote plant growth, which has consequently become a noticeable feature around or above a decomposing cadaver (Gill-King, 1997; Carter and Tibbett, 2008; Forbes, 2008). As stated by Forbes (2008), unutilized ammonium ions can undergo either nitrification or denitrification in soil. Nitrification is the oxidation of the ammonium ion via nitrite into nitrate and this process can be divided into two steps (Eq. 1.7–1.9) (Killham, 1994):

1. Ammonium ion oxidation to nitrite by Gram-negative *Nitrosomonas* spp.

$$NH_4^+ + O_2 + H^+ + 2e^- \rightarrow \underset{\text{Hydroxylamine}}{HN_2OH} + H_2O \tag{1.7}$$

$$\underset{\text{Hydroxylamine}}{HN_2OH} + H_2O \rightarrow \underset{\text{Nitrite}}{NO_2^-} + 5H^+ + 4e^- \tag{1.8}$$

2. Nitrite oxidation by Gram-negative *Nitrobacter* spp.

$$\underset{\text{Nitrite}}{NO_2^-} + H_2O \rightarrow H_2O \cdot NO_2^- \rightarrow \underset{\text{Nitrate}}{NO_3^-} + 2H^+ \tag{1.9}$$

These bacteria are sensitive to changes in environmental pH with *Nitrosomonas* spp. proliferating between pH 7 and 9, while *Nitrobacter* spp. are favoured at pH values between 5 and 8 (Forbes, 2008).

Carbohydrate Decomposition

Cadaver carbohydrates such as glycogen are catabolized microbially to glucose monomers, which in turn can be mineralized to water and carbon dioxide or oxidized to various alcohols and organic acids (Forbes, 2008). For example, the aerobic catabolism of sucrose by fungi produces citric, oxalic, and glucuronic acids, while the anaerobic *Clostridium* spp. catabolize carbohydrates to alcohols and organic acids, such as acetic, butyric, and lactic. The acidic conditions in proximity to a decomposing cadaver have been attributed to these by-products (Forbes, 2008; Janaway et al., 2009). Additional bacterial catabolic products include: gases, such as hydrogen, hydrogen sulfide and methane; alcohols, such as ethanol and butanol; and acetone (Forbes, 2008; Janaway et al., 2009). According to reports by Collison (2005) and Ziavrou et al. (2005), determination of antemortem blood alcohol concentrations remains a problem for pathologists and toxicologists due to postmortem bacterial production of ethanol.

Lipid Decomposition

Human adipose tissue is composed of 60%–80% lipids, with water accounting for the balance. Lipids in turn are comprised of approximately 90%–99% triglycerides (triacylglycerol), which are unchained fatty acid esters of glycerol. Monounsaturated $C_{18:1}$ oleic acid is the most abundant fatty acid in adipose tissue, followed by polyunsaturated $C_{18:2}$ linoleic acid and monounsaturated $C_{16:1}$ palmitoleic acid. The corresponding saturated $C_{16:0}$ palmitic acid is also present (Forbes, 2008). Rothschild et al. (1996) reported that the fat content of a cadaver was hydrolyzed by intrinsic lipases to fatty acid metabolites, which in turn were either oxidized or hydrolyzed under aerobic or anaerobic conditions, respectively.

In the presence of oxygen, unsaturated fatty acids are converted to ketones and aldehydes by bacteria and fungi (Forbes, 2008). In contrast, both saturated and unsaturated fatty acids undergo bacterial hydrolysis and hydrogenation under anaerobic conditions. For example, Clostridia produce lipolytic enzymes that facilitate anaerobic hydrogenation and hydrolysis. *Clostridium perfringens*, a major agent of cadaver decomposition, has been isolated from the gastrointestinal tract for its strong proteolytic, lipolytic, and saccharolytic abilities (Forbes, 2008; Janaway et al., 2009). This bacterium is also found in soils exemplifying its involvement in grave cadaver decomposition (Forbes, 2008). The reduction of cadaver fatty tissues to fatty acids depends greatly on moisture content, more particularly water activity, and catabolic enzyme activity (Forbes, 2008; Janaway et al., 2009).

ADIPOCERE

Various workers have described adipocere as "grave wax" or "corpse wax" (Forbes, 2008; Ubelaker and Zarenko, 2011; Schoenen and Schoenen, 2013) with its definition based on morphological characteristics. Thus Gill-King (1997) defined it as a "greyish white caseous material," Janaway et al. (2009) defined it as a "waxy substance," while Schoenen and Schoenen (2013) described it as a "whitish, soft-smeary up to firm-crumbly, inodorous, mouldy or putrid smelling, fatty feeling lipid bulk." Independent of definition, the basis of adipocere formation, as largely agreed by various researchers, is the hydrolysis and hydrogenation of adipose tissue (Forbes et al., 2005a; Ubelaker and Zarenko, 2011; Schoenen and Schoenen, 2013). Bacterial activities in a temperature range of 22–38°C, in a damp and anaerobic environment, have been reported to enhance its formation (Forbes, 2008; Schoenen and Schoenen, 2013; Kasuda et al., 2016). As reported by Ubelaker and Zarenko (2011), adipocere is an essential taphonomic phenomenon due to its:

1. Preservative characteristics of soft tissues;
2. Ability to reveal constitutional and environmental factors that may prove valuable in forensic investigation; and
3. Complicating role in the determination of PMI due to its preservative characteristics.

Adipocere formation follows triglyceride hydrolysis to free fatty acids with the unsaturated fatty acids converted to saturated fatty acids (Gill-King, 1997). For example, oleic acid hydrolysis and oxidation result in a palmitic acid concentration increase, while hydrogenation of its double bond results in the formation of 10-hydroxystearic acid, which is subsequently dehydrogenated to oxo-stearic acid (Forbes, 2008).

The major components of adipocere, as described by Forbes et al. (2005a; 2005b) and Ueland et al. (2014), are a mixture of saturated fatty acids (stearic, palmitic, and myristic), unsaturated fatty acids (lanoleic, palmitoleic, and oleic), and their calcium salts. According to Gill-King (1997), free fatty acids can attach to interstitial fluid potassium and sodium ions at a "slightly alkaline pH." As reported by Gill-King (1997), the identification of fatty acid calcium salts as adipocere components from grave site samples was attributed to potassium and sodium ion displacement (Eq. 1.10).

$$\underset{\substack{\text{Sodium stearate}\\ \text{(soluble)}}}{2\,C_{17}H_{35}C(=O)O^{-}Na^{+}} + Ca^{2+} \longrightarrow \underset{\substack{\text{Calcium stearate}\\ \text{(insoluble)}}}{(C_{17}H_{35}COO^{-})_2Ca} + 2Na^{+} \qquad (1.10)$$

In summary, adipocere formation occurs where there are cadaver fatty tissues or even a minimal fat content such as in internal organs such as the heart, liver, and kidneys (Forbes et al., 2005a, 2005b; Kasuda et al., 2016). As reported by Forbes (2008), *C. perfringens* growth and production of lecithinase stimulate adipocere formation in anoxic environments. Ueland et al. (2014) reported a dominance of Gram-negative bacteria at the later stages of adipocere formation and theorized that this group outcompeted the Gram-positive bacteria over time. With the exception of hot, dry soils, adipocere can be formed in a range of ecosystems. Subsequent adipocere decomposition, as reported by Pfeiffer et al. (1998), may be attributed to Gram-positive bacteria such as *Bacillus*, *Cellulomonas*, and *Nocardia* species.

TRANSDISCIPLINARY FORENSIC SCIENCE

The different stages of decomposition are summarized in Fig. 1.2 (see also Chapters 2 and 3). Although they are not entirely distinct but characterized instead by some overlaps, the sequential occurrences of the decompositional phases, concomitant with their respective metabolic by-products, are well accepted. Therefore there is considerable potential to study their unique attendant (epi)necrobiomes. As a result, understanding the succession of total and functional microbial communities that are responsible for and affected by cadaver/proxy decomposition can be used to predict, infer, and calculate PMI and TSB interval. Also there is potential to target different biomolecules and in different parts/organs/tissues of the body, as in thanatomicrobiome profiling, for example, to reflect the available multi-, cross-, and transdisciplinary methods (Fig. 1.2; see also Fig. 3.2), and the different stages of decomposition regarding PMI, $_{min}$PMI, and PMSI.

Overall, studying the order of decomposition, successional substrates, and probable microbial consortia should be matched with investigation of the sequential macrobial populations and chemical moieties (i.e., liquid and gaseous volatile organic compounds). Thus overlaps of forensic ecogenomics, forensic botany, forensic entomology, and forensic chemistry (Fig. 1.3), among others, should facilitate appropriately robust cross-, multi-, and transdisciplinary knowledge development during forensic research. This will ultimately inform real scenes of crime, add to comprehensive intelligence gathering, enhance postmortem and TSB estimations and increase success rates for retribution. As deliberated in Chapter 9, success of this pathway will be more realizable if researchers, practitioners, and scene of crime officers collaborate on existing real crime scenes.

EMERGENT APPLICATIONS OF MICROBIAL ECOLOGY TOOLS

Forensically, soil is viewed as important crime scene evidence (Bull et al., 2006; Petraco et al., 2008; Woods et al., 2014), hence it is typically characterized physicochemically to link suspects to known crime scenes. Therefore physico- and biochemical analysis such as pH, volatile organic compound concentration determinations, and dynamics of different soil nutrients, e.g., CO_2 evolution, ninhydrin-N, total N, total C, have been applied including PMI estimations (e.g., Benninger et al., 2008; Vass et al., 1992, 2002). However,

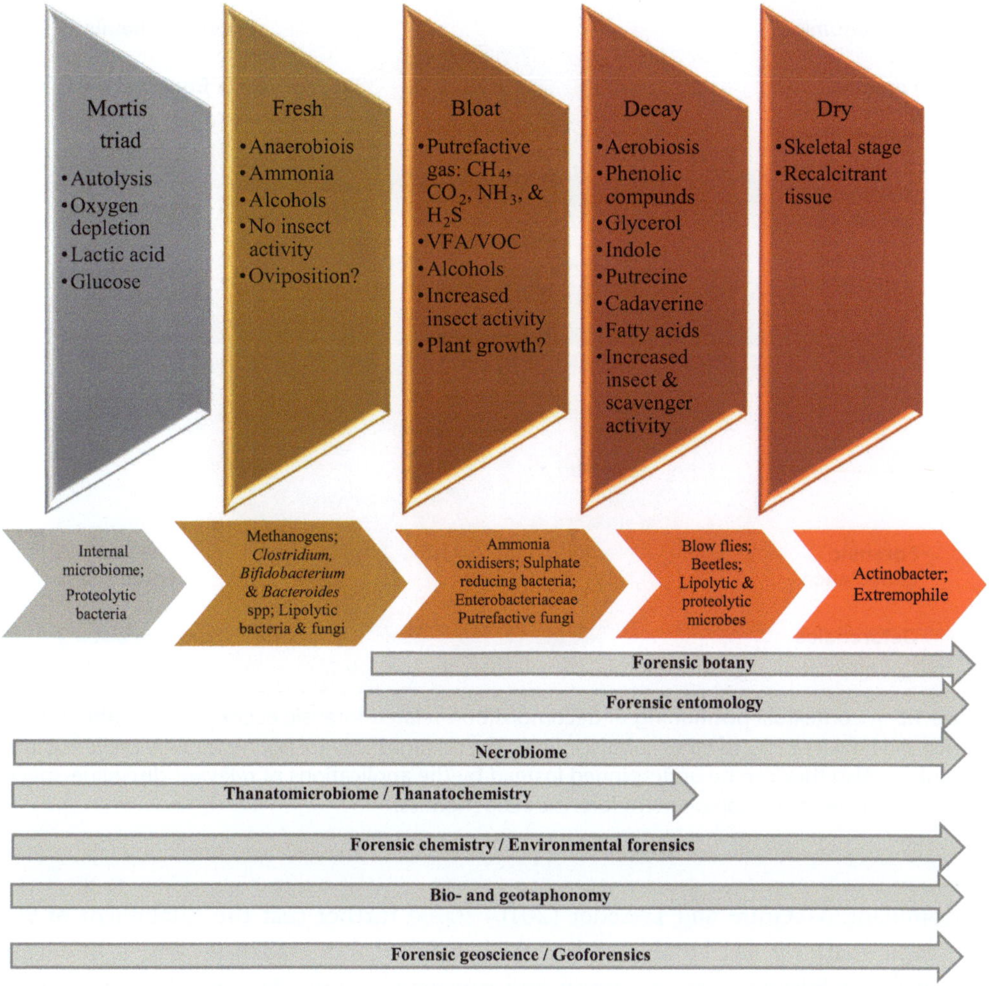

Figure 1.2 Temporal occurrence of postmortem changes and/or stages, some of their known metabolic by-products, example functional microbial communities that can be studied in decomposition-related forensic ecogenomics, and the parallel forensic subdisciplines that can be applied toward enhanced postmortem and postburial interval determinations. The stages are compiled from different literature sources but with some alignment to Brooks (2016) for expedient cross-referencing. Full acknowledgment is made that the stages, hence their attendant metabolic products and macro-/microbial activities, are characterized by overlaps. *VFA*, Volatile fatty acid; *VOC*, volatile organic compound.

soil microbiological profiling as part of the crime scene toolkit lags considerably behind approaches such as forensic geoscience, geoforensics, forensic entomology, and forensic chemistry—including the use of cadaver dogs to locate clandestine burials.

According to several researchers such as Maier and Pepper (2009), terrestrial ecosystems are inhabited by billions of microorganisms where bacteria are often the most

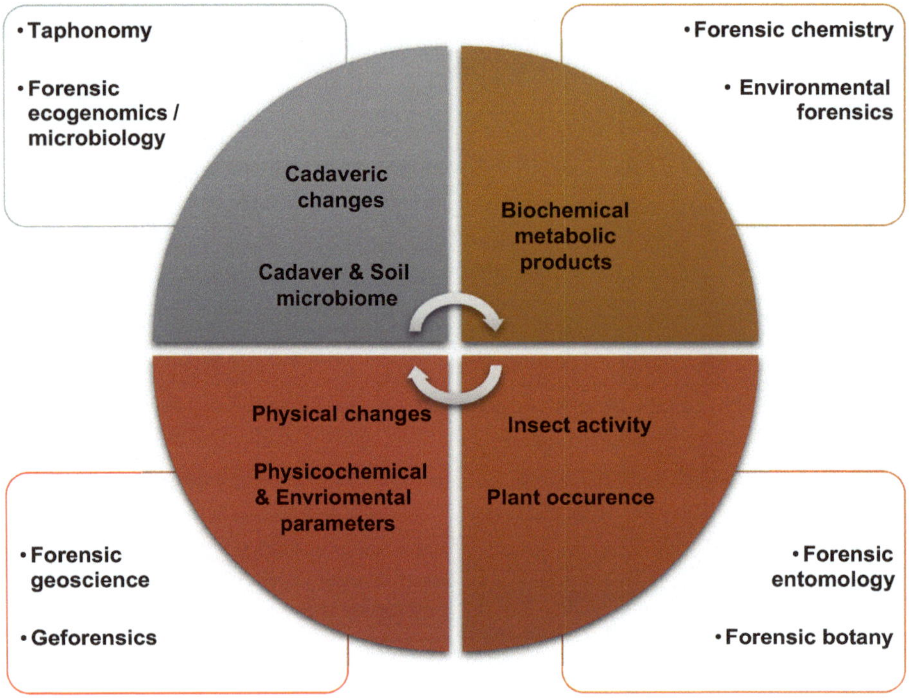

Figure 1.3 A contextual positioning of decomposition-related forensic ecogenomics within forensic science and how it relates to other subdisciplines. The relationships are not necessarily cyclic but interdependent. Also they can be underpinned instead by the applications of relevant discipline-specific tools that align with and complement forensic ecogenomics.

predominant. McGuire and Treseder (2010) stated further that the catabolism of 90% of organic matter is attributable to bacterial and fungal degradation, which underpins their well-established roles in carbon and nitrogen cycling. As a result, and although accurate PMI and PBI estimation within (soil) ecosystems can be particularly challenging, emergent research in forensic ecogenomics/microbiology is illustrating how microbial communities of the cadaver or taphonomic proxies and the surrounding environments can be analyzed for potential use in scenes of crime. Therefore the impact of cadaver decomposition on ecosystem function and microbial consortia dynamics, parallel with the impact of the surrounding (microbial) ecology on the rate of cadaver decomposition, are being explored as mirror parameters to enhance determinations for PMI and TSB interval.

Recognition of the utility and applicability of microbiological methods including culture-based and culture-independent (molecular) approaches has led to multiple research initiatives to test/show their potential to expand existing methods for PMI estimation. Although different biomolecules can be targeted, fatty acids and nucleic acids are most commonly used as also in general is microbial ecology. Naturally, and as in other disciplines, full cognizance of the applicability, strengths, and weaknesses of the techniques must be made before they can be adopted for forensic analyses.

For example, the principles of two whole-cell fatty acid analytical techniques, phospholipid fatty acid (PLFA) and fatty acid methyl ester (FAME), are discussed in Chapter 7. Their strengths and limitations have been considered briefly within microbial ecology in general and forensic ecogenomics in particular. Therefore their forensic applicability has been demonstrated by researchers such as Parkinson et al. (2009) and Breton et al. (2016). In parallel is a discourse on DNA-based techniques, which are most popular, with next-generation sequencing (NGS) the most adopted platform. Research on these techniques has been made subsequently within different forensic ecogenomic contexts in relation to animal models and different parts/tissues of animals; at laboratory scale indoors or outdoors; and in the cadaver decomposition island aboveground or in the subsurface. The studies that were published at the time of writing are therefore summarized in Table 1.1.

As in other soil microbial ecology disciplines, the most used techniques in forensic ecogenomics to date are denaturing gradient gel electrophoresis, terminal restriction fragment length polymorphism, PLFA and FAME, and single-strand conformation polymorphism. Advances in molecular techniques have led subsequently to the creation and use of high-throughput parallel sequencing tools referred to as NGS technologies, which can resolve complex environmental, microbial communities (Crippen et al., 2015; Singh and Crippen, 2015). The most widely used tools include: Roche-454 pyrosequencing; Illumina (HiSeq/Miseq); and Ion-torrent (Allen and LaMontagne, 2015). Each technique incorporates nucleotides or oligonucleotides at the blunt end of each fragmented DNA strand. There are, however, limitations of the various techniques as highlighted in Table 1.2.

Table 1.2 Advantages and disadvantages of various next-generation sequencing platforms

Sequence platform	Method	Approximate sequence length (bp)	Advantages	Disadvantages
Roche-454	Pyrosequencing	400	High throughput, longer sequence length	High error rate because of homopolymers
Illumina (HiSeq/MiSeq)	Sequencing by synthesis	150	High throughput, lower error rate	Short sequence length
Ion-torrent	Semiconductor sequencing technology	400	High throughput, faster, and cheaper per run	High error rate because of homopolymers

SUMMARY AND FUTURE WORK

"Forensic ecogenomics" is a designation that is most probably interchangeable with "microbioforensics" and "forensic microbiology." Irrespective of their provenance, these terms and disciplines highlight the need to develop, understand, and apply microbiology knowledge in crime scene investigation. Specifically, forensic ecogenomics aims to elucidate the role of microbial/macrobial communities and the application of a wide range of attendant ecophysiology analyses to inform novel forensic research and ultimately expand the crime scene investigative toolkit. It entails the use of established and cutting-edge techniques for cross-, multi-, and transdisciplinary investigations by soil scientists, microbial ecologists, molecular biologists, forensic scientists, and ultimately crime scene investigators or practitioners. It is envisaged that as a subdiscipline, forensic ecogenomics will be applicable for research and pre- and postmortem investigations in microbial fingerprinting, PMI, PMSI, and PBI estimations, and clandestine grave location. Its full realization will be subject to comprehensive collaborative research initiatives that are also informed by parallel forensic botany, forensic chemistry, forensic entomology, and forensic geoscience/geoforensics, for example.

Therefore this compilation aims to highlight the existing research efforts that are underpinned by forensic ecogenomics, the knowledge development milestones to date, the related contextual investigations or potential, the existing knowledge gaps, and therefore future research questions that should be addressed to realize the applicability of the subdiscipline. Since all forensic research is underpinned by human taphonomy, Chapter 2 presents a historical and contemporary discourse on bio- and geotaphonomy with details on the different stages of human decomposition. The themes are explored further in Chapter 3 where the strengths, applicabilities, and limitations of different PMI estimation methods are also considered. A proposal for method management and application to potentially enhance PMI determinations is also made. In keeping with the wider theme of the forensic ecogenomics text, Chapter 3 also highlights the new (micro-) biological methods that are expanding and/or should extend forensic science in general and PMI estimations in particular.

As introduced in Chapter 2, the deliberations on the use of human taphonomic surrogates in the absence of ethical frameworks that permit the use of human remains are considered further in Chapter 4. Therefore although the domestic pig (*Sus scrofa domesticus*) is accepted by most researchers as the appropriate taphonomic proxy for the human body, decomposition studies have to date used different animal models. The chapter explores the implications of these differences, the importance of species choice, appropriate/correct use of taxonomic nomenclature, and achievements made in related subdisciplines, especially forensic entomology, which can be replicated/adopted in forensic ecogenomics. Finally, the requisite research and knowledge development to test and validate the transferability and applicability of mammalian proxy-derived findings to real crime scenarios involving human remains are discussed.

The necrobiome is defined as all the microorganisms, invertebrates, vertebrates, and plants associated with a decomposing organism. Since most forensic ecogenomic/microbiology research has to date focused on microbial (bacterial) communities, Chapter 5 explores their role in PMI estimation. Thus the aim is to discuss the microbial ecology techniques applied currently to study specifically the dynamics of microbial communities that characterize the body postmortem and during decomposition, and then those in the surrounding ecosystem, which are affected by the decomposition processes. Future multidisciplinary necrobiome research should consider the wider "necrobiome" definition and elucidate how the dynamic distributions and functions of all decomposition-related macroorganisms (plant, insects, scavengers) in turn affect the structure and composition of the microbial communities of the cadaver/taphonomic proxy and the surrounding soil (and water).

Chapter 6 develops key themes as introduced in Chapter 4 with a dedicated discussion of the roles of specific organs and tissue types in efficient and/or alternative approaches for PMI analysis. Briefly, "thanatomicrobiome" is a relatively new term/concept that encapsulates investigations on temporal and successional microbial community dynamics in the circulatory system in particular, following death, deposition, and/or burial. Also different organs are being used in research to elucidate whether thanatomicrobiome profiling in one organ can facilitate enhanced PMI estimations better than another, especially when applied parallel to established autopsy techniques. Overall, investigations of these processes are being advanced considerably by the application of cutting-edge forensic ecogenomic techniques.

As in microbial ecology, the discipline from which multiple techniques are being adopted/adapted for forensic ecogenomics, most studies of the cadaver/mammalian proxy and soil necrobiome, and the thanatomicrobiome, have focused largely on bacterial profiling. Although not in a dedicated chapter, the significant roles of fungi in mycology-based forensic ecogenomics (mycoforensics) were explored earlier and are discussed in other parts of the book (e.g., Chapters 3 and 7). Therefore informed debates and investigations must be pursued with the sole aim of ensuring that studies in fungal community dynamics are made parallel to those on bacteria. Also the role of fungi in the degradation of specific tissues, e.g., hair and bones, nutrient cycling as a whole, and plant matter decomposition, as also deliberated in Chapter 7 regarding differentiating for clandestine burials, must be reflected for an all-inclusive application of forensic ecogenomics, particularly in real crime scenarios. Furthermore, soil pH, a key parameter for ecosystem function, will have a direct impact on fungal community dynamics regarding occurrence, abundance, and structure. These will have direct implications for subsurface decomposition, for example, and hence PMI and PBI determinations in general.

Used widely in microbial ecology, high-throughput NGS platforms have now been adopted rapidly by forensic researchers as proposed previously (Finley et al.,

2015a, 2015b; Kuiper, 2016; Ralebitso-Senior et al., 2016) to explore: the effects/response of the human microbiome on/to decomposition; the impacts of decomposition on environmental microbial communities; the influence of the surrounding environment on cadaver decomposition; and the potential role of all three dynamics in estimating PMI/PBI. Notwithstanding this, a whole suite of microbial ecology techniques is available to expand fully the interesting diagnostic interface between microecophysiology, forensics, and biological anthropology. Also decomposition-based forensic ecogenomic research has to date focused mainly on aboveground terrestrial ecosystems (soils) with very few studies published on the subsurface. Therefore Chapter 7 emphasizes the importance of studies that are as close to real crime scene investigations as possible and hence presents a mesocosm experimental design and findings to elucidate how body decomposition affects different soil microbial communities belowground.

Since most crime investigations lead to court, the potentials and limitations of implementing experimental findings in real crime scenes in particular is appraised critically in Chapter 8. Admittedly, the critique is limited to the perspectives of contributors that were available and their respective professional experiences. Nevertheless, the acceptability of different forensic sciences and their associated methods, including forensic ecogenomics, for subsequent use in court proceedings are considered within historical perspectives where relevant. To reflect the unique challenges and opportunities that are likely to arise from different legal systems, this chapter has multiple contributors with perspectives from China, the Netherlands, Turkey, and the United Kingdom.

Future Work

As highlighted previously (Ralebitso-Senior et al., 2016), the strengths and weaknesses of different forensic ecogenomic/microbiology techniques must be recognized fully. It is only through comprehensive analyses of their limitations, and addressing these, that their potential impacts will be realized for subsequent adoption into an updated crime scene investigative toolkit. Furthermore, "*the importance of concerted (global) efforts*" was highlighted and these are being reflected by initiatives such as the Human Postmortem Microbiome Project (Chapter 6). Also, and as posited in Chapters 4 and 8, collaborative research and case work between teams with/without access to human tissue facilities and police forces should be made parallel to human taphonomic proxy studies to test and validate knowledge transfer to real scenes of crime.

Succinct reflections have been presented on the current ethical and legislative frameworks that direct all research work on human remains (Chapters 2 and 4), existing case studies and cases where forensic scientists have informed police investigations and court proceedings (Chapter 8), and how all these should inform forensic ecogenomics research to then make the discipline relevant for real crime scenes and the courts. In summary therefore are the following key themes or aims that should be explored in future forensic ecogenomics research and case work, which are also identified in the subsequent chapters and summarized in Chapter 9:

1. Comparisons between mammalian surrogates;
2. Assessments of knowledge transfer from animal model-based studies to human remains;
3. Knowledge development using different organs and types of tissue;
4. Ecosystem dynamics during surface and subsurface decomposition;
5. Method development, assessment, optimization, and validation;
6. Transdisciplinary investigations at the interface of forensic ecogenomics with, for example, forensic chemistry and forensic entomology regarding insect–(epi)necrobiome interaction;
7. Collaborative work between researchers, practitioners, and scenes of crime officers; and
8. Further national/global discussions and efforts for ethical framework developments toward the establishment of human taphonomic facilities.

REFERENCES

Aaspõllu, A., Lillsaar, T., Tummeleht, L., Simm, J., Metsis, M., 2011. Can microbes on skin help linking persons and crimes? Forensic Science International: Genetics Supplement Series 3 (1), e269–270.

Aitkenhead-Peterson, J.A., Owings, C.G., Alexander, M.B., Larison, N., Bytheway, J.A., 2012. Mapping the lateral extent of human cadaver decomposition with soil chemistry. Forensic Science International 216, 127–134.

Alaeddini, R., Walsh, S.J., Abbas, A., 2010. Forensic implications of genetic analyses from degraded DNA—a review. Forensic Science International: Genetics 4 (3), 148–157.

Allen, M.S., LaMontagne, M.G., 2015. Microbial genetics and systematics. In: Benbow, E.M., Tomberlin, J.K., Tarone, A.M. (Eds.), Carrion Ecology, Evolution, and Their Applications. CRC Press, Boca Raton, pp. 403–419.

Arnaldos, M.I., García, M.D., Romera, E., Presa, J.J., Luna, A., 2005. Estimation of postmortem interval in real cases based on experimentally obtained entomological evidence. Forensic Science International 149, 57–65.

Bellini, E., Ambrosio, E., Zotti, M., Nucci, G., Gabbrielli, M., Vanezis, P., 2016. The usefulness of cadaveric fungi as an investigation tool. The American Journal of Forensic Medicine and Pathology 37 (1), 23.

Benbow, M.E., Lewis, A.J., Tomberlin, J.K., Pechal, J.L., 2013. Seasonal necrophagous insect community assembly during vertebrate carrion decomposition. Journal of Medical Entomology 50 (2), 440–450.

Benbow, M.E., Pechal, J.L., Lang, J.M., Erb, R., Wallace, J.R., 2015. The potential of high-throughput metagenomic sequencing of aquatic bacterial communities to estimate the postmortem submersion interval. Journal of Forensic Sciences 60 (6), 1500–1510.

Benninger, L.A., Carter, D.O., Forbes, S.L., 2008. The biochemical alteration of soil beneath a decomposing carcass. Forensic Science International 180 (2–3), 70–75.

Benschop, C.C.G., Quaak, F.C.A., Boon, M.E., Sijen, T., Kuiper, I., 2012. Vaginal microbial flora analysis by next generation sequencing and microarrays; can microbes indicate vaginal origin in a forensic context? International Journal of Legal Medicine 126, 303–310.

Bergmann, R.C., Ralebitso-Senior, T.K., Thompson, T.J.U., 2014. An RNA-based analysis of changes in biodiversity indices in response to *Sus scrofa* domesticus decomposition. Forensic Science International 241, 190–194.

Bock, J., Norris, D., 1997. Forensic botany: an under-utilized resource. Journal of Forensic Sciences 42 (3), 364–367.

Breton, H., Kirkwood, A.E., Carter, D.O., Forbes, S.L., 2016. The impact of carrion decomposition on the fatty acid methyl ester (FAME) profiles of soil microbial communities in southern Canada. Canadian Society of Forensic Science Journal 49 (1), 1–18.

Bristow, J., Simms, Z., Randolph-Quinney, P., 2011. Taphonomy. In: Black, S., Ferguson, E. (Eds.), Forensic Anthropology 2000 to 2010, pp. 279–317 Boca Raton.

Brooks, J.W., 2016. Postmortem changes in animal carcasses and estimation of the postmortem interval. Veterinary Pathology 53 (5), 929–940.

Budowle, B., 2004. Genetics and attribution issues that confront the microbial forensics field. Forensic Science International 146, S185–S188.

Budowle, B., Schutzer, S., Breeze, R., 2005. Microbial Forensics, first ed. Academic Press, p. 448.

Bull, P.A., Parker, A., Morgan, R.M., 2006. The forensic analysis of soils and sediment taken from the cast of a footprint. Forensic Science International 162 (1–3), 6–12.

Campobasso, C.P., Della, G.D., Introna, F., 2001. Factors affecting decomposition and Diptera colonization. Forensic Science International 120, 18–27.

Can, I., Javan, G.T., Pozhitkov, A.E., Noble, P.A., 2014. Distinctive thanatomicrobiome signatures found in the blood and internal organs of humans. Journal of Microbiological Methods 106, 1–7.

Carter, D.O., Tibbett, M., 2008. Cadaver decomposition and soil: processes. In: Tibbett, M., Carter, D.O. (Eds.), Soil Analysis in Forensic Taphonomy: Chemical and Biological Effect of Buried Human Remains. CRC Press, Boca Raton, pp. 29–52.

Carter, D.O., Metcalf, J.L., Bibat, A., Knight, R., 2015. Seasonal variation of postmortem microbial communities. Forensic Science, Medicine & Pathology 11 (2), 202–207.

Carter, D.O., Tibbett, M., 2006. Microbial decomposition of skeletal muscle tissue (*Ovis aries*) in a sandy loam soil at different temperatures. Soil Biology & Biochemistry 38, 1139–1145.

Carter, D.O., Tibbett, M., 2003. Taphonomic mycota: fungi with forensic potential. Journal of Forensic Science 48 (1), 168–171.

Carter, D.O., Tomberlin, J.K., Benbow, M.E., Metcalf, J.L. (Eds.), 2017. Forensic Microbiology. Wiley, West Sussex.

Carter, D.O., Yellowlees, D., Tibbett, M., 2010. Moisture can be the dominant parameter governing cadaver decomposition in soil. Forensic Science International 200 (1–3), 60–66.

Carvalho, L.M., Thyssen, P.J., Linhares, A.X., Palhares, F.A., 2000. A checklist of arthropods associated with pig carrion and human corpses in Southeastern Brazil. Memórias do Instituto Oswaldo Cruz 95 (1), 135–138.

Chen, Y.Q., Cai, J.F., Wen, J.F., 2009. Advances in the studies of postmortem interval estimation by the levels of chemical components in human vitreous humor after death. Fa Yi Xue Za Zhi 25 (1), 53–56.

Chimutsa, M., Olakanye, A.O., Thompson, T.J., Ralebitso-Senior, T.K., 2015. Soil fungal community shift evaluation as a potential cadaver decomposition indicator. Forensic Science International 17, 155–159.

Chun, L.P., Miguel, M.J., Junkins, E.N., Forbes, S.L., Carter, D.O., 2015. An initial investigation into the ecology of culturable aerobic postmortem bacteria. Science & Justice 55 (6), 394–401.

Clark, M.A., Worrell, M.B., Pless, J.E., 1997. Postmortem changes in soft tissues. In: Haglund, W.D., Sorg, M.H. (Eds.), Forensic Taphonomy: The Postmortem Fate of Human Remains. CRC Press, Boca Raton, pp. 151–164.

Cobaugh, K.L., Schaeffer, S.M., DeBruyn, J.M., 2015. Functional and structural succession of soil microbial communities below decomposing human cadavers. PLoS One 10 (6), e0130201.

Collison, I.B., 2005. Elevated postmortem ethanol concentrations in an insulin-dependent diabetic. Journal of Analytical Toxicology 29 (7), 762–764.

Coyle, H.M., 2004. Forensic Botany: Principles and Applications to Criminal Casework. CRC Press, Boca Raton.

Crippen, T.L., Benbow, E.M., Pechal, J.L., 2015. Microbial interactions during carrion decomposition. In: Benbow, E.M., Tomberlin, J.K., Tarone, A.M. (Eds.), Carrion Ecology, Evolution, and Their Applications. CPC Press, Boca Raton, pp. 31–63.

Damann, F.E., Carter, D.O., 2013. Human decomposition ecology and postmortem microbiology. In: Pokines, J., Symes, S.A. (Eds.), Manual of Forensic Taphonomy. CRC Press, Boca Raton, pp. 37–49.

Dekeirsschieter, J., Verheggen, F., Gohy, M., Hubrecht, F., Bourguignon, L., Lognay, G., Haubruge, E., 2009. Cadaveric volatile organic compounds released by decaying pig carcasses (*Sus domesticus* L.) in different biotopes. Forensic Science International 189 (1), 46–53.

Denier, V.G., 1940. Carcass temperatures and their relation to winter blowfly populations and activity in the Southwest. Journal of Economic Entomology 33 (5), 166–170.

Dent, B.B., Forbes, S.L., Stuart, B.H., 2004. Review of human decomposition process in soil. Environmental Geology 45 (4), 576–585.

Damann, F.E., Tanittaisong, A., Carter, D.O., 2012. Potential carcass enrichment of the University of Tennessee Anthropology Research Facility: a baseline survey of edaphic features. Forensic Science International 222, 4–10.

Dickson, G.C., Poulter, R.T.M., Maas, E.W., Probert, P.K., Kieser, J.A., 2011. Marine bacterial succession as a potential indicator of postmortem submersion interval. Forensic Science International 209 (1–3), 1–10.

Dillon, L., 1995. Forensic Entomology: The Use of Insects in Death Investigations to Determine Elapsed Time since Death. Canadian Police Research Centre, Ottawa.

Donaldson, A.E., Lamont, I.L., 2013. Biochemistry changes that occur after death: potential markers for determining post-mortem interval. PLoS One 8 (11), e82011.

Ferri, G., Alù, M., Corradini, B., Beduschi, G., 2009. Forensic botany: species identification of botanical trace evidence using a multigene barcoding approach. International Journal of Legal Medicine 123 (5), 395–401.

Fierer, N., Lauber, C.L., Zhou, N., McDonald, D., Costello, E.K., Knight, R., 2010. Forensic identification using skin microbial communities. Proceedings of the National Academy of Sciences USA 107 (14), 6477–6481.

Finley, S.J., Benbow, M.E., Javan, G.T., 2015a. Potential applications of soil microbial ecology and next-generation sequencing in criminal investigations. Applied Soil Ecology 88, 69–78.

Finley, S.J., Benbow, M.E., Javan, G.T., 2015b. Microbial communities associated with human decomposition and their potential use as postmortem clocks. International Journal of Legal Medicine 129 (3), 623–632.

Finley, S.J., Pechal, J.L., Benbow, M.E., Robertson, B.K., Javan, G.T., 2016. Microbial signatures of cadaver gravesoil during decomposition. Microbial Ecology 71 (3), 524–529.

Forbes, S.L., Dent, B.B., Stuart, B.H., 2005a. The effect of soil type on adipocere formation. Forensic Science International 154 (1), 35–43.

Forbes, S.L., Dent, B.B., Stuart, B.H., 2005b. The effect of the method of burial on adipocere formation. Forensic Science International 154 (1), 44–52.

Forbes, S.L., 2008. Decomposition chemistry in a burial environment. In: Tibbett, M., Carter, D.O. (Eds.), Soil Analysis in Forensic Taphonomy: Chemical and Biological Effects of Buried Human Remains. CRC Press, Boca Raton, pp. 203–224.

Forbes, S.L., Carter, D.O., 2015. Processes and mechanisms of death and decomposition of vertebrate carrion. In: Benbow, E.M., Tomberlin, J.K., Tarone, A.M. (Eds.), Carrion Ecology, Evolution, and Their Applications, pp. 13–30 Boca Raton.

Forbes, S.L., Perrault, K.A., 2014. Decomposition odour profiling in the air and soil surrounding vertebrate carrion. PLoS One 9 (4), e95107.

Ghannoum, M., 2016. The mycobiome. The Scientist. http://www.the-scientist.com/?articles.view/articleNo/45153/title/The-Mycobiome/.

Gill-King, H., 1997. Chemical and ultrastructural aspects of decomposition. In: Haglund, W.D., Sorg, M.H. (Eds.), Forensic Taphonomy: The Postmortem Fate of Human Remains. CRC Press, Boca Raton, pp. 93–108.

Goga, H., 2012. Comparison of bacterial DNA profiles of footwear insoles and soles of feet for the forensic discrimination of footwear owners. International Journal of Legal Medicine 126, 815–823.

Gunn, A., 2009. Essential Forensic Biology, second ed. John Wiley and Sons, West Sussex.

Guo, J., Fu, X., Liao, H., Hu, Z., Long, L., Yan, W., Ding, Y., Zha, L., Guo, Y., Yan, J., Chang, Y., 2016. Potential use of bacterial community succession for estimating post-mortem interval as revealed by high-throughput sequencing. Scientific Reports 6, 24197.

Habtom, H., Demaneche, S., Dawson, L.A., Azulay, C., Matan, O., Robe, P., Gafny, R., Simonet, P., Jurkevitch, E., Pasternak, Z., 2017. Soil characterisation by bacterial community analysis for forensic applications: a quantitative comparison of environmental technologies. Forensic Science International 26, 21–29.

Haglund, W.D., Sorg, M.H. (Eds.), 1997. Forensic Taphonomy: The Post Mortem Fate of Human Remains. CRC Press, Boca Raton, pp. 405–413.

Hauther, K.A., Cobaugh, K.L., Jantz, L.M., Sparer, T.E., DeBruyn, J.M., 2015. Estimating time since death from postmortem human gut microbial communities. Journal of Forensic Sciences 60 (5), 1234–1240.

Hawksworth, D.L., Wiltshire, P.E.J., 2011. Forensic mycology: the use of fungi in criminal investigations. Forensic Science International 206 (1–3), 1–11.

Hawksworth, D.L., Wiltshire, P.E.J., 2015. Forensic mycology: current perspectives. Research and Reports in Forensic Medical Science 5, 75–83.

Hayman, J., Oxenham, M., 2016. Human Body Decomposition. Academic Press, London.

Hobischak, N.R., VanLaerhoven, S.L., Anderson, G.S., 2006. Successional patterns of diversity in insect fauna on carrion in sun and shade in the boreal forest region of Canada, near Edmonton, Alberta. Canadian Entomologist 138 (3), 376–383.

Hopkins, D.W., Wiltshire, P.E., Turner, B.D., 2000. Microbial characteristics of soil graves: an investigation at the interface of soil microbiology and forensic science. Applied Soil Ecology 14 (3), 283–288.

Howard, G.T., Duos, B., Watson-Horzelski, E.J., 2010. Characterization of the soil microbial community associated with the decomposition of swine carcass. International Biodeterioration and Biodegradation 64 (4), 300–304.

Hyde, E.R., Haarmann, D.P., Lynne, A.M., Bucheli, S.R., Petrosino, J.F., 2013. The living dead: bacterial community structure of a cadaver at the onset and end of the bloat stage of decomposition. PLoS One 8 (10), e77733.

Hyde, E.R., Haarmann, D.P., Petrosino, J.F., Lynne, A.M., Bucheli, S.R., 2015. Initial insights into bacterial succession during human decomposition. International Journal of Legal Medicine 129 (3), 661–671.

Iancu, L., Cater, D.O., Junkins, E.N., Purcarea, C., 2015. Using bacterial and necrophagous insects dynamics for post-mortem interval estimation during cold season: novel case study in Romania. Forensic Science International 254, 106–117.

Ishii, K., Hitosugi, M., Yagichi, T., Tokudome, S., 2007. The importance of forensic mycology. Legal Medicine 9, 287.

Javan, G.T., Finley, S.J., Can, I., Wilkinson, J.E., Hanson, J.D., Tarone, A.M., 2016. Human thanatomicrobiome succession and time since death. Scientific Reports 6, 29598. http://dx.doi.org/10.1038/srep29598.

Janaway, R.C., 1996. The decay of buried human remains and their associated materials. In: Hunter, J., Roberts, C., Martin, A. (Eds.), Studies in Crime: An Introduction to Forensic Archaeology. B.T. Batsford Ltd., London, pp. 58–85.

Janaway, R.C., Percival, S.L., Wilson, A.S., 2009. Decomposition of human remains. In: Percival, S.L. (Ed.), Microbiology and Aging: Clinical Manifestations. Springer, New York, pp. 313–334.

Kasuda, S., Kudo, R., Yuui, K., Imai, H., Nakata, M., Hatake, K., 2016. An autopsy case of complete adipocere formation. Legal Medicine 18, 49–51.

Kasper, J., Mumm, R., Ruther, J., 2012. The composition of carcass volatile profiles in relation to storage time and climate conditions. Forensic Science International 223 (1–3), 64–71.

Killham, K., 1994. The ecology of soil nutrient cycling. In: Killham, K. (Ed.), Soil Ecology. Cambridge University Press, Cambridge, pp. 89–150.

Knight, L.D., Presnell, S.E., 2005. Death by sewer gas: case report of a double fatality and review of the literature. The American Journal of Forensic Medicine and Pathology 26 (2), 181–185.

Kuiper, I., 2016. Microbial forensics: next-generation sequencing as catalyst. EMBO Reports 17 (8), 1085–1087.

Lauber, C.L., Metcalf, J.L., Keepers, K., Ackermann, G., Carter, D.O., Knight, R., 2014. Vertebrate decomposition is accelerated by soil microbes. Applied and Environmental Microbiology 80 (16), 4920–4929.

LeBlanc, H.N., Logan, J.G., 2010. Exploiting insect olfaction in forensic entomology. In: Amendt, J., Goff, M.L., Campobasso, C.P., Grassberger, M. (Eds.), Current Concepts in Forensic Entomology. Springer, Dordrecht, pp. 205–221.

Lerner, A., Shor, Y., Vinokurov, A., Okon, Y., Jurkevitch, E., 2006. Can denaturing gradient gel electrophoresis (DGGE) analysis of amplified 16S rDNA of soil bacterial populations be used in forensic investigations? Soil Biology & Biochemistry 38, 1188–1192.

Ma, Q., Fonseca, A., Liu, W., Fields, A.T., Pimsler, M.L., Spindola, A.F., Tarone, A.M., Crippen, T.L., Tomberlin, J.K., Wood, T.K., 2012. *Proteus mirabilis* interkingdom swarming signals attract blow flies. The ISME Journal 6 (7), 1356–1366.

Maier, R.M., Pepper, I.L., 2009. Bacterial communities in natural ecosystems. In: Maier, R.M., Pepper, I.L., Gerba, C.P. (Eds.), Environmental Microbiology, second ed. Academic Press, London, pp. 347–356.

Mann, R.W., Bass, W.M., Meadows, L., 1990. Time since death and decomposition of the human body: variables and observations in case and experimental field studies. Journal of Forensic Sciences 35, 103–111.

McGuire, K.L., Treseder, K.K., 2010. Microbial communities and their relevance for ecosystem models: decomposition as a case study. Soil Biology & Biochemistry 42, 529–535.

Menezes, R.G., Kanchan, T., Lobo, S.W., Jain, A., Bhat, N.B., Rao, N.G., 2008. Cadaveric fungi: not yet an established forensic tool. Journal of Forensic and Legal Medicine 15, 124–126.

Metcalf, J.L., Parfrey, L.W., Gonzalez, A., Lauber, C.L., Knights, D., Ackermann, G., Humphrey, G.C., Gebert, M.J., Van Treuren, W., Berg-Lyons, D., Keepers, K., 2013. A microbial clock provides an accurate estimate of the postmortem interval in a mouse model system. Elife 2, e01104.

Metcalf, J.L., Xu, Z.Z., Weiss, S., Lax, S., Van Treuren, W., Hyde, E.R., Song, S.J., Amir, A., Larsen, P., Sangwan, N., Haarmann, D., 2016. Microbial community assembly and metabolic function during mammalian corpse decomposition. Science 351 (6269), 158–162.

Moreno, L.I., Mills, D., Fetscher, J., John-Williams, K., Meadows-Jantz, L., McCord, B., 2011. The application of amplicon length heterogeneity PCR (LH-PCR) for monitoring the dynamics of soil microbial communities associated with cadaver decomposition. Journal of Microbiological Methods 84, 388–393.

Nishi, E., Tashiro, Y., Sakai, K., 2015. Discrimination among individuals using terminal restriction fragment length polymorphism profiling of bacteria derived from forensic evidence. International Journal of Legal Medicine 129, 425–433.

Olakanye, A.O., Thompson, T.J.U., Ralebitso-Senior, T.K., 2014. Changes to soil bacterial profiles as a result of *Sus scrofa* domesticus decomposition. Forensic Science International 245, 101–106.

Olakanye, A.O., Thompson, T., Ralebitso-Senior, T.K., 2015. Shifts in soil biodiversity – a forensic comparison between *Sus scrofa domesticus* and vegetation decomposition. Science & Justice 55 (6), 402–407.

Olakanye, A.O., Ralebitso-Senior, T.K., 2017. Subsurface decomposition analysis reveals shifts in soil necrobiome community structure. Forensic Science International –Genetics (Submitted).

Olakanye, A.O., Nelson, A., Ralebitso-Senior, T.K., 2017. A comparative *in situ* decomposition study using still born piglets and leaf litter from a deciduous forest. Forensic Science International (Submitted).

Paczkowski, S., Maibaum, F., Paczkowska, M., Schütz, S., 2012. Decaying mouse volatiles perceived by *Calliphora vicina* Rob.-Desv. Journal of Forensic Sciences 57 (6), 1497–1506.

Parkinson, R.A., Dias, K.R., Horswell, J., Greenwood, P., Banning, N., Tibbett, M., Vass, A.A., 2009. Microbial community analysis of human decomposition on soil. In: Ritz, K., Dawson, L.A., Miller, D. (Eds.), Criminal and Environmental Soil Forensics. Springer, New York, pp. 379–394.

Pechal, J.L., Crippen, T.L., Benbow, M.E., Tarone, A.M., Dowd, S., Tomberlin, J.K., 2014. The potential use of bacterial community succession in forensics as described by high throughput metagenomic sequencing. International Journal of Legal Medicine 128 (1), 193–205.

Pechal, J.L., Crippen, T.L., Tarone, A.M., Lewis, A.J., Tomberlin, J.K., Benbow, M.E., 2013. Microbial community functional change during vertebrate carrion decomposition. PLoS One 8 (11), e79035.

Petraco, N., Kubic, T.A., Petraco, N.D., 2008. Case studies in forensic soil examinations. Forensic Science International 178 (2–3), e23–e27.

Petrisor, I.G., Parkinson, R.A., Horswell, J., Waters, J.M., Burgoyne, L.A., Catcheside, D.E.A., Dejonghe, W., Leys, N., Vanbroekhoven, K., Pattnaik, P., Graves, D., 2006. Microbial forensics. In: Morrison, R.D., Murphy, B.L. (Eds.), Environmental Forensics: Contaminant Specific Guide. Academic Press, pp. 227–257.

Pfeiffer, S., Milne, S., Stevenson, R.M., 1998. The natural decomposition of adipocere. Journal of Forensic Science 43 (2), 368–370.

Ralebitso-Senior, T.K., Thompson, T.J.U., Carney, H.E., 2016. Microbial ecogenomics and forensic archaeology: new methods for investigating clandestine grave sites. Human Remains & Violence 2 (1), 41–57.

Rothschild, M.A., Schmidt, V., Schneider, V., 1996. Adipocere – problems in estimating the length of time since death. Medical Law 15 (2), 329–335.

Ruffell, A., 2010. Forensic pedology, forensic geology, forensic geoscience, geoforensics and soil forensics. Forensic Science International 202, 9–12.

Ruffell, A., McKinley, J., 2005. Forensic geoscience: applications of geology, geomorphology and geophysics to criminal investigations. Earth Science Review 69, 235–247.

Sabucedo, A.J., Furton, K.G., 2003. Estimation of postmortem interval using the protein marker cardiac Troponin I. Forensic Science International 134 (1), 11–16.

Sharanowski, B.J., Walker, E.G., Anderson, G.S., 2008. Insect succession and decomposition patterns on shaded and sunlit carrion in Saskatchewan in three different seasons. Forensic Science International 179 (2–3), 219–240.

Schmidtmann, E.T., Martin, P.A., 1992. Relationship between selected bacteria and the growth of immature house flies, *Musca domestica*, in an axenic test system. Journal of Medical Entomology 29 (2), 232–235.

Schoenen, D., Schoenen, H., 2013. Adipocere formation—the result of insufficient microbial degradation. Forensic Science International 226 (1–3), 301–306.

Schultz, J.J., Martin, M.M., 2012. Monitoring controlled graves representing common burial scenarios with ground penetrating radar. Journal of Applied Geophysics 83, 74–89.

Sidrim, J.J.C., Moreira Filho, R.E., Cordeiro, R.A., Rocha, R.A., Caetano, E.P., Monteiro, A.J., Brilhante, R.S.N., 2010. Fungal microbiota dynamics as a postmortem investigation tool: focus on Aspergillus, Peninillium and Candida species. Journal of Applied Microbiology 108 (5), 1751–1756.

Singh, B., Crippen, T.L., 2015. Methodologies in forensic and decomposition microbiology. In: Tomberlin, J.K., Benbow, E.M. (Eds.), Forensic Entomology: International Dimensions and Frontiers. CRC Press, Boca Raton, pp. 249–262.

Statheropoulos, M., Agapiou, A., Spiliopoulou, C., Pallis, G.C., Sianos, E., 2007. Environmental aspects of VOCs evolved in the early stages of human decomposition. Science of the Total Environment 385 (1), 221–227.

Statheropoulos, M., Spiliopoulou, C., Agapiou, A., 2005. A study of volatile organic compounds evolved from the decaying human body. Forensic Science International 153 (2), 147–155.

Stokes, K.L., Forbes, S.L., Tibbett, M., 2009. Freezing skeletal muscle tissue does not affect its decomposition in soil: evidence from temporal changes in tissue mass, microbial activity and soil chemistry based on excised samples. Forensic Science International 183, 6–13.

Tibbett, M., 2008. The basics of forensic taphonomy: understanding cadaver decomposition in terrestial gravesites. In: Oxenham, M. (Ed.), Forensic Approaches to Death, Disaster and Abuse. Australian Academic Press, Bowen Hills, pp. 29–36.

Tibbett, M., Carter, D.O., 2003. Mushroom and taphonomy: the fungi that mark woodland graves. Mycologist 17 (1), 20–24.

Tomberlin, J.K., Benbow, E.M., 2015. Forensic Entomology: International Dimensions and Frontiers. CRC Press, Florida.

Tomberlin, J.K., Crippen, T.L., Tarone, A.M., Singh, B., Adams, K., Rezenom, Y.H., Benbow, M.E., Flores, M., Longnecker, M., Pechal, J.L., Russell, D.H., Beier, R.C., Wood, T.K., 2012. Interkingdom responses of flies to bacteria mediated by fly physiology and bacterial quorum sensing. Animal Behaviour 84 (6), 1449–1456.

Tranchida, M.C., Centeno, N.D., Cabello, M.N., 2014. Soil fungi: their potential use as a forensic tool. Journal of Forensic Sciences 59 (3), 785–789.

Ubelaker, D.H., Zarenko, K.M., 2011. Adipocere: what is known after two centuries of research. Forensic Science International 208 (1–3), 167–172.

Ueland, M., Breton, H.A., Forbes, S.L., 2014. Bacterial populations associated with early-stage adipocere formation in lacustrine waters. International Journal of Legal Medicine 128 (2), 379–387.

Uitdehaag, S.C.A., Quaak, F.C.A., Kuiper, I., 2016. Soil comparisons using small soil traces, a case report. In: Kars, H., van den Eijkel, L. (Eds.), Soil in Criminal and Environmental Forensics; Proceedings of the Soil Forensics Special 6th European Academy of Forensic Science Conference. Editors, The Hague. ISBN: 978-3-319-33113-3, pp. 61–69.

Ururahy-Rodrigues, A., Rafael, J.A., Wanderley, R.F., Marques, H., Pujol-Luz, J.R., 2008. *Coprophanaeus lancifer* (Linnaeus, 1767) (Coleoptera, Scarabaeidae) activity moves a man-size pig carcass: relevant data for forensic taphonomy. Forensic Science International 182 (1–3), e19–e22.

van Belle, L.E., Carter, D.O., Forbes, S.L., 2009. Measurement of ninhydrin reactive nitrogen influx into gravesoil during aboveground and belowground carcass (*Sus domesticus*) decomposition. Forensic Science International 193 (1–3), 37–41.

Vass, A.A., 2012. Odor mortis. Forensic Science International 222 (1), 234–241.

Vass, A.A., Barshick, S.A., Sega, G., Caton, J., Skeen, J.T., Love, J.C., Synstelien, J.A., 2002. Decomposition chemistry of human remains: a new methodology for determining the postmortem interval. Journal of Forensic Sciences 47 (3), 542–553.

Vass, A.A., Eckenrode, B.A., Thompson, C.V., Wolf, D.A., Synstelien, J.A., Burnett, M.N., Dulgerian, N., Smith, R.R., 2004. Decompositional odor analysis database. Journal of Forensic Science 49 (4), 1–10.

Vass, A.A., Smith, R.R., Thompson, C.V., Burnett, M.N., Dulgerian, N., Eckenrode, B.A., 2008. Odor analysis of decomposing buried human remains. Journal of Forensic Sciences 53 (2), 384–391.

Vass, A.A., Bass, W.M., Wolt, J.D., Foss, J.E., Ammons, J.T., 1992. Time since death determinations of human cadavers using soil solution. Journal of Forensic Science 37 (5), 1236–1253.

Ward, J., Peakall, R., Gilmore, S.R., Robertson, J., 2005. A molecular identification system for grasses: a novel technology for forensic botany. Forensic Science International 152, 121–131.

Weiss, S., Carter, D.O., Metcalf, J.L., Knight, R., 2016. Carcass mass has little influence on the structure of gravesoil microbial communities. International Journal of Legal Medicine 130 (1), 253–263.

Woods, B., Lennard, C., Kirkbride, P.K., Robertson, J., 2014. Soil examination for a forensic trace evidence laboratory-Part 1: spectroscopic techniques. Forensic Science International 245, 187–194.

Zhou, C., Byard, R.W., 2011. Factors and processes causing accelerated decomposition in human cadavers – an overview. Journal of Forensic and Legal Medicine 18 (1), 6–9.

Ziavrou, K., Boumba, V.A., Vougiouklakis, T.G., 2005. Insights into the origin of postmortem ethanol. International Journal of Toxicology 24 (2), 69–77.

FURTHER READING

Horswell, J., Cordiner, S.J., Maas, E.W., Martin, T.M., Sutherland, K.B., Speir, T.W., Nogales, B., Osborn, A.M., 2002. Forensic comparison of soils by bacterial community DNA profiling. Journal of Forensic Science 47 (2), 350–353.

Zhang, L., Guo, J.J., Peng, Y.L., Xie, D., Guo, Y.D., Yan, J., Zha, L., Cai, J.F., 2016. Bacterial succession on rat carcasses and applications for PMI estimation. Fa Yi Xue Za Zhi 32 (1), 1–6.

CHAPTER 2

Forensic Taphonomy

Amy E. Rattenbury
Wrexham Glyndŵr University, Wrexham, United Kingdom

INTRODUCTION TO TAPHONOMY AND TAPHONOMIC RESEARCH

The Role of Taphonomy

Taphonomy comes from the Greek word taphos (τάφος) meaning grave, but has more commonly been accepted as the study of an organism from the time of its death to the point of its discovery. A multifaceted area, it incorporates decomposition, burial, transportations, and the chemical, physical, and biological factors that go alongside. Originally classified as a subdiscipline of paleontology, the study of taphonomy, under this specific title, was first recognized by Professor J.A. Efremov of the Soviet Academy of Sciences in Moscow (Efremov, 1940). He has been credited by many with founding the field when he studied the transition of animal remains from the biosphere to the lithosphere. However, texts recognizing differences in postmortem degradation, such as the impact of soil type and temperature, date back to 1927 (Weigelt, 1927).

Within paleontology the discipline is focused around the preservation of remains and, more specifically, the process of fossilization. This recognized the importance of identifying the features of taphonomy to better understand the environment and conditions in which the remains were recovered, but also suggested how factors of the living organism could be determined by changes that occur after its death. A significant factor in many aspects of forensic investigation is chronology and reconstruction. Haglund and Sorg (2002) recognized that taphonomic studies can provide an insight to this by focusing on four distinct phases: time before death, death, deposition, and recovery. Dirkmaat et al. (2008) then suggested that forensic taphonomy is a key development in forensics, particularly in relation to the area of anthropology.

Forensic taphonomy has a somewhat checkered research history with several plausible reasons proposed. The most significant of these appear to be: the lack of human specimens available for research; limited awareness of its application in criminal justice; and limited collaboration between those investigating deaths and biological anthropology specialists (Haglund and Sorg, 1997). Very few facilities exist globally to investigate this area, with the use of human remains research being almost entirely constrained to the United States. An additional factor may be that historically, and still to some extent, many bodies are found and recovered very quickly after death, such as in road traffic

Forensic Ecogenomics
ISBN 978-0-12-809360-3
http://dx.doi.org/10.1016/B978-0-12-809360-3.00002-3

accidents or in medical institutions, meaning a great deal of anthropological or taphonomic expertise was not readily required.

Aspects of pathology, anthropology, and archeology all feed into the multidisciplinary area that is now recognized as an integral part of death investigation; an amalgamation of other subjects used for the purposes of examining contemporary human remains (Haglund and Sorg, 2002). Like other forensic specialisms, the area of forensic taphonomy sees the rules and knowledge of its original discipline made relevant in legal settings for use in court and for the investigation of crimes. Taphonomy has applications for the location of remains, supporting the identification of the deceased, helping to establish cause of death, and determination of postmortem intervals (PMIs). The PMI can be estimated by a variety of methods, each with its own limitations, and therefore a collection of data from both direct and indirect methods is often used to narrow down this period. Many methods are suggested throughout the chapter, including the use of features such as *rigor mortis* or the growth rates of entomological species; however, there is still a great degree of variability in the accuracy of these methods. One thing that is universally agreed upon is that as the PMI increases, the accuracy of any estimations decreases (Christensen et al., 2014).

The role of a forensic taphonomist is not only diverse, but evolutionary as well, which can help to make links between these areas to then provide a comprehensive investigation into the circumstances surrounding death. A clear definition of taphonomy is probably best summarized by Schotsmans et al. (2017) who considered the broader spectrum of its role in archeology, paleobiology, and the forensic context. Most previous attempts to encapsulate the term have focused on elements of degradation or preservation up until the point of recovery. Instead, Schotsmans and colleagues propose that taphonomy should be an assessment of all peri- and postmortem processes, inclusive of recovery, storage, and stages of analysis. By examining all aspects of these stages, a better understanding of the scope of forensic analysis in taphonomy can be gained. This separates taphonomy into two further subdisciplines: biotaphonomy and geotaphonomy.

Biotaphonomy is focused around aspects such as decomposition, preservation, and modification. Several variables constantly affect the biotaphonomic action occurring. There are external factors that are both abiotic, such as climate, and biotic, such as animal activity, as well as individual factors such as height and weight. With prolonged deterioration, there is leeching of material into the deposition environment and this is where we enter the remit of geotaphonomy. The cadaver itself forms a microenvironment caused by its decay, integration or any scattering, complex trophic phases that can initiate variations to the chemistry and ecology of the surrounding environment. Differences that characterize this environment, such as weather, microbiology, and body coverings, all form a significant impact on the taphonomic processes, some of which can act as a catalyst to the overall process of decomposition (Lyman, 1994).

Although different aims have been suggested for the focus of forensic taphonomy, a general consensus is that it should deal with a reconstruction of perimortem events to determine the time since death and any factors that may have impacted on the remains (Beary and Lyman, 2012; Komar and Buikstar, 2008). Although the field still has its critics, it is an important discipline and further decomposition studies are still required.

Taphonomic Research Facilities

Founded in 1980 by Dr. William Bass, the Anthropological Research Facility at the University of Tennessee in the United States was for many years the only one of its kind in the world. It pioneered the use of human cadavers for its decomposition research and allowed for some of the first comparisons of experimental data with real-life forensic situations. Working with bodies that had been donated to the facility for research, various conditions were recreated to simulate burial and deposition contexts and allowed the decomposition process to be studied closely. This research paved the way for many other decomposition studies and made it possible to better understand entomological activity, as well as the significance of environmental factors such as body coverings, burial environment, and the effect scavengers might have on the body (Shirley et al., 2011). Experimental data from this facility has been integral to many of the details to be explored later in this chapter.

To provide different geographical contexts, similar facilities have opened elsewhere such as at the University of Western Carolina. Also there are now six such facilities across North America and one in Sydney, Australia. Early in 2017 the first human research facility was approved in Europe in Amsterdam. The Academic Medical Center Cemetery will focus entirely on subsurface decomposition. By providing a comparison for experiments with differences in environments and land typography, it is possible to better understand the factors that effect and disrupt the decomposition process (Jones and Whitaker, 2009).

Animal Analogs

In many experimental studies, animals are used as analogs when human remains are either unavailable or unlicensed. At research facilities across the globe, such as the Wrexham Glyndŵr University's Forensic Science and Crime Scene Research Area, other easily accessible mammals are used in the place of human cadavers. Most research is commonly conducted on pigs, rabbits, mice, or rats, either dealing with the carcass as a whole or select anatomic sections, for example, trotters. The choice of these is often dependent on the cost, availability, and scale of the experiment (Stokes et al., 2013). Unfortunately, however, this has resulted in questions with regards to transferability when much of the data collected from studies conducted on nonhuman remains are utilized in death scene investigation.

Turner and Wiltshire (1999), Notter et al. (2009), and Stokes et al. (2013) have all recorded disparities in outcomes from the use of pigs as human analogs with the latter revealing that none of the analogs utilized had similar results when measuring decomposition to those obtained when testing on human remains in a subsurface soil environment. Research looking at the use of pigs and rabbits in comparison to human cadavers across different seasons has showed that their use as analogs does not yield the transferable results originally anticipated (Dautartas et al., 2016). The research, which was presented to the American Academy of Forensic Science, summarized that the decomposition of pigs was quicker than that of both humans and rabbits in spring and summer. Initially, rabbit decomposition was the slowest overall until the point of peak maggot activity, which showed significant progression over a 24-h period. The results of the winter study shed light on the scavenging preferences of local wildlife with human remains being consumed initially. Finally, one of the most notable conclusions was the degree of variation within the human subject group. Both the rates of pig and rabbit decomposition were consistent within the samples, while human remains decomposition proved much more variable and therefore harder to predict.

Ethical and Legal Factors

Many ethical issues are raised when considering the use of human remains for research purposes. Thus any experimentation that makes use of cadavers must be highly regulated (Stokes et al., 2013). Existing legislation in the United Kingdom prevents any form of taphonomic experimentation to be performed on human tissue, as governed by the Human Tissue Authority (HTA), hence there is a significant push from academics in the field to begin discussions with the HTA surrounding the current legislation. At present, the Human Tissues Act (2004) states that human cadavers can be used acceptably for medical purposes. Nevertheless, this process is highly regulated with only designated hospital training centers being approved at universities subject to agreements on the nature of all donor testing and approval by a research ethics committee before any cadaver donations can be accepted. According to McNeill (1993), this was essential to ensure that not only are legal requirements met, but any cultural and religious wishes of those donating would always be upheld.

As well as the legal issues, previous attempts to establish human research facilities for forensic research in the United Kingdom have been met with a number of objections. One of the most notable attempts to establish a facility was in 2010 when Omega Supplies Ltd. put forward funds to support a facility in Lincolnshire (Williams, 2015). However, concerns over location and availability of cadavers were raised as well as a lack of public support for the proposal. To mitigate for the last issue, public opinion surveys have been launched to better inform UK citizens and address their worries and concerns. For example, research from Staffordshire University in 2014 revealed an overwhelming recognition from the public that there is a need for a UK-based human research facility, with 92% agreeing that a center should be established (Witt and Cassella, 2014). In contrast, there was less conviction when participants were asked for their opinions on funding, security, and if they would be happy for the bodies of their loved ones to be donated. A more contemporary survey has been launched by the University of Huddersfield, which is targeting over 1000 UK adults, although no results have been published as yet.

STAGES OF DECOMPOSITION

Postmortem Changes

At the point of death, when circulatory, respiratory, and neurological functions cease, both the body as an entity and the cells contained within it begin a transition into a state of decay. Although consisting of a series of relatively predictable events, the entire decomposition process is highly susceptible to environmental influence, which can cause significant variations in not only the detectable changes but also the time periods in which they occur. Numerous factors such as temperature and scavenging contribute to the rate of decomposition, and as a result significant research has been undertaken in an attempt to establish specific correlations between the intrinsic and external influences (see also Chapter 3). It is well accepted that the taphonomic changes present will generally fit into either putrefaction or arrested decay, which is determined by the aforementioned factors (Schotsmans et al., 2017). Internally, reduced concentrations of cellular oxygen initiate the process of autolysis, or self-digestion. Often, oviposition by certain entomological species, such as the necrophagous blow flies, will occur within minutes of death, with eggs laid on the body, typically within natural orifices or wounds (Martinez et al., 2007; Pokines and Symes, 2013).

Autolysis

Decomposition begins initially within the abdomen because of the high diversity and abundance of hydrolytic enzymes from the liver, stomach, and pancreas, which begin to break down cells and tissues. The decreased concentrations of oxygen in the body, along with the increase of carbon dioxide and other waste products, cause a shift in pH within cells. This leads to a subsequent decreased integrity of the cellular membranes, resulting in enzymes being released and denaturing the remaining membrane molecules (Gill-King, 1997).

Many of these microscopic and chemical changes are not observed easily at this stage without histological testing. This confirms the degradation of the cell structure and provides evidence of cell necrosis. Often more macroscopic characteristics such as clouding in the cornea, cooling of the body or other observable characteristics can be noted externally (Pokines and Symes, 2013). Overall, many features of both putrefaction and autolysis occur simultaneously and therefore it can be difficult to attribute them to the separate processes. Technically, however, autolysis is enzyme driven with putrefaction resulting in the activity of bacteria. Notwithstanding these differences, both features contribute to the overall taphonomic changes witnessed in the cadaver.

Algor Mortis

Algor mortis, the cooling of the body postmortem, is the result of a cessation in thermoregulation. As body temperature is controlled by the hypothalamus, this homeostatic feature can no longer be maintained after death. Thus the body temperature will begin to change toward the ambient temperature of the room or surroundings in which the remains are found. This occurs through radiation, convection, conduction, and, if the subject is wet, evaporation. Most commonly, the body temperature decreases, although in more extreme climates an increase in cadaver temperature may result. Consequently, temperature change can play a particularly important role in establishing the PMI, which in turn helps to reconstruct the chronology and circumstances surrounding death (Guharaj, 2003).

Although a generally accepted principle is that body temperature decreases by an average of 1°C per hour, research findings suggest that this process can be delayed by up to 3 h in the initial postmortem period (Al-Alousi et al., 2002). Newton's Law of Cooling states that the larger the temperature difference between an object and its surrounding, the quicker it will cool. However, it has been well accepted that this pattern should not be adapted for cadavers with Rainy (1868) first recording that cadaveric cooling did not occur in this fashion. This was later attributed to the continuation of metabolic processes and the complexities of interior and surface cooling, resulting in nonuniform changes across the body being recorded (Joseph and Schickele, 1970). Numerous formulae have been suggested over the last century taking this into account, each with varying degrees of accuracy noted but all of which faced problems in their application to field work due to differences predicted by body position, location or temperature reading, or the presence of clothing (Glaister, 1942; Marshall and Hoare, 1962). It has also been noted that such standardized curves may not take into account other factors such as natural differences in body temperature at the time of death, wind speed, and surface area-to-volume ratio. For example, thinner individuals tend to cool much more quickly. Individual variations such as these have led to suggestions that this PMI estimation approach holds little value when applied to human remains in real criminal investigations (Sutherland et al., 2013).

One of the most renowned tools for PMI estimations from body temperature is the nomogram method. The approach adopts separate graphs that are provided for ambient temperatures above and below 23 °C and considerations such as clothing and water can be taken into account with the lag phase also corrected for (Henssge, 1988). To militate against the numerous environmental uncertainties, a more sophisticated formula was subsequently designed to factor in multiple crime scene variables into the "Henssge equation." This formula facilitates more objective calculations as it does not focus on an exact time of death but rather a PMI range of 5.3 h. Although less precise, this novel technique, which is now available through smartphone application technology, has increased accuracy and functionality at crime scenes (Madea, 2015).

Concerns over the use of *algor mortis* as a feasible method for PMI estimation remain particularly for death scenes where significant abdominal trauma or potential sexual assault has occurred. This is because the methods for measuring postmortem body temperature rely on the penetration of internal organs or rectal thermometer readings, which can be either impossible or unsuitable depending on the nature of the crime. Additionally, depending on the amount of microbial and entomological activity, accurate body temperatures cannot always be established as maggot masses and bacteria activity may generate heat. Therefore the use of body temperature as a method for determining PMI should be restricted to fresh remains.

Livor Mortis

Another characteristic of the fresh stage of decomposition is the appearance and fixation of *livor mortis*, also known as hypostasis or lividity. As for *algor mortis*, lividity is a result of normal bodily functions ceasing, but with a focus on the lack of circulation and oxygen depletion. Normally observed within 2 h of death, but sometimes as quickly as the first 20 min, lividity is a characteristic discoloration to the skin caused by the pooling of blood (Dhawane and Dhoble, 2016).

Without cardiac contractions to keep it moving, blood, whose oxygen has dissociated from its hemoglobin, collects in the lower parts of the body causing the skin to appear red or dark purple. Initially, blood remains fluid due to the presence of plasmin, a fibrinolytic enzyme that prevents coagulation by reducing fibrinogen levels. Thus blood can be moved easily and forced out of different parts of the body due to pressure caused by contact with surfaces, such as a hard floor, or around tight-fitting ligatures. Sometimes even aspects of clothing such as elasticated waistbands can cause enough pressure to leave white voids within the tissue staining. This unique patterning becomes fixed on the skin due to hemolysis within 12 h and can prove a very useful tool in determining the location, position, and any postmortem movement of the body. Nevertheless, the timing and presence of *livor mortis* is highly unreliable for accurate use in PMI determination. Although studies have been conducted on their potential use, spectrophotometry and colorimetry are still extremely limited in their practical capacity (Usumoto et al., 2010).

Lividity is not a feature that is only restricted to the external remains and there have been many reported cases of blood pooling within specific organs such as the heart or lungs (Ishida et al., 2011, 2015). Care must be taken therefore when analyzing and interpreting this internal discoloration as it should not be confused with features caused by hemorrhaging. A secondary effect of hypostasis is a characteristic known as pallor. As blood begins to pool, it drains away from capillaries close to the skin's surface on the superior aspects of the body. Much like the paling complexion as a heat preservation mechanism in living individuals, a color loss can be observed in the skin resulting in a more grayed appearance, hence the term "deathly pale" (Pounder, 2000).

Rigor Mortis

Rigor mortis is possibly one of the most well known of the taphonomic changes and is the process that causes the muscles in the body to stiffen resulting in rigidity due to a range of chemical changes in the muscle structure. Muscle fibers, which in life move because of sliding filament theory, rely on the conversion of ATP to ADP. After death, when respiration ceases, the intracellular pH decreases due to the production of lactic and pyruvic acid. The anaerobic glycolysis of glycogen in the muscles causes glycogen depletion and thus reduced ATP concentrations. Also calcium leaks into the sarcomere, where the protein filaments of actin and myosin are present in an alternating arrangement, where calcium then binds allowing for a cross-linkage to occur between the filaments. This causes a pulling motion along the length of the muscle causing it to become shorter and more rigid. In a living individual, ATP would be used to dissociate the cross-linking in the fibers and as a result the rigidity associated with the change would be reversed, whereas it becomes fixed postmortem (Powers, 2005).

First noticed in the small muscle groups such as in the hands and face, rigor can take hold within 3 to 4 h and normally extends across the large muscle groups also within the first 12 h after death, causing the entire body to become stiff. Variations in this time period are observed particularly in individuals who may have decreased levels of ATP at the point of death. This could be caused by exercise or strenuous activity in the perimortem period around the time of death (Madea, 2015). *Rigor mortis* can also be helpful in the reconstruction of the postmortem period by preserving the positioning of the body and in some circumstances showing if any attempt has been made to move the body. However, this type of interpretation is very much time dependent and relies on rigor still being present at the time the body is discovered. The point at which this rigidity reverses and the stiffness passes is extremely variable because of significant differences in the volume of muscle in the remains. However, the body generally returns to a fully flaccid state after 36 h from the time of death, although this can increase by up to 10 days in refrigerated remains (Varetto and Curto, 2005). The exact cause of the breakdown on the cross-linked bonds is not well established, although it is generally credited to enzyme action and the increased cellular breakdown occurring throughout the body.

Since *rigor mortis* occurs in a somewhat predictable pattern, it has been suggested that it can be used to estimate the PMI in combination with body temperature. Knight and Saukko (2004) presented a timeline allowing for bodies categorized as stiff/flaccid and warm/cold to be dated as dead for less than 3 h, 3–8 h, 8–36 h, and more than 36 h. However, due to the variations in both *algor* and *rigor mortis* this method is best not used for anything more than a primary indication.

Bloat Stage

As the primary autolytic stage ends, the body has become a nutrient-rich, acidic, and anaerobic environment. Additionally, the normal defense mechanisms, such as the immunological response against foreign agents, have ceased. This allows exogenous and endogenous microorganisms to thrive inside and on the cadaver. Many of these are natural populations from inside the body but others may migrate in from the surrounding environment. These increased microbial communities start to break down body tissues, producing gases and other metabolic by-products that are responsible for the bloating and unpleasant odor that are characteristic of this stage. Overall, the complex biological molecules within the soft tissue are broken down by the microbes into liquids and gases resulting in an overall loss of integrity and structure (Dent et al., 2004).

The majority of this activity starts in the digestive system, which contains a range of microbial species such as *Staphylococcus epidermidis*, *Clostridium perfringens*, and *Escherichia coli*. One of the significant observable changes of this stage is the increased production of gases such as hydrogen sulfide, methane, ammonia, and sulfur dioxide. The sulfur plays a particularly interesting role when, in combination with hemolysis, it forms sulfhemoglobin, which is observed as a green discoloration of the skin. This color change often begins around the lower abdomen but as bacterial numbers increase rapidly and spread throughout blood vessels it causes them to appear much darker. The distinct coloration pattern resembles that of marble and so the phrase "marbling" was coined. In individuals who were suffering from bacterial infections at the time of death the increased numbers present in the body can also contribute to the putrefactive process (Yamaguchi et al., 2015).

Autolytic action spreads as the microorganisms, which are now colonizing the cadaver, migrate throughout the body. As the rate of autolysis increases the volume of gas also increases and causes the body, and most notably the stomach, to bloat and become distended (Statheropoulos et al., 2011). Blisters, known as bullae, also appear across the skin, filling with gases, decomposition fluids, or both. This buildup creates pressure within the tissues and the body as a whole causing gases to escape. Initially, this occurs through the body's natural orifices or through injuries such as sharp force trauma, which may have been inflicted ante-, peri-, and postmortem. In many cases the combination of increased pressure and degradation of tissue causes bonds between the dermis and epidermis to break down. This causes skin slippage where skin sloughs off exposing the moist, pink basal layers beneath (Boddington et al., 1987). When perforation occurs, this allows the body to rapidly purge fluids and gases into the surrounding environment resulting in a more noticeable and pungent smell.

Active and Advanced Decay

As the integrity of the body is compromised, the decompositional fluids that are released into the surrounding environment, particularly soil, create a unique nutrient-rich cadaver decomposition island (CDI) around the body (Carter et al., 2007). The boundaries of the CDI will change with time as the purged leachate continues to spread away from the body laterally and vertically through the soil. In many cases the CDI environment is not initially conducive to plant life and can be phytotoxic to the local vegetation also as a result of the introduction of vast microbial populations. Although these biophysicochemical properties change over time, it can take up to a year for the vegetation to improve, hence the result of the CDI can still persist even when the remains have been removed (Aitkenhead-Peterson et al., 2012).

This stage is also characterized by a significant surge in entomological activity with blow fly eggs hatching into larvae and additional species being drawn to the body to feed due to the increased surface area of the cadaver. The larvae mature and eventually migrate away from the body to pupate and this results in a second wave of adult flies that colonize the cadaver with further eggs lain to then hatch into larvae. This infestation and succession of numerous species consume the corpse, vastly increasing the rate of decomposition, and it is during this active stage that the biggest decrease in biomass occurs (Singh et al., 2016). Consequently, a significant amount of data is available on the rates and sequence of insect activity, which often prove useful in PMI determination.

When entomological species are present it is possible to use their growth patterns to determine a PMI bracket. Unlike human development, entomological species require specific threshold temperatures for growth. Accumulated degree days (ADD) are a measurement of the total heat, above the threshold temperature, that has been recorded. By considering average daily temperatures, it is possible to convert ADD to calendar days, giving a range in which death is estimated to have occurred. Although accumulated degree hours would be ideal for increased accuracy, the parameter relies on average hourly temperatures for the potential postmortem period, which are seldom available. There are, as with all PMI estimation methods, several limitations that can impact on the accuracy and feasibility of ADD. These include the proximity of the thermometer to the location of recovery, microclimates, and heavy reliance on the availability of entomological samples to analyze (Dabbs, 2010).

The advanced decay stage occurs when the body has lost most of its mass and has begun to dry. At this stage, entomological activity is greatly reduced and fluids have either evaporated or drained from the body (Martinez et al., 2007). The discontinuities in the skin have allowed for oxygen to be introduced, meaning that degradation by aerobic organisms, such as fungi, can begin. At this point an increase in certain chemicals, such as sodium, potassium, nitrogen, calcium, and magnesium, in the soil of the CDI is seen. Although it can be difficult to determine discrete points at which one stage of decomposition ends and the next begins, a surge in vegetative growth on the boarder of the CDI has been suggested as one such marker for the transition from decay to the dry remains stage (Carter et al., 2007).

Skeletal Stage

The final stage of decomposition is the skeletal stage, which is the point at which all soft tissue has been fully decomposed and only the bones remain. Bones are a crystalline matrix formed of carbonated hydroxyapatite (HAP), which also contains collagen; this combination gives the bones their flexibility and strength. Ligaments, tendons, and periosteal tags will initially remain adhered to the bones but, often with the assistance of faunal activity, these too break down causing the skeleton to begin to disarticulate (Dupras et al., 2012). The bones themselves will also begin to decompose through a process of diagenesis. In its simplest construct, diagenesis relates to any form of naturally occurring bone modification that may impact on its structure, chemistry, or molecular content. Its focus is on three major factors: physical, chemical, and biological features. The latter is the one that has been studied the least.

Several processes are at play when considering the breakdown of bone, namely, physical fracturing, degradation by microbes, dissolution in wet or acidic environments, and decalcification. The process of weathering was best summarized by Behrensmeyer (1978) in her six-stage bone degradation scoring system, which is still used today. This system focuses on the extent of cracking and splintering because of water lost through evaporation once decomposition of the protective soft tissue covering has occurred. Additionally, as temperature fluctuates throughout the day and night, the bone too will heat and cool. This can cause repeated expansion and contraction of the bone resulting in the formation of microfractures.

Initially, the fresh bone will be ivory in color but as it is exposed to the sun it becomes bleached. Another impact on bone is the presence of vegetation. In subsurface remains, acid from plant roots can etch the bones as well as the root growth causing mechanical weathering to the skeleton. When bones are deposited in wet conditions, such as saturated soil or in water burials, certain mineral components can begin to disintegrate. Both soil and aquatic conditions will be discussed in detail later but one notable change is that, in acidic environments, HAP becomes soluble (Boaks et al., 2014). Additionally, material can be taken into the bone from the surrounding environments due to the porosity of the bone. This can cause the bone to darken as it takes on the color of the surrounding soil. In exposed remains, moss or lichen can grow on the surface; the impact this has on erosion is currently unknown. However, moss can cause staining on the bone (Fig. 2.1).

ENVIRONMENTAL INFLUENCES

Temperature

Temperature has one of the most significant effects on the rate of decomposition. As it increases, the kinetic energy present and available for enzyme migration results in a greater chance of enzyme substrate collisions. Most enzymes will see an increase in

Figure 2.1 ***Bone weathering on pigs' skulls.*** In the figure the remains on the left were left to decompose in a shallow burial environment. Evidence of color leaching from surrounding soil is present. The remains on the right were left to decompose on the surface. Evidence of bone bleaching and staining because of moss growth is present. Both samples were deposited fresh and left for the same time periods at the Forensic Science and Crime Scene Research Area, Wrexham Glyndŵr University, Wrexham, United Kingdom.

action of 50%–100% with temperature increases of just 10°C. While all enzymes have an optimum functional temperature, they also have a wider threshold range within which their catabolic or metabolic activity occurs (Ball et al., 2011). Some deposition environments are not supportive of the traditional putrefactive decay and as a result a different process of decomposition is seen. If temperatures exceed specific thresholds, then enzymes may denature causing the cadaver to go into a state of arrested decay. Inversely, as temperatures decrease, energy levels also decrease and bacteria and enzymes become dormant. For example, Micozzi and Pless (1997) noted that bacterial growth is reduced significantly below 12°C and stops completely below 5°C.

In extremely cold conditions bodies may freeze, drastically altering the normal pattern of decomposition because the process of freezing alters the microstructures within the body. Specifically, a substantial proportion of the water is drawn out of the cells forming ice crystals at −5°C with the cytoplasm also affected if temperatures drop by a further 5°C. This causes the cells to either freeze internally or shrink. Overall, the process results in less intercellular diffusion and therefore the autolytic and putrefactive processes do not spread throughout the body. Freezing may also cause disruption to intercellular connections, which may cause softening and liquefaction upon thawing. Thawing begins in the external tissue cells and, unlike in remains that have never been frozen, decomposition begins superficially with internal organs remaining relatively preserved (Roberts and Dabbs, 2015).

Vass (2011) proposes that temperature, along with humidity, could be used as a method of determining the PMI more accurately. As a result, decompositional PMI estimations and formulae were developed through analyses performed for over 20 years in the Anthropological Research Facility in Tennessee. However, a Canadian study by Cockle and Bell (2015), which used corpses with known PMIs, found that formerly acknowledged scales considerably misjudged the PMI of bodies exposed to colder temperatures, suggesting a much shorter timeframe than that recorded. This indicated that the developed PMI formulae may not be transferrable to geographically different areas with different climates, with disparities between Tennessee and the United Kingdom one of many examples. Cooler climates or seasonal differences also show a reduced rate of entomological activity resulting in an increased timeframe for soft tissue consumption and therefore a significantly longer time for a body to reach the skeletal stage.

According to Turpin (2017), freezing can potentially be an extremely destructive process for skeletal remains. Specifically, water in the porous cortical can expand by up to 10% as temperatures decrease toward freezing and consequently create pressure in the pores, pushing the bone apart. If the bones undergo freeze–thaw cycles then the water will refreeze in different locations, increase pore sizes, and cause micro-, and sometimes macro-, fractures. If bones remain frozen then the traditional weathering process cannot occur because water is trapped within the structure and therefore cannot evaporate.

Mummification

Another extreme case of arrested decay is the natural mummification process where the preserved cadaver resists decay for a prolonged period while still maintaining features of its living appearance (Aufderheide, 2003). The condition typically occurs in arid, hot or dry, environments. In locations such as chimneys, attics, basements, or other closed environments, mummification results in less destructive changes, which result in the desiccated tissue becoming significantly more preserved. Typically, the skin stretches tightly and becomes brittle with a dark leathery appearance believed to be caused by oxidation. Also water is lost from the body causing internal organs to shrink parallel to an overall reduction in stature. As this type of decay is often a dry process, the pungent smells due to the release of gases and decompositional fluids during putrefaction are not present. Therefore this absence of a decomposition indicator can lead to an extended period between death and recovery as in the case presented by Hänsch (1974). In this example, the mummified remains of a man were found over a year after he had disappeared from his family home. He was recovered subsequently from a hanging position in the cellar of a house that had been occupied the entire time.

Bog Bodies

Across northern Europe a number of highly preserved remains have been recovered from peat bogs and so the phenomena of "bog bodies" were discovered. These remains have spanned vast time periods with some dating back to prehistoric times. The inherent conditions within the peat bogs can make them microbially sterile and acidic environments in which very little organic material, including plant matter, decomposes. This material inhibits oxygenation of the water deep within the peat, creating a unique anaerobic environment (Lynnerup, 2015).

Sphagnum, a type of moss associated with peat, plays a key part in creating the extraordinary preservative environment. The presence of sphagnan, a polysaccharide derived from the sphagnum moss as it turns into peat, is fundamental to the formation of bog bodies. Biodegradation of the moss creates humic acids, which react with bacterial digestive enzymes and makes them inactive. It also causes a tanning process due to a Maillard reaction (Lynnerup, 2015). This reaction expels water from the body's tissue and collagen fibers begin to cross-link, making them resistant to degradation. As a result, the skin "tans" giving it a distinctive dark, leathery appearance with hair and nails well preserved. In some cases, internal organs and stomach contents have also been preserved in the specimens recovered (Pestka et al., 2010).

Adipocere

Another feature of natural preservation is caused by the formation of adipocere, which is the saponification of lipids in the body by bacteria. It is most frequently witnessed in humid, anaerobic environments such as burials in water-saturated soils. The formation of this tissue can be observed as early as 2 weeks postmortem but formation that covers the full cadaver may take several years (Yan et al., 2001). Originally believed to occur only in aqueous environments, it is now understood that there is sufficient water within the body for the saturated fatty acids to hydrogenate and hydrolyze into adipocere, where the release of fatty acids limits decomposition and inhibits bacterial growth. When fresh, adipocere is characterized by the smell of ammonia and a soft, wet, greasy appearance. Over time it dries out forming a gray or white crumbly appearance, hence the name "grave wax" (Nushida et al., 2008).

In anaerobic environments, *Clostridium perfringens* produces lecithinase, which, along with warm temperatures, facilitates the development of adipocere. The optimum conditions for the catalytic enzymes are mildly alkaline pH and between 22°C and 40°C (Fiedler et al., 2004; Forbes et al., 2005) Generally, adipocere is more commonly found on juvenile or female remains due to the elevated levels of subcutaneous fat in these body types. However, adipocere is not restricted to forming solely in locations with elevated fat content, hence there is evidence of saponification occurring within organs and other tissues where fat has diffused to (Kumar et al., 2009). This translocation occurs because fats liquefy as they are catabolized. Adipocere will eventually degrade once exposed to aerobic conditions but this process is very slow (Fiedler et al., 2015).

Water Burials

Water-based decomposition, with the marked presence of adipocere, *cutis anserina*, and skin maceration, creates postmortem profiles rarely presented with land-based decay.

However, the presence of these characteristics on bodies recovered from water is not necessarily indicative of death in water, i.e., drowning. Specifically, *cutis anserina* is caused by *rigor mortis* in the erector pilae muscles of the dermis with the skin adopting a pimpled appearance similar to that of goose bumps. Additionally, the skin becomes wrinkled and swells, particularly in the extreme aspects of the limbs. The palms and soles show evidence of skin maceration or washerwoman's skin (Pounder, 2005). Ayers (2010) compared decomposition in different types of water during a pilot study in Texas and recorded that salt water delayed the decomposition process when compared to specimens found in fresh water. Furthermore, the rate of decomposition in water was half that on land, although there was no differentiation here between fresh or salt water. This is particularly interesting, however, when considering that the delay in decomposition could result in the recovery of a more intact body and therefore a greater chance of identification (Tuller et al., 2008).

When a body first enters the water, it will float due to the air trapped in the lungs or in clothing. Over time the air trapped within the body escapes and the remains begin to sink toward the bed of the water. Reflotation then occurs typically as gases build up during putrefaction. During the period of floating, parts of the cadaver will protrude above the water surface, causing different decomposition environments to occur within the same corpse. Although most of the body will stay submerged, it is an opportunity for insects or larger, nonaquatic scavengers to consume the remains (Dilen, 1984).

O'Brien (1997) proposed a sequence of postmortem events while studying the water action of a lake. He differentiated between four seasonal periods and noted that these would each impact upon the submergence and flotation intervals of remains. He established a sequence for underwater decomposition, which was summarized into five main phases and two substages: float, initial sinking, reflotation, differential decomposition, and secondary sinking (either free or snagged). Conversely, Payne and King (1972) studied submerged fetal pig remains in freshwater environments and suggested six distinct stages of the decomposition process, which did not match those identified by O'Brien. This separated decomposition into submerged fresh, early floating, floating decay, bloated deterioration, floating remains, and sunken remains. Neither of the two classification approaches included timeframes for each of these decomposition periods, instead overarching sequences of events were merely observed. Additionally, subsequent research questioned the universal applicability of O'Brien's floating sequence with suggestions that this area still requires significant research (Ayers, 2010).

If comprehensive data can be collected on variables such as body size, as suggested by Sutherland et al. (2013), and compared with similar research also incorporating coverings, then a better understanding of their impact on both the rate of decomposition and any disruption to "normal" movement patterns can be established (Matuszewski et al., 2014). Also the local aquatic physicochemical conditions, including temperature, will have a direct impact on the decompositional processes, sequence of events, or both. For example, marine temperatures for UK waters in winter range typically between 6 and 10°C. As a consequence, different and more appropriate models may be required for specific stages such as skeletalization than that originally established in Texas, where the climate and faunal community in the water are significantly different.

Similar to when bones became exposed on terrestrial surfaces, bone bleaching can occur in submerged remains as well. Very little is currently known about the timeframe for this process but it can be differentiated from sun bleaching by the lack of cracking and a more uniform coverage (Pokines and Higgs, 2015). Aquatic bleaching occurs because of chemical reactions, particularly in saline water. Typically, bones absorb sodium and chlorine from the water, in the form of salts, when submerged for prolonged periods of time such as a number of years. As the bones dry, either due to being washed to the bank or because of recovery, the salt begins to form large crystals that cause fractures. It is important therefore that skeletal remains that are recovered from salt water environments are stored in similar salt water conditions until they are processed (Hedges, 2002).

Clandestine Burials

Burials are a common method chosen for the disposal of remains in homicide cases and a large number of these are clandestine, or close to the surface. Similar to surface decomposition, the decomposing remains will have an impact on the surrounding soil, although a greater influence is seen on the body from the soil environment with subsurface burial. The combination of chemical, biological, and geological conditions in a location contributes to the characteristics of the burial environment and all subsequent postmortem changes (Tibbett and Carter, 2008).

The first ever forensic study using cadavers was an experiment on the effects of subsurface burial at a range of depths from 1 to 4 ft (Rodriguez and Bass, 1985). The study found that decomposition rates were generally slower than in surface deposits with an increased degree of preservation observed at greater depths. Currently, there is limited research and literature available on burial decomposition, particularly when looking at short-term interment, as it can be difficult to monitor changes accurately without repeated exhumation of the buried materials. This cycle of data collection would introduce the subject to air repeatedly and therefore not be reflective of protracted or permanent burial conditions. Also it would disrupt the soil, fauna, and flora, which are known to reflect changes around clandestine burials. Changes to surface vegetation have been recorded both in studies and anecdotal observations at crime scenes. As described by Tibbett and Carter (2008) while discussing CDIs, death of vegetation may also occur due to phytotoxicity with buried remains as leachates dispersed throughout the surrounding soil. However, as protein metabolism occurs in the corpse, ammonia leaches out and is converted to ammonium, which can be used by plants. Another feature of botanical change is the colonization of new and different plant species at the grave site where their seeds may have been exposed to more favorable conditions, either through the digging process or because of the change in soil alkalinity.

There have been cases that utilized the growth of perennial plants through remains as a method for determining the PMI. For example, Courtin and Fairgrieve (2004) used growth rings as applied in the field of dendrochronology to date the age of a black spruce branch (*Picae mariana*) and therefore provided a minimum time period in which the plant has been associated with the remains. However, this is not a true PMI measurement, rather a time since deposition estimation and thus the method is rarely used. In contrast, analysis of the gravesoil is probably the best way to estimate PMI once entomological activity has decreased. Particular chemicals within the soil can be detected and their concentrations used to estimate ADD. An example of such forensic chemical analyses is measurement of change is the presence of ninhydrin-reactive nitrogen (NRN). Consistent concentrations are seen in NRN with both winter and summer decomposition and its concentrations can remain elevated for up to a year (Van Belle et al., 2009). This could provide indications of a burial location even if the remains have subsequently been removed. A general principle is that 1 week of surface decomposition is equivalent to 8 weeks in the subsurface, even when the environmental temperature is the same. Much of this is attributed to soil pH, which may inhibit bacterial growth, the enclosed environment, which limits the amount of aerobic decomposition, and the protection from insects and scavenging activity.

Scavenging

Although buried remains are mostly well protected from scavengers, increases in temperature result in soil drying and cracking, allowing volatile organic compounds (VOCs), the chemicals responsible for the distinctive smell associated with death and decomposition, to escape. These can then draw scavengers to the area. One of the greatest complications in the recovery and analysis of accessible remains is the impact of scavengers (Young et al., 2014). Exposed soft tissue could become food for scavengers such as rats, birds, or different species of canids, particularly at times when other food sources are scarce (Brown et al., 2006). Although scavenging populations and species differ significantly around the world, an experiment conducted in the United Kingdom showed that, while the remains of rats were fully accessible to all species, the only animals to feed on the cadavers were foxes, crows, and magpies (Inger et al., 2016). This may be because of the small body size of the analog in comparison to human remains, and the unlikely occurrence of cannibalism by scavenging rats.

Larger, carnivorous predators are known to disarticulate bodies and transport sections of remains, often limbs, away from the initial deposition or burial sites. Here, the knowledge of the forensic taphonomist on feeding and dispersal patterns of native scavengers is invaluable in the coordination of any search and recovery efforts. A large proportion of this disarticulation and scattering of remains is due to the feeding preferences of the animals, the presence of other, larger scavengers, and simple anatomical considerations. Some scavengers have teeth and claws better adapted for cutting through flesh, while others are simply larger and stronger, allowing them to drag or carry remains. This can, however, leave trailing evidence, such as decompositional fluids emitting VOCs, across the ground surface, which can aid in the search and recovery process (Komar, 1999).

Highly trained cadaver dogs, animals with extremely sensitive olfactory systems, are capable of detecting human remains based on the chemical profile produced by the VOCs. Research is progressing to develop and test portable devices that can detect and measure these VOC profiles. For example, the Lightweight Analyzer for Buried Remains And Decomposition Odor Recognition, a self-contained detection tool, was designed for field use to provide data comparable with that of gas chromatography-mass spectrometry (Vass et al., 2010). Unfortunately, the results available so far have not proved as accurate or reliable as the human remains detection dogs.

DEVELOPING TECHNIQUES OF DATING REMAINS

Vitreous Humor

Because the eye is a closed environment that is isolated from other aspects of the body, it is of particular interest in PMI estimations. The vitreous humor contained within the eyeball appears transparent and gelatinous but as the retina degrades potassium begins to leak into it. This increase in the concentration of potassium occurs at a steady rate and hence it is possible to estimate the PMI based on analysis of this fluid, provided that care is taken in the extraction process to avoid contamination with other cellular fragments, which may impact on the values analyzed (Garg et al., 2004). By use of linear regression equations, the PMI can be estimated from a known potassium concentration. However, this technique still has its critiques and is not a universally accepted method. Testing by Barmate and Dhawane (2013), which analyzed samples from over 200 cases with known PMIs, concluded that, although still useful, the method was not as accurate as initially proposed.

DNA Degradation

Cellular DNA begins and continues to degrade throughout the autolytic and putrefactive stages of decomposition. Therefore there have been suggestions that the rate at which this degradation occurs may be helpful in PMI assessment. Although environmental factors such as humidity and temperature have also been proven to effect the process, extensive research has indicated that studying the interaction between bones and their environment, and the subsequent degradation of DNA, can aid PMI determinations. Two seminal studies utilizing luminol, which is routinely used in presumptive blood testing, identified the presence and extent of hemoglobin that is protected within the structural integrity of the bone (Creamer and Buck, 2009; Introna et al., 1999). These showed a strong correlation between short PMIs and intense luminescence. However, the analysis of this intensity is somewhat subjective and both studies had limited samples. Nevertheless, the researchers suggested that although not considered an effective measure for PMI estimation yet, there was potential for further study of the approach.

Total Body Score

The use of a rigorous scoring system for the categorization of decay stages was long demanded and over the years the total body score (TBS) system has been well publicized in studies on human and animal remains. A significant number of these refer to the system that was first employed by Megyesi et al. (2005). The formula used for TBS was based on a total of 66 cases across the United States, and offers a prediction on the required ADDs to reach the TBS, which is allocated by the observer. A limitation with the TBS approach is that few details on its application, which seem to be very subjective, have been provided in other studies that use the system. This should raise concerns of replicability and accuracy as dedicated research is somewhat limited on this aspect. Nevertheless, the method has been adapted for use in a number of studies since suggesting peer support for the system and confidence in its results is present (Henssge and Madea, 2007), while further improvements have also been proposed (Moffatt et al., 2016).

A study by Vass (2011) aimed to develop a novel approach to TBS by producing a formula that was less subjective. The approach was identified as a "universal" solution to the PMI problem with the hope of improving on the Megyesi method. Two formulae were developed specifically for aerobic decomposition and anaerobic decomposition. Both formulae have been applied successfully to case work and appear to work consistently across Mid-Eastern America, although they can only be utilized in preskeletal PMI estimations.

The development of a single method that can be used universally to calculate PMI with a consistent degree of accuracy is simply not feasible due to the diversity of conditions that can be encountered when dealing with remains. As with many areas, a multidisciplinary approach will offer the best estimations in terms of accuracy and application. There is no doubt that further work is necessary to develop more climate-specific formulae, which can be used subsequently in combination with numerous other methods, some of which have been discussed here. Naturally, there is also the increasing demand for more and larger studies that utilize human remains to be undertaken.

REFERENCES

Aitkenhead-Peterson, J.A., Owings, C.G., Alexander, M.B., Larison, N., Bytheway, J.A., 2012. Mapping the lateral extent of human cadaver decomposition with soil chemistry. Forensic Science International 216 (1–3), 127–134.

Al-Alousi, L.M., Anderson, R.A., Worster, D.M., Land, D.V., 2002. Factors influencing the precision of estimating the postmortem interval using the triple-exponential formulae (TEF). Part II. A study of the effect of body temperature at the moment of death on the postmortem brain, liver and rectal cooling in 117 forensic cases. Forensic Science International 125 (2–3), 231–236.

Aufderheide, A., 2003. The Scientific Study of Mummies. Cambridge University Press, Cambridge.

Ayers, L.E., 2010. Differential Decomposition in Terrestrial, Freshwater, and Saltwater Environments: A Pilot Study (Theses and Dissertations). Texas State University.

Ball, D.W., Hill, J.W., Scott, R.J., 2011. Amino acids, proteins and enzymes. In: The Basics of General Organic and Biological Chemistry. Saylor Foundation, Washington.

Barmate, N.S., Dhawane, S.G., 2013. A correlation study of time since death by vitreous potassium with postmortem changes. Journal of Forensic Medicine and Toxicology 14 (2).

Beary, M.O., Lyman, R.L., 2012. The use of taphonomy in forensic anthropology: past trends and future prospects. In: Dirkmaat, D.C. (Ed.), A Companion to Forensic Anthropology. Wiley-Blackwell Publishing, Chichester.

Behrensmeyer, A.K., 1978. Taphonomic and ecologic information from bone weathering. Paleobiology 4, 150–162.

Boaks, A., Siwek, D., Mortazavi, F., 2014. The temporal degradation of bone collagen: a histochemical approach. Forensic Science International 24, 104–110.

Boddington, A., Garland, A.N., Janaway, R.C., 1987. Death, Decay and Reconstruction: Approaches to Archaeology and Forensic Science, first ed. Manchester University Press, Manchester.

Brown, O.J.F., Field, J., Letnic, M., 2006. Variation in the taphonomic effect of scavengers in semi-arid Australia linked to rainfall and the El Niño Southern Oscillation. International Journal of Osteoarchaeology 16 (2), 165–176.

Carter, D.O., Yellowlees, D., Tibbett, M., 2007. Cadaver decomposition in terrestrial ecosystems. Naturwissenschaften 94 (1), 12–24.

Christensen, A.M., Passalacqua, N.V., Bartelink, E.J., 2014. Forensic Anthropology: Current Methods and Practice. Academic Press, San Diego.

Cockle, D.L., Bell, L.S., 2015. Human decomposition and the reliability of a "universal" model for post mortem interval estimations. Forensic Science International 253, 136.e1–136.e9.

Courtin, G.M., Fairgrieve, S.I., 2004. Estimation of postmortem interval (PMI) as revealed through the analysis of annual growth in woody tissue. Journal of Forensic Sciences 49, 781–783.

Creamer, J.I., Buck, A.M., 2009. The assaying of haemoglobin using luminol chemiluminescence and its application to the dating of human skeletal remains. Luminescence 24, 311–316.

Dabbs, G.R., 2010. Caution! All data are not created equal: the hazards of using National Weather Service data for calculating accumulated degree days. Forensic Science International 202 (1–3), e49–e52.

Dautartas, A.M., Steadman, D.W., Mundorff, A.Z., Jantz, L.M., Vidoli, G.M., 2016. A Comparison of Seasonal Decomposition Patterns between Human and Non-human Animal Models. 68th Annual Scientific Meeting of the American Academy of Forensic Sciences. Nevada, Las Vegas.

Dent, B.B., Forbes, S.L., Stuart, B.H., 2004. Review of human decomposition process in soil. Environmental Geology 45, 576–585.

Dhawane, S.G., Dhoble, S.V., 2016. Estimation of time since death from post mortem lividity: easy and simple method. International Journal of Scientific Research 5 (3).

Dilen, D.R., 1984. The motion of floating and submerged objects in the Chattahoochee River, Atlanta, GA. Journal of Forensic Sciences 29, 1027–1037.

Dirkmaat, D.C., Cabo, L., Ousley, S.D., Symes, S.A., 2008. New perspectives in forensic anthropology. American Journal of Physical Anthropology (suppl. 47), 33–52.

Dupras, T.L., Schultz, J.J., Wheeler, S.M., Williams, L.J., 2012. Forensic Recovery of Human Remains, second ed. CRC Press, Florida.

Efremov, J.A., 1940. Taphonomy: new branch of paleontology. Pan-American Geologist LXXIV (2), 81–93.

Fiedler, S., Schneckenberger, K., Graw, M., 2004. Characterization of soils containing adipocere. Archives of Environmental Contamination and Toxicology 47 (4), 561–568.

Fiedler, S., Berns, A.E., Schwark, L., Woelk, A.T., Graw, M., 2015. The chemistry of death: adipocere degradation in modern graveyards. Forensic Science International 257, 320–328.

Forbes, S.L., Stuart, B.H., Dent, B.B., 2005. The effect of the method of burial on adipocere formation. Forensic Science International 154 (1), 44–52.

Garg, V., Oberoi, S.S., Gorea, R.K., Kaur, K., 2004. Changes in the levels of vitreous potassium with increasing time since death. Journal of Indian Academy of Forensic Medicine 26 (4), 136–139.

Gill-King, H., 1997. Chemical and ultrastructural aspects of decomposition. In: Haglund, W.D., Sorg, M.H. (Eds.), Forensic Taphonomy: The Postmortem Fate of Human Remains, first ed. CRC Press, Washington, D. C.
Glaister, J., 1942. Medical Jurisprudence and Toxicology, seventh ed. E & S Livingstone, Edinburgh.
Guharaj, P.V., 2003. Forensic Medicine, second ed. Longman Orient, Hyderabad, pp. 61–62.
Haglund, W.D., Sorg, M.H., 1997. Forensic Taphonomy: The Postmortem Fate of Human Remains. CRC Press, Boca Raton, Florida.
Haglund, W.D., Sorg, M.H., 2002. Advances in Forensic Taphonomy, Method Theory and Archaeological Perspectives. CRC Press, Boca Raton, Florida.
Hänsch, C., 1974. An unusual case of body mummification. Zeitschrift für Rechtsmedizin 75, 225–227.
Hedges, R.E.M., 2002. Bone diagenesis: an overview of processes. Archeometry 44 (3), 319–328.
Henssge, C., 1988. Death time estimation in case work 1. The rectal temperature time of death nomogram. Forensic Science International 38, 209–236.
Henssge, C., Madea, B., 2007. Estimation of the time since death. Forensic Science International 165 (2–3), 182–184.
Human Tissues Act. 2004. c.30.
Inger, R., Cox, D.T., Per, E., Norton, B.A., Gaston, K.J., 2016. Ecological role of vertebrate scavengers in urban ecosystems in the UK. Ecology and Evolution 6 (19), 7015–7023.
Introna, F., Vella, G.D., Campobasso, C.P., 1999. Determination of postmortem interval from old skeletal remains by image analysis of luminol test results. Journal of Forensic Sciences 44 (3), 535–538.
Ishida, M., Gonoi, W., Hagiwara, K., Takazawa, Y., Akahane, M., Fukayama, M., Ohtomo, K., 2011. Hypostasis in the heart and great vessels of non-traumatic in-hospital death cases on postmortem computed tomography: relationship to antemortem blood tests. Legal Medicine 13 (6), 280–285.
Ishida, M., Gonoi, W., Okuma, H., Shirota, G., Shintani, Y., Abe, H., Takazawa, Y., Fukayama, M., Ohtomo, K., 2015. Common postmortem computed tomography findings following atraumatic death: differentiation between normal postmortem changes and pathologic lesions. Korean Journal of Radiology 16 (4), 798–809.
Jones, D.G., Whitaker, M.I., 2009. Speaking for the Dead: The Human Body in Biology and Medicine, second ed. Ashgate Publishing Limited, Surrey.
Joseph, A.E., Schickele, E., 1970. A general method for assessing factors controlling postmortem cooling. Journal of Forensic Sciences 15 (3), 364–391.
Knight, B., Saukko, P., 2004. Knight's Forensic Pathology, third ed. Hodder Arnold, London.
Komar, D., 1999. The use of cadaver dogs in locating scattered, scavenged human remains: preliminary field test results. Journal of Forensic Sciences 44 (2), 405–408.
Komar, D.A., Buikstar, J.E., 2008. Forensic Anthropology: Contemporary Theory and Practice. Oxford University Press, New York.
Kumar, T.S.M., Monteiro, F.N.P., Bhagavath, P., Bakkannavar, S.M., 2009. Early adipocere formation: a case report and review of literature. Journal of Forensic and Legal Medicine 16, 475–477.
Lyman, R.L., 1994. Vertebrate Taphonomy. Cambridge University Press, Cambridge.
Lynnerup, N., 2015. Bog bodies. Anatomical Record, Hoboken 298 (6).
Madea, B., 2015. Estimation of Time Since Death, third ed. CRC Press, Boca Raton, FL.
Marshall, T.K., Hoare, F.E., 1962. Estimating the time of death. The rectal cooling after death and its mathematical expression. Journal of Forensic Sciences 7 (1), 56–81.
Martinez, E., Duque, P., Wolff, M., 2007. Succession pattern of carrion-feeding insects in paramo, Colombia. Forensic Science International 166 (2–3), 182–189.
Matuszewski, S., Konwerski, S., Fratczak, K., Szafalowicz, M., 2014. Effect of body mass and clothing on decomposition of pig carcasses. International Journal of Legal Medicine 128 (6), 1039–1048.
McNeill, P.M., 1993. The Ethics and Politics of Human Experimentation, first ed. Cambridge University Press, Cambridge.
Megyesi, M., Nawrocki, S., Haskell, N., 2005. Using accumulated degree-days to estimate the postmortem interval from decomposed human remains. Journal of Forensic Sciences 50, 1–9.
Micozzi, M.S., Pless, J., 1997. Frozen environments and soft tissue preservation. In: Haglund, W.D., Sorg, M.H. (Eds.), Forensic Taphonomy: The Postmortem Fate of Human Remains. CRC Press, Boca Raton, Florida, pp. 171–180.

Moffatt, C., Simmons, T., Lynch-Aird, J., 2016. An improved equation for TBS and ADD: establishing a realiable postmortem interval framework for casework and experimental studies. Journal of Forensic Sciences 61, S201–S207.

Notter, S.J., Stuart, B.H., Rowe, R., Langlois, N., 2009. The initial changes of fat deposits during the decomposition of human and pig remains. Journal of Forensic Sciences 54 (1), 195–201.

Nushida, H., Adachi, J., Takeuchi, A., Asano, M., Ueno, Y., 2008. Adipocere formation via hydrogenation of linoleic acid in a victim kept under dry concealment. Forensic Science International 175 (2–3), 160–165.

O'Brien, T.G., 1997. Movement of bodies in lake Ontario. In: Haglund, W.D., Sorg, M.H. (Eds.), Forensic Taphonomy: The Postmortem Fate of Human Remains. CRC Press, Boca Raton, Florida, pp. 171–180.

Payne, J.A., King, E.W., 1972. Insect succession and decomposition of pig carcasses in water. Journal of the Georgia Entomological Society 7 (3), 153–162.

Pestka, J.M., Barvencik, F., Beil, F.T., Marshall, R.P., Jopp, E., Schilling, A.F., Bauerochse, A., Fansa, M., Püschel, K., Amling, M., 2010. Skeletal analysis and comparison of bog bodies from Northern European peat bogs. Naturwissenschaften 97 (4), 393–402.

Pokines, J.T., Higgs, N., 2015. Macroscopic taphonomic alterations to human bone recovered from marine environments. Journal of Forensic Identification 65 (6), 953–984.

Pokines, J.T., Symes, S.A., 2013. Manual of Forensic Taphonomy, first ed. CRC Press, Washington DC.

Pounder, D.J., 2000. Postmortem interval. In: Siegel, J.A., Saukko, P.J., Knupfer, G.C. (Eds.), Encyclopedia of Forensic Sciences. Academic, San Diego, pp. 1167–1172.

Pounder, D.J., 2005. Autopsy findings: drowning. Encyclopedia of Forensic and Legal Medicine 227–232.

Powers, R.H., 2005. The decomposition of human remains: a biochemical perspective. In: Rich, J., Dean, D.E., Powers, R.H. (Eds.), Forensic Medicine of the Lower Extremity: Human Identification and Trauma Analysis of the Thigh, Leg and Foot. Humana Press, Totowa, NJ, pp. 3–15.

Rainy, H., 1868. On the cooling of dead bodies as indicating the length of time since death. The Glasgow Medical Journal 1, 323–330.

Roberts, L.G., Dabbs, G.R., 2015. A taphonomic study exploring the differences in decomposition rate and manner between frozen and never frozen domestic pigs (*Sus scrofa*). Journal of Forensic Sciences 60 (3), 588–594.

Rodriguez, W.C., Bass, W.M., 1985. Decomposition of buried bodies and methods that may aid in their location. Journal of Forensic Sciences 30 (3), 836–852.

Schotsmans, E.M.J., Marquez-Grant, N., Forbes, S.L., 2017. Taphonomy of Human Remains: Forensic Analysis of the Dead and the Depositional Environment. Wiley, Chichester.

Shirley, N.R., Wilson, R.J., Jantz, L.M., 2011. Cadaver use at the University of Tennessee's Anthropological Research Facility. Clinical Anatomy 24 (3), 372–380.

Singh, R., Sharma, S., Sharma, A., 2016. Determination of post-burial interval using entomology: a review. Journal of Forensic and Legal Medicine 42, 37–40.

Statheropoulos, M., Agapiou, A., Zorba, E., Mikedi, K., Karma, S., Pallis, G.C., Eliopoulos, C., Spiliopoulou, C., 2011. Combined chemical and optical methods for monitoring the early decay stages of surrogate human models. Forensic Science International 210 (1–3), 154–163.

Stokes, K.L., Forbes, S.L., Tibbett, M., 2013. Human versus animal: contrasting decomposition dynamics of mammalian analogues in experimental taphonomy. Journal of Forensic Science 58 (3), 583–591.

Sutherland, A., Myburgh, J., Steyn, M., Becker, P.J., 2013. The effect of body size on the rate of decomposition in a temperate region of South Africa. Forensic Science International 231, 257–262.

Tibbett, M., Carter, D.O., 2008. Soil Analysis in Forensic Taphonomy: Chemical and Biological Effects of Buried Human Remains, first ed. CRC Press, Florida.

Tuller, H., Hofmeister, U., Daley, S., 2008. Spatial analysis of mass grave mapping data to assist in the reassociation of disarticulated and commingled human remains. In: Adams, B.J., Byrd, J.E. (Eds.), Recovery, Analysis, and Identification of Commingled Human Remains. Humana Press, Totowa.

Turner, B., Wiltshire, P., 1999. Experimental validation of forensic evidence: a study of the decomposition of buried pigs in a heavy clay soil. Forensic Science International 101 (2), 113–122.

Turpin, C., 2017. The micro-taphonomy of cold: differential microcracking in response to experimental cold-stresses. Journal of Forensic Sciences. http://dx.doi.org/10.1111/1556-4029.13406. (Epub).

Usumoto, Y., Hikiji, W., Sameshima, N., Kudo, K., Tsuji, A., Ikeda, N., 2010. Estimation of postmortem interval based on the spectrophotometric analysis of postmortem lividity. Legal Medicine 12 (1), 19–22.
Van Belle, L.E., Carter, D.O., Forbes, S.L., 2009. Measurement of ninhydrin reactive nitrogen influx into gravesoil during aboveground and belowground carcass (*Sus domesticus*) decomposition. Forensic Science International 193 (1–3), 37–41.
Varetto, L., Curto, O., 2005. Long persistence of rigor mortis at constant low temperature. Forensic Science International 147 (1), 31–34.
Vass, A.A., 2011. The elusive universal post-mortem interval formula. Forensic Science International 204, 34–40.
Vass, A.A., Thompson, M.S., Wise, M., 2010. A new forensics tool: development of an advanced sensor for detecting clandestine graves. U.S. Department of Justice.
Weigelt, J., 1927. Recent Vertebrate Carcasses and Their Paleobiological Implications. (J. Schaefer, Trans). The University of Chigago Press, Chigago.
Williams, A., 2015. Coming to a field near you? The "body farms" where human remains decompose in the name of Science. The Conversation.
Witt, I., Cassella, J.P., 2014. The Feasibility of a United Kingdom Human Taphonomic Research Facility. 10th Forrest Conference, Newcastle.
Yamaguchi, R., Makino, Y., Chiba, F., Motomura, A., Inokuchi, G., Yajima, D., Iwase, H., 2015. Fatal *Clostridium perfringens* septicaemia suggest by postmortem computed tomography: a medico-legal autopsy case report. Forensic Science International 253, e4–e9.
Yan, F., Mcnally, R., Kontanis, E.J., Sadik, O.A., 2001. Preliminary qualitative investigation of postmortem adipocere formation. Journal of Forensic Science 46, 609–614.
Young, A., Stillman, R., Smith, M.J., Korstjens, A.H., 2014. Scavenging in northwestern Europe: a survey of UK police specialist search officers. Policing 7.

CHAPTER 3

The Method Debate: A State-of-the-Art Analysis of PMI Estimation Techniques

Chawki Bisker, T. Komang Ralebitso-Senior
Teesside University, Tees Valley, United Kingdom

INTRODUCTION

The fascination with the changes that a decaying cadaver undergoes extends back to antiquity when people searched for meanings to death and decomposition, while the attraction to this natural phenomenon resulted in speculations and tales among primeval, medieval, and even modern societies (Manhein, 1997). Long before the establishment of forensic science as a proper discipline, 18th century physicians established the science that explores the changes in decaying human cadavers in an attempt to treat patients suffering from "putrid diseases." This was later named "Taphonomy" by the Russian paleontologist Ivan Efremov (1940). Today, the term and discipline have a broader meaning and focus on cadaver decomposition and related death scene materials (Janaway et al., 2009). Considerable interest is still generated by decomposition, especially among the scientific community, which focuses mainly on understanding the underpinning processes in ecological and forensic contexts.

The scientific community has long been interested in understanding the different aspects associated with human decomposition toward developing reliable tools for the estimation of postmortem interval (PMI). This is reflected by the large number of research investigations on this topic, which led to the development and application of a variety of techniques dedicated to the determination of time since death (Mathur and Agrawal, 2011; Marín-Roldan et al., 2013; Bilheux et al., 2015). Nevertheless, there is still a gap in the knowledge about cadaver decomposition, especially from a microbiological perspective. The determination of PMI is fundamental to investigations when death is unwitnessed as knowing the victim's exact time of death provides insight into the circumstances of death, permits the reconstruction of a death scenario, and facilitates the confirmation of witnesses' testimonies and suspects' alibis (Sachdeva et al., 2011).

A range of decomposition phenomena linked to phases of decay has been studied and used as routine PMI estimation tools. These include *rigor mortis* (cadaver stiffening), *livor mortis* (cadaveric hypostasis), *algor mortis* (cadaver cooling), and supravitality (Henssge et al., 1984), among others. These methods are, however, mostly applicable during the early hours to days after death and often lack the accuracy and reliability needed to withstand

Forensic Ecogenomics
ISBN 978-0-12-809360-3
http://dx.doi.org/10.1016/B978-0-12-809360-3.00003-5

scrutiny in court (Tibbett, 2008; Pittner et al., 2016a). In fact, a robust PMI estimation tool is expected to be precise, reliable, and practical for potential use in situ, taking into consideration the various factors affecting decomposition to allow the best estimation possible.

In summary, the lack of practical, robust, and accurate methods for PMI estimation, despite more than 100 years of efforts to optimize current techniques and/or develop new ones, necessitates further research (Kaliszan et al., 2009). The major deficiency resides in the intermediate phase of decomposition, which corresponds to the decay of soft tissue (Pittner et al., 2016a), as the error margin in PMI estimation increases with time elapsed, causing higher inaccuracy. For example, Kaliszan et al. (2009) reported an error margin of more than 2 h during the first 6 h postmortem. This increased up to 4.5 h by the end of the first day and caused higher inaccuracies in PMI assessment after that time period, even when using a combination of methods. Furthermore, current time since death assessment tools are affected considerably by environmental factors with limited capacity for high accuracy in estimations.

CADAVER DECOMPOSITION

Decomposition is a variable complex process that involves inner changes of the decaying body together with the action of endogenous and exogenous organisms (Pinheiro, 2006). During this process, soft tissues progressively liquefy due to the cadaver's own enzymes and microbiologically driven changes (Carter and Tibbett, 2008; Janaway et al., 2009). Although decay will lead eventually to the loss of soft tissue, residual organic material such as collagen may survive for several hundreds of years under certain conditions (Carter and Tibbett, 2008). Payne et al. (1968) classified decomposition processes into three major periods: an early phase from death to the bloat stage; an intermediate phase until advanced decay; and a late phase that comprises disintegration and skeletization of the cadaver. Other researchers (Galloway et al., 1989; Goff, 2009; Hau et al., 2014) divided this environment-dependent and highly variable process into five different phases: fresh, bloat (early decomposition), active decay (decay), advanced decay (postdecay), and skeletization (extreme decomposition). Although these are a convenient means for decomposition stage assessment, they are not always discernible as their supposedly distinctive characteristics usually blend with one another (Pinheiro, 2006).

Death marks the onset of the fresh stage where once the heart stops functioning and blood circulation and oxygen supply cease, causing anoxia in the body (Swann et al., 2010). The cadaver becomes flaccid and undergoes autolysis and the associated triad of subsequent changes known as *livor*, *rigor*, and *algor mortis* (Gill-King, 1997; Janaway et al., 2009; Lee, 2009). During *livor mortis*, usually called lividity (Goff, 2009), blood is drained by gravity to the lower parts of the cadaver and the accumulation of blood deoxyhemoglobin through lack of oxygen causes the skin color to change to dark blue/deep purple (Hau et al., 2014), although this discoloring may vary in some cases (Krompecher, 2002).

Within hours, the degradation of ATP and accumulation of calcium ions in muscle fibers lead to myosin and actin binding in the muscles and therefore stiffening (Swift, 2006; Goff, 2009; Janaway et al., 2009) in a process called *rigor mortis*. Due to their lower ATP contents, the small muscles solidify first so there is sequential tissue stiffening of the body progressing downward, starting from the jaws and eyelids, followed by the neck, trunk, and limbs until the total stiffening of the cadaver (Gill-King, 1997). However, this has been contradicted by Kobayashi et al. (2001) who stated that the *rigor mortis* sequence is not affected by muscle size, and Kobayashi (2002) who suggested that cadaveric stiffening evolution down the body might be governed by temperature and fiber type proportions in muscle tissues.

Cadaveric cooling (*algor mortis*) is a physical process that happens when the ambient temperature is lower than body temperature. During this process the cadaver loses its heat to the external environment until temperature equilibrium is reached (Myburgh, 2010). *Algor mortis* may be influenced by the presence of clothing or other material. Also small and/or thin cadavers tend to cool down faster than tall and/or obese ones (Shkrum and Ramsay, 2007; Smart and Kaliszan, 2012). Furthermore, the cooling rate may be affected by antemortem medical conditions such as fever, brain injury, heat stroke, hyperthyroidism, sepsis, drugs, and toxins together with the age of the deceased, antemortem physical activity, stress, and cause of death (Smart and Kaliszan, 2012).

Autolysis is a postmortem self-digestion process driven by intrinsic enzymes (Janaway et al., 2009). Only perceptible at the histological level at the beginning, it can subsequently cause blisters to form on the skin (Vass et al., 2002). Typically, cell acidity increases due to an increase in carbon dioxide, rupturing lysosomes and discharging their enzymes into the cells (Parkinson et al., 2009). Once released, the hydrolytic enzymes denature membranes and molecules, leading to cell breakdown and content diffusion (Zhou and Byard, 2011). Autolysis is affected considerably by environmental factors such as temperature and moisture (Carter et al., 2010) and can start during the minutes following death (Gill-King, 1997). Organs with high contents and concentrations of water, enzymes, or ATP are highly vulnerable to autolysis and may undergo this process more rapidly than the remaining cells of the cadaver (Vass et al., 2002; Swann et al., 2010).

In general, autolysis tissue anoxia promotes the growth of anaerobes in the digestive and respiratory systems and leads to the production of gases and organic acids from fats, carbohydrates, and peptides. The microbial-induced accumulation of gases causes distention of the cadaver and marks the beginning of the bloat stage (Vass et al., 2002). This starts usually in the abdominal region before progressing to the whole body (Gennard, 2007; Hau et al., 2014) where it is associated with the distinctive decay odor, skin marbling (Shkrum and Ramsay, 2007), and blister formation. In some cases, the *stratum corneum* detaches (Lee, 2009), especially from the hands and feet, and causes what is known commonly as glove formation or skin slippage (Shkrum and Ramsay, 2007).

Furthermore, gas accumulation inside the cadaver causes fluids to purge through natural orifices and may even rupture the skin in extreme cases (Vass et al., 2002). Fluids diffusion into the soil leads to the restoration of aerobiosis, marking the onset of the fast-decomposition stage called active decay (Carter and Tibbett, 2008). During this stage, insect activity reaches a peak and cadaver-associated vegetation dies (Hopkins, 2008); in addition, soil microorganisms, insects, and scavengers access the body's inner parts through the skin and accelerate its decomposition. Once the cadaver's tissues decompose and fluids drain into the soil, the decay rate decreases considerably and advanced decay starts. This stage is discernible by decaying carcass caving and bone visibility. Decomposition odor is weak and recalcitrant tissues such as hair, bones, cartilage, and desiccated tissues remain (Dekeirsschieter et al., 2009).

The skeletal or dry remains stage is characterized by the increased visibility of bones together with the absence of odor and loss of body tissue with the exception of dry skin and cartilage. The decay rate drops markedly at this stage and complete bone decomposition may take up to 30 years in temperate regions (Ross and Cunningham, 2011), or even longer in some cases. Overall, decomposition rate is not uniform for the whole cadaver, hence the head and limbs usually decay faster than the body trunk due to their richness in labile soft tissue (Braig and Perotti, 2009).

Exogenous Organisms in Decomposition

Autolysis and putrefaction are the major changes of decay. Autolysis is macroscopically unapparent and occurs independently from the action of any exogenous organisms. Its action is then completed by microorganisms and enzymes present in the tissues and/or other organisms attracted by cellular catabolic products (Vass et al., 2002). Under conducive environmental conditions, flies may be the first to colonize the corpse and lay their eggs, whereas microorganisms and scavengers dominate when the weather is unsuitable for insect activity. According to Mann et al. (1990), Calliphoridae (blow flies) usually reach the cadaver within seconds of death in cases of aboveground decomposition or when the cadaver is accessible before burial, while gravid blow flies detect its scent from several miles away. Insects may colonize the decaying body or its remains over time. High numbers of eggs are laid on the cadaver's natural orifices and wounds, with larvae apparent after 1–2 days depending on environmental conditions such as temperature and humidity (Carter et al., 2007). Once larvae evolve into maggots, cadaver soft tissue destruction accelerates. Even mummified tissue and bone are attacked by insects and scavengers, which can excavate cadavers, especially from shallow burials. This results in extensive tissue loss, grave aeration, and accelerated decay (Haglund, 1997). DeVault et al. (2003) reported that scavengers can consume up to 75% (w/w) of the decomposing cadaver in the presence of insects and microorganisms and potentially the entire cadaver in their absence.

Following death, the immune system remains active for more than 48 h, which accounts for the absence of microorganisms in the cadaver tissues during the first day

(Janaway, 1996). Once the immune system is overcome, the body microorganisms, especially those of the lungs and gastrointestinal system, proliferate and colonize local tissues and then the whole body through the lymphatic and vascular conduits (Carter and Tibbett, 2008; Paczkowski and Schütz, 2011). Due to the very quick decrease in tissue redox potential following death, anaerobic bacteria generally increase and become predominant over obligate aerobes.

In general, body changes lead to the proliferation of indigenous microbiota, which accelerate decomposition (Vass, 2001). In particular, the action of a few bacteria such as Streptococci, Enterobacteriae, and *Clostridium* spp. in the gastrointestinal tract has been reported during the first days of putrefaction (Carter and Tibbett, 2008; Janaway et al., 2009). Putrefaction changes, essentially due to the transformation of hemoglobin by anaerobic microbial communities of the bowel, are noticeable 48–72 h after death on the abdomen before they spread to the whole body. Usually, the production of hydrogen sulfide within 7 days after death causes the transformation of hemoglobin into sulfhemoglobin (Goff, 2009) with accumulation of this greenish pigment in blood resulting in a gradual greenish marbling of the body skin starting from the anterior abdominal wall skin (Madea and Kernbach-Wighton, 2013). During this process, high volumes of various gases such as hydrogen, hydrogen sulfide, methane, carbon dioxide, mercaptans, sulfur dioxide, and ammonia are produced by microbial metabolic activity and autolysis (Clark et al., 1997). Other by-products including indole, skatole, volatile fatty acids, hydrocarbons, and various phenol, nitrogen, and sulfur-containing molecules are also produced by fermentation (Vass et al., 2002; Janaway et al., 2009). Together with these, cadaverine and putrescine are responsible for the characteristic decay smell, while accumulation of gases and molecules causes body swelling (Hau et al., 2014).

Overall, microorganisms play significant roles in human decomposition. This is more obvious in new-born deceased who, in certain cases, do not undergo bloating due to the relative absence of gut microorganisms (McQuinn, 2011). In wounded cadavers and where death is caused by high numbers of infecting bacteria, the decomposition rate is faster than in unwounded/uninfected bodies (Zhou and Byard, 2011). Soil microorganisms also affect heavily the decomposition rate, hence Lauber et al. (2014), for example, reported a two to three times faster decomposition in mice placed on nonsterile soil compared to those decaying on sterile soil.

The introduction of a cadaver is a physical disturbance to soil that causes an increase in telluric bacterial and fungal community activity and an initial shift in their composition (Kim et al., 2013). Ferrenberg et al. (2015) suggested that long-term physical disturbance and climate change may cause similar shifts in soil communities. There is evidence that microorganisms are essential to cadaver organic residue recycling, although very little is known about the associated microbial communities' structures. Cobaugh et al. (2015) reported the persistence of human-associated microbial species in soil, which are very distinct and scarce in nature and so make them possible biomarkers of human decomposition.

Other organisms such as plants, fungi, and termites have also been reported. Fungi are usually observed on exposed parts of decaying bodies and the surrounding soil in cases of aboveground decomposition. On rare occasions they have been detected in the intestines and body cavities (Sagara et al., 2008). Queiroz et al. (2016) evidenced for the first time the activity of termites, capable of degrading bones, even on nonfossilized human remains.

Factors Affecting Decomposition

Death is the beginning of a series of changes in the body leading to its decay through two major processes: autolysis and putrefaction (Shirley et al., 2011). The study of these changes helps investigators assess time-since-death, although a variety of parameters may accelerate or limit decay, making PMI estimation even more challenging. The rates of autolysis and putrefaction depend on different factors, which are related either directly to the cadaver or indirectly to its surrounding environment (Zhou and Byard, 2011).

Decomposition rate varies significantly depending on a range of factors including: the environment; cadaver antemortem condition and perimortem disease treatment (Hayman and Oxenham, 2016); the presence of clothing; death location and circumstances; soil properties and topography; type and depth of burial; presence of oxygen; humidity; cadaver exposition to exogenous organisms including soil microbes, insects, plants, and scavengers; temperature; embalming; and type of coffin (DiMaio and DiMaio, 2001; Pinheiro, 2006; Tumer et al., 2013; Lauber et al., 2014). Also cadaver condition can determine the decay rate (Pinheiro, 2006) since, in the same burial setting, decomposition is often slower in fleshy and unwounded cadavers than in skinny or wounded bodies. Autolysis and putrefaction can be accelerated by high initial core temperature caused by antemortem medical conditions including fever, localized or generalized sepsis, diabetes mellitus, obesity, and drugs consumption (Zhou and Byard, 2011). External factors such as temperature, moisture, and oxygen availability affect decay rate significantly (Carter et al., 2010). Temperature is particularly important as it determines microbial growth and multiplication on and around the body. Warm temperatures accelerate the decomposition processes, which are delayed or even stopped at low temperatures because of inhibitory effects on some enzymes and microorganisms (Mann et al., 1990; Olakanye et al., 2015). Also reduced oxygen availability inhibits the growth of some microorganisms and their circulation inside the cadaver (Janaway et al., 2009), which may promote cadaver preservation.

Decay is slower in burial settings due to the limited actions of plants, insects, and scavengers. According to Mann et al. (1990), the impact of soil type on decomposition is of minor importance within the first 2 years of burial. In contrast, Wilson et al. (2007) suggested that, together with other parameters, soil has a significant effect on decay. They reported that decomposition occurred more rapidly in porous, permeable, and light soils due to the action of water and oxygen, together with decomposition gases such as hydrogen sulfide, methane, ammonia, and carbon dioxide. Furthermore, bacterial inoculation and insulation provision for exothermic decomposition may accelerate decomposition (Janaway et al., 2009). Outdoors, decomposition may be accelerated by high ambient temperature and humidity during summer months, the local climate, fire, in-vehicle death, carbon monoxide, and entrapment (Zhou and Byard, 2011; Tumer et al., 2013). These researchers added that the main indoor causes of accelerated body decay are central heating, bath, sauna, shower, excessive bedding, electric blankets, fire, and refrigeration delay and failure.

The preservation of a decaying body can occur under certain environmental conditions. For example, rapid evaporation of body water may cause mummification to start 2–3 days after death. First noticed at the body extremities, this desiccation process can be complete or partial, and turns the skin dark brown, leathery, and stiff. In some cases, mummification may even reach the internal organs (Hau et al., 2014). It usually occurs in dry, ventilated locations with low humidity, often indoors or following burial in crypts (Schotsmans et al., 2011; Madea and Kernbach-Wighton, 2013). Generally, the bodies shrink by losing their tissue mass and so last for long periods of time without change (Hau et al., 2014). This phenomenon can also be promoted by coarse soils or quicklime (Carter et al., 2007; Schotsmans et al., 2011) and low moisture content, which hinders microbial catabolism (Carter et al., 2010). Typically, mummification is more likely to be observed in thin cadavers with relatively low muscle and adipose tissue and new-born babies.

Anaerobiosis and high soil moisture content can cause cadaver saponification (Pfeiffer et al., 1998) and contribute therefore to the preservation of its tissues and sometimes protects organs from microorganisms, insects, and scavengers (Durães et al., 2010). This process produces adipocere or the fat of graveyards (Byard, 2016a), a yellowish white to gray waxy substance (Ubelaker and Zarenko, 2011) attributable to the hydration, oxidation, or hydrogenation of unsaturated fatty acids and their transformation into saturated moieties (Notter et al., 2009; Hau et al., 2014). Generally, saponification is a long process that requires months or even years to complete. Cadavers of females, babies, and old or obese people are the most likely to undergo saponification (Schotsmans et al., 2011). Cadavers can also stay well preserved for long periods of time in other conditions such as cryotic soils at or below freezing point (permafrost bodies) and swamplands (bog bodies) (Madea and Kernbach-Wighton, 2013).

Microorganisms spread easily in moist areas of the body. Additionally, wounds, burns, and lacerations rupture the cadaver skin, facilitating microbial access to the body where they potentially accelerate decomposition (Zhou and Byard, 2011). Surface and internal temperatures, which are generally higher in burned cadavers, typically lead to higher larvae activity, generating more heat and therefore accelerated decomposition (Chin et al., 2008). This is in accordance with Avila and Goff (1998) who noticed a high attraction of calliphorid flies to burned pig carcasses resulting in a slightly faster decomposition. Gruenthal et al. (2012) reported a high variation in decomposition rates between parts of the same body charred at different temperatures and attributed the difference in decomposition speed to their degrees of burning. The main findings were that light charring dehydrated the skin and limited access to cadaver internal parts, while heavy charring cracked the skin, exposed tissue, and caused seepage (Gruenthal et al., 2012). Also fluids and odors emitted from heavily charred cadavers were more likely to attract arthropods and accelerate the decomposition rate.

POSTMORTEM INTERVAL ESTIMATION

Against this background, and because of multiple and complex interacting parameters, a panoply of techniques and approaches have been used to understand the decomposition processes, estimate PMI, or explore the potential to identify clandestine graves. For decades, scientists have attempted to develop reliable and accurate methods to assess time since death; however, no perfect tool has yet been developed. Most research initiatives have to date focused on relatively fresh cadavers since it is accepted that the longer the time of death, the less accurate the PMI estimation. The methods that have been evaluated are summarized in Table 3.1.

Furthermore, parameters such as CO_2–C evolution, ninhydrin reactive nitrogen, microbial biomass carbon, cadaver mass loss, and entomological patterns have been used often to assess decomposition rate in a variety of locations including cars, soil surface, and following burial (Carter and Tibbett, 2008; Spicka et al., 2011; Sharma et al., 2015). Most studies, however, were centered on the roles played by terrestrial insects (Carter and Tibbett, 2008) and scavengers (DeVault et al., 2003), while gravesoil processes have received limited attention.

Crime/death scene soil is usually considered as associative evidence. This echoes the outdated, yet widespread, forensic community vision of soil being passive (Ralebitso-Senior et al., 2016). Soil is, in fact, dynamic and is affected by environmental changes such as pollution and disturbance (Brookes, 1995). Considering that animal death in an ecosystem is a disturbance, the biochemical and physical characteristics of soil have the potential to be used for criminal investigations. For this purpose, biology, ecology, and chemistry have been considered for the development of PMI estimation and clandestine grave localization tools (Carter and Tibbett, 2008). Although some of these methods have been successful in some real casework, most are still being researched and developed.

Parallel to their development and application, other researchers and practitioners have proposed the importance of classifying PMI estimation tools. For example, Kaliszan et al. (2009) divided the current PMI evaluation techniques into temperature-based approaches, which are useful for early PMI estimation during the first 24 h, and methods based on the estimation of cadaveric processes, from early to late. In contrast, Madea (2013) classified the methods, depending on the timing of the processes, into Group 1 and Group 2

Table 3.1 Summary of the biochemical, physicochemical, physiological, microbial, and molecular methods that have been used to estimate postmortem interval between 1999 and early 2017

Method/method group	Cadaver area, tissue, or condition	Key findings including projected PMI estimation accuracy	References
Immunohistochemical detection	Insulin	P: <29 days; N: >12 days	Wehner et al. (1999, 2000, 2001a,b)
	Thyroglobulin	P (<12 days); N (>6 days)	
	Glucagon	P (<14 days); N (>7 days)	
	Calcitonin	P (<13 days); N (>4 days)	
H-Magnetic resonance spectroscopy	Brain tissue	<3 days on animal model	Ith et al. (2002)
Point-based decomposition scoring	Whole cadaver	ND	Megyesi et al. (2005)
Phospholipid fatty acid analysis	Soil	ND	Parkinson et al. (2009)
RNA degradation analysis	Tooth pulp	<84 days <21 days	Young et al. (2013), Sampaio-Silva et al. (2013), and Poór et al. (2016)
Laser-induced breakdown spectroscopy	Skeletal muscle	ND	Marín-Roldan et al. (2013)
Microbial community profiling	Soil/body	ND	Damann et al. (2015), Parkinson et al. (2009), and Hauther et al. (2015)
Analysis of botanical samples	Bryophytes, plant roots		Lancia et al. (2013) and Cardoso et al. (2010)
Neutron radiography	Muscles, lungs, and bones	ND	Bilheux et al. (2015)
Tomographic imagery	Intracardiac hypostasis	>12 h; error: ±2 h	Zerbini et al. (2016)
Thanatochemistry, supravitality	Vitreous humor; whole cadaver	Early stages	Salam et al. (2012), Madea (2013), Cantürk et al. (2016), and Kaszynski et al. (2016)
Mortis triad		Early stages	Krompecher (2002), Madea (2013), and Mathur and Agrawal (2011)
Volatile organic compounds analysis	Pig carcass	ND	Paczkowski et al. (2015) and Forbes et al. (2016)
Albumin concentration	Cerebrospinal fluid	>2 h and <72 h; error: ±1–4 h	Parmar and Menon (2015)
Morphological and histological changes	Eye lens	>24 h and <96 h	Prieto-Bonete et al. (2015)
Cholesterol concentration	Median nerve	<48 h	Vacchiano et al. (2016)
Total body decomposition score	Whole cadaver	<14 days	Hayman and Oxenham (2017)
Estimation of the postmortem degradation of protein markers	Skeletal muscle	ND	Sabucedo and Furton (2003), Poloz and O'day (2009), and Pittner et al. (2016a, b)

N, negative; *ND*, not determined; *P*, positive.

for tools based on detectable antemortem changes and those reliant on postmortem changes, respectively (Fig. 3.1). Specifically, Group 1 gives an insight into the approximate time of survival—a good example is the assessment of wound age. Group 2 consists of most methods intended to estimate time since death. Generally, these can be clustered according to the nature of the after-death processes into:

1. Predominantly physical—*livor* and *algor mortis*;
2. Metabolic—enzymatic activity, fluctuations in metabolite concentrations;

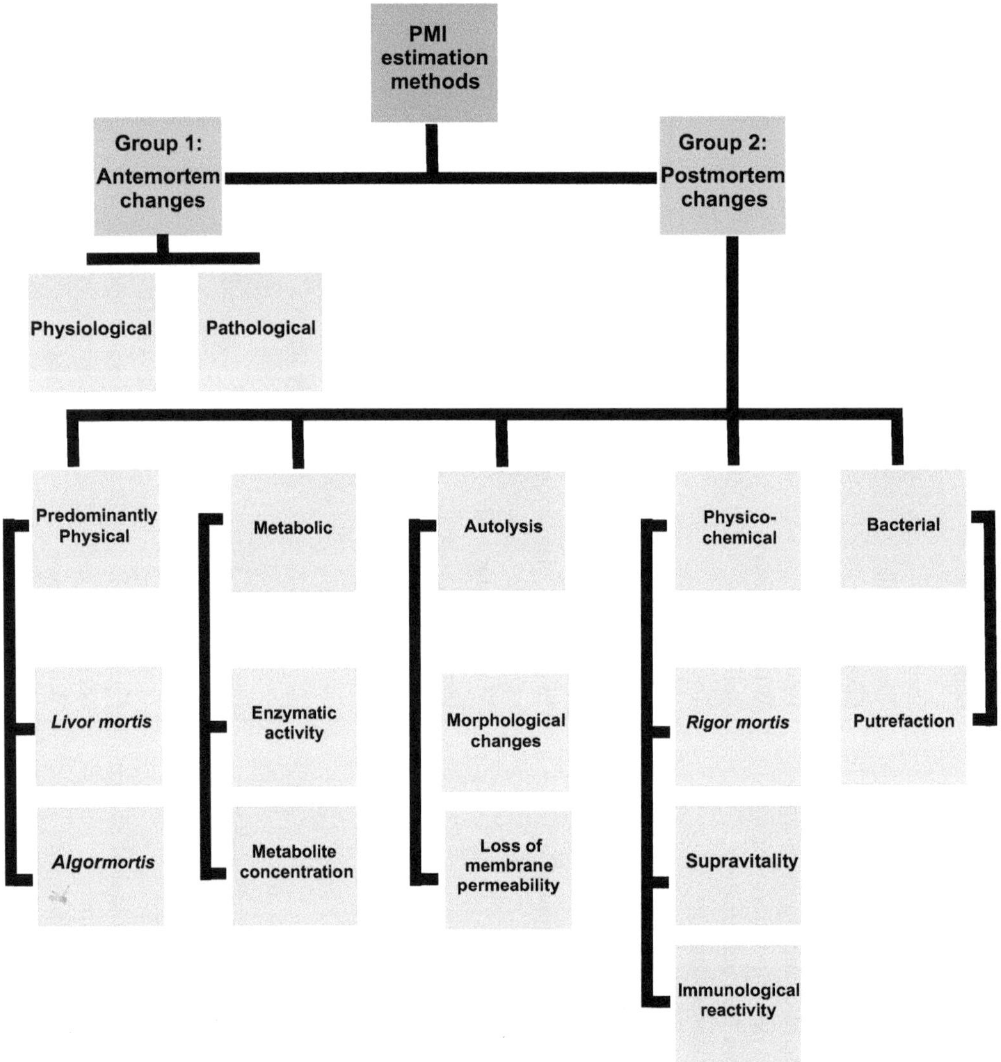

Figure 3.1 Schematic interpretation of postmortem interval (PMI) estimation methods classification as described by Madea (2013).

3. Autolytic—morphological changes;
4. Physicochemical—*rigor mortis*, supravital, and immunological reactivity; and
5. Bacterial—putrefaction.

We suggest a classification strategy that, in contrast to the approaches cited earlier, makes a distinction between real (proper) PMI estimation that may also take into account new scientific disciplines and auxiliary methods (Fig. 3.2). Categorizing these into three classes affords two major groups according to the perspective or focus and a third comprising auxiliary tools used to assess time of survival and to complement other methods. Thus time-since-death methods can be designed or developed to: assess impacts on the cadaver due to its inherent internal changes (Class I) and external factors (Class II); and (III) collect auxiliary intelligence. This classification has the potential to facilitate unencumbered and informed decision making on which PMI tool(s) to use relative to the specific case being investigated.

Class I PMI Methods: Assessment of Cadaver Inner Changes

Livor Mortis

Livor mortis starts immediately after the cessation of blood circulation. Adelson (1952) reported the appearance of minor signs on specific parts of the cadaver 30 min after death, which become fully discernible after 3–4 h and fixed in 8–12 h. In contrast, Polson (1985) stated that these first appear 30 min to 2 h after death and become completely developed after 6–12 h. Typically, the color shifts and patterns will often not disappear entirely even when the cadaver is transported or repositioned. Moreover, these are not normally observable on areas in contact with solid surfaces due to the compression of blood vessels (Krompecher, 2002). This highlights the utility of *livor mortis* in postmortem interval delimitation, death scenario reconstruction, and cause of death assessment, especially in cases such as hypothermia, carbon monoxide poisoning, and cyanide intoxication. The use of spectrophotometry, such as tristimulus colorimetry, was suggested by Vanezis and Trujillo (1996) for PMI estimation up to 48 h, while an equation was proposed by Usumoto et al. (2010) for time of death assessment within 72 h postmortem.

Rigor Mortis

Cadaveric stiffening is used for PMI estimation during the early phase after death. It is a natural process that occurs due to ATP degradation, a drop in pH, and accumulation of calcium ions (Goff, 2009). Its onset and duration vary considerably depending on the deceased's medical condition, environmental temperature, and antemortem metabolic activity, and is typically faster with vigorous antemortem activity (Krompecher, 2002; Goff, 2009). *Rigor mortis* changes appear about 2–6 h after death in temperate climates and reach a peak at 12 h. After 24–84 h, the corpse starts to loosen due to the effects of putrefactive of alkaline liquids until it becomes flaccid again (Carter and Tibbett, 2008; Goff, 2009; Janaway et al., 2009). This is marginally different from the report by

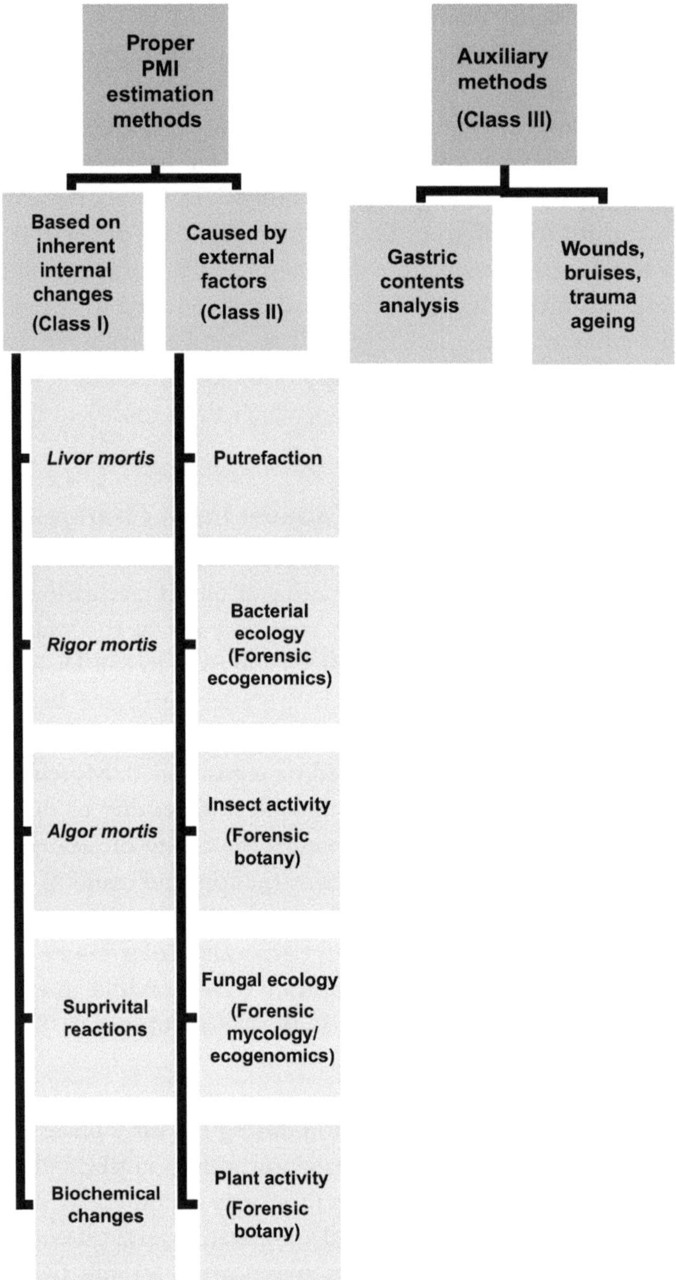

Figure 3.2 Suggested classification of postmortem interval (PMI) estimation methods.

Mathur and Agrawal (2011) who described *rigor mortis* as starting to appear 2–4 h after death, being completely discernible after 6–12 h, and then disappearing gradually up to around 72 h after death.

Algor Mortis

Algor mortis is applicable largely up to 24 h after death (Mathur and Agrawal, 2011). In this process, cadaver temperature decreases gradually by convection, radiation, conduction, and fluid evaporation (Myburgh, 2010) until it reaches an equilibrium with the environment often after 18–20 h (Fisher, 2004). The difference in temperature between the cadaver and its environment is the determining factor of the cooling rate (Reddy and Lowenstein, 2011), hence a bigger difference in temperature between the surrounding environment and the body leads to more rapid cooling (Hau et al., 2014; Shkrum and Ramsay, 2007). Usually, body temperature is maintained stable for 30 min to 1 h after death before starting to decrease, although this can persist for 5 h in extreme cases. According to Marshall (1969), metabolism, heat production, and body surface tissues are the main determinants for this initial delay in cooling.

Although the first reports on this widely used PMI assessment tool date back to the first half of the 19th century (Kaliszan et al., 2009), it has limitations that must be considered when applied. For example, cooling evaluation is applicable only in temperate and cool weather conditions; it is region specific and cannot be used for any geographically disparate areas. In particular, cooling rate is governed primarily by environmental temperature (Shkrum and Ramsay, 2007; Reddy and Lowenstein, 2011; Hau et al., 2014) together with the cadaver condition (Smart and Kaliszan, 2012). As a result, rectal temperature measurement is the most used technique in practice because of the minimal impacts of environmental conditions on this part of the body. Nevertheless, alternative approaches are described in the literature including assessing the temperature of the ear, nostril, axilla, brain, eyeball, and abdominal skin surface (Kaliszan et al., 2009). An illustration of this is the use of cooling dummies specifically for cases or studies where the cooling conditions need to be determined. The composition of the dummies enables good precision in reproducing a cadaver's cooling pattern and therefore helps assess the PMI with potentially increased confidence (Henssge, 1992; Althaus and Henssge, 1999).

Supravital Reactions

Supravitality is defined as the human tissue survival period beyond resuscitation during which tissues are still sensitive to mechanical, electrical, or pharmacological stimuli (Madea, 2016). The association between PMI and muscular response was established by Moulds et al. (1977) who applied electrical stimuli for direct excitation of skeletal muscles. Therefore supravital reactions comprise skeletal muscle excitability by mechanical or electrical stimuli and pharmacological excitability of the iris. These responses result from metabolic activity and/or continuity up to 20h after death, mainly due to anaerobic glycolysis and creatine kinase reaction. Supravitality is affected by factors such as antemortem illness and medical treatment, drug consumption, temperature fluctuations, and climate. Nonetheless, supravital reactions are observable on undamaged, unburnt cadavers without difficulty, hence their use as a practical tool for PMI estimation during the early phase of decomposition (Madea, 2016).

The iris muscle can be excited by pharmacological stimuli up to 46h after death. This reaction to stimuli has been used for PMI estimation after subconjunctival injection of drugs such as epinephrine, norepinephrine, acetylcholine, atropine, cyclopentolate, and tropicamide. Another practical tool for the estimation of early PMI up to 8–12h after death is based on the idiomuscular contraction of skeletal muscles in response to mechanical stimulation, which was first observed in vitro by Dowler in 1846 (Warther et al., 2012). According to Henssge and Madea (2004), Zsako's phenomenon is observable during the first 2–3h after death and entails the propagation of muscular fiber excitation in response to mechanical stimuli. This phenomenon is followed by local idiomuscular contraction.

Electrical stimulation is an additional supravital reaction of forensic value. First described during the 18th century, this phenomenon received much interest and was used for the assessment of PMI by Prokop in 1960. Although different muscles had been explored including skeletal, iris, and heart muscles, the most widely used for the assessment of time since death by means of electrical excitability is the *orbicularis oculi*. This approach was described by Klein and Klein in 1978 after conducting large-scale examination and statistical analysis (Henssge and Madea, 2004).

Biochemical Changes

Chemical methods for death time estimation have received a lot of attention from the scientific community since the second half of the 20th century. This interest is ongoing as exemplified by consistent initiatives to optimize and/or develop increasingly reliable methods. Potassium concentration in the vitreous humor (VH) is arguably the most documented biochemical parameter for PMI estimation due to its location in the body and its lower susceptibility to autolytic changes (Belsey and Flanagan, 2016). Zilg et al. (2015) suggested a PMI estimation model based on potassium concentration in VH corrected for age and temperature. This was optimized by Kokavec et al. (2016) who included a calibration step using antemortem vitreous samples. Rognum et al. (1991) suggested measuring hypoxanthine concentration in the VH with the approach developed further by Rognum et al. (2016) who recommended an estimation combining potassium, hypoxanthine, and ambient temperature for enhanced precision. Also parameters such as sodium, calcium, glucose, cardiac troponin I, calmodulin-binding proteins, glucagon, lactate, malate and lactate dehydrogenase, 3-methoxytyramine, creatinine, and urea were explored in body fluids including VH, cerebrospinal fluid or blood, and organs such as the heart, liver, spleen, lung, and brain (Sparks et al., 1986, 1989; Gos and Raszeja,

1993; Wehner et al., 2001b; Sabucedo and Furton, 2003; Swain et al., 2015; Belsey and Flanagan, 2016).

Cingolani et al. (1994) used an immunohistochemical, ultrastructural, and cytochemical approach to assess the autolytic changes of the skin to estimate time of death up to 12 h postmortem, while Ishikawa et al. (2006) suggested the utility of the adenohypophysis immunohistochemical analysis for PMI evaluation up to 20 days after death. Also Wehner et al. (1999, 2000, 2001a) proposed methods based on the immunohistochemical detection of insulin, thyroglobulin, and calcitonin, respectively. For postmortem estimation based on molecular analysis, Cina (1994) proposed a method that relied on DNA degradation assessment by flow cytometry using spleen samples. The approach was tested subsequently by Di Nunno et al. (1998) and reported to be reliable up to 72 h. Furthermore, Sampaio-Silva et al. (2013) characterized RNA degradation rates in various tissues and developed a mathematical model for time since death estimation to supplement current methods.

Despite considerable research investments to develop these PMI estimation methods, most have little or inadequate practical value in real crime scenes or routine laboratory work because of their inherently limited accuracy, robustness, consistency, and reliability. Nevertheless, some of the approaches afford acceptable approximations of the PMI and have potential applicability in forensic cases especially when used in combination with other techniques. As a result, researchers have proposed several novel chemical- and biomolecule-based methods, especially during the last decade, with more research required for these to become established. For example, Kaszynski et al. (2016) used mice to illustrate the applicability of gas chromatography-mass spectrometry for biochemical profiling of the low molecular weight metabolites in serum and muscles to estimate time since death.

Human skeletal muscles are abundant, accessible, and protected from external contamination. Their decomposition is slower than that of internal organs yet faster than cartilage and bone, which makes them ideal for intermediate PMI estimation. Consequently, Pittner et al. (2016a,b) developed and applied a new method for PMI determination based on muscle protein degradation assessment by Western blotting and casein zymography on 40 real forensic cases. The authors identified specific proteins such as desmin, cTnT, and Calpain 1, and their respective catabolic metabolites, which had demonstrable potential for the evaluation of time since death. In parallel, Lee et al. (2016) used a preliminary study to suggest the use of lateral flow assay as a tool to determine and measure protein markers of time since death. Additional approaches recommended post-2010 include measurements of the median nerve cholesterol concentration (Vacchiano et al., 2016) and electrical skin conductivity changes (Cantürk et al., 2016), while Hayman and Oxenham (2017) suggested the development of PMI estimation models based on total body decomposition scores.

Molecular techniques include gene expression analyses of the "biological clock" to estimate the time of death (Kimura et al., 2011). Poór et al. (2016) implemented a pilot study with the analysis of RNA degradation in human dental pulp using reverse transcription polymerase chain reaction. The researchers identified this as a promising approach since it facilitated PMI estimation with high statistical confidence during the first 21 days after death. Also Van den Berge et al. (2016) demonstrated the ability of DNA and RNA to be used for profiling of human cadavers buried for long periods of time (4–42 years), while Lv et al. (2016) described and validated an accurate mathematical model for the estimation of time since death based on RNA degradation that was applicable at different temperatures (10, 20, and 30°C).

Class II PMI Methods: Assessment of Cadaver Changes Due to External Factors

Putrefaction/Postmortem Decomposition

Putrefaction is defined as the breakdown of the cadaver's soft tissues and disintegration of their proteins, fats, sugars, and nucleic acids into their building blocks (i.e., amino acids, ketones, glucose, amines). This environment-dependent and microbial-led process is recognizable from changes in the color of the cadaver and the production of liquefaction fluids and gases (Mathur and Agrawal, 2011). Marbling is first observable on the abdomen 36–72 h after death before its sequential spread all over the body. Blisters form on the skin and the abdominal wall swells due to gas accumulation, followed by other parts of the cadaver. At high body temperatures (above 26°C), putrefaction and bloating occur within a day and 2–3 days after death, respectively. Putrefactive changes in terrestrial environments may be used for crude estimations of time since death; however, precaution is essential since this process is highly affected by the surrounding environment and weather fluctuations and therefore varies considerably. In contrast, putrefactive change examination may facilitate a good indication of time since death for submerged cadavers due to the constancy of the water temperature for a relatively long time (Madea, 2016).

Bacterial and Site Ecology: Forensic Ecogenomics

Microbial communities associated with gravesoil have the potential to be used as a tool to estimate time since death (Finley et al., 2015). For example, Metcalf et al. (2013) and Olakanye et al. (2015) reported a consistent shift of the microbial communities in response to the decomposition of domestic pigs as human surrogates. Metcalf et al. (2016) described the appearance of decomposing microorganisms in a predictable order, which may be used to estimate time since death. Guo et al. (2016) sequenced 16S rRNA gene amplicons from rectal and buccal samples of dead and live rats to use the bacterial community shifts to estimate time since death. The rectal bacterial communities, which were initially similar, became gradually more analogous with progressive decomposition of the cadavers. These studies reflect the increasing application of culture-based and molecular analyses in novel forensic contexts (see also Chapters 1 and 5–7). For example, forensic ecogenomics is an emerging discipline at the interface of microbiology, archaeology, and forensics. It is developed to further understand decomposition site ecology by measuring the effect of decomposition on the surrounding environment and/or the effect of the site on decomposition to facilitate forensic investigations (Chimutsa et al., 2015; Ralebitso-Senior et al., 2016) (see also Chapter 1).

Insect Activity: Forensic Entomology

Forensic entomology is a widely used technique for the estimation of time since death, based on the study of the lifecycles of cadaver-eating insects. Despite its usefulness, this technique has investigative limitations such as the dependence upon environmental factors, regional fauna, and type of burial (Pittner et al., 2016a). Also conditions such as darkness, cold weather, water, and belowground burial hinder insect activity (Gennard, 2007) and therefore prevent the use of forensic entomology by investigators. As a consequence, other techniques based on chemical, biochemical, molecular, physical, and supravital reactions have been developed to improve the accuracy of current PMI estimation methods or invent new tools.

Fungal Activity and Ecology: Forensic Mycology/Ecogenomics

Fungi play a major role in terrestrial environment decomposition and are therefore likely to have a significant effect on cadaver decomposition (Bruns et al., 1991). Various authors reported the presence of fungi on and inside cadavers (Hitosugi et al., 2006; Ishii et al., 2006; Tranchida et al., 2014), although little is known about their specific role in decomposition and the different species of decomposers involved (Carter et al., 2007).

Van de Voorde and Van Dijck were probably the first researchers to use cadaveric fungi for PMI estimation in 1982 by assessing the growth of isolates collected from a cadaver and incubated at the same ambient temperature. The estimation was subsequently checked and confirmed against the suspect's confessions. Similarly, Ishii et al. (2006) studied fungal growth on a mummified cadaver and bones and highlighted their value as geographical markers and potential PMI assessment tools, while Janaway et al. (2009) reported an early presence of this glade on decaying bodies and the presence of molds after 1-week postmortem. Parkinson et al. (2009) used terminal restriction fragment length polymorphism to monitor the fungal community changes during human aboveground decomposition, and noticed some successional patterns with the progression of decay. Similarly, Fu et al. (2015) investigated the use of internal transcribed spacer analysis to study the fungal community's shift patterns in decomposing rats, and reported a significant difference in richness and abundance that might be used for PMI estimation.

According to Hawksworth and Wiltshire (2011), fungal multiplication and growth are affected considerably by the surrounding environment. Therefore PMI estimation should take temperature and humidity records into consideration. In general, more case studies, using different approaches, are needed to give forensic mycology more value as a forensic tool.

Plant Activity: Forensic Botany

Behrensmeyer (1978) and Vass (2001) highlighted the role played by plants in the decomposition of remains. In fact, roots accelerate decomposition possibly via physical bone degradation and fragmentation, and the action of acids associated with decaying plant roots. Overall, the growth rate of plants may be used to estimate time since burial in cases of clandestine burial or when human remains have been translocated.

The usual PMI estimation tools are mostly ineffective in assessing time since death of highly decomposed or skeletonized bodies. As a result, investigators rely on intelligence, testimonies, and information collected from the cadaver and crime scene to assess time of death during this phase of decomposition. Cardoso et al. (2010) reported a case where they estimated the minimum PMI of a skeletonized cadaver discovered in a forest by evaluating the growth rate of bryophytes and vascular plants recovered from the cadaver together with its remains and clothing analysis. Similarly, Lancia et al. (2013) estimated the minimum time since death of a skeletonized skull by assessing the development of a colony of the bryophyte *Leptodyctium riparium* (Hedw.) Warnst on it. Notwithstanding these examples of its applicability, this tool is circumstantial and needs expert knowledge in botany. Its application relies on the adherence of the bryophytes and their growth on the bone remains. This colonization may be delayed by the persistence of soft tissues, the surrounding environmental factors, or the temporal physical protection of the cadaver. Therefore researchers recommended that it should be used cautiously.

Class III PMI Auxiliary Methods

Besides the abovementioned classes of tools, there are other techniques usually used by forensic practitioners to determine time since death, reconstruct the death scenario, and estimate the survival time or moment at which the victim was known to be still alive. These can be adopted to complement true PMI estimation tools to provide more comprehensive and conclusive metadata during research initiatives, real crime investigations, and ultimately court cases.

Gastric Contents Analysis

The analysis of gastric contents and their distribution in the stomach and intestines has been used as a forensic tool in death investigations (Madea, 2016). Notwithstanding this, and in contrast to those discussed earlier, this method does not afford PMI estimation. Instead it gives insight into the approximate time elapsed between the victim's final meal and death. The approach relies on intelligence gathered by investigators to know the time and size of the ultimate meal to give a good estimate, although it is possible to make an estimation based on the type of the last meal (Madea and Kernbach-Wighton, 2013). A variety of scientific methods such as radiology, ferromagnetic traces, absorption kinetics of oral solutes, ultrasound, aspiration, and radioisotopes have been used in forensic contexts to analyze the gastric content of the deceased. Nonetheless, the accuracy of gastric content analysis can be affected by illness, stress, infections, drug consumption, and type of food ingested, which may accelerate or hinder gastric emptying (Byard, 2016b).

Wounds, Bruises, and Trauma Aging

Wound or bruise age may be defined by the time elapsed between the occurrence of the injury and death time. Wounds, bruises, and trauma are often examined and their regeneration assessed by pathologists to determine the cause of death, conclude if the injuries were ante- or postmortem, and assess the survival time, which may help estimate time since death. This approach is based on the assessment of a highly variable biological phenomenon, regeneration, which is affected by the severity of the injuries and their location on the body. Therefore it is very difficult to estimate wound age with precision (Byard, 2016b).

SUMMARY

In a forensic context, PMI estimation methods are tools used to understand the circumstances of death, confirm testimonies, and help solve crimes. Despite multiple attempts, the development of an accurate PMI estimation tool remains one of the major challenges that face the forensic community. This is mainly because PMI determination is influenced by a sequence of external factors such as microbial, insect, and scavenging activities together with edaphic and environmental parameters. It also depends on cadaver endogenous factors such as corpulence and cause of death (Bilheux et al., 2015). The forensic sciences have seen the introduction of revolutionary protocols, mostly borrowed from other disciplines (Ralebitso-Senior et al., 2016). Notwithstanding the wide variety of techniques and approaches adopted, a precise and practical method for PMI estimation is yet to be developed.

Although most techniques are mainly of academic value and therefore potentially impractical in real scenarios, they enrich the current knowledge base and orientate researchers to the most valuable approaches. The majority of current methods are context specific, and lack the reliability and precision to be applied in different forensic cases. Also they are based largely on the analysis of the metabolic and putrefactive changes of the cadaver, which depend on intrinsic parameters related to the physiological state of the deceased and local environmental factors. It is vital therefore to consider the bias caused by these determinative parameters, avoid/minimize reliance on individual methods for PMI assessment, and instead adopt multidisciplinary approaches to mitigate the inherent errors related to each single method.

Although combining different PMI evaluation methods may be relatively effective for increased estimation accuracy, the choice of the techniques to use should reflect the specificity of the case being investigated. Additionally, it is crucial to correlate the PMI calculations to data collected from intelligence, evidence from the cadaver and the surrounding environment, and eventual testimonies, as this will allow for the results to be confirmed and checked against different sources. Another approach would be to develop new tools that are not affected by environmental fluctuations, or those using parts of the body that are protected physically from the external environment, such as the VH or DNA, which are theoretically less affected by variations. This principle is questionable, however, since the decomposing cadaver cells undergo autolysis simultaneously, and putrefactive changes sequentially (Janaway et al., 2009; Hau et al., 2014).

Recent advances in molecular biology, biochemistry, computer modeling, data analysis, and medical visualization should facilitate the optimization of current methods. This is dependent upon and will be realized through more case studies, which should be designed to include corrective factors, incorporate robust and relevant statistical analyses, validate adopted methods, and therefore confirm the theoretical feasibility and practicality of the techniques in real-life applications. Also the new technologies may afford the exploration of novel parameters that were previously challenging to study, with the ultimate aim of finding a definitive PMI estimation tool. In summary, this chapter has considered a wide range of cadaver-focused biochemical, physicochemical, physiological, microbial, and molecular PMI estimation techniques with those developed within specific forensic subdisciplines deliberated in Chapters 5–7. Furthermore, the reader is referred to relevant compilations by other researchers and practitioners for a more expansive discourse on the specific topics, disciplines, and contexts presented in this chapter.

REFERENCES

Adelson, L., 1952. Pathologic findings in patients dead of common poison. American Journal of Clinical Pathology 22 (6), 509–519.

Althaus, L., Henssge, C., 1999. Rectal temperature time of death nomogram: sudden change of ambient temperature. Forensic Science International 99 (3), 171–178.

Avila, F.W., Goff, M.L., 1998. Arthropod succession patterns onto burnt carrion in two contrasting habitats in the Hawaiian Islands. Journal of Forensic Science 43 (3), 581–586.

Behrensmeyer, A.K., 1978. Taphonomic and ecologic information from bone weathering. Paleobiology 4, 150–162.

Belsey, S., Flanagan, R., 2016. Postmortem biochemistry: current applications. Journal of Forensic and Legal Medicine 41, 49–57.

Bilheux, H.Z., Cekanova, M., Vass, A.A., Nichols, T.L., Bilheux, J.C., Donnell, R.L., Finochiarro, V., 2015. A novel approach to determine postmortem interval using neutron radiography. Forensic Science International 251, 11–21.

Braig, H.R., Perotti, M.A., 2009. Carcases and mites. Experimental and Applied Acarology 49 (1), 45–84.

Brookes, P.C., 1995. The use of microbial parameters in monitoring soil pollution by heavy metals. Biology and Fertility of Soils 19, 269–279.

Bruns, T., White, T., Taylor, J., 1991. Fungal molecular systematics. Annual Review of Ecology and Systematics 22, 525–564.

Byard, R.W., 2016a. Adipocere-the fat of graveyards. The American Journal of Forensic Medicine and Pathology 37 (3), 208–210.

Byard, R.W., 2016b. Timing: the Achilles heel of forensic pathology. Forensic Science, Medicine and Pathology 1–2.

Cantürk, İ., Karabiber, F., Çelik, S., Şahin, M.F., Yağmur, F., Kara, S., 2016. An experimental evaluation of electrical skin conductivity changes in postmortem interval and its assessment for time of death estimation. Computers in Biology and Medicine 69, 92–96.

Cardoso, H.F.V., Santos, A., Dias, R., Garcia, C., Pinto, M., Sérgio, C., Magalhães, T., 2010. Establishing a minimum postmortem interval of human remains in an advanced state of skeletonization using the growth rate of bryophytes and plant roots. International Journal of Legal Medicine 124 (5), 451–456.

Carter, D.O., Tibbett, M., 2008. Cadaver decomposition and soil: processes. In: Tibbett, M., Carter, D.O. (Eds.), Soil Analysis in Forensic Taphonomy: Chemical and Biological Effect of Buried Human Remains. CRC Press, Boca Raton, USA, pp. 29–52.

Carter, D.O., Yellowlees, D., Tibbett, M., 2007. Cadaver decomposition in terrestrial ecosystems. Naturwissenschaften 94 (1), 12–24.

Carter, D.O., Yellowlees, D., Tibbett, M., 2010. Moisture can be the dominant environmental parameter governing cadaver decomposition in soil. Forensic Science International 200, 60–66.

Chimutsa, M., Olakanye, A.O., Thompson, T.J.U., Ralebitso-Senior, T.K., 2015. Soil fungal community shift evaluation as a potential cadaver decomposition indicator. Forensic Science International 257, 155–159.

Chin, H.C., Marwi, M.A., Salleh, A.F.M., Jeffery, J., Kurahashi, H., Omar, B., 2008. Study of insect succession and rate of decomposition on a partially burned pig carcass in an oil palm plantation in Malaysia. Tropical Biomedicine 25 (3), 202–208.

Cina, S., 1994. Flow cytometric evaluation of DNA degradation: a predictor of postmortem interval? American Journal of Forensic Medicine & Pathology 15 (4), 300–302.

Cingolani, M., Osculati, A., Tombolini, A., Tagliabracci, A., Ghimentonm, C., Ferrara, S.D., 1994. Morphology of sweat glands in determining time of death. International Journal of Legal Medicine 107 (3), 132–140.

Clark, M.A., Worrell, M.B., Pless, J.E., 1997. Postmortem changes in soft tissues. In: Haglund, W.D., Sorg, M.H. (Eds.), Forensic Taphonomy: The Postmortem Fate of Human Remains. CRC Press, Boca Raton, USA, pp. 151–164.

Cobaugh, K.L., Schaeffer, S.M., De Bruyn, J.M., 2015. Functional and structural succession of soil microbial communities below decomposing human cadavers. Public Library of Science 10 (6), e0130201.

Damann, F.E., Williams, D.E., Layton, A.C., 2015. Potential use of bacterial community succession in decaying human bone for estimating postmortem interval. Journal of Forensic Sciences 60 (4), 844–850.

Dekeirsschieter, J., Verheggen, F., Gohy, M., Hubrecht, F., Bourguignon, L., Lognay, G., Haubruge, E., 2009. Cadaveric volatile organic compounds released by decaying pig carcasses (*Sus domesticus* L.) in different biotopes. Forensic Science International 189 (1), 46–53.

DeVault, T.L., Rhodes, O.E., Shivik, J.A., 2003. Scavenging by vertebrates: behavioural, ecological and evolutionary perspectives on an important energy transfer pathway in terrestrial ecosystems. Oikos 102, 225–234.

Di Nunno, N., Costantinides, F., Bernasconi, P., Bottin, C., Melato, M., 1998. Is flow cytometric evaluation of DNA degradation a reliable method to investigate the early postmortem period? The American Journal of Forensic Medicine and Pathology 19 (1), 50–53.

DiMaio, D., DiMaio, V.J., 2001. Time of death. In: DiMaio, D., DiMaio, V.J. (Eds.), Forensic Pathology, second ed. CRC Press, Boca Raton, Florida, pp. 21–41.

Durães, N., Cortez, D., Algarra, M., Sánchez, F.G., Rodríguez-Borges, J.E., Bobos, I., Da Silva, J.C.G., 2010. Comparison of adipocere formation in four soil types of the Porto (Portugal) district. Forensic Science International 195 (1), e161–e168.

Efremov, I.A., 1940. Taphonomy: a new branch of paleontology. Pan-American Geologist 74 (2), 81–93.

Ferrenberg, S., Reed, S.C., Belnap, J., 2015. Climate change and physical disturbance cause similar community shifts in biological soil crusts. Proceedings of the National Academy of Sciences 112 (39), 12116–12121.

Finley, S.J., Benbow, M.E., Javan, G.T., 2015. Potential applications of soil microbial ecology and next-generation sequencing in criminal investigations. Applied Soil Ecology 88, 69–78.

Fisher, B.A.J., 2004. Techniques of Crime Scene Investigation, seventh ed. CRC Press, New York, USA, pp. 433–435.
Forbes, S.L., Troobnikoff, A.N., Ueland, M., Nizio, K.D., Perrault, K.A., 2016. Profiling the decomposition odour at the grave surface before and after probing. Forensic Science International 259, 193–199.
Fu, X.L., Guo, J.J., Zhu, Z.Y., Ding, Z.Y., Zha, L., Cai, J.F., 2015. The potential use of fungi community in postmortem interval estimation in China. Forensic Science International Genetics Supplement Series 5, e476–e478.
Galloway, A., Birkby, W.H., Jones, A.M., Henry, T.E., Parks, B.O., 1989. Decay rates of human remains in an arid environment. Journal of Forensic Sciences 34 (3), 607–616.
Gennard, D.E., 2007. Forensic Entomology: An Introduction. John Wiley & Sons Ltd., West Sussex, England, pp. 3–12.
Gill-King, H., 1997. Chemical and ultrastructural aspects of decomposition. In: Haglund, W.D., Sorg, M.H. (Eds.), Forensic Taphonomy: The Postmortem Fate of Human Remains. CRC Press, Boca Raton, USA, pp. 93–108.
Goff, M.L., 2009. Early post-mortem changes and stages of decomposition in exposed cadavers. Experimental and Applied Acarology 49, 21–36.
Gos, T., Raszeja, S., 1993. Postmortem activity of lactate and malate dehydrogenase in human liver in relation to time after death. International Journal of Legal Medicine 106 (1), 25–29.
Gruenthal, A., Moffatt, C., Simmons, T., 2012. Differential decomposition patterns in charred versus uncharred remains. Journal of Forensic Sciences 57 (1), 12–18.
Guo, J., Fu, X., Liao, H., Hu, Z., Long, L., Yan, W., Ding, Y., Zha, L., Guo, Y., Yan, J., Chang, Y., Cai, J., 2016. Potential use of bacterial community succession for estimating post-mortem interval as revealed by high-throughput sequencing. Scientific Reports 6.
Haglund, W.D., 1997. Dogs and coyotes: postmortem involvement with human remains. In: Haglund, W.D., Sorg, M.H. (Eds.), Forensic Taphonomy: The Postmortem Fate of Human Remains. CRC Press, Boca Raton, USA, pp. 367–381.
Hau, T.C., Hamzah, N.H., Lian, H.H., Amir Hamzah, S.P.A., 2014. Decomposition process and post mortem changes: review. Sains Malaysiana 43 (12), 1873–1882.
Hauther, K.A., Cobaugh, K.L., Jantz, L.M., 2015. Estimating time since death from postmortem human gut microbial communities. Journal of Forensic Science 60, 1234–1240.
Hawksworth, D.L., Wiltshire, P.E., 2011. Forensic mycology: the use of fungi in criminal investigations. Forensic Science International 206 (1), 1–11.
Hayman, J., Oxenham, M., 2016. Peri-mortem disease treatment: a little known cause of error in the estimation of the time since death in decomposing human remains. Australian Journal of Forensic Sciences 48 (2), 171–185.
Hayman, J., Oxenham, M., 2017. Estimation of the time since death in decomposed bodies found in Australian conditions. Australian Journal of Forensic Sciences 49 (1), 31–44.
Henssge, C., Madea, B., 2004. Estimation of the time since death in the early post-mortem period. Forensic Science International 144 (2), 167–175.
Henssge, C., 1992. Rectal temperature time of death nomogram: dependence of corrective factors on the body weight under stronger thermic insulation conditions. Forensic science international 54 (1), 51–66.
Henssge, C., Lunkenheimer, P.P., Salomon, O., Madea, B., 1984. Supravital electrical excitability of muscles. Journal of Legal Medicine 93 (3), 165–174.
Hitosugi, M., Kiyoshi, I., Takashi, Y., Yuichi, C., Akira, K., Masahito, K., Toshiaki, N., Shogo, T., 2006. Fungi can be a useful forensic tool. Legal Medicine 8 (4), 240–242.
Hopkins, D.W., 2008. The role of soil organisms in terrestrial decomposition. In: Tibbett, M., Carter, D.O. (Eds.), Soil Analysis in Forensic Taphonomy. CRC Press, pp. 53–66.
Ishii, K., Hitosugi, M., Kido, M., Yaguchi, T., Nishimura, K., Hosoya, T., Tokudome, S., 2006. Analysis of fungi detected in human cadavers. Legal Medicine 8 (3), 188–190.
Ishikawa, T., Zhu, B., Li, D., Zhao, D., Michiue, T., Maeda, H., 2006. Postmortem stability of pituitary hormones in the human adenohypophysis. Legal Medicine 8 (1), 34–38.
Ith, M., Bigler, P., Scheurer, E., Kreis, R., Hofmann, L., Dirnhofer, R., Boesch, C., 2002. Observation and identification of metabolites emerging during postmortem decomposition of brain tissue by means of *in situ* 1H-magnetic resonance spectroscopy. Magnetic Resonance in Medicine 48, 915–920.

Janaway, R.C., 1996. The decay of buried human remains and their associated materials. In: Hunter, J., Roberts, C., Martin, A. (Eds.), Studies in Crime: An Introduction to Forensic Archaeology. Batesford, London, UK, pp. 58–85.

Janaway, R.C., Percival, S.L., Wilson, A.S., 2009. Decomposition of human remains. In: Percival, S.L. (Ed.), Microbiology and Aging, Clinical Manifestations. Springer Science+Business Media, New York, USA, pp. 313–334.

Kaliszan, M., Hauser, R., Kernbach-Wighton, G., 2009. Estimation of the time of death based on the assessment of post mortem processes with emphasis on body cooling. Legal Medicine 11, 111–117.

Kaszynski, R.H., Nishiumi, S., Azuma, T., Yoshida, M., Kondo, T., Takahashi, M., Asano, M., Ueno, Y., 2016. Postmortem interval estimation: a novel approach utilizing gas chromatography/mass spectrometry-based biochemical profiling. Analytical and Bioanalytical Chemistry 408 (12), 3103–3112.

Kim, M., Heo, E., Kang, H., Adams, J., 2013. Changes in soil bacterial community structure with increasing disturbance frequency. Microbial Ecology 66, 171–181.

Kimura, A., Ishida, Y., Hayashi, T., Nosaka, M., Kondo, T., 2011. Estimating time of death based on the biological clock. International Journal of Legal Medicine 125 (3), 385–391.

Kobayashi, M., July–December 2002. Why does rigor mortis progress downwards? Anil Aggrawal's Internet Journal of Forensic Medicine and Toxicology 3 (2). http://www.anilaggrawal.com/ij/vol_003_no_002/papers/paper001.html Published July 1, 2002.

Kobayashi, M., Ikegaya, H., Takase, I., Hatanaka, K., Sakurada, K., Iwase, H., 2001. Development of rigor mortis is not affected by muscle volume. Forensic Science International 117 (3), 213–219.

Kokavec, J., Min, S.H., Tan, M.H., Gilhotra, J.S., Newland, H.S., Durkin, S.R., Grigg, J., Casson, R.J., 2016. Biochemical analysis of the living human vitreous. Clinical & Experimental Ophthalmology 44 (7), 597–609.

Krompecher, T., 2002. Rigor mortis: estimation of the time since death by evaluation of cadaveric rigidity. In: Knight, B. (Ed.), The Estimation of the Time since Death in the Early Postmortem Period, second ed. Edward Arnold, London, UK, pp. 144–160.

Lancia, M., Conforti, F., Aleffi, M., Caccianiga, M., Bacci, M., Rossi, R., 2013. The use of *Leptodyctium riparium* (Hedw.) *Warnst* in the estimation of minimum postmortem interval. Journal of Forensic Sciences 58 (s1), s239–s242.

Lauber, C.L., Metcalf, J.L., Keepers, K., Ackermann, G., Carter, D.O., Knight, R., 2014. Vertebrate decomposition is accelerated by soil microbes. Applied and Environmental Microbiology 80 (16), 4920–4929.

Lee, D., Yang, K., Hwang, J., Kang, H., Lee, S., Choi, S., Shin, J., Jang, I., An, H., Chung, H., Jung, H., Choi, J., 2016. Degradation of kidney and psoas muscle proteins as indicators of post-mortem interval in a rat model, with use of lateral flow technology. PLoS One 11 (8), e0160557.

Lee, G.M., 2009. Early post-mortem changes and stages of decomposition in exposed cadavers. Experimental and Applied Acarology 49 (1), 21–36.

Lv, Y., Ma, J., Pan, H., Zhang, H., Li, W., Xue, A., Wang, H., Ma, K., Chen, L., 2016. RNA degradation as described by a mathematical model for postmortem interval determination. Journal of Forensic and Legal Medicine 44, 43–52.

Madea, B., 2013. Estimation of the time since death. In: Siegel, J.A., Saukko, P.J., Houck, M.M. (Eds.), Encyclopedia of Forensic Sciences. Academic Press, Waltham, USA, pp. 229–238.

Madea, B., 2016. Methods for determining time of death. Forensic Science, Medicine and Pathology 12 (4), 451–485.

Madea, B., Kernbach-Wighton, G., 2013. Early and late postmortem changes. In: Siegel, J.A., Saukko, P.J., Houck, M.M. (Eds.), Encyclopedia of Forensic Sciences. Academic Press, Waltham, USA, pp. 217–228.

Manhein, M.H., 1997. Decomposition rate of deliberate burials. In: Haglund, W.D., Sorg, M.H. (Eds.), Forensic Taphonomy: The Postmortem Fate of Human Remains. CRC Press, Boca Raton, USA, pp. 469–481.

Mann, R.W., Bass, W.M., Meadows, L., 1990. Time since death and decomposition of the human body: variables and observations in case and experimental field studies. Journal of Forensic Science 35, 103–111.

Marín-Roldan, A., Manzoor, S., Moncayo, S., Navarro-Villoslada, F., Izquierdo-Hornillos, R.C., Caceres, J.O., 2013. Determination of the postmortem interval by laser induced breakdown spectroscopy using swine skeletal muscles. Spectrochimica Acta Part B: Atomic Spectroscopy 88, 186–191.

Marshall, T.K., 1969. The use of body temperature in estimating the time of death and its limitations. Medicine, Science and the Law 9 (3), 178–182.
Mathur, A., Agrawal, Y.K., 2011. An overview of methods used for estimation of time since death. Australian Journal of Forensic Sciences 43 (4), 275–285.
McQuinn, B.C., 2011. Impact of Embalming and Burial on Decomposition Rates and Diffusion of Volatile Fatty Acids in Kentucky (MSc thesis) Eastern Kentucky University. Available at: http://etd.lsu.edu/docs/available/etd-04252011-180855/unrestricted/McQuinn_Thesis.pdf.
Megyesi, M.S., Nawrocki, S.P., Haskell, N.H., 2005. Using accumulated degree-days to estimate the post-mortem interval from decomposed human remains. Journal of Forensic Sciences 50 (3), 1–9.
Metcalf, J.L., Xu, Z.Z., Weiss, S., Lax, S., Van Treuren, W., Hyde, E.R., Song, S.J., Amir, A., Larsen, P., Sangwan, N., Haarmann, D., 2016. Microbial community assembly and metabolic function during mammalian corpse decomposition. Science 351 (6269), 158–162.
Metcalf, J.L., Parfrey, L.W., Gonzalez, A., Lauber, C.L., Knights, D., Ackermann, G., Humphrey, G.C., Gebert, M.J., Van Treuren, W., Berg-Lyons, D., Keepers, K., Guo, Y., Bullard, J., Fierer, N., Carter, D.O., Knight, R., 2013. A microbial clock provides an accurate estimate of the postmortem interval in a mouse model system. eLife 2, e01104.
Moulds, R.F.W., Young, A., Jones, D.A., Edwards, R.H.T., 1977. A study of the contractility, biochemistry and morphology of an isolated preparation of human skeletal muscle. Clinical Science and Molecular Medicine 52, 291–297.
Myburgh, J., 2010. Estimating the Post-mortem Interval Using Accumulated Degree-Days in a South African Setting (Thesis) University of Pretoria Available at: http://repository.up.ac.za/handle/2263/25700.
Notter, S.J., Stuart, B.H., Rowe, R., Langlois, N., 2009. The initial changes of fat deposits during the decomposition of human and pig remains. Journal of Forensic Sciences 54 (1), 195–201.
Olakanye, A.O., Thompson, T., Ralebitso-Senior, T.K., 2015. Shifts in soil biodiversity—a forensic comparison between *Sus scrofa domesticus* and vegetation decomposition. Science & Justice 55 (6), 402–407.
Paczkowski, S., Nicke, S., Ziegenhagen, H., Schütz, S., 2015. Volatile emission of decomposing pig carcasses (*Sus scrofa domesticus* L.) as an indicator for the postmortem interval. Journal of Forensic Science 60 (1), 130–137.
Paczkowski, S., Schütz, S., 2011. Post-mortem volatiles of vertebrate tissue. Applied Microbiology and Biotechnology 91 (4), 917–935.
Parkinson, R.A., Dias, K.R., Horswell, J., Greenwood, P., Banning, N., Tibbett, M., Vass, A.A., 2009. Microbial community analysis of human decomposition on soil. In: Ritz, K., Dawson, L., Miller, D. (Eds.), Criminal and Environmental Soil Forensics. Springer, Netherlands, pp. 379–394.
Parmar, A.K., Menon, S.K., 2015. Estimation of postmortem interval through albumin in CSF by simple dye binding method. Science & Justice 55 (6), 388–393.
Payne, J.A., King, E.W., Beinhart, G., 1968. Arthropod succession and decomposition of buried pigs. Nature 219, 1180–1181.
Pfeiffer, S., Milne, S., Stevenson, R.M., 1998. The natural decomposition of adipocere. Journal of Forensic Sciences 43 (2), 368–370.
Pinheiro, J., 2006. Decay process of a cadaver. In: Schmitt, A., Cunha, E., Pinheiro, J. (Eds.), Forensic Anthropology and Medicine: Complementary Sciences from Recovery to Cause of Death. Humana Press Inc., Totowa, New Jersey, pp. 85–116.
Pittner, S., Ehrenfellner, B., Monticelli, F.C., Zissler, A., Sänger, A.M., Stoiber, W., Steinbacher, P., 2016a. Postmortem muscle protein degradation in humans as a tool for PMI delimitation. International Journal of Legal Medicine 130 (6), 1547–1555.
Pittner, S., Ehrenfellner, B., Zissler, A., Racher, V., Trutschnig, W., Bathke, A.C., Sänger, A.M., Stoiber, W., Steinbacher, P., Monticelli, F.C., 2016b. First application of a protein-based approach for time since death estimation. International Journal of Legal Medicine 1–5.
Poloz, Y.O., O'Day, D.H., 2009. Determining time of death: temperature-dependent postmortem changes in calcineurin A, MARCKS, CaMKII, and protein phosphatase 2A in mouse. International Journal of Legal Medicine 123 (4), 305–314.
Polson, C.J., 1985. The signs of death. In: Polson, C.J., Gee, D., Knight, B. (Eds.), The Essentials of Forensic Medicine, fourth ed. Pergamon Press, Oxford, UK, pp. 3–39.

Poór, V.S., Lukács, D., Nagy, T., Rácz, E., Sipos, K., 2016. The rate of RNA degradation in human dental pulp reveals post-mortem interval. International Journal of Legal Medicine 130 (3), 615–619.
Prieto-Bonete, G., Perez-Carceles, M.D., Luna, A., 2015. Morphological and histological changes in eye lens: possible application for estimating postmortem interval. Legal Medicine 17 (6), 437–442.
Queiroz, R.A., Soriano, E.P., Carvalho, M.V.D., Caldas-Junior, A.F., Souza, E.H.A., Coelho-Junior, L.G.T.M., Campello, R.I.C., Almeida, A.C., Farias, R.C.A.P., Vasconcellos, A., 2016. First forensic records of termite activity on non-fossilized human bones in Brazil. Brazilian Journal of Biology. http://dx.doi.org/10.1590/1519-6984.11415.
Ralebitso-Senior, T.K., Thompson, T.J.U., Carney, H.E., 2016. Microbial ecogenomics and forensic archaeology: new methods for investigating clandestine gravesites. Human Remains and Violence: An Interdisciplinary Journal 2 (1), 41–57.
Reddy, K., Lowenstein, E.J., 2011. Forensics in dermatology: part I. Journal of the American Academy of Dermatology 64 (5), 801–808.
Rognum, T.O., Hauge, S., Øyasaeter, S., Saugstad, O.D., 1991. A new biochemical method for estimation of postmortem time. Forensic Science International 51 (1), 139–146.
Rognum, T.O., Holmen, S., Musse, M.A., Dahlberg, P.S., Stray-Pedersen, A., Saugstad, O.D., Opdal, S.H., 2016. Estimation of time since death by vitreous humor hypoxanthine, potassium, and ambient temperature. Forensic Science International 262, 160–165.
Ross, A.H., Cunningham, S.L., 2011. Time-since-death and bone weathering in a tropical environment. Forensic Science International 204 (1), 126–133.
Sabucedo, A.J., Furton, K.G., 2003. Estimation of postmortem interval using the protein marker cardiac Troponin I. Forensic Science International 134 (1), 11–16.
Sachdeva, N., Rani, Y., Singh, R., Murari, A., 2011. Estimation of post-mortem interval from the changes in vitreous biochemistry. Journal of Indian Academy of Forensic Medicine 33 (2), 171–174.
Sagara, N., Yamanaka, T., Tibbett, M., 2008. Soil fungi associated with graves and latrines: toward a forensic mycology. In: Tibbett, M., Carter, D.O. (Eds.), Soil Analysis in Forensic Taphonomy: Chemical and Biological Effect of Buried Human Remains. CRC Press, Boca Raton, USA, pp. 67–107.
Salam, H.A., Shaat, E.A., Aziz, M.H.A., Sheta, A.A.M., Hussein, H.A.S.M., 2012. Estimation of postmortem interval using thanatochemistry and postmortem changes. Alexandria Journal of Medicine 48 (4), 335–344.
Sampaio-Silva, F., Magalhães, T., Carvalho, F., Dinis-Oliveira, R., Silvestre, R., 2013. Profiling of RNA degradation for estimation of post morterm interval. PLoS One 8 (2), e56507.
Schotsmans, E.M.J., Van De Voorde, W., De Winne, J., Wilson, A.S., 2011. The impact of shallow burial on differential decomposition to the body: a temperate case study. Forensic Science International 206 (1), e43–e48.
Sharma, R., Kumar, G.R., Gaur, J.R., 2015. Various methods for the estimation of the postmortem interval from Calliphoridae: a review. Egyptian Journal of Forensic Sciences 5 (1), 1–12.
Shirley, N.R., Wilson, R.J., Jantz, L.M., 2011. Cadaver use at the University of Tennessee's Anthropological Research Facility. Clinical Anatomy 24, 372–380.
Shkrum, M.J., Ramsay, D.A., 2007. Postmortem changes. In: Shkrum, M.J., Ramsay, D.A. (Eds.), Forensic Pathology of Trauma: Common Problems for the Pathologist. Humana Press Inc., Totowa, USA, pp. 23–56.
Smart, J.L., Kaliszan, M., 2012. The post mortem temperature plateau and its role in the estimation of time of death: a review. Legal Medicine 14 (2), 55–62.
Sparks, D.L., Oeltgen, P.R., Kryseio, R.J., Hunsaker, J.C., 1989. Comparison of chemical methods for determining postmortem interval. Journal of Forensic Sciences 34 (1), 197–206.
Sparks, D.L., Slevin, J.T., Hunsaker, J.C., 1986. 3-Methoxytyramine in the putamen as a gauge of the postmortem interval. Journal of Forensic Sciences 31 (3), 962–971.
Spicka, A., Johnson, R., Bushing, J., Higley, L.G., Carter, D.O., 2011. Carcass mass can influence rate of decomposition and release of ninhydrin-reactive nitrogen into gravesoil. Forensic Science International 209 (1), 80–85.
Swain, R., Kumar, A., Sahoo, J., Lakshmy, R., Gupta, S., Bhardwaj, D., Pandey, R., 2015. Estimation of postmortem interval: a comparison between cerebrospinal fluid and vitreous humour chemistry. Journal of Forensic and Legal Medicine 36, 144–148.
Swann, L., Forbes, S., Lewis, S., 2010. Analytical separations of mammalian decomposition products for forensic science: a review. Analytica Chimica Acta 682, 9–22.

Swift, B., 2006. The timing of death. In: Rutty, G.N. (Ed.), Essentials of Autopsy Practice: Current Methods and Modern Trends. Springer, New York, USA, pp. 189–214.

Tibbett, M., 2008. The basics of forensic taphonomy: understanding cadaver decomposition in terrestrial gravesites. In: Oxenham, M. (Ed.), Forensic Approaches to Death, Disaster and Abuse. Australian Academic Press, Sidney, Australia, pp. 29–36.

Tranchida, M.C., Centeno, N.D., Cabello, M.N., 2014. Soil fungi: their potential use as a forensic tool. Journal of Forensic Sciences 59 (3), 785–789.

Tumer, A., Karacaoglu, E., Namli, A., Keten, A., Farasat, S., Akcan, R., Sert, O., Odabasi, A., 2013. Effects of different types of soil on decomposition: an experimental study. Legal Medicine 15, 149–156.

Ubelaker, D.H., Zarenko, K.M., 2011. Adipocere: what is known after over two centuries of research. Forensic Science International 208 (1), 167–172.

Usumoto, Y., Hikiji, W., Sameshima, N., Kudo, K., Tsuji, A., Ikeda, N., 2010. Estimation of postmortem interval based on the spectrophotometric analysis of postmortem lividity. Legal Medicine 12 (1), 19–22.

Vacchiano, G., Maldonado, A.L., Ros, M.M., Di Lorenzo, P., Pieri, M., 2016. The cholesterol levels in median nerve and post-mortem interval evaluation. Forensic Science International 265, 29–33.

Van de Voorde, H., Van Dijck, P.J., 1982. Determination of the time of death by fungal growth. Zeitschrift für Rechtsmedizin 89 (2), 75–80.

Van den Berge, M., Wiskerke, D., Gerretsen, R.R.R., Tabak, J., Sijen, T., 2016. DNA and RNA profiling of excavated human remains with varying postmortem intervals. International Journal of Legal Medicine 130 (6), 1471–1480.

Vanezis, P., Trujillo, O., 1996. Evaluation of hypostasis using a colorimeter measuring system and its application to assessment of the post-mortem interval (time of death). Forensic Science International 78 (1), 19–20.

Vass, A.A., 2001. Beyond the grave – understanding human decomposition. Microbiology Today 28, 190–192.

Vass, A.A., Barshick, S.A., Sega, G., Caton, J., Skeen, J.T., Love, J.C., Synstelien, J.A., 2002. Decomposition chemistry of human remains: a new methodology for determining the postmortem interval. Journal of Forensic Sciences 47, 542–553.

Warther, S., Sehner, S., Raupach, T., Püschel, K., Anders, S., 2012. Estimation of the time since death: post-mortem contractions of human skeletal muscles following mechanical stimulation (idiomuscular contraction). International Journal of Legal Medicine 126 (3), 399–405.

Wehner, F., Wehner, H.D., Schieffer, M.C., Subke, J., 1999. Delimitation of the time of death by immunohistochemical detection of insulin in pancreatic β-cells. Forensic Science International 105, 161–169.

Wehner, F., Wehner, H.D., Subke, J., 2000. Delimitation of the time of death by immunohistochemical detection of thyroglobulin. Forensic Science International 110 (3), 199–206.

Wehner, F., Wehner, H.D., Subke, J., 2001a. Delimitation of the time of death by immunohistochemical detection of calcitonin. Forensic Science International 122, 89–94.

Wehner, F., Wehner, H.D., Subke, J., 2001b. Delimitation of the time of death by immunohistochemical detection of glucagon in pancreatic α-cells. Forensic Science International 124, 192–199.

Wilson, A.S., Janaway, R.C., Holland, A.D., Dodson, H.I., Baran, E., Pollard, A.M., Tobin, D.J., 2007. Modelling the buried human body environment in upland climes using three contrasting field sites. Forensic Science International 169, 6–18.

Young, S.T., Wells, J.D., Hobbs, G.R., Bishop, C.B., 2013. Estimating postmortem interval using RNA degradation and morphological changes in tooth pulp. Forensic Science International 229, 163.e1–163.e6.

Zerbini, T., da Silva, L.F.F., Lobato-Baptista, P.A., Ikari, E.S., Rodrigues de Araujo, M., de André, C.D.S., da Motta Singer, J., da Rocha, F.M.M., Junior, E.A., Pasqualucci, C.A.G., Saldiva, P.H.N., 2016. Estimation of post mortem interval by tomographic images of intra-cardiac hypostasis. Journal of Forensic and Legal Medicine 38, 111–115.

Zhou, C., Byard, R.W., 2011. Factors and processes causing accelerated decomposition in human cadavers – an overview. Journal of Forensic and Legal Medicine 18 (1), 6–9.

Zilg, B., Bernard, S., Alkass, K., Berg, S., Druid, H., 2015. A new model for the estimation of time of death from vitreous potassium levels corrected for age and temperature. Forensic Science International 254, 158–166.

CHAPTER 4

Implications of the Investigative Animal Model

T. Komang Ralebitso-Senior[1], Michael K.P. Pyle[2]
[1]Teesside University, Tees Valley, United Kingdom; [2]London, United Kingdom

INTRODUCTION

The roles of postmortem interval (PMI), postmortem submersion interval (PMSI), and time since burial/postburial interval (PBI) determinations in solving crimes that involve human remains, and the need to increase the accuracy of these essential parameters, are well recognized. This has resulted in multiple, extensive research, and modeling initiatives, sometimes with case studies, to illustrate new methods for improved accuracy. Parallel to this has been the acceptance that a wide range of biological (macro- and microbial), chemical, geological, and physical parameters influence postmortem processes and hence PMI/PMSI/PBI estimations. All these undertakings have resulted in the emergence of several subdisciplines in forensic science, each with its own tools, though overlaps also occur. Briefly, the impacts of environmental and physicochemical parameters (Carter et al., 2008; Zhou and Byard, 2011), cadaver size/mass (Spicka et al., 2011; Suckling et al., 2016; Weiss et al., 2016), injury (Cross and Simmons, 2010; Micozzi, 1986; Niederegger et al., 2017), insect activity (Alajmi et al., 2016; Al-Mesbah et al., 2012; Barton and Evans, 2017; Rodriguez and Bass, 1983), season (Payne, 1965), scavenger activity (DeVault et al., 2004), clothing (Matuszewski et al., 2014), shelter (Centeno et al., 2002), the ecosystem (Dent et al., 2004; Dickson et al., 2011), and microbial activity (Carter and Tibbett, 2006; Crippen and Singh, 2015; Howard et al., 2010; Lauber et al., 2014) on human cadaver or taphonomic proxy decomposition have led to geoforensics, bio-/geotaphonomy, forensic chemistry, forensic entomology, forensic botany, mycoforensics, and forensic microbiology/forensic ecogenomics. The relatively new application of microbiological and/or (molecular) microbial ecology analyses has then led to novel developments in the last topic(s). Since extensive research has generated a wealth of data and knowledge within the subdiscipline, our discourse in the chapter draws on and makes parallels with forensic entomology where relevant.

Irrespective of subdiscipline, all forensic science studies intended to inform real crime investigations on human remains, including determining PMI, PMSI, and PBI, must follow specific ethical guidelines. Therefore, and as posited by many researchers (e.g., Benbow and Pechal, 2017; Cockle and Bell, 2015; Finley et al., 2016; Hyde et al., 2017;

Forensic Ecogenomics
ISBN 978-0-12-809360-3
http://dx.doi.org/10.1016/B978-0-12-809360-3.00004-7

Stokes et al., 2013), the ideal for all forensic research is to use human cadavers, where the studied decomposing material generates information and knowledge that is directly relevant to PMI, PMSI, and PBI calculations, and clandestine burial location in real crime scenes. Nevertheless, ethical and legal frameworks, including the sourcing of human cadaveric materials, parallel with historical and current policy statements, mean that this ideal is not always feasible in parts of the world.

Challenges for Investigations and Proof-of-Concept

Currently, known human taphonomic facilities (HTFs) have been established in two countries where cadavers of individuals who bequeathed their bodies to scientific research are used, subject to appropriate ethical approval. These include six in the United States: (1) the Anthropological Research Facility at the University of Tennessee; (2) the Forensic Osteology Research Station of the University of Western Carolina; (3) the Forensic Anthropology Research Facility at Texas State University; (4) the South East Texas Applied Forensic Science Facility at Sam Houston State University; (5) the Complex for Forensic Anthropology Research at Southern Illinois University; and (6) the Forensic Investigation Research Station at Colorado Mesa University. The first HTF outside the United States, the Australian Facility for Taphonomic Experimental Research at the University of Technology, Sydney, Australia, opened in 2015.

Further facilities are at different stages of conceptualization and implementation and they include the University of South Florida's Facility for Outdoor Experimental Research and Training and/or Florida Forensic Institute for Research, Security and Tactical Training—a joint venture with Pasco County Sheriff's Office; the Institute of Criminological and Forensic Sciences at California University of Pennsylvania's Grace Lair Farm facility; and the Fox Valley Technical College's Public Safety Training Center in Wisconsin. Finally, the first European HTF is due to be established at the Academic Medical Centre Cemetery, Amsterdam, the Netherlands (Enserink, 2017).

Potential Solutions

In contrast to the trend in the United States, and despite several deliberations (e.g., Cross et al., 2010), no HTFs exist in the United Kingdom or other parts of Europe with unique climates, as at the time of writing. Notwithstanding this, the recognized need for dedicated research facilities is exemplified by initiatives such as those at Cranfield University, University of Huddersfield, University of Central Lancashire (Taphonomic Research in Anthropology: Centre for Experimental Studies), and Wrexham Glyndŵr University in Wales (Forensic Science and Crime Scene Research Area), where mammalian analogs are used as approved by the UK Department for Environment, Food, and Rural Affairs.

Parallel to these establishments, researchers use accepted human taphonomic proxies in different-sized lysimeters, either outdoors or indoors and sometimes under controlled conditions, for fundamental investigative work. These initiatives must also be subject to ethical clearance by the relevant universities, research institutes, and funding councils. Although a key limitation of the mammalian analog approach is the translation and applicability of the research data to humans and real crime investigations, multiple benefits are gained. These include, but are not limited to, the increased potential for: (1) replication during research, hence higher levels of confidence in the findings—this is important especially in relation to known soil heterogeneity even at small biogeographies; (2) reproducibility and repeatability between studies; (3) cost efficiency during scale-up; and (4) simultaneous and factorial study designs for comparative assessments of the effects of multiple parameters, such as the use of the same human taphonomic proxy (animal) species with different soil types, different mammalian surrogates in the same soils, geographical locations, climatic conditions, and seasons.

Overall, the need for relatively high degrees of consistency and comparability between studies, as also recognized in forensic entomology (e.g., Tomberlin et al., 2012), must be implemented in forensic ecogenomics/forensic microbiology. The use of human taphonomic proxies (Armstrong et al., 2016; Human Tissue Act, 2004; Parkinson et al., 2009; Swann et al., 2010) facilitates this, provided that the correct animal model is used (Cockle and Bell, 2015) and validated (Lossi et al., 2016; Tomberlin and Benbow, 2015), and full cognizance of the caveats and limitations of these approaches is made. Also key decisions need to be made on the investigative animal models generally and for forensic ecogenomics specifically. For example, are findings on the impacts of decomposition on the surrounding terrestrial ecosystem when using mice (*Mus musculus* Linnaeus), the brown rat (*Rattus rattus*), the laboratory-bred rat (Sprague–Dawley rat; *Rattus norvegicus* Berkenhout), sheep (*Ovis aries* Linnaeus), rabbits (*Oryctolagus cuniculus*), cattle (*Bos taurus* Linnaeus), or suids/swine interchangeable? Specifically, and since suids are often the mammalian surrogate of choice, what significance should be attached to the particular species used regarding *Sus scrofa domesticus* Erxleben and *Sus scrofa* Linnaeus (Payne, 1965)? So, are all species the same and equal (Schoenly et al., 2007; Stokes et al., 2013)?

Finally, and as discussed expansively in Chapter 6, analyses of microbial community ecological succession for potential forensic investigations can adopt components of a cadaver or human proxy instead of the whole animal. Thus thanatomicrobiome research involves the use of postmortem samples from the circulatory (blood) and lymphatic systems, the gastrointestinal tract, and internal organs such as the brain, liver, heart, and spleen (Hyde et al., 2013; Tuomisto et al., 2013a; Can et al., 2014). According to Tuomisto et al. (2013a) and Can et al. (2014), the liver and pericardial fluids are the ideal tissues to sample for subsequent thanatomicrobiome profiling as a tool for PMI estimation.

In the absence of the requisite ethical and legal infrastructure, thanatomicrobiome-based forensic ecogenomics will probably continue to rely on suids, which as omnivores are expected to have a similar gut microbiota, fat distribution, and minimal hair coverage as humans (Howard et al., 2010; Swann et al., 2010). Although they resemble humans sufficiently as whole organisms, Stokes et al. (2013) demonstrated that using parts of *S. scrofa* may render the decomposition process dissimilar to that of human cadavers. Briefly, the researchers investigated the decomposition of skeletal muscle tissues from different animals and reported that ovine tissue shared most of the measured parameters in common with human tissue. Therefore further research is required to identify a taphonomic proxy that is most reflective of the human body, particularly when using organs or tissue instead of the whole animal model.

Implications of Study Design

Once the decision has been made on the mammalian surrogate species, a key consideration is the experimental design in relation to analyzing the impacts of decomposition on the surface or subsurface substrata, particularly in soils. To date, most studies have focused on the aboveground necrobiome with only a few published on belowground impacts (see also Chapters 1 and 7). As deliberated earlier, several research groups have reported that key parameters including temperature, precipitation, scavengers, and insects will have a direct impact on the decomposition rate. Typically, the rate of decay is slower in the subsurface due to limited sunlight and scavenger access, and with cooler soil temperatures. These differences will consequently determine the effects on the surrounding macro- and microbial ecology dynamics and hence the applicability of ecological measures for PMI and PBI estimations. Therefore forensic ecogenomics-based analyses for these important intervals will be more informative to real crime scenarios if comparative studies have also been made between surface and subsurface conditions. Further studies can then explore the effects of interment at different depths.

Additional questions to be posed on a given animal model include: size/mass; age; freshly slaughtered or decomposed; refrigerated or frozen; temperature and duration of refrigeration and/or freezing; interment while frozen or frozen/thawed; whole, organs, or tissues of organism; and ground/minced. Ultimately, all these parameters have direct importance and implications for knowledge development on the effects of the cadaver/carrion microbiome on decomposition generally and the dynamics of the surrounding (soil) ecosystem specifically. Further considerations are required for sampling strategies and analytical methods particularly when the research findings are intended to start to inform protocols that will be adopted in principle in real scenes of crime and court proceedings. Therefore several researchers (Adlam and Simmons, 2007; Benbow and Pechal, 2017; Fiene et al., 2014; Pasternak et al., 2012; Schoenly et al., 2007; Michaud et al., 2012; Moffatt et al., 2016; Quaak and Kuiper, 2011; Wells et al., 2015) have presented seminal discourses across different forensic subdisciplines on key challenges such as: sampling of gravesoils, for example, with or without disturbance of the interred materials; methods for sample collection, handling, processing, and storage; analytical techniques, e.g., choosing from several nucleic acid extraction protocols, polymerase chain reaction primers and conditions, downstream profiling tools (denaturing gradient gel electrophoresis, terminal restriction fragment length polymorphism), and next-generation sequencing platforms and protocols; and data and statistical analyses (see also Chapter 1).

WHAT'S IN A NAME? DOMESTICATION OF SUIDS/SWINE (*SUS DOMESTICUS* ERXLEBEN) AND CATTLE (*BOS TAURUS* LINNAEUS)

The domestication of species as livestock is a process that has led to changes in both phenotypic variation, influenced by the desirability of phenotypes per human needs, and geographic distribution, influenced by human dispersal patterns (Krause-Kyora et al., 2013; Ottoni et al., 2013). The phylogenetic development of domestic species was, and is, therefore a nonlinear process, where monophyly is not always present. Mitochondrial DNA (mtDNA) and Y chromosomal haplotype analyses have demonstrated that the most commonly used human taphonomic proxies, *Sus* spp (Larson et al., 2005; Ramírez et al., 2009), *Bos* spp. (Achilli et al., 2009; Loftus et al., 1994), and *Ovis* spp (Guo et al., 2005; Hiendleder et al., 1998, 2002; Meadows et al., 2006), derive from two or more ancestral, wild species, and/or subspecies lineages.

Genetic analyses also indicated hybridization and introgression within and between the transitional subspecies progenitors of modern domesticates and wild species during conservation, population management, and selective breeding (Vilà et al., 2005). For example, modern breeds of domesticated suids/swine (*S. scrofa domesticus* Erxleben), which are native to Europe and North America, are a hybrid of the species *S. scrofa* (Linnaeus), the Eurasian wild boar, the subspecies *Sus scrofa scrofa* (Linnaeus), the central European boar, and earlier transitional forms of *S. scrofa domesticus* (Giuffra et al., 2000; Larson et al., 2005; Scandura et al., 2011; Frantz et al., 2012, 2013). In contrast, the independently domesticated Asian clade of Suidae are usually considered descendants of *Sus scrofa vittatus* (Boie), the banded pig now found native only to Indonesia and the Thai-Malay Peninsula of South East Asia (Giuffra et al., 2000; Larson et al., 2005). Several different subspecies of progenitorial wild boar (*S. scrofa*) are, however, recognized as contributing to the multiphyletic nature of various worldwide breeds, races, and strains of domestic pig. This includes: *Sus scrofa meridionalis* (Forsyth Major), the Mediterranean boar; *Sus scrofa algira* (Loche), the North African boar; *Sus scrofa attila* (Thomas), the Carpathian boar; and the Indian boar, *Sus scrofa cristatus* (Wagner) (Larson et al., 2005; Mayer, 1998).

Similarly, it is hypothesized that human migration-led cattle dispersal, predomestication selection pressures, and the independent domestication of two different subspecies of Auroch (*Bos primigenius* Bojanus) gave rise to the two phenotypically different subspecies of domestic bovine cattle, *Bos taurus taurus* (Linnaeus) and *Bos taurus indicus* (Linnaeus), also known as *Bos primigenius taurus* and *Bos primigenius indicus*, respectively (Ajmone-Marsan et al., 2010; Bradley et al., 1998; Xu et al., 2015). Eurafrican and Indian domesticates have taurine mtDNA lineage originating in the Fertile Crescent and indicine originating in the Indus Valley, respectively (Ajmone-Marsan et al., 2010). Evidence of hybridization between *B. primigenius* bulls and cows with both *B. taurus* subspecies, along with between the subspecies, leading to indicine introgression into *B. taurus taurus*, was suggested by molecular analysis of the Y chromosome (Beja-Pereira et al., 2006; Bollongino et al., 2006; Bradley et al., 1998; Freeman et al., 2006; Götherström et al., 2005). Furthermore, molecular evidence suggests selective interspecific hybridization and interbreeding of *B. taurus taurus* and *B. taurus indicus* with the gaur or Indian bison (*Bos gaurus* Smith), the domestic (*Bos grunniens* Linnaeus), and wild (*Bos mutus* Przewalski) yak, and several other progenitors capable of producing fertile offspring. This also includes hybridization of *B. taurus taurus* with *Bison* spp., water buffalo of the genus *Bubalus*, and the African or Cape buffalo (*Syncerus caffer* Sparrman).

The different, polyphyletic, domesticate subspecies, including domesticated suids and cattle as described earlier, do not fall into the recognized and consistent system of binomial Linnaean taxonomy. As a result, nomenclatural treatment is often inconsistent, both between authors and within publications by the same author. For example, domestic pigs are commonly interchangeably and indiscriminately referred to binomially as both the genus and species, *S. scrofa* (Linnaeus); genus and subspecies, *Sus domestica* (Erxleben); or trinomially as genus, species, and subspecies, *S. scrofa domesticus* (Erxleben). The method proposed by Gautier (1993) is to name modern domesticates as subspecies of their wild progenitors. Nonetheless, there is a level of subjectivity with regard to the justified usage of taxonomic nomenclature—where levels of the taxonomic hierarchy are described and named, and can be subsequently moved, expanded upon, or removed by different interpretations.

As domesticated species and their progenitors are recognizably different entities, it is appropriate for our purposes to nomenclaturally separate them. A focus on detail, and the correct use of the nomenclature of domestic species commonly used in forensic ecogenomics, allowing for comparability, consistency, and repeatability among and between studies, is therefore recommended to account for potential variation caused by inter- and intra-specificity and subspecificity. It seems reasonable therefore to suggest that forensic ecogenomic studies adapt and utilize a consistent, established, internationally recognized, Linnaean Latin binomenclatural approach to the description of taphonomic proxies in publications—avoiding the sole use of vernacular where possible. This approach should differentiate (*sensu amplo*; Odening, 1979) between the wild progenitors of modern domesticates, for example, avoiding the misstated use of *S. scrofa* when referring to domestic pigs, and account for nomenclatural homonymy, e.g., the use of *Bos indicus* when referring to domestic indicine as opposed to taurine cattle, *B. taurus*. It is suggested further that supplementary information regarding the breeds, stocks, and strains of multiphyletic domesticates, such as *S. domesticus*, is also recorded.

IMPLICATIONS OF STUDY DESIGN: FRESHLY SLAUGHTERED VERSUS FROZEN/THAWED ANIMAL MODELS

There is currently a paucity of knowledge regarding the implications of freezing and thawing on the decomposition of carrion, which may be subjected to low environmental temperatures, with information available only from the results of a limited number of studies (Micozzi, 1996, 1986; Roberts and Dabbs, 2015; Stokes et al., 2009, Table 4.1). The decay of cadavers and human taphonomic proxy animal models, organs, and tissues used in forensic ecogenomic research is usually a result of chemical reactions mediated by microbial and endogenous enzymes. It is also common practice to extend the useful life of animal models and media by periodic storage at low temperatures. It is important therefore to consider the implications of the effect of both low environmental temperatures and this deliberate low-temperature storage on the premortem microbiome, the postmortem necrobiome, and the decomposition of animal models, organs, and tissues. Furthermore, it is pertinent to consider the effect of the aforementioned on decomposition rates, and the reliability of methods of PMI estimation including, but not limited to, forensic ecogenomics.

Although the acceleration of the decomposition process in frozen/thawed carrion was first noted by Micozzi (1986) and Catts (1991), the use of frozen/thawed animal models, organs, and tissues is applied widely in decomposition studies within forensic taphonomy. Similarly managed materials are also used as rearing substrates in forensic entomological studies pertaining to the development of forensically relevant dipteran species—often for PMI estimation. It is essential therefore to consider human taphonomic proxy animal models, organs, and tissues used in forensic ecogenomic studies using similar approaches to those commonly adopted in food microbiology/science. This is particularly important in relation to the nature of these proxies at the onset of research programs, and the substantial effect of indigenous carrion microbiome on both decomposition and ecosystem dynamics. For example, the use of fresh versus frozen/thawed animal models, organs, and tissues may hinder accurate timing and tracking of the decomposition process and affect the development of forensically important insect species, thus potentially invalidating determinations of the estimated PMI (Micozzi, 1986, 1996; Roberts and Dabbs, 2015).

Where molecular microbial analyses are to be applied, storage at and below −20°C is typically adopted to inhibit microbial viability, growth, and proliferation, with the metabolic processes of nonpsychrophilic and nonextremophilic strains most likely inhibited irreversibly. Therefore members of the premortem microbiome and necrobiome for which these storage conditions are bacteriocidal instead of bacteriostatic, for example, will have potentially little or no impact on carrion decomposition processes or changes in the microbial ecology and dynamics of the surrounding gravesoil ecosystem. Consequently, these components will have minimal relevance to forensic ecogenomic profiling of the necrobiome, thanatomicrobiome, epinecrotic microbial communities, or the gravesoil

Table 4.1 Summary of mammalian taphonomic proxy species and their organ/tissue type, state of refrigeration, and the forensically important diptera used in comparative developmental studies between 2004 and 2016

Taphonomic proxy species	Tissue type	State	Dipteran species	Publication
Bos taurus (Linnaeus, 1758)	Adductor, biceps (femoris), semitendinosus, and semimembranosus muscle	Frozen/thawed	*Hermetia illucens*	Harnden and Tomberlin (2016)
	Biceps (femoris) muscle	Frozen/thawed	*Megaselia scalaris*	Thomas et al. (2016)
	Cerebral (brain)	Fresh	*Lucilia sericata*; *Protophormia terranovae*	El-Moaty and Kheirallah (2013) and Warren and Anderson (2009)
	Gastric (stomach)	Fresh	*Chrysomya albiceps*; *Chrysomya megacephala*; *Chrysomya putoria*	Thyssen et al. (2014)
	Hepatic (liver)	Fresh	*C. albiceps*; *C. megacephala*; *C. putoria*; *L. sericata*	El-Moaty and Kheirallah (2013) and Thyssen et al. (2014)
		Frozen/thawed	*Calliphora vicina*; *Calliphora vomitoria*; *P. terranovae*	Niederegger et al. (2013) and Warren and Anderson (2009)
		Unknown	*L. sericata*	Clark et al. (2006)
	Intestinal	Fresh	*L. sericata*	El-Moaty and Kheirallah (2013)
	Lingual (tongue)	Fresh	*C. albiceps*; *C. megacephala*; *C. putoria*	Thyssen et al. (2014)
	Myocardial (cardiac)	Fresh	*L. sericata*	El-Moaty and Kheirallah (2013)
		Frozen/thawed	*P. terranovae*	Warren and Anderson (2009)
		Unknown	*L. sericata*	Clark et al. (2006)
	Pulmonary (lung)	Fresh	*L. sericata*	El-Moaty and Kheirallah (2013)
		Unknown	*L. sericata*	Clark et al. (2006)
	Renal (kidney)	Fresh	*L. sericata*	El-Moaty and Kheirallah (2013)
	Unknown muscle	Fresh	*C. albiceps*; *C. megacephala*; *C. putoria*	Thyssen et al. (2014)
		Fresh ground/minced	*L. sericata*	El-Moaty and Kheirallah (2013)
		Frozen/thawed	*P. terranovae*	Warren and Anderson (2009)
		Frozen/thawed ground/minced	*C. vicina*; *C. vomitoria*	Niederegger et al. (2013)

B. taurus/Sus scrofa domesticus	Unknown muscle	Frozen/thawed ground/minced	*C. vicina; C. vomitoria*	Niederegger et al. (2013)
Canis lupus familiaris	Unknown muscle	Frozen/thawed	*Chrysomya rufifacies*	Flores et al. (2014)
Equus ferus caballus	Gluteal muscle	Frozen/thawed	*C. rufifacies; Cochliomyia macellaria*	Boatright and Tomberlin (2010) and Flores et al. (2014)
Gallus gallus domesticus	Myocardial	Fresh	*C. albiceps; C. megacephala; C. putoria*	Thyssen et al. (2014)
Meleagris gallopavo	Pectoral muscle	Frozen/thawed	*C. vicina; C. vomitoria*	Niederegger et al. (2013)
	Unknown muscle	Frozen/thawed ground/minced	*C. vicina; C. vomitoria*	Niederegger et al. (2013)
Odocoileus virginianus	Unknown muscle	Frozen/thawed ground/minced	*Phormia regina*	Wilson et al. (2014)
Ovis aries	Cerebral	Fresh	*Calliphora augar; Lucilia cuprina*	Day and Wallman (2006b)
	Hepatic	Fresh	*C. augar; L. cuprina*	Day and Wallman (2006a,b)
		Frozen/thawed	*C. augar*	Day and Wallman (2006a)
	Loin muscle with associated adipose (fat) and epithelial (skin)	Fresh	*C. augar; L. cuprina*	Day and Wallman (2006b)
Rattus norvegicus	Whole organism	Frozen/thawed	*P. terranovae*	Warren and Anderson (2009)

Continued

Table 4.1 Summary of mammalian taphonomic proxy species and their organ/tissue type, state of refrigeration, and the forensically important diptera used in comparative developmental studies between 2004 and 2016—cont'd

Taphonomic proxy species	Tissue type	State	Dipteran species	Publication
S. scrofa domesticus	Adductor, biceps (femoris), semitendinosus, and semimembranosus muscle	Frozen/thawed	*H. illucens*	Harnden and Tomberlin (2016)
	Abdominal adipose	Fresh	*C. albiceps*	Beuter and Mendes (2013)
	Biceps (femoris) muscle	Frozen/thawed	*M. scalaris*	Thomas et al. (2016)
	Buccal (cheek) muscle	Fresh	*C. vomitoria*	Ireland and Turner (2006)
	Cerebral	Fresh	*C. vomitoria*; *C. albiceps*	Beuter and Mendes (2013) and Ireland and Turner (2006)
		Frozen/thawed	*C. vicina*	Kaneshrajah and Turner (2004)
	Hepatic	Decomposed for 7 days (anaerobically in vacuum packaging)	*C. vicina*	Richards et al. (2013)
		Fresh	*C. vicina*; *C. vomitoria*; *C. albiceps*	Beuter and Mendes (2013), Ireland and Turner (2006) and Richards et al. (2013)
		Fresh ground/minced	*C. vicina*	Richards et al. (2013)
		Frozen/thawed	*C. vicina*; *C. vomitoria*	Bernhardt et al. (2016), Kaneshrajah and Turner (2004), Niederegger et al. (2013) and Richards et al. (2013)
		Unknown	*L. sericata*	Clark et al. (2006)
	Loin muscle	Frozen/thawed	*C. vicina*; *C. rufifacies*; *C. macellaria*	Bernhardt et al. (2016), Boatright and Tomberlin (2010) and Flores et al. (2014)
	Myocardial	Frozen/thawed	*C. vicina*	Kaneshrajah and Turner (2004)
		Unknown	*L. sericata*	Clark et al. (2006)
	Pulmonary	Frozen/thawed	*C. vicina*	Kaneshrajah and Turner (2004)
		Unknown	*L. sericata*	Clark et al. (2006)
	Renal	Frozen/thawed	*C. vicina*	Kaneshrajah and Turner (2004)
	Unknown muscle	Fresh ground/minced	*C. albiceps*	Beuter and Mendes (2013)
		Frozen/thawed ground/minced	*C. vicina*; *C. vomitoria*; *P. regina*	Bernhardt et al. (2016), Niederegger et al. (2013) and Wilson et al. (2014)

microbiome. Notwithstanding, these communities cannot be dismissed completely, as their biomolecules—DNA, RNA, and lipids—will not necessarily be wholly denatured and may therefore still contribute to any molecular-based analyses, including denaturing gradient gel electrophoresis, terminal restriction length polymorphism, fatty acid methyl ester profiling, phospholipid fatty acid analysis, and next-generation sequencing methods.

As commonly demonstrated in food microbiology/science, most organs and tissues begin to freeze within the temperature range of −0.5 to −3°C, with the freezing point lower than that of water due to the presence of solutes. As water is converted to ice during freezing, the concentration of solutes increases, thus decreasing its freezing point still further so that even at temperatures as low as −60°C some water may remain supercooled but unfrozen (Adams et al., 2015). The extracellular nature of ice formation, along with high extracellular osmotic pressure, mechanically damages and dehydrates bacterial cells. Cold shock—damage to bacterial cell membranes caused by membrane lipid phase changes—also creates hydrophilic pores through which cytoplasmic contents can leak. This, concomitant with increases in single-strand breaks in DNA and changes in the ionic strength and pH of water because of freezing, disrupts further the structure, function, and stability of numerous bacterial cell components and biomolecules (Adams et al., 2015; Ali et al., 2015; Leygonie et al., 2012). For example, a decrease in pH from 5.79 to 5.49 caused by water loss, increased solute concentration (Leygonie et al., 2012), and protein denaturation and oxidation have also been observed (Ali et al., 2015). Furthermore, Ali et al. (2015) reported that the freezing and thawing of *Gallus domesticus* (Linnaeus, 1758) pectoral muscle tissue caused a number of physicochemical and protein oxidative effects. Specifically, the freeze/thaw cycle resulted in statistically significant ($P < .05$) protein oxidation, as evidenced by an increase in carbonyl concentration from 1.90 to 3.63 nmol/mg, and decreased sulfhydryl content. Differential scanning calorimetry and sodium dodecyl sulfate polyacrylamide gel electrophoresis further indicated denaturation of the myofibrillar proteins myosin and actin. Also ionic and hydrophobic interactions in myofibrillar protein networks have been affected by the changes in water volume (Ali et al., 2015; Leygonie et al., 2012).

During freezing, key inhibitory factors include low temperature and low water activity, which are produced by the removal of water from organs and tissues in the form of ice. Similar to domestic freezers with foods stored at temperatures where microbial growth is possible (above −10°C), the microbial communities that grow on frozen human analogs, organs, or tissues are most probably not those associated typically with decomposition, but psychrophiles and extremophiles tolerant of reduced temperatures and water activity. Therefore microbial viability during and after thawing is dependent on the specific conditions of freezing and thawing, the type of proxy, the organs or tissues, and the initial compositions of their microbiomes. Notwithstanding this, microbial survival rates between 5% and 70% have been recorded in the literature, with bacterial spores virtually unaffected by freezing and most Gram-positive bacteria relatively resistant (Adams et al., 2015). Typically, survival or viability rates increase with rapid freezing where exposure to high solute concentrations is minimized, while Gram-negative bacteria exhibit the highest sensitivity to the freezing process. The formation of large ice crystals and prolonged exposure to high osmotic pressure during the freezing process also damages the cells of the proxy, organ, or tissue being used. This has direct consequences for forensic entomology studies on decomposition and production of oviposition/insect developmental media, with considerable paucity of knowledge for the forensic ecogenomics context. Although it makes microbial growth inhibition more efficient, the slow rate of freezing in domestic freezers also causes greater textural deterioration of organs and tissues upon thawing through increased exposure to high solute concentrations.

Thawing is a slower process than freezing where the exterior and interior materials reach thawing temperature at different times. This time lag allows the growth of psychrophilic and mesophilic bacteria at low and intermediate thawing temperatures, respectively, on exterior surfaces, while the interior remains frozen (Adams et al., 2015). Thus the developing micro/necrobiome of frozen/thawed human surrogates, organs, or tissues will differ from that of fresh material due to the selective effects of freezing and thawing (Pechal et al., 2017). This was illustrated seminally by Micozzi (1986) who found that frozen/thawed *R. norvegicus* (Berkenhout) were increasingly susceptible to aerobic decomposition of the skin and external surfaces, whereas anaerobic decomposition/putrefaction proceeded from within in freshly killed nonfrozen *R. norvegicus*. The author concluded that freezing and subsequent thawing possibly diminished the capacity of intestinal bacteria to lead the postmortem decomposition/putrefaction process, with decomposition due predominantly to colonization by gravesoil microbial communities (Micozzi, 1986, 1996). Using frozen/thawed animal models, Micozzi (1986) further observed the mechanical disruption of tissues, weakening of skin and connective tissue, and increased rates of disarticulation of the temporomandibular, cervical, and lumbar vertebral, costovertebral, sternocostal, lumbosacral, sacroiliac, and pelvis/hip joints (Micozzi, 1996). These were consistent with the textural deterioration associated with domestic freezing.

Textural deterioration in particular was also observed by Stokes et al. (2009) who carried out a study to ascertain the effect of freezing on *S. scrofa domesticus* (Erxleben) skeletal muscle tissue decomposition and changes in associated soil chemistry under controlled laboratory conditions. Morphological changes including marked increases in the percentage of both longitudinal and transverse interstitial spaces, and areas containing no tissue, were noted in refrigerated and frozen/thawed *S. scrofa domesticus* muscle tissue. The percentage of longitudinal interstitial spaces increased from 0.82% in fresh samples to 11.49% and 24.02% after refrigeration and freezing, respectively. Similarly, the percentage of transverse interstitial spaces increased from 13.29% in fresh samples to

30.66% after freezing. Furthermore, 1.5 g and 1 cm^3 portions of *S. scrofa domesticus* muscle tissue were frozen at −20°C or refrigerated at 4°C before interment in microcosms containing 100 g of 40 mm deep sieved sandy soil adjusted to 50% water holding capacity, the optimal for microbial activity in a soil system (Stokes et al., 2009). Freezing was found to have no significant impact on either decomposition or soil chemistry when compared to unfrozen samples. However, the interment of skeletal muscle tissue contrasted soil-only controls without muscle tissue and recorded statistically significant impacts on the microbial activity (carbon dioxide respiration) and chemistry of the surrounding soil including: pH, electroconductivity, ammonium, nitrate, phosphate, and potassium.

Reduced tissue integrity and enhanced aerobic decomposition by freezing and subsequent thawing, as previously discussed (Micozzi, 1986; Stokes et al., 2009), has also been thought to accelerate the growth of larvae in forensic entomological studies using frozen/thawed oviposition and developmental substrates (Day and Wallman, 2006b; Richards et al., 2013). As a result, the effect of the freezing and thawing of ovine (*O. aries* Linnaeus) (Day and Wallman, 2006b) and porcine (*S. scrofa domesticus* Erxleben) (Richards et al., 2013) hepatic tissue used as developmental substrate by larval *Calliphora augur* (Fabricius) and *Calliphora vicina* (Robineau-Desvoidy), respectively, was investigated to facilitate the standardization and quality assessment of forensic entomological techniques. The authors concluded that freezing to −20°C overnight with subsequent thawing had no observable effect on the growth of *C. augur* larvae, with full migration of postfeeding larvae and pupariation occurring at the same time for both treatments. Nevertheless, marginal differences were detected where larvae grown on frozen/thawed tissue achieved maximum mean length and the postfeeding stage a day earlier than those grown on fresh tissue. Notwithstanding this, no statistically significant differences were recorded in the body lengths of larvae on each treatment at a 1% level, with only one pair of larvae exhibiting mathematically significant differences at a 5% level.

It is noteworthy, however, that the 50 g samples of "fresh" ovine hepatic tissue used by Day and Wallman (2006b) were refrigerated at 4°C overnight prior to acclimatization to room temperature and the commencement of this study. Similar to freezing, refrigeration can change both the nature and rate of decay since low temperatures and physiological changes, including tissue degradation, select for microbiomes dominated by psychrophiles through the prevention of mesophilic growth and disruption of metabolic processes. Mesophiles that survive bacteriostatic refrigeration at 4°C may persist, recover, and resume growth should conditions later become favorable during thawing to room temperature.

It is suggested therefore that the selective effects of freezing and refrigeration may have led to the microbiome and tissue integrity of the "fresh" samples used in this study differing from nonrefrigerated fresh samples. Also these samples may have been characterized by microbiomes and tissue degradation highly similar to that of the frozen/

thawed samples. These parameters may have accounted potentially for the nonstatistically significant differences in the data recorded by Day and Wallman (2006b). It is suggested further that future investigations should use fresh unrefrigerated media whenever possible to elucidate the effects of freezing and thawing, and potentially adopt concurrent entomological, microbiological, and microbial ecological analyses of both the necrobiome and gravesoil biota.

POTENTIAL FOR ORGAN/TISSUE-BASED RESEARCH

As with knowledge development and pursuance in other topics, forensic science is driven by multi-, cross-, and transdisciplinary research and practice initiatives, with forensic ecogenomics and forensic microbiology examples of emergent subdisciplines. Thus tools that are used in existing investigative forensic subdisciplines and practices, such as forensic entomology, must underpin these novel areas of research particularly since a comprehensive crime scene investigation would most probably adopt these and other relevant existing protocols. Therefore advances in forensic ecogenomics with potential for applications in real crime scenes will be realized fully with the adoption of animal species that are used typically in forensic entomology.

Forensic entomology, in its broadest sense, is the application of insect or other arthropod evidence to legal investigations (Catts and Goff, 1992; Greenberg, 1991). The discipline's most frequent and key role is the estimation of the minimum time since death or minimum PMI ($_{min}$PMI), which is achieved through the analysis of insect evidence collected at crime scenes. Typically, the estimation of $_{min}$PMI applies thermal-summation models that are derived from experimentally determined, species-specific laboratory data of the developmental rates of immature dipteran as primary carrion colonizers. Thus $_{min}$PMI is generally expressed as accumulated degree hours or days that are required to reach developmental landmarks, weights, lengths, and/or lifecycle stages (Harvey et al., 2016). The common assumption is that insect colonization occurs post- rather than premortem. Consequently, the minimum time since insect colonization, or post-colonization interval ($_{min}$PCI), is calculated and used to infer $_{min}$PMI (Amendt et al., 2011, 2007). Understanding, accounting, and correcting for many factors, both abiotic and biotic, which may affect the development of immature insects is therefore essential to ensure accuracy when estimating $_{min}$PCI and ultimately $_{min}$PMI within this forensic subdiscipline (Amendt et al., 2011; Tomberlin et al., 2011a, 2011b; Villet et al., 2009).

Therefore adoption and exchange of standards, experimental procedures, and protocols across forensic entomology and forensic ecogenomics would afford comparability and consistency across studies. This is an objective that has been pursued internationally within the forensic entomology field to address the NRC Committee on Identifying the Needs of the Forensic Sciences Community (2009) report, which highlighted the necessity for increased accuracy in the forensic sciences to meet the Daubert standard—used by US courts to evaluate expert scientific evidence. This necessity was mirrored by both the UK House of Commons Science and Technology Committee (2016) Forensic Science Strategy Report and a review of forensic science research by UK Home Office Chief Scientific Advisor Professor Silverman (2011) subsequent to the closure of the Forensic Science Service.

Within the field of forensic entomology, several studies have been performed using organs or tissues from various taphonomic proxy species. Assessment of the use of animal tissues as surrogates for human tissues is, however, needed for standardization of the substrates used as oviposition and rearing substrates in forensic entomology, and subsequently investigative models in forensic ecogenomics and microbiology. The applicability and value of the data generated from using these animals for human cadaver contexts, particularly ground/minced porcine (*S. scrofa domesticus* Linnaeus) muscle tissue, was illustrated by Bernhardt et al. (2016). The researchers recorded no statistically significant differences between human tissue-reared *C. vicina* (Robineau-Desvoidy) and those reared on ground/minced porcine muscle tissue ($P < .001$). Instead, slower development resulted in *C. vicina* larvae when reared on other porcine and bovine hepatic tissue. To our knowledge, this was the first study to investigate directly how such developmental data, derived from the growth of a forensically important species on human tissue, was potentially applicable and appropriate for the estimation of $_{min}$PMI.

In contrast, studies on the development of immature Calliphoridae of forensic importance have previously entailed organs and/or tissues from several mammalian human taphonomic proxy species with marked differences recorded between them. These included bovine (*B. taurus*); canine (*Canis lupus familiaris*); cervine (*Odocoileus virginianus*); equine (*Equus ferus caballus*); galline (*Gallus gallus domesticus*); meleagrine (*Meleagris gallopavo*); ovine (*O. aries*); and porcine (*S. scrofa domesticus*). For example, a seminal study by Kaneshrajah and Turner (2004) revealed that the development of *C. vicina* was affected directly by the different types of organ or tissue. Similarly, Clark et al. (2006) observed that immature *Lucilia sericata* (Meigen) developed statistically significantly quicker when reared on porcine instead of bovine tissues, and on pulmonary and myocardial tissue in comparison to hepatic tissue. El-Moaty and Kheirallah (2013) reported similar trends for the development rates of *L. sericata* on cerebral, hepatic, renal, muscle, and intestinal tissues. A number of subsequent studies have provided further evidence that these species of forensic importance develop at considerably different rates when reared on the same, and different, tissue types sourced from different animal species (Beuter and Mendes, 2013; Boatright and Tomberlin, 2010; Day and Wallman, 2006a; Flores et al., 2014; Harnden and Tomberlin, 2016; Ireland and Turner, 2006; Niederegger et al., 2013; Rabêlo et al., 2011; Thomas et al., 2016; Thyssen et al., 2014; Warren and Anderson, 2009; Wilson et al., 2014).

Further research has been pursued in this area particularly to compare dipteran development in: whole fresh versus frozen/thawed ovine and porcine hepatic tissue

(Day and Wallman, 2006b; Richards et al., 2013); whole fresh or frozen/thawed substrate tissues versus ground/minced tissues (Bernhardt et al., 2016; Beuter and Mendes, 2013; El-Moaty and Kheirallah, 2013; Niederegger et al., 2013; Richards et al., 2013); and whole fresh porcine liver versus porcine liver allowed to decompose for 7 days (Richards et al., 2013). Specifically, Richards et al. (2013) reared *C. vicina* (Robineau-Desvoidy) larvae on fresh minced, fresh whole, thawed-from-frozen whole, and decomposed whole porcine liver, and found that the rate of development on whole porcine liver, which was allowed to decompose inside vacuum packaging for 7 days at 21 ± 2°C, was significantly lower than on all other diets. This difference accounted for as much as 30 h or 55.4% of total development for mid-sized larvae, and 71 h (35.0%) and 58 h (14.6%) when using times to pupariation and eclosion, respectively. Nevertheless, with the exception of the foregoing, significant differences were not observed between the other diets as also reported by Day and Wallman (2006b). Furthermore, Richards et al. (2013) indicated that first, second, and early third instar larvae were the life stages that were affected adversely but with no statistically significant difference in the pupal stage length of larvae when reared on decomposed liver. The researchers attributed this to pupariation and pupation being regulated by developmental processes rather than diet. Also larger or older larvae are most likely to be exposed naturally to decomposed substrates and hence best adapted to tolerate these conditions.

The decomposition of the liver used by Richards et al. (2013) is assumed to have been caused by anaerobic bacteria due to storage inside vacuum packaging for 7 days. Vacuum and modified-atmosphere packing of meat have been reported to cause changes in associated microbial communities (Adams et al., 2015). For example, the absence of oxygen, accumulation of carbon dioxide, and retention of moisture in vacuum packaging inhibits fast-growing, Gram-negative aerobes including the Pseudomonadaceae. These conditions select and enrich for a microbial community composition dominated by obligate and facultative Gram-positive bacteria including Clostridia and Enterobacteriaceae with particular abundance of lactic acid bacteria of the genera *Lactobacillus*, *Carnobacterium*, and *Leuconostoc*. These are metabolically less versatile, grow slower, and reach lower populations than the Gram-negative aerobes (Adams et al., 2015). In summary, Richards et al. (2013) suggested that the development rate of *C. vicina* (Robineau-Desvoidy) larvae reared on liver tissue that is allowed to decompose aerobically may therefore differ.

Overall, the factors discussed previously may influence data accuracy and subsequent application in the estimation of $_{min}$PMI. Therefore it is imperative that they are considered and accounted for within the emergent field of forensic ecogenomics and related disciplines. For example, the key role of body tissue type in $_{min}$PMI calculation particularly within forensic entomology identifies this as an important area for pursuance in forensic ecogenomics. Typically, the media and methods used for rearing forensically important dipteran species, including in laboratory-based decomposition studies, are selected on the basis of cost effectiveness and ease of use, leading to the adoption of different animal model species and tissue types with possibly little regard for representativeness. This approach must be militated against if the novel forensic subdisciplines and their attendant toolkits are to be applicable in real crime scenes.

Considerable achievements have been made with forensic ecogenomic studies using whole cadaver or mammalian surrogates aboveground and in the subsurface (Chapter 1; Table 1.1). Established and emergent initiatives have also used organs and/or different types of tissue as decompositional substrates to understand the process and its utility in PMI determinations. These include adipose (fat), cerebral (brain), gastric (stomach), hepatic (liver), intestinal, pulmonary (lungs), renal (kidney), and muscle tissue. The last can then be biceps, buccal (cheek), gluteal, lingual (tongue), loin (with and without associated adipose and epithelial tissue), and myocardial (cardiac/heart) muscles. Therefore Table 4.2 expands on Table 1.1 to highlight published studies where different organs, tissues, and cells from human cadavers and/or taphonomic proxies were used as substrates. The contexts of the investigations are specified using both the established and newly designated forensic subdisciplines, even if not by the primary authors.

Overall, the use and value of organs, tissue, and artificial media instead of complete cadavers and proxies in forensic ecogenomics is probably justifiable for three key reasons. First, autopsies typically entail the examination of specific organs/tissue for PMI estimations and to establish conditions such as health, toxicology, and the last meal (Swift, 2006). Second, studies of individual organs and tissue types afford expediency in addressing key investigative questions since they decompose more rapidly than whole bodies or mammalian analogs. This is exemplified elegantly by several studies (see also Chapter 6), which suggested that PMI analysis could be established also by targeting specific organs (Hauther et al., 2015; Ith et al., 2002). Third, knowledge development in medical contexts (Huh et al., 2013; Williamson et al., 2013) is being advanced through research initiatives that model or mimic otherwise complex (eco)systems where key parameters are controlled each in turn, sequentially, and then collectively. It is reasonable therefore that artificial media that facilitate multiple, parallel, and reproducible experiments can be made similarly in forensic ecogenomics. For example, human gene chips for the human body or different parts thereof, as illustrated by Bergström et al. (2012), Paliy and Agans (2012), and Zoetendal et al. (2008), can be developed using the wealth of information in national and global databases such as the Human Microbiome Project (The Human Microbiome Project Consortium, 2012; Turnbaugh et al., 2007) and, even more appropriately, the Human Postmortem Microbiome Project. Therefore although admittedly an ambitious and long-term goal, postmortem microbiome chips could be developed for high-throughput analysis where the occurrence, dominance, and distribution of likely "microbial clocks" could be determined for more consistent, standardized, and accurate PMI estimations.

Table 4.2 Examples of studies that used organs and tissues from human cadavers or mammalian surrogates for research in different forensic subdisciplines

Animal model	Organ/tissue	Target communities/ discipline	Research team
Ovis aries	Skeletal muscle tissue	Biotaphonomy, geotaphonomy, soil necrobiome	Haslam and Tibbett (2009)
Sus scrofa	Skeletal muscle tissue	Biotaphonomy, geotaphonomy, soil necrobiome	Stokes et al. (2009)
BALB/c mice	Skin, heart, spleen, femoral quadriceps, liver, pancreas, stomach, and lungs	Molecular forensic pathology	Sampaio-Silva et al. (2013)
Human (*Homo sapiens*), pork (*S. scrofa*), beef (*Bos taurus*), lamb (*O. aries*)	Skeletal muscle tissue	Biotaphonomy, geotaphonomy, soil necrobiome	Stokes et al. (2013)
Human (*H. sapiens*)	Fecal samples from rectum and cecum	Postmortem forensic microbiology, forensic ecogenomics	Tuomisto et al. (2013a)
Human (*H. sapiens*)	Liver, mesenteric lymph node, pericardial fluid, portal vein, peripheral vein	Postmortem forensic microbiology, forensic ecogenomics	Tuomisto et al. (2013b)
Human (*H. sapiens*)	Blood, muscle tissue	Forensic molecular analysis	Hansen et al. (2014)
Domestic pig (*Sus scrofa domesticus*)	Leg	Soil necrobiome, forensic ecogenomics	Olakanye et al. (2014)
Human (*H. sapiens*)	Bones	Thanatomicrobiome	Damann et al. (2015)
Human (*H. sapiens*)	Proximal large intestines	Thanatomicrobiome	Hauther et al. (2015)
Domestic pig (*S. scrofa domesticus*)	Skeletal muscle	Soil necrobiome, forensic ecogenomics	Olakanye et al. (2015)
Human (*H. sapiens*)	Blood, buccal cavity, brain, heart, liver, and spleen	Thanatomicrobiome	Javan et al. (2016)

FUTURE RESEARCH QUESTIONS AND INITIATIVES

To date, considerable achievements have been made particularly in bio-/geotaphonomy, forensic chemistry, forensic entomology, and geoforensics. As established in real cases or proposed in the literature and case studies, some of these milestones reflect how the disciplines are already applied or have potential utility in real crime scenes (see also Chapter 8).

It is essential therefore that parallel and/or complementary initiatives in forensic ecogenomic/microbiology research and application adopt the knowledge that is developed in these and other relevant/related forensic subdisciplines. Ultimately, there must be concerted and complementary efforts to address standardization requirements and potentially meet the objectives identified and/or proposed by relevant stakeholders including, but not limited to, policy developers, scenes of crime officers, and government committees.

Due to ethical guidelines and legal frameworks in different countries, research on the role of body decomposition in PMI and time since burial calculations using human cadavers is not always possible. As a result, different mammalian taphonomic surrogates are used with choice of the animal model dependent largely on availability, cost, and study design regarding scale, replication, and repeatability. Notwithstanding the attendant wealth of developed and emerging knowledge and understanding, a key question remains on the utility and transferability of these data to the investigations of real scenes of crime involving human remains. Therefore future forensic (ecogenomics) science research and case studies should compare epinecrotic or necrobiome profiles, including those of the cadaver decomposition islands, using human cadavers and different taphonomic proxies in parallel. As exemplified by Schoenly et al. (2007), making and understanding these parallels between, for example, gravesoils that are impacted by animal model and human cadaver decomposition will validate the use of suids/swine in particular, until the relevant ethical and legal frameworks are in place globally.

OTHER SPECIES STUDIED IN RELATED CONTEXTS

Although outwith the main thrust of this chapter, decompositional processes, how they are influenced by different biophysicochemical parameters, and their impacts on the surrounding (terrestrial) ecosystems, have been investigated in other nonforensic contexts. Therefore an interesting research and knowledge pursuance question is: does (observational) information from the decompositions of vertebrate carrion such as canine (dog), deer (*Cervus nippon*, *Capreolus capreolus*; Young et al., 2014), equine (horse), buffalo, and bison (Reeb et al., 2011) have any applicability and value to the human cadaver context? Therefore can conclusions be drawn from nonforensic ecogenomics studies or observations be used for human forensic investigations? Is this valid and/or justifiable knowledge transfer?

REFERENCES

Achilli, A., Bonfiglio, S., Olivieri, A., et al., 2009. The multifaceted origin of taurine cattle reflected by the mitochondrial genome. PLoS One 4.

Adams, M.R., Moss, M.O., McClure, P., 2015. Food Microbiology, fourth ed. The Royal Society of Chemistry, Cambridge, UK.

Adlam, R.E., Simmons, T., 2007. The effect of repeated physical disturbance on soft tissue decomposition: are taphonomic studies an accurate reflection of decomposition? Journal of Forensic Sciences 52, 1007–1014.

Ajmone-Marsan, P., Garcia, J.F., Lenstra, J.A., et al., 2010. On the origin of cattle: how aurochs became cattle and colonized the world. Evolutionary Anthropology 19, 148–157.

Alajmi, R.A., AlGhufaili, H., Farrukh, A., Alijohani, H., Mashaly, A.M.A., 2016. First report of necrophagous insects on human corpses in Riyadh, Saudi Arabia. Journal of Medical Entomology 53 (6), 1276–1282.

Ali, S., Zhang, W., Rajput, N., et al., 2015. Effect of multiple freeze-thaw cycles on the quality of chicken breast meat. Food Chemistry 173, 808–814.

Al-Mesbah, H., Moffatt, C., El-Azazy, O.M., Majeed, Q.A., 2012. The decomposition of rabbit carcass and associated necrophagous Diptera in Kuwait. Forensic Science International 217 (1–3), 27–31.

Amendt, J., Campobasso, C.P., Gaudry, E., et al., 2007. Best practice in forensic entomology—standards and guidelines. International Journal of Legal Medicine 121, 90–104.

Amendt, J., Richards, C.S., Campobasso, C.P., et al., 2011. Forensic entomology: applications and limitations. Forensic Science, Medicine, and Pathology 7, 379–392.

Armstrong, P., Nizio, K.D., Perrault, K.A., Forbes, S.L., 2016. Establishing the volatile profile of pig carcasses as analogues for human decomposition during the early postmortem period. Heliyon 2 (2), 70–77.

Barton, P.S., Evans, M.J., 2017. Insect diversity meets ecosystem function: different effects of habitat and insects on carrion decomposition. Ecological Entomology. http://dx.doi.org/10.1111/een.12395.

Beja-Pereira, A., Caramelli, D., Lalueza-Fox, C., et al., 2006. The origin of European cattle: evidence from modern and ancient DNA. Proceedings of the National Academy of Sciences of the United States of America 103, 8113–8118.

Benbow, M.E., Pechal, J.L., 2017. Approaches and considerations for forensic microbiology decomposition. In: Carter, D.O., Tomberlin, J.K., Benbow, M.E., Metcalf, J.L. (Eds.), Forensic Microbiology. Wiley, West Sussex, pp. 56–70.

Bergström, A., Licht, T.R., Wilcks, A., Andersen, J.B., Schmidt, L.R., Grønlund, H.A., Vigsnaes, L.K., Michaelsen, K.F., Bahl, M.I., 2012. Introducing GUt low-density array (GULDA): a validated approach for qPCR-based intestinal microbial community analysis. FEMS Microbiology Letters 337 (1), 38–47.

Bernhardt, V., Schomerus, C., Verhoff, M.A., et al., 2016. Of pigs and men—comparing the development of *Calliphora vicina* (Diptera: Calliphoridae) on human and porcine tissue. International Journal of Legal Medicine 131.

Beuter, L., Mendes, J., 2013. Development of *Chrysomya albiceps* (Wiedemann) (Diptera: Calliphoridae) in different pig tissues. Neotropical Entomology 42, 426–430.

Boatright, S.A., Tomberlin, J.K., 2010. Effects of temperature and tissue type on the development of *Cochliomyia macellaria* (Diptera: Calliphoridae). Journal of Medical Entomology 47, 917–923.

Bollongino, R., Edwards, C.J., Alt, K.W., et al., 2006. Early history of European domestic cattle as revealed by ancient DNA. Biology Letters 2, 155–159.

Bradley, D.G., Loftus, R.T., Cunningham, P., et al., 1998. Genetics and domestic cattle origins. Evolutionary Anthropology: Issues, News, and Reviews 6, 79–86.

Can, I., Javan, G.T., Pozhitkov, A.E., Noble, P.A., 2014. Distinctive thanatomicrobiome signatures found in the blood and internal organs of humans. Journal of Microbiological Methods 106, 1–7.

Carter, D.O., Tibbett, M., 2006. Microbial decomposition of skeletal muscle tissue (*Ovis aries*) in a sandy loam soil at different temperatures. Soil Biology & Biochemistry 38, 1139–1145.

Carter, D.O., Yellowlees, D., Tibbett, M., 2008. Temperature affects microbial decomposition of cadavers (*Rattus rattus*) in contrasting soils. Applied Soil Ecology 40, 129–137.

Catts, E.P., 1991. Analyzing entomological data. In: Catts, E.P., Haskell, N. (Eds.), Entomology and Death: A Procedural Guide. Joyce's Print Shop. Clemson, pp. 124–137.

Catts, E.P., Goff, M.L., 1992. Forensic entomology in criminal investigations. Annual Review of Entomology 37, 253–272.

Centeno, N., Maldonado, M., Oliva, A., 2002. Seasonal patterns of arthropods occurring on sheltered and unsheltered pig carcasses in Buenos Aires Province (Argentina). Forensic Science International 126 (1), 63–70.

Clark, K., Evans, L., Wall, R., 2006. Growth rates of the blowfly, *Lucilia sericata*, on different body tissues. Forensic Science International 156, 145–149.

Cockle, D.L., Bell, L.S., 2015. Human decomposition and the reliability of a "universal" model for post mortem interval estimations. Forensic Science International 253, 136.e1–136.e9.

Committee, H. of C.S. and T., 2016. Forensic Science Strategy: Fourth Report of Session 2016-2017. House of Commons.
Crippen, T.L., Singh, B., 2015. Forensic and decomposition microbiology. In: Tomberlin, J.K., Benbow, M.E. (Eds.), Forensic Entomology International Dimensions and Frontiers. CRC Press, Boca Raton, pp. 249–262.
Cross, P., Simmons, T., 2010. The influence of penetrative trauma on the rate of decomposition. Journal of Forensic Sciences 55 (2), 295–301.
Cross, P., Simmons, T., Cunliffe, R., Chatfield, L., 2010. Establishing a taphonomic research facility in the United Kingdom. Forensic Science Policy & Management 1 (4), 187–191.
Damann, F.E., Williams, D.E., Layton, A.C., 2015. Potential use of bacterial community succession in decaying human bone for estimating postmortem interval. Journal of Forensic Sciences 60 (4), 844–850.
Day, D.M., Wallman, J.F., 2006a. Influence of substrate tissue type on larval growth in Calliphora augur and *Lucilia cuprina* (Diptera: Calliphoridae). Journal of Forensic Sciences 51, 657–663.
Day, D.M., Wallman, J.F., 2006b. A comparison of frozen/thawed and fresh food substrates in development of *Calliphora augur* (Diptera: Calliphoridae) larvae. International Journal of Legal Medicine 120, 391–394.
Dent, B.B., Forbes, S.L., Stuart, B.H., 2004. Review of human decomposition processes in soil. Environmental Geology 45 (4), 576–585.
DeVault, T.L., Brisbin Jr., I.L., Rhodes Jr., O.E., 2004. Factors influencing the acquisition of rodent carrion by vertebrate scavengers and decomposers. Canadian Journal of Zoology 82, 502–509.
Dickson, G.C., Poulter, R.T.M., Maas, E.W., Probert, P.K., Kieser, J.A., 2011. Marine bacterial succession as a potential indicator of postmortem submersion interval. Forensic Science International 209 (1), 1–10.
El-Moaty, Z.A., Kheirallah, A.E.M., 2013. Developmental variation of the blow fly *Lucilia sericata* (Meigen, 1826) (Diptera: Calliphoridae) by different substrate tissue types. Journal of Asia-Pacific Entomology 16, 297–300.
Enserink, M., 2017. Amsterdam to host Europe's first 'forensic cemetery'. Science Magazine. http://dx.doi.org/10.1126/science.aal0637.
Fiene, J.G., Sword, G.A., VanLaerhoven, S.L., Tarone, A.M., 2014. The role of spatial aggregation in forensic entomology. Journal of Medical Entomology 51 (1), 1–9.
Finley, S.J., Pechal, J.L., Benbow, M.E., Robertson, B.K., Javan, G.T., 2016. Microbial signatures of cadaver gravesoil during decomposition. Microbial Ecology 71 (3), 524–529.
Flores, M., Longnecker, M., Tomberlin, J.K., 2014. Effects of temperature and tissue type on *Chrysomya rufifacies* (Diptera: Calliphoridae) (Macquart) development. Forensic Science International 245, 24–29.
Frantz, A.C., Massei, G., Burke, T., 2012. Genetic evidence for past hybridisation between domestic pigs and English wild boars. Conservation Genetics 13, 1355–1364.
Frantz, A.C., Zachos, F.E., Kirschning, J., et al., 2013. Genetic evidence for introgression between domestic pigs and wild boars (sus scrofa) in Belgium and Luxembourg: a comparative approach with multiple marker systems. Biological Journal of the Linnean Society 110, 104–115.
Freeman, A.R., Bradley, D.G., Nagda, S., et al., 2006. Combination of multiple microsatellite data sets to investigate genetic diversity and admixture of domestic cattle. Animal Genetics 37, 1–9.
Gautier, A., 1993. "What's in a name?" A short history of the Latin and other labels proposed for domestic animals. In: Clason, A., Payne, S., Uerpmann, H.-P. (Eds.), Skeletons in Her Cupboard. Festschrift for Juliet Clutton-Brock. Oxbow, Oxford. Monograph no. 34.
Giuffra, E., Kijas, J.M.H., Amarger, V., et al., 2000. The origin of the domestic pig: independent domestication and subsequent introgression. Genetics 154, 1785–1791.
Götherström, A., Anderung, C., Hellborg, L., et al., 2005. Cattle domestication in the Near East was followed by hybridization with aurochs bulls in Europe. Proceedings. Biological Sciences/The Royal Society 272, 2345–2350.
Greenberg, B., 1991. Flies as forensic indicators. Journal of Medical Entomology 28, 565–577.
Guo, J., Du, L.X., Ma, Y.H., et al., 2005. A novel maternal lineage revealed in sheep (*Ovis aries*). Animal Genetics 36, 331–336.
Hansen, J., Lesnikova, I., Funder, A.M., Banner, J., 2014. DNA and RNA analysis of blood and muscle from bodies with variable postmortem intervals. Forensic Science, Medicine, and Pathology 10 (3), 322–328.

Harnden, L.M., Tomberlin, J.K., 2016. Effects of temperature and diet on black soldier fly, *Hermetia illucens* (L.) (Diptera: Stratiomyidae), development. Forensic Science International 109–116.

Haslam, T.C., Tibbett, M., 2009. Soils of contrasting pH affect the decomposition of buried mammalian (*Ovis aries*) skeletal muscle tissue. Journal of Forensic Sciences 54 (4), 900–904.

Harvey, M.L., Gasz, N.E., Voss, S.C., 2016. Entomology-based methods for estimation of postmortem interval. Research and Reports in Forensic Medical Science 6, 1–9.

Hauther, K.A., Cobaugh, K.L., Jantz, L.M., 2015. Estimating time since death from postmortem human gut microbial communities. Journal of Forensic Science 60, 1234–1240.

Hiendleder, S., Kaupe, B., Wassmuth, R., et al., 2002. Molecular analysis of wild and domestic sheep questions current nomenclature and provides evidence for domestication from two different subspecies. Proceedings of the Royal Society B: Biological Sciences 269, 893–904.

Hiendleder, S., Mainz, K., Plante, Y., et al., 1998. Analysis of mitochondrial DNA indicates that domestic sheep are derived from two different ancestral maternal sources: No evidence for contributions from urial and argali sheep. Journal of Heredity 89, 113–120.

Howard, G.T., Duos, B., Watson-Horzelski, E.J., 2010. Characterization of the soil microbial community associated with the decomposition of a swine carcass. International Biodeterioration & Biodegradation 64 (4), 300–304.

Huh, D., Kim, H.J., Fraser, J.P., Shea, D.E., Khan, M., Bahinski, A., Hamilton, G.A., Ingber, D.E., 2013. Microfabrication of human organs-on-chips. Nature Protocols 8 (11), 2135–2157.

Human Tissue Act. 2004. c30. http://www.legislation.gov.uk/ukpga/2004/30/contents.

Hyde, E.R., Haarmann, D.P., Lynne, A.M., Bucheli, S.R., Petrosino, J.F., 2013. The living dead: bacterial community structure of a cadaver at the onset and end of the bloat stage of decomposition. PloS One 8 (10), e77733.

Hyde, E.R., Metcalf, J.L., Bucheli, S.R., Lynne, A.M., Knight, R., 2017. Microbial communities associated with decomposing corpses. In: Carter, D.O., Tomberlin, J.K., Benbow, M.E., Metcalf, J.L. (Eds.), Forensic Microbiology. Wiley, West Sussex, pp. 245–273.

Ireland, S., Turner, B.D., 2006. The effects of larval crowding and food type on the size and development of the blowfly, *Calliphora vomitoria*. Forensic Science International 159, 175–181.

Ith, M., Bigler, P., Scheurer, E., Kreis, R., Hofmann, L., Dirnhofer, R., Boesch, C., 2002. Observation and identification of metabolites emerging during postmortem decomposition of brain tissue by means of in situ 1H-magnetic resonance spectroscopy. Magnetic Resonance in Medicine 48, 915–920.

Javan, G.T., Finley, S.J., Can, I., Wilkinson, J.E., Hanson, J.D., Tarone, A.M., 2016. Human thanatomicrobiome succession and time since death. Scientific Reports 6, 29598. http://dx.doi.org/10.1038/srep29598.

Kaneshrajah, G., Turner, B.D., 2004. *Calliphora vicina* larvae grow at different rates on different body tissues. International Journal of Legal Medicine 118, 242–244.

Krause-Kyora, B., Makarewicz, C., Evin, A., et al., 2013. Use of domesticated pigs by Mesolithic hunter-gatherers in northwestern Europe. Nature Communications 4, 2348.

Larson, G., Dobney, K., Albarella, U., et al., 2005. Worldwide phylogeography of wild boar reveals multiple centers of pig domestication. Science (New York, N.Y.) 307, 1618–1621.

Lauber, C.L., Metcalf, J.L., Keepers, K., Ackermann, G., Carter, D.O., Knight, R., 2014. Vertebrate decomposition is accelerated by soil microbes. Applied and Environmental Microbiology 80 (16), 4920–4929.

Leygonie, C., Britz, T.J., Hoffman, L.C., 2012. Impact of freezing and thawing on the quality of meat: review. Meat Science 91, 93–98.

Loftus, R.T., MacHugh, D.E., Bradley, D.G., et al., 1994. Evidence for two independent domestications of cattle. Proceedings of the National Academy of Sciences of the United States of America 91, 2757–2761.

Lossi, L., D'Angelo, L., De Girolamo, P., Merighi, A., 2016. Anatomical features for an adequate choice of experimental animal model in biomedicine: II. Small laboratory rodents, rabbit, and pig. Annals of Anatomy 204, 11–28.

Matuszewski, S., Konwerski, S., Fratczak, K., Szafalowicz, M., 2014. Effect of body mass and clothing on decomposition of pig carcasses. International Journal of Legal Medicine 128 (6), 1039–1048.

Mayer, J.J., 1998. Evaluation of molar size as a basis for distinguishing wild boar from domestic swine: employing the present to decipher the past. MASCA Research Papers in Science and Archaeology 15, 39–53.

Meadows, J.R.S., Hanotte, O., Drögemüller, C., et al., 2006. Globally dispersed Y chromosomal haplotypes in wild and domestic sheep. Animal Genetics 37, 444–453.
Michaud, J.-P., Schoenly, K.G., Moreau, G., 2012. Sampling flies or sampling flaws? Experimetnal design and inference strength in forensic entomology. Journal of Medical Entomology 49, 1–10.
Micozzi, M.S., 1996. Frozen environments and soft tissue preservation. In: Haglund, W.D., Sorg, M.H. (Eds.), Forensic Taphonomy: The Postmortem Fate of Human Remains. CRC Press, Boca Raton, pp. 171–180.
Micozzi, M.S., 1986. Experimental study of postmortem change under field conditions: effects of freezing, thawing, and mechanical injury. Journal of Forensic Sciences 31, 953–961.
Moffatt, C., Simmons, T., Lynch-Aird, J., 2016. An improved equation for TBS and ADD: establishing a reliable postmortem interval framework for casework and experimental studies. Journal of Forensic Sciences 61, S201–S207.
Niederegger, S., Steube, X., Tiltmann, P., Mall, G., 2017. Decomposition rate of intact and injured piglet cadavers. Rechtsmedizin 27, 8–15. http://dx.doi.org/10.1007/s00194-016-0137-7.
Niederegger, S., Wartenberg, N., Spiess, R., et al., 2013. Influence of food substrates on the development of the blowflies *Calliphora vicina* and *Calliphora vomitoria* (Diptera, Calliphoridae). Parasitology Research 112, 2847–2853.
NRC Committee on Identifying the Needs of the Forensic Sciences Community, 2009. Strengthening Forensic Science in the United States: A Path Forward. The National Academies Press.
Odening, K., 1979. Zur Taxonomie und Benennung der Haustier. Zoologische Garten 49, 89–103.
Olakanye, A.O., Thompson, T., Ralebitso-Senior, T.K., 2014. Changes to soil bacterial profiles as a result of *Sus scrofa domesticus* decomposition. Forensic Science International 245, 101–106.
Olakanye, A.O., Thompson, T., Ralebitso-Senior, T.K., 2015. Shifts in soil biodiversity – a forensic comparison between *Sus scrofa domesticus* and vegetation decomposition. Science & Justice 55 (6), 402–407.
Ottoni, C., Girdland Flink, L., Evin, A., et al., 2013. Pig domestication and human-mediated dispersal in western eurasia revealed through ancient DNA and geometric morphometrics. Molecular Biology and Evolution 30, 824–832.
Paliy, O., Agans, R., 2012. Application of phylogenetic microarrays to interrogation of human microbiota. FEMS Microbiology Ecology 79 (1), 2–11.
Parkinson, R.A., Dias, K.R., Horswell, J., Greenwood, P., Banning, N., Tibbett, M., Vass, A.A., 2009. Microbial community analysis of human decomposition on soil. In: Ritz, K., Dawson, L.A., Miller, D. (Eds.), Criminal and Environmental Soil Forensics. Springer, New York, pp. 379–394.
Pasternak, Z., Al-Ashhab, A., Gatica, J., Gafny, R., Avraham, S., Frenk, S., Minz, D., Gillo, O., Jurkevitch, E., 2012. Optimization of molecular methods and statistical procedures for forensic fingerprinting of microbial soil communities. International Research Journal of Microbiology 3 (11), 363–372.
Payne, J.A., 1965. A summer carrion study of the baby pig *Sus scrofa* Linnaeus. Ecology 46 (5), 592–602.
Pechal, J.L., Schmidt, C.J., Jordan, H.R., et al., 2017. Frozen: thawing and its effects on the postmortem microbiome in two pediatric cases. Journal of Forensic Sciences. http://dx.doi.org/10.1111/1556-4029.13419.
Quaak, F.C.A., Kuiper, I., 2011. Statistical analysis of bacterial t-RFLP profiles in forensic soil comparisons. Forensic Science International 210 (1–3), 96–101.
Rabêlo, K.C.N., Thyssen, P.J., Salgado, R.L., et al., 2011. Bionomics of two forensically important blowfly species *Chrysomya megacephala* and *Chrysomya putoria* (Diptera: Calliphoridae) reared on four types of diet. Forensic Science International 210, 257–262.
Ramírez, O., Ojeda, A., Tomàs, A., et al., 2009. Integrating Y-chromosome, mitochondrial, and autosomal data to analyze the origin of pig breeds. Molecular Biology and Evolution 26, 2061–2072.
Reeb, V., Kolel, A., McDermott, T.R., Bhattacharya, D., 2011. Good to the bone: microbial community thrives within bone cavities of a bison carcass at Yellowstone National Park. Environmental Microbiology 13 (9), 2403–2415.
Richards, C.S., Rowlinson, C.C., Cuttiford, L., et al., 2013. Decomposed liver has a significantly adverse affect on the development rate of the blowfly *Calliphora vicina*. International Journal of Legal Medicine 127, 259–262.
Rodriguez, W.C., Bass, W.M., 1983. Insect activity and its relationship to decay rates of human cadavers in East Tennessee. Journal of Forensic Sciences 28 (2), 423–432.

Roberts, L.G., Dabbs, G.R., 2015. A taphonomic study exploring the differences in decomposition rate and manner between frozen and never frozen domestic pigs (*Sus scrofa*). Journal of Forensic Sciences 60, 588–594.

Sampaio-Silva, F., Magalhães, T., Carvalho, F., Dinis-Oliveira, R.J., Silvestre, R., 2013. Profiling of RNA degradation for estimation of post morterm interval. Plos One 8 (2), e56507.

Scandura, M., Iacolina, L., Apollonio, M., 2011. Genetic diversity in the European wild boar *Sus scrofa*: phylogeography, population structure and wild x domestic hybridization. Mammal Review 41, 125–137.

Schoenly, K., Haskell, N., Hall, R., Gbur, J., 2007. Comparative performance and complementarity of four sampling methods and arthropod preference tests from human and porcine remains at the forensic anthropology center in Knoxville, Tennessee. Journal of Medical Entomology 44 (5), 881–894.

Silverman, B., 2011. Research and Development in Forensic Science: A Review. The Home Office, pp. 1–24.

Spicka, A., Johnson, R., Bushing, J., Higley, L.G., Carter, D.O., 2011. Carcass mass can influence rate of decomposition and release of ninhydrin-reactive nitrogen. Forensic Science International 209 (1–3), 80–85.

Stokes, K.L., Forbes, S.L., Tibbett, M., 2009. Freezing skeletal muscle tissue does not affect its decomposition in soil: evidence from temporal changes in tissue mass, microbial activity and soil chemistry based on excised samples. Forensic Science International 183, 6–13.

Stokes, K.L., Tibbett, M., Forbes, S.L., 2013. Human versus animal: contrasting decomposition dynamics of mammalian analogues in experimental Taphonomy. Journal of Forensic Sciences 58 (3), 583–591.

Suckling, J.K., Spradley, M.K., Godde, K., 2016. A longitudinal study on human outdoor decomposition in Central Texas. Journal of Forensic Sciences 61 (1), 19–25.

Swann, L.M., Forbes, S.L., Lewis, S.W., 2010. Analytical separations of mammalian decomposition products for forensic science: a review. Analytica Chimica Acta 682 (suppl. 1–2), 9–22.

Swift, B., 2006. The timing of death. In: Rutty, G.N. (Ed.), Essentials of Autopsy Practice: Current Methods and Modern Trends. Springer, New York, USA, pp. 189–214.

The Human Microbiome Project Consortium, 2012. Structure, function and diversity of the healthy human microbiome. Nature 486 (7402), 207–214.

Thomas, J.K., Sanford, M.R., Longnecker, M., et al., 2016. Effects of temperature and tissue type on the development of *Megaselia scalaris* (Diptera: Phoridae). Journal of Medical Entomology 53, 519–525.

Thyssen, P.J., de Souza, C.M., Shimamoto, P.M., et al., 2014. Rates of development of immatures of three species of *Chrysomya* (Diptera: Calliphoridae) reared in different types of animal tissues: implications for estimating the postmortem interval. Parasitology Research 113, 3373–3380.

Tomberlin, J.K., Benbow, M.E., Tarone, A.M., et al., 2011a. Basic research in evolution and ecology enhances forensics. Trends in Ecology & Evolution 26, 53–55.

Tomberlin, J.K., Mohr, R.M., Benbow, M.E., et al., 2011b. A roadmap for bridging basic and applied research in forensic entomology. Annual Review of Entomology 56, 401–421.

Tomberlin, J.K., Crippen, T.L., Tarone, A.M., Singh, B., Adams, K., Rezenom, Y.H., Benbow, M.E., Flores, M., Longnecker, M., Pechal, J.L., Russell, D.H., Beier, R.C., Wood, T.K., 2012. Interkingdom responses of flies to bacteria mediated by fly physiology and bacterial quorum sensing. Animal Behaviour 84 (6), 1449–1456.

Tomberlin, J.K., Benbow, E.M., 2015. Forensic Entomology: International Dimensions and Frontiers. CRC Press, Florida.

Tuomisto, S., Karhunen, P.J., Pessi, T., 2013a. Time-dependent post mortem changes in the composition of intestinal bacteria using real-time quantitative PCR. Gut Pathogens 5 (1), 35.

Tuomisto, S., Karhunen, P.J., Vuento, R., Aittoniemi, J., Pessi, T., 2013b. Evaluation of postmortem bacterial migration using culturing and real-time quantitative PCR. Journal of Forensic Sciences 58 (4), 910–916.

Turnbaugh, P.J., Ley, R.E., Hamady, M., Fraser-Liggett, C., Knight, R., Gordon, J.I., 2007. The human microbiome project: exploring the microbial part of ourselves in a changing world. Nature 449 (7164), 804–810.

Vilà, C., Seddon, J., Ellegren, H., 2005. Genes of domestic mammals augmented by backcrossing with wild ancestors. Trends in Genetics 21, 214–218.

Villet, M.H., Richards, C.S., Midgley, J.M., 2009. Contemporary precision, bias and accuracy of minimum post-mortem intervals estimated using development of carrion-feeding insects. In: Amendt, J., Campobasso, C.P., Goff, M.L., et al. (Eds.), Current Concepts in Forensic Entomology. Springer, Dordrecht, pp. 109–137.

Warren, J.A., Anderson, G.S., 2009. A comparison of development times for Protophormia terraenovae (RD) reared on different food substrates. Canadian Society of Forensic Science Journal 42, 161–171.

Weiss, S., Carter, D.O., Metcalf, J.L., Knight, R., 2016. Carcass mass has little influence on the structure of gravesoil microbial communities. International Journal of Legal Medicine 130 (1), 253–263.

Wells, J.D., Lecheta, M.C., Moura, M.O., LaMotte, L.R., 2015. An evaluation of sampling methods used to produce insect growth models for postmortem interval estimation. International Journal of Legal Medicine 129 (2), 405–410.

Williamson, A., Singh, S., Fernekorn, U., Schober, A., 2013. The future of the patient-specific Body-on-a-chip. Lab on a Chip 13 (18), 3471–3480.

Wilson, J.M., Lafon, N.W., Kreitlow, K.L.T., et al., 2014. Comparing growth of pork- and venison-reared *Phormia regina* (Diptera: Calliphoridae) for the application of forensic entomology to wildlife poaching. Journal of Medical Entomology 51, 1067–1072.

Xu, L., Bickhart, D.M., Cole, J.B., et al., 2015. Genomic signatures reveal new evidences for selection of important traits in domestic cattle. Molecular Biology and Evolution 32, 711–725.

Young, A., Stillman, R., Smith, M.J., Korstjens, A.H., 2014. An experimental study of vertebrate scavenging behavior in a northwest European woodland context. Journal of Forensic Sciences 59 (0), 1333–1342.

Zhou, C., Byard, R.W., 2011. Factors and processes causing accelerated decomposition in human cadavers – an overview. Journal of Forensic and Legal Medicine 18 (1), 6–9.

Zoetendal, E.G., Rajilić-Stojanović, M., de Vos, W.M., 2008. High-throughput diversity and functionality analysis of the gastrointestinal tract microbiota. Gut 57, 1605–1615.

CHAPTER 5

The Role of the Microbiome in PMI Estimation

Jifeng Cai, Yadong Guo, Lagabaiyila Zha, Juanjuan Guo
Central South University, Changsha, PR China

INTRODUCTION

A corpse begins to decompose a few minutes after death with numerous organisms such as insects, bacteria, fungi, and animals using the carrion as a nutrient source. The activities of these organisms are the major forces of decomposition, where insects and microorganisms in particular play a vital role in the removal of soft tissues and can consume approximately 80% of the carcass mass (Spicka et al., 2011). Also the decomposition-associated microbial community (microbiome) plays an important ecological role, as decomposition is critical to nutrient cycling and energy flow (Carter et al., 2007). The process of decomposition is affected further by many environmental factors including temperature, humidity, light, oxygen, and soil pH. Although forensic entomology is studied widely and used to estimate postmortem interval (PMI) or time since death (TSD), forensic scientists/researchers are attempting to find more accurate methods by analyzing the microbial communities of mammal cadavers, human corpses, and gravesoils. As a result, studies have documented that temporal successions in microbial community composition and structure have the potential to be used as a "microbial clock" to estimate PMI (Finley et al., 2015).

The main purpose of this chapter is to introduce the role of the microbiome of decomposition in PMI estimation, hence two major roles of these microbial communities will be discussed: the ecological functions and forensic applications. The chapter will begin with a discussion of the necrobiome, especially the insects, vertebrate scavengers, and microbes, followed by the environmental factors influencing decay and the interactions between the decomposer organisms. A comprehensive review is then provided on the development of methods used to analyze bacteria and how microbes of carrion decomposition may influence the surrounding terrestrial ecosystems in particular. Finally, the chapter summarizes recent advances and findings in microbial community studies during the process of carrion decomposition and discusses the potential use of microbial communities in PMI estimation. The microorganisms that are discussed largely in this chapter are bacteria, although cognizance is made of the dynamics and functions of fungi in the process of decomposition.

Forensic Ecogenomics
ISBN 978-0-12-809360-3
http://dx.doi.org/10.1016/B978-0-12-809360-3.00005-9

THE NECROBIOME

Decomposition begins immediately after death (approximately 4 min) through autolysis or self-digestion, which can break down cells and tissues (Vass, 2001). The process is both chemical and biological with microorganisms, invertebrates, vertebrates, and plants as participants in carrion decomposition. Generally, all the organisms associated with decomposing remains of heterotrophic biomass, including animal carrion and human corpses, are defined as the necrobiome (Benbow et al., 2013).

Various kinds of arthropods and sarcosaprophagous insects are attracted to carcasses or terrestrial carrions and most belong to the orders Diptera (flies) and Coleoptera (beetles) (Byrd and Castner, 2010). Diptera is dominant in early decomposition and Coleoptera in advanced decay and dry stages (Carvalho et al., 2000; Wolff et al., 2001). Many insects utilize the carrion organic material as food resources and oviposition sites directly, while others (e.g., part of Silphidae) use cadavers as a habitat where they find other insects attracted to the carrion as food sources (Campobasso et al., 2001; Gibbs and Stanton, 2001; Benbow et al., 2013). As a result, Smith (1986) used the feeding habits of arthropods associated with corpses to divide them into four categories: necrophagous species, predator and parasites on the necrophagous species, omnivorous species, and adventive species (Table 5.1). In the terrestrial environment, necrophagous insect larvae are responsible for the majority of the rapid carcass decomposition during the active decay and advanced decay stages (Payne, 1965; Centeno et al., 2002; Benbow et al., 2013).

Microorganisms are very diverse and include all bacteria and archaea, most protozoa, some species of fungi and algae, and certain microscopic animals and plants. An enormous number of microorganisms exist in terrestrial, atmospheric, and aquatic environments and live together on and within other creatures. Shortly after death, microbes (bacteria, fungi, and protozoa) begin to digest the body from the inside out. It is these microorganisms that metabolize the body's macromolecules (carbohydrates, proteins, lipids, and nucleic acids) into gas, liquids, and simple molecules (Vass, 2001; Forbes, 2008). These microorganisms are the main force in the putrefaction or bloat stage, which alters the appearance of the carcasses significantly. Typically, a green discoloration appears while various gases, including hydrogen sulfide, carbon dioxide, methane, ammonia, sulfur dioxide, and hydrogen, are released into the surrounding environment (Vass, 2001; Forbes, 2008).

Scavenging refers to the carnivorous and herbivorous feeding behavior in which scavengers feed on the carcasses. Some invertebrates such as burying beetles, blow flies, crayfish, or marine crustaceans are considered to scavenge carcasses (Burkepile et al., 2006). Most common vertebrate scavengers are vultures, raccoons, and feral pigs (DeVault and Rhodes, 2002; Reeves, 2009; Spradley et al., 2012). Also, according to Haglund (1997a,b) and Rippley et al. (2012), some predators such as big cats, rodents, dogs, and coyotes, which are not usually considered as scavengers, may occasionally scavenge carrion.

Table 5.1 The ecological classification of sarcosaprophagous insects (Smith, 1986; Wolff et al., 2001)

Category	Order	Family
Necrophagous	Coleoptera	Dermestidae
		Scarabaeidae
		Silphidae
	Diptera	Caliphoridae
		Muscidae
		Sarcophagidae
	Hymenoptera	Formicidae
Predators and parasites	Coleoptera	Carabidae
		Cleridae
		Histeridae
		Silphidae
		Staphylinidae
	Dermaptera	Forficulidae
	Diptera	Syrphidae
	Hemiptera	Gelastocoridae
	Hymenoptera	Vespidae
Omnivorous	Blattodea	Blattidae
	Coleoptera	
	Hymenoptera	Formicidae
		Vespidae
Adventive	Coleoptera	Nitidulidae
		Passalidae
	Hemiptera	Coreidae
	Hymenoptera	Halictidae
	Lepidoptera	Hesperiidae

Key Environmental Factors That Affect the Necrobiome

Decomposition is a complex process affected by a variety of biotic—the cadaver itself, microbes, insects, and carnivores—and abiotic—temperature, humidity, oxygen, and light—factors. The abiotic or environmental factors may impact the decomposition rate by influencing the necrobiome or affect the necrobiome dynamics with a subsequent effect on specific decomposition process rates. For example, bacterial replication and the activity of invertebrates and vertebrates are dependent on optimum temperature with the most favorable temperature range for putrefaction being between 21°C and 38°C. Furthermore, higher temperatures can increase necrobiome activity whereby their enhancement of the odor of putrefying bodies attracts more insects and carnivores (Zhou and Byard, 2011; Kasper et al., 2012). Although the majority of bacteria can tolerate low temperatures and survive cold weather, their proliferation and metabolic activities are suppressed between 0°C and 5°C, and cell division occurs at a time near to infinity (Micozzi, 1997). Consequently, Melvin et al. (1984) reported that microorganisms migrated through the small intestine wall slowly in low-temperature conditions (2–3 h at 37°C compared to 72 h at 4°C) and only a few species appeared on the gut surface.

Vertebrates remove less tissue mass with increased temperature. A study by DeVault et al. (2004) revealed that 49% of small-mammal carcasses were scavenged in cool weather (5.8–17°C) and only 19% were scavenged in warm weather (22.6–27.8°C). Blow fly activity was found on carcasses when the temperature exceeded 40–60°F (Denier, 1940). In contrast, insect growth and development are limited in cold environments, and even death occurs. This was exemplified by Smith (1986) who observed that *Calliphora* eggs failed to hatch below 4°C and their larvae failed to pupate below 16°C and over 30°C. In general, the death points for different insects change widely and range from −15°C to −30°C (Knipling and Sullivan, 1957).

Humidity is another key factor mediating the growth and abundance of bacteria and insects. The lack of moisture in both soft tissue and the surrounding environment typically restricts microbial activity, causes desiccation of fly eggs, and inhibits larval growth (Forbes and Carter, 2016). For example, few adults of *Fannia canicularis* and *Fannia femoralis* (Diptera: Muscidae) oviposited when manure moisture content was below 45% (Mullens et al., 2002). Also egg eclosion and adult emergence success of the *Hermetia illucens* (Diptera: Stratiomyidae) increased as relative humidity rose from 25% to 70%, and the higher humidity-enhanced larvae development (Holmes et al., 2012). Compared to the cold/dry conditions, carcass-related volatiles were emitted earlier, in higher amounts, and in a greater diversity under warm/humid conditions (Kasper et al., 2012), subsequently attracting more arthropods and vertebrate scavengers.

Invertebrates, vertebrates, plants, and aerobic bacteria all require oxygen for respiration and energy production. Bacteria can be classified as aerobes (obligate and microaerophiles) and anaerobes (obligate, facultative, and aerotolerant) according to their requirements for oxygen. After oxygen deprivation in the gut, facultative and obligate anaerobes metabolize the available substrates using organic carbon fermentation pathways (Cammack et al., 2016), which generate considerable amounts and types of gases and fluids. After the purging, in the subsequent influx of oxygen, the anaerobes decrease in relative abundance, while aerobes and facultative anaerobes increase.

According to Smith (1986), light can interfere with fly activity. Specifically, *Calliphora* adults prefer shade conditions, while *Lucilia* and *Sarcophaga* adults prefer sunlight, which can affect the patterns and distributions of insects present on a carcass. Shade can promote the oviposition of blow flies and increase larvae activity (Dillon, 1995). Larval masses can be on the surface of a carcass in the shade but will often colonize darker environments within the body cavity of a carcass that is under direct sunlight (Bass, 1997). Also larvae remove internal soft tissues and leave the skin as a protective barrier from sunlight, which can protect the larvae surfaces from desiccation. Overall, several studies (e.g., Hobischak et al., 2006; Sharanowski et al., 2008) have shown that sun-exposed carrions support higher insect species abundance than shaded carrions.

In terrestrial habitats, several other environmental factors including the state of dress, surrounding vegetation, soil components, and soil pH can affect the necrobiome of a decomposing human corpse (Damann and Carter, 2014; Benbow et al., 2016). In summary, the many factors that influence the process of decomposition present a considerable challenge for researchers that study the necrobiome and its dynamics.

Interactions Between Necrobiome Communities

Microbes, invertebrates, and vertebrate scavengers all utilize vertebrate carrion as a nutrient resource. These organisms engage in complicated interactions such as competition and symbiosis, not only between different taxonomic and phylogenetic groups but also among the same species. Insect competition occurs in three ways: intraspecific competition (within a species), interspecific competition (between species), and predators and parasites (Smith, 1986). The arthropod community structure succession on carrion is partly explained by the intraspecific competition (Norris, 1965; Hanski and Kuusela, 1977). For example, predaceous insects use the necrophagous larvae or adults as food resources and some second and third instars (e.g., *Chrysomya*, *Hydrotaea*, and *Ophyra*) can become predators (Smith, 1986).

Insect colonization and larvae development may decrease bacteria taxon richness via direct or indirect competitive interactions (Pechal et al., 2013). Flies or other insects bring microorganisms to the corpse, which also influence the microbe taxon richness and relative abundance through competition (Boer et al., 2006; Mille–Lindblom et al., 2006). Also blow flies can impact microbial species directly through chemical secretions that have antibiotic properties (Sherman et al., 2000; Mumcuoglu et al., 2001). Furthermore, vertebrate scavengers transfer microorganisms that are adhered onto their feet, fur, or feathers. In contrast, microbial communities can produce toxins (e.g., botulin toxin) to prevent competition by scavengers that feed on vertebrate carrion (Janzen, 1977). Therefore Burkepile et al. (2006) found that microbe-laden fish carrion was four times less likely to be scavenged by large consumers than fresh carrion in a coastal marine ecosystem. However, some vertebrate scavengers have been well adapted and possess the mechanisms to compete against the carcass-colonizing microorganisms (DeVault et al., 2003).

In addition to competition, the multiple micro- and macroorganisms that constitute the necrobiome have mutually beneficial interactions. For example, insects can facilitate microbe-based decomposition where carrion tissue digestion by insects produces many substrates that are more bioavailable for utilization by microorganisms. These processes can be affected further by abiotic/environmental parameters. Consequently, Payne (1965) and Janzen (1977) reported that carrion tended to mummify rather than decompose at summer temperatures when insects were excluded. Similarly, bacteria and other microbes are vital for the development of many species of flies and other insects as exemplified by fly larvae that obtain amino acids from a variety of bacteria. *M. domestica* larvae cannot develop to third instars in a completely sterile environment and different bacteria species showed a wide range of impacts on the growth and development of larvae (Schmidtmann and Martin, 1992; Watson et al., 1993; Zurek et al., 2000; Rochon et al., 2004). Microbes including bacteria, fungi, and protozoa metabolize carrion organic matter and release volatile organic compounds (VOCs) as by-products. Burkepile et al. (2006) found significant differences in the attraction of arthropods between bacteria-inhabited and bacteria-free cadavers. Also some compositions of VOCs, e.g., dimethyl disulfide and dimethyl trisulfide, were confirmed to have an attractive activity to *Musca domestica*, *Calliphora vicina*, and *Thanatophilus sinuatus* adults (Kelling, 2001; Paczkowski et al., 2012; Dekeirsschieter et al., 2013). Blow flies may use VOCs as signals for arrival patterns and behavior such as oviposition (LeBlanc and Logan, 2010; Ma et al., 2012; Tomberlin et al., 2012). VOC chemical cues are also considered as a mechanism that assists mammals (e.g., *Boiga irregularis*) to locate carrion (Shivik and Clark, 1997; Shivik, 1999).

TECHNIQUE DEVELOPMENT FOR BACTERIAL IDENTIFICATION

Historically, identification of bacteria was based on morphological characterization with preliminary classification achieved through culture on media, individual colony analysis and selection, specimen glass slide production, staining, and microscopy examination. Subsequently, physiological and biochemical experiments are carried out and these include aerobic/anaerobic or oxidation/fermentative characterization, substrate utilization analysis, degradation, and metabolic capacity determinations, with serological tests used sometimes to initiate specific strain/species identification. These methods have several drawbacks: they can be used only for organisms that can be cultured in vitro; identification results may be imprecise due to the limited number of existing biochemical and phenotypic tests; and some strains exhibit unique biochemical properties that make it difficult to achieve species differentiation by biochemical or morphological characterization. Finally, only 0.1%–1% of the total microorganisms in the biosphere are culturable (Amann et al., 1995), hence several molecular and culture-independent methods have been invented to overcome the limitations of traditional bacterial identification.

The 16S rRNA gene, a sequence that is approximately 1550 bp long comprising nine variable and nine conserved regions, is used commonly for taxonomic identification of bacteria (Petrosino et al., 2009). The conserved region of the 16S rRNA gene is highly conserved between different bacteria and can be used in phylogenetic analysis (Weisburg et al., 1991; Woese and Fox, 1977), while the hypervariable regions can provide specific signature sequences for identification at the species level (Kolbert and Persing, 1999; Clarridge III, 2004). For some time, Sanger sequencing facilitated comparative analysis of the 16S rRNA gene sequence and subsequent development of the microbial genome database (Jenks, 1998). Although this DNA-sequencing method was more accurate than morphological and biochemical tests, it was culture based with well-recognized limitations. As a result, culture-independent, PCR-based, and length heterogeneity-based methods were used widely to study bacterial community structure based on the 16S rRNA gene. They included restriction fragment length polymorphism (RFLP) (Dymock et al., 1996; Suau et al., 1999), ribosomal intergenic spacer analysis (Borneman and Triplett, 1997; Sigler et al., 2002; Sigler and Zeyer, 2002), denaturing gradient gel electrophoresis (Muyzer et al., 1993; Schabereiter-Gurtner et al., 2001), and real-time quantitative polymerase chain reaction (qPCR) (Suzuki et al., 2000; Bizhang et al., 2011).

Notwithstanding this, the techniques require the development of 16S rRNA/DNA libraries of microbial flora through cloning and sequencing, and creation of phylogenetic trees to obtain limited microbial diversity information, which is time consuming and costly. In contrast, next-generation sequencing (NGS) technology, also called high-throughput sequencing, was developed in 2005 and greatly reduced the human, material, and time costs. The technology has since developed rapidly and presently affords largely reliable simultaneous identification of bacterial community members at the genus level (Crippen and Singh, 2015). Also the United States National Institutes of Health initiated the Human Microbiome Project in 2007, aimed at identifying and characterizing the human microbiome and analyzing its role in human health and disease (Turnbaugh et al., 2007). This project led to the boom of microbial community research using the NGS technique.

As discussed earlier, bacteria are considered a major driving force for the decomposition of human cadavers and animal carcasses. As a result, numerous scientists have used various methods to investigate the bacteria associated with decomposition to estimate PMI. Initially, traditional culture-dependent methods were used, but these are time consuming and labor intensive, particularly bacterial isolation, which limits comprehensive determinations of the numbers and types of species that colonize cadavers (Staley and Konopka, 1985; Amann, 2000; Vass, 2001). Therefore RFLP (Parkinson et al., 2009), real-time qPCR (Howard et al., 2010; Tuomisto et al., 2013a,b; Hauther et al., 2015), and Sanger sequencing (Howard et al., 2010; Dickson et al., 2011; Chun et al., 2015) were used to identify bacterial taxa that were dominant in carrion decomposition studies. Since 2013, forensic scientists have used NGS to study postmortem microbial variations and attempted to elucidate the relationship between bacteria communities and death time (Hyde et al., 2013; Metcalf et al., 2013; Pechal et al., 2013, 2014; Lauber et al., 2014; Benbow et al., 2015; Carter et al., 2015; Cobaugh et al., 2015; Damann et al., 2015; Hyde et al., 2015; Finley et al., 2016; Guo et al., 2016; Metcalf et al., 2016; Weiss et al., 2016) (see also Chapter 1).

ECOLOGICAL EFFECTS OF MICROORGANISMS INVOLVED IN DECOMPOSITION

Many vertebrates die in the terrestrial environment. Their decompositions release multiple compounds into the surrounding soil, water, and atmosphere with subsequently considerable impacts on terrestrial ecosystems in particular. Also Forbes and

Carter (2016) stated that independent of their species, i.e., pig or mouse, carcasses can influence the environment significantly, although different cadaver sizes may lead to different degrees of impact (see also Chapter 4).

Dent et al. (2004) reviewed the human decomposition processes in soil and explained the likely pathways of protein, fat, carbohydrate, and bone decomposition. Protein can be broken down into ephenolic substances such as skatole and indole, and gases including carbon dioxide, hydrogen sulfide, ammonia, and methane. Glycerol and fatty acids can become shorter-chain saturated fatty acids by microbial metabolic activities. During burial, and hence subsurface decomposition under anaerobic conditions, microorganisms break down carbohydrates into various acids (lactic acid, butyric acid, and acetic acid), alcohols (butyl alcohol, ethyl alcohol, and acetone), and gases (methane, hydrogen, and hydrogen sulfide) via fermentative pathways. These metabolites are released into the soil to participate in biogeochemical cycling and make the soil rich in nutrients. For carcasses placed on the soil surface, ammonia-rich fluids permeate the soil after cadaver rupture, resulting in extreme and significant effects on nitrogen concentrations and pH of gravesoil (Metcalf et al., 2016). As a result, Carter et al. (2007) defined the highly fertile area created by a decaying carcass as a "cadaver (or carcass) decomposition island" (CDI). Smaller cadavers tend to be consumed ex situ and adult or large cadavers tend to be consumed partly in situ (Coe, 1978; Towne, 2000). Consequently, cadaveric materials are more likely to enter the soil horizon when the cadavers are large and not carried away by scavengers. Therefore Towne (2000) observed that larger carcasses can increase inorganic nitrogen concentration in the underlying soil significantly and change the vegetation pattern for up to 5 years.

As discussed previously, microorganisms can metabolize all organic matter in cadavers, forming and releasing VOCs into the surrounding environment. Forbes and Perrault (2014) identified 249 VOCs from pig carcasses placed on the soil surface and only 58 compounds were common to both air and soil samples collected around the carcasses. They detected more VOCs in soil (207) than in air (100), which they ascribed to the indigenous soil microbial communities or adsorption of VOCs to soil particles, causing longer retention. Vass et al. (2004) identified 424 specific VOCs associated with human decomposition postburial and classified them into eight major classes: cyclic hydrocarbons; noncyclic hydrocarbons; nitrogen compounds; oxygen compounds; acids/esters; halogen compounds; sulfur compounds; and miscellaneous. Although the corpses were buried, many of the compounds produced during decomposition migrated to the surface at detectable levels. Sulfur compound volumes were increased only during the early stages (first few years) of postburial decomposition, while cyclic/noncyclic hydrocarbons, oxygen compounds, and halogen compounds were detectable for a longer time, up to 12 years. The research team (Vass et al., 2008, Vass, 2012) advanced the knowledge base on VOCs associated with burial human decomposition and improved further the Decompositional Odor Analysis Database.

Other studies (Statheropoulos et al., 2005, 2007) detected fewer VOCs (approximately 80 and 30 substances in 2005 and 2007, respectively) during the early stages of decay of human remains. Nevertheless, both studies showed maximum concentrations for dimethyl disulfide. Eleven VOCs were considered as a "common core" and included ethanol, 2-propanone, dimethyl disulfide, methyl benzene, octane, 2-butanone, methyl ethyl disulfide, dimethyl trisulfide, and *o*-, *m*-, and *p*-xylenes (Statheropoulos et al., 2007). Overall, VOCs have been reported to be electrophysiologically active to insects. For example, the sulfur compounds, dimethyl trisulfide and dimethyl disulfide, have been identified as some of the most important cues that are used by flies to find sources of odor and trace decayed food or dead vertebrates (Kelling, 2001; Paczkowski et al., 2012; Dekeirsschieter et al., 2013). Thus Kelling (2001) used dimethyl disulfide at 0.001–10 mg and all the concentrations were electrophysiological active to *M. domestica*. Paczkowski et al. (2012) diluted (10^{-2} to 10^{-9}) dimethyl trisulfide and dimethyl disulfide and reported that female *C. vicina* could find the compounds at very low concentrations of 10^{-9} for dimethyl trisulfide and 10^{-8} for dimethyl disulfide. Finally, Dekeirsschieter et al. (2013) used 100 ng and 1 μg of dimethyl disulfide with both concentrations attracting *T. sinuatus* females, while the 100 ng concentration attracted males of the species specifically.

Carrion decomposition not only affects the chemical characteristics of the surrounding environment but also increases local biodiversity. As a cadaver decomposes, its microbiome may be incorporated into the microbial community of the soil below (Finley et al., 2015). After carcass rupture events, the microbial richness on the soil surface increases rapidly, and the decomposition-associated microbial communities can have long-term influences on soil dynamics (Finley et al., 2016). Cobaugh et al. (2015) observed that the richness and diversity of the bacterial communities in CDI soils increased statistically significantly only in the final decomposition stage, at least 87 days postmortem. Also they found several human-specific bacterial taxa in the surrounding soil samples. Specifically, Bacteroides, Staphylococcus, and Enterococcus were recorded during the active decay stage, whereas Lactobacillus, Phascolarctobacterium, and Eggerthella appeared during the early advanced decay stage. In general, Bacteroides persisted in the soils during decomposition. After removing the cadavers from soil surface, the taxa remained high for the first 4 days, decreased by day 126, and were not detected at day 204. At the same time, indigenous soil microbial communities can increase carrion decomposition rates. For example, Lauber et al. (2014) reported that laboratory-reared mice (*M. musculus*, strain B6C3F1) cadavers decomposed statistically significantly slower in sterilized soil (rapture occurred between days 13 and 20) than on the soils with an intact microbial community (rapture occurred between days 6 and 9).

ADVANCES IN DECOMPOSITION-ASSOCIATED BACTERIAL COMMUNITY STUDIES AND PMI ESTIMATION

According to Amendt et al. (2007), for example, PMI refers to the time interval between death and recovery of the body. It is hugely important and meaningful to determine TSD or PMI in forensic practices. Conventionally, PMI estimation relied on the physical changes that occur after death, including *algor mortis*, *livor mortis*, *rigor mortis*, and supravital activity, which are well recognized as early postmortem phenomena. Numerous techniques have been employed subsequently for estimating the PMI of mammalian remains, such as DNA/RNA degradation (Sampaio-Silva et al., 2013; Hansen et al., 2014), ATP degradation (Mao et al., 2013), and chemical examination of body tissues and/or fluids (Mikami et al., 1994; Elmas et al., 2002; Donaldson and Lamont, 2013). Nonetheless, these approaches have limitations, hence their application for accurate PMI estimation remains a challenge. As a result, alternative methods and disciplines have been developed and applied for estimating PMI. In particular, a major force of decomposition has been considered, hence forensic entomology, which is based on the development rate of insect larvae and arthropod community compositional and successional patterns (Smith, 1986; Campobasso and Introna, 2001), has been used widely. As observed by several authors (e.g., Vass, 2001; Zhang et al., 2016), few studies have investigated bacterial communities during carrion decomposition using traditional culture-based methods. Instead, research on bacterial community dynamics during cadaver and carrion decomposition and gravesoils has gained considerable momentum in the past 3 years due to the advanced high-throughput NGS technique.

The studies using traditional methods identified several bacteria associated with carrion decomposition, and recorded shifts from aerobic to anaerobic components due to the depletion of oxygen. Melvin et al. (1984) stated that *Staphylococcus* species first migrated from the small intestine, followed by coliform and fungi, then coliform and anaerobes. Vass (2001) observed a shift from aerobic bacteria (*Staphylococcus*, *Candida*, *Malasseria*, *Bacillus*, and *Streptococcus* spp.) in early decomposition stages to anaerobic bacteria (micrococci, coliforms, diphtheroids, and *Clostridium* spp.) as decomposition progressed. Also Zhang et al. (2016) observed that *Staphylococcus* and *Neisseria* spp., which were predominant in the early PMI, were replaced by *Flavobacterium* spp., *Pseudomonas* spp., and *Lactobacillus casei* in late PMI. Similar shifts from aerobes to anaerobes were also observed in studies that employed NGS techniques (Hyde et al., 2013; Cobaugh et al., 2015; Guo et al., 2016). Metcalf et al. (2013) made a medium-term study (48 days) and found that endogenous and facultative anaerobes (e.g., *Lactobacillus* and *Bacteroides* spp.) increased in the abdominal cavity during the bloat stage (approximately days 6–9). After rupture occurred (approximately 9 days after the start of the experiment), the predominance of these taxa decreased considerably, and aerobes including *Pseudochrobactrum* and *Ochrobactrum*, dominated due to exposure of the abdominal cavity to oxygen.

The Human Microbiome Project (2012) reported that the microbial communities of the human body differed in composition relative to different sites and parts of the body. Specifically, Proteobacteria and Firmicutes are the dominant phyla in the bacterial communities of the buccal mucosa, while Bacteroidetes and Firmicutes are dominant in stool specimens, as also demonstrated in carrion decomposition studies (Hyde et al., 2013, 2015; Guo et al., 2016). As carrion decomposed, their bacterial communities showed statistically significant temporal variations and became more similar to each other across body sites (Metcalf et al., 2013, 2016; Guo et al., 2016). Nonetheless, the studies that employed NGS techniques showed a high variability of the bacterial community pattern of carrion decomposition at different taxonomic levels of phylum, family, and genus. For example, Guo et al. (2016) found that Proteobacteria, particularly Gammaproteobacteria, replaced Firmicutes and Bacteroidetes as the dominant phyla during early decomposition in the mouth and rectum, respectively, but became the most dominant phylum in both the buccal cavity and rectum in late decomposition. In contrast, Pechal et al. (2014) reported that the relative abundances of Proteobacteria and Firmicutes decreased and increased, respectively, as carcasses decomposed. Additionally, bacterial taxon richness decreased as decomposition progressed (Pechal et al., 2014; Guo et al., 2016), which could result from insect colonization and subsequent utilization of the carrion.

Several bacteria have been identified as useful to estimate PMI by using animal decomposition models. Metcalf et al. (2013) studied the necrobiome of mice (*M. musculus*, strain B6C3F1) and highlighted the most changeable bacterial taxa during decomposition: Clostridiaceae and Enterococcaceae of the abdominal cavity increased in abundance, while Lactobacillaceae, Bacteroidaceae, and Lachnospiraceae decreased; Alcaligenaceae, Sphingobacteriaceae, and Xanthomonadaceae of the skin increased in abundance, while Campylobacteraceae and Pseudomonadaceae decreased. Pechal et al. (2014) observed that Bacteroidaceae and Moraxellaceae were significant indicators during the initial sampling of three decomposing swines, while Bacillaceae and Clostridiales Incertae Sedis XI statistically significantly represented the communities on day 5 postmortem (advanced decay stage). Using Sprague—Dawley rats as decomposition models, Guo et al. (2016) suggested that the dominance of five specific genera in the mouth (*Myroides*, *Proteus*, *Streptococcus*, *Ignatzschineria*, and *Acinetobacter*) and six different others in the rectum (*Phascolarctobacterium*, *Ignatzschineria*, *Escherichia*, *Bacteroidales*, *Prevotella*, and *Proteus*) revealed obvious distinct trends during decomposition and could therefore suggest their potential to estimate PMI.

Several studies investigated the bacterial community structure and composition during decomposition using human corpses. For example, Hyde et al. (2013) found that the oral swab and scrape prebloat samples from the human corpse STAFS 2011-016 had statistically significant percentages of Firmicutes, Bacteriodetes, and Actinobacteria, while the end-bloat scrape sample was predominated by Firmicutes followed by Proteobacteria for the same human cadaver. For human cadaver STAFS 2011-006, the oral prebloat swab sample was predominated by Firmicutes, while the scrape sample was predominated by Proteobacteria, and the mouth end-bloat scrape was very similar to the prebloat mouth swab. In 2015, the same research team (Hyde et al., 2015) used two human cadavers again and found that Proteobacteria that dominated the skin and mouth samples decreased in abundance during the later phases of decomposition, with Firmicutes and Actinobacteria increasing. In contrast, Firmicutes and Bacteroidetes were the most abundant phyla in the fecal samples before purge with Proteobacteria predominant after purge until the drier phases when Firmicutes and Actinobacteria increased in abundance.

Similar to carcasses, bacterial communities in gravesoils showed significant temporal succession during, and as a result of, the decomposition process (e.g., Olakanye et al., 2014,2015,2017) (see also Chapter 7). Metcalf et al. (2013) found that Alphaproteobacteria abundance, mainly the Rhizobiales, increased with sampling time and became the most abundant soil phylum in the postrupture stage. Cobaugh et al. (2015) reported that Proteobacteria and Firmicutes increased and dominated the soil bacterial community composition with reduced Acidobacteria abundances during decomposition. In particular, Xanthomonadaceae, Caulobacteraceae, Sphingobacteriaceae, Aurantimonadaceae, and Sphingomonadaceae were the top five taxa whose abundances increased markedly in the soil just beneath decomposing cadavers. Finley et al. (2016) discovered that Rhodospirillales, Burkholderiales, and Lactobacillales had an overall increase in relative abundance for surface cadavers throughout decomposition timelines, while Rhizobiales and Chthoniobacterales decreased in relative abundance. In contrast, the buried cadaver soils maintained consistent compositions over a decomposition period of nearly a year. Weiss et al. (2016) found that the abundance of Candidatus, Chthoniobacteraceae, Gaiellaceae, Acidobacteria, and Rhodoplanes decreased during decomposition while Planococcaceae, Sporosarcina, Ignatzschineria, and Chitinophagaceae increased.

To build on these findings, Pechal et al. (2014) developed random forest models that used bacterial taxa to estimate physiological time—the time since placement of remains in the field—and proposed a framework of how epinecrotic bacterial community data could be used in casework (Fig. 5.1). Their findings identified four phyla (Bacteroidetes, Proteobacteria, Actinobacteria, Firmicutes) and seven families (Campylobacteraceae, Moraxellaceae, Aerococcaceae, Micrococcaceae, Clostridiales Incertae Sedis XI, Comamonadaceae, Fusobacteriaceae) as potentially important predictors of estimating physiological time.

Similarly, Metcalf et al. (2013) stated that microbial communities of the head skin can estimate PMI with errors as little as 3.30 ± 2.52 days (mean absolute error $\pm$ standard deviation) for a timeframe of 0–34 days. According to Metcalf et al. (2013), skin and soil microbial community data can be more informative for estimating PMI than the abdominal cavity. The researchers reached this conclusion in a study where the major microbial community changes corresponding to rupture occurred at different times for replicate corpses, which increased the PMI errors (about 8 days) and reduced the usefulness of abdominal data for PMI estimation. Furthermore, the research team (Metcalf et al., 2016) used microbial community dynamics data to demonstrate that PMI estimates with errors of about 2–3 days could be determined for the first 2 weeks of decomposition. Also two experiments both indicated that microbial community data derived from sequencing the 16S, 18S, and ITS genes performed similarly in PMI estimation and may be more highly informative in the earlier decomposition stages. Although the

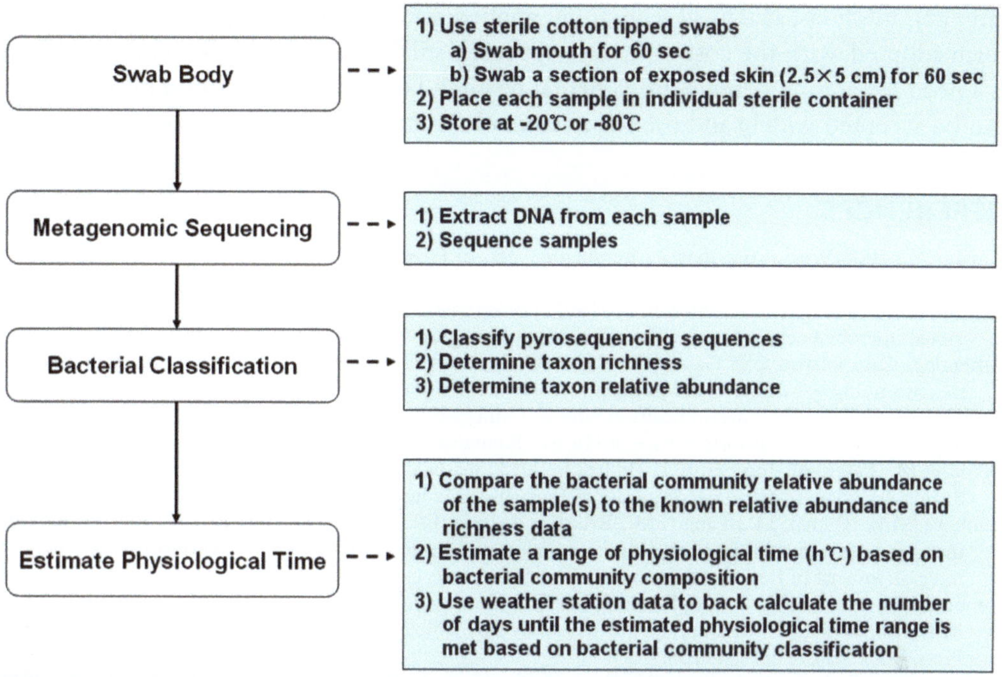

Figure 5.1 Framework for utilizing bacterial communities to estimate physiological time (Pechal et al., 2014).

improvement was not statistically significant, Metcalf et al. (2013) also stated that combining both 16S and 18S datasets resulted in the best estimates of PMI.

CONCLUSION

This chapter generally defined the necrobiome, identified the common organisms that constitute the necrobiome, and discussed the environmental factors that may influence necrobiome and the interactions between its constituent organisms. The development of bacterial identification techniques as applied to study the necrobiome was considered briefly. Finally, the ecological functions and forensic applications of decomposition-associated microbial—mainly bacterial—community dynamics were discussed. Overall, the chapter dedicated a considerable section to summarize the recent decay-associated microbiome studies that employed high-throughput NGS approaches in particular and aimed to estimate PMI accurately. Although numerous studies have highlighted the role of bacterial communities in PMI estimation, some obstacles remain for practical forensic use. In particular, considerable variations exist between investigations due to human cadaver and/or animal model used, environmental parameters/conditions, biotic factors, sampling methods, analytical techniques applied, and high-throughput sequencing platform adopted, with the cost of the last approach still largely prohibitive. Therefore there is a need for comprehensive fundamental research before bacterial community profiling can be accepted widely and used as a standard forensic tool for PMI estimation.

REFERENCES

Amann, R., 2000. Who is out there? Microbial Aspects of Diversity Systematic and Applied Microbiology 23 (1), 1–8.

Amann, R.I., Ludwig, W., Schleifer, K.H., 1995. Phylogenetic identification and in situ detection of individual microbial cells without cultivation. Microbiological Reviews 59 (1), 143–169.

Amendt, J., Campobasso, C.P., Gaudry, E., Reiter, C., LeBlanc, H.N., Hall, M.J., 2007. Best practice in forensic entomology—standards and guidelines. International Journal of Legal Medicine 121 (2), 90–104.

Bass, W.M., 1997. Outdoor decomposition rates in Tennessee. In: Haglund, W.D., Sorg, M.H. (Eds.), Forensic Taphonomy: The Postmortem Fate of Human Remains. CRC Press, Boca Raton, pp. 181–186.

Benbow, M., Lewis, A., Tomberlin, J., Pechal, J., 2013. Seasonal necrophagous insect community assembly during vertebrate carrion decomposition. Journal of Medical Entomology 50 (2), 440–450.

Benbow, M.E., Pechal, J.L., Lang, J.M., Erb, R., Wallace, J.R., 2015. The potential of high-throughput metagenomic sequencing of aquatic bacterial communities to estimate the postmortem submersion interval. Journal of Forensic Sciences 60 (6), 1500–1510.

Benbow, M.E., Pechal, J.L., Molar, R.M., 2016. Community and landscape ecology of carrion. In: Benbow, M.E., Tomberlin, J.K., Tarone, A.M. (Eds.), Carrion Ecology, Evolution, and Their Applications. CRC Press, Boca Raton, pp. 151–185.

Bizhang, M., Ellerbrock, B.I., Preza, D., Raab, W.H., Singh, P., Beikler, T., Henrich, B., Zimmer, S., 2011. Detection of nine microorganisms from the initial carious root lesions using a TaqMan-based real-time PCR. Oral Diseases 17 (7), 642–652.

Boer, W., Folman, L.B., Summerbell, R.C., Boddy, L., 2006. Living in a fungal world: impact of fungi on soil bacterial niche development. FEMS Microbiology Reviews 29 (4), 795–811.

Borneman, J., Triplett, E.W., 1997. Molecular microbial diversity in soils from eastern Amazonia: evidence for unusual microorganisms and microbial population shifts associated with deforestation. Applied and Environmental Microbiology 63 (7), 2647–2653.

Burkepile, D.E., Parker, J.D., Woodson, C.B., Mills, H.J., Kubanek, J., Sobecky, P.A., Hay, M.E., 2006. Chemically mediated competition between microbes and animals: microbes as consumers in food webs. Ecology 87 (11), 2821–2831.

Byrd, J., Castner, J., 2010. Forensic Entomology: The Utility of Arthropods in Legal Investigations. CRC Press, Boca Raton.

Cammack, J.A., Pimsler, M.L., Crippen, T.L., Tomberlin, J.K., 2016. Chemical ecology of vertebrate carrion. In: Benbow, M.E., Tomberlin, J.K., Tarone, A.M. (Eds.), Carrion Ecology, Evolution, and Their Applications. CRC Press, Boca Raton, pp. 187–203.

Campobasso, C.P., Introna, F., 2001. The forensic entomologist in the context of the forensic pathologist's role. Forensic Science International 120 (1), 132–139.

Campobasso, C.P., Vella, G.D., Introna, F., 2001. Factors affecting decomposition and Diptera colonization. Forensic Science International 120 (1–2), 18–27.

Carter, D.O., Metcalf, J.L., Bibat, A., Knight, R., 2015. Seasonal variation of postmortem microbial communities. Forensic Science, Medicine, and Pathology 11 (2), 202–207.

Carter, D.O., Yellowlees, D., Tibbett, M., 2007. Cadaver decomposition in terrestrial ecosystems. Die Naturwissenschaften 94 (1), 12–24.

Carvalho, L.M., Thyssen, P.J., Linhares, A.X., Palhares, F.A., 2000. A checklist of arthropods associated with pig carrion and human corpses in Southeastern Brazil. Memórias do Instituto Oswaldo Cruz 95 (1), 135–138.

Centeno, N., Maldonado, M., Oliva, A., 2002. Seasonal patterns of arthropods occurring on sheltered and unsheltered pig carcasses in Buenos Aires Province (Argentina). Forensic Science International 126 (1), 63–70.

Chun, L.P., Miguel, M.J., Junkins, E.N., Forbes, S.L., Carter, D.O., 2015. An initial investigation into the ecology of culturable aerobic postmortem bacteria. Science & Justice 55 (6), 394–401.
Clarridge III, J.E., 2004. Impact of 16S rRNA gene sequence analysis for identification of bacteria on clinical microbiology and infectious diseases. Clinical Microbiology Reviews 17 (4), 840–862.
Cobaugh, K.L., Schaeffer, S.M., DeBruyn, J.M., 2015. Functional and structural succession of soil microbial communities below decomposing human cadavers. PLoS One 10 (6), e0130201.
Coe, M., 1978. The decomposition of elephant carcasses in the Tsavo (East) National Park, Kenya. Journal of Arid Environments 1 (1), 71–86.
Crippen, T.L., Singh, B., 2015. Forensic and decomposition microbiology. In: Tomberlin, J.K., Benbow, M.E. (Eds.), Forensic Entomology International Dimensions and Frontiers. CRC Press, Boca Raton, pp. 249–262.
Damann, F.E., Carter, D.O., 2014. Human decomposition ecology and postmortem microbiology. In: Pokines, J.T., Symes, S.A. (Eds.), Manual of Forensic Taphonomy. CRC Press, Boca Raton, pp. 37–50.
Damann, F.E., Williams, D.E., Layton, A.C., 2015. Potential use of bacterial community succession in decaying human bone for estimating postmortem interval. Journal of Forensic Sciences 60 (4), 844–850.
Dekeirsschieter, J., Frederickx, C., Lognay, G., Brostaux, Y., Verheggen, F.J., Haubruge, E., 2013. Electrophysiological and behavioral responses of *Thanatophilus sinuatus* Fabricius (Coleoptera: Silphidae) to selected cadaveric volatile organic compounds. Journal of Forensic Sciences 58 (4), 917–923.
Denier, V.G., 1940. Carcass temperatures and their relation to winter blowfly populations and activity in the Southwest. Journal of Economic Entomology 33 (5), 166–170.
Dent, B.B., Forbes, S.L., Stuart, B.H., 2004. Review of human decomposition processes in soil. Environmental Geology 45 (4), 576–585.
DeVault, T.L., Brisbin, L.L., Rhodes, O.E., 2004. Factors influencing the acquisition of rodent carrion by vertebrate scavengers and decomposers. Canadian Journal of Zoology 82 (3), 502–509.
DeVault, T.L., Rhodes, O.E., 2002. Identification of vertebrate scavengers of small mammal carcasses in a forested landscape. Acta Theriologica 47 (2), 185–192.
DeVault, T.L., Rhodes, O.E., Shivik, J.A., 2003. Scavenging by vertebrates: behavioral, ecological, and evolutionary perspectives on an important energy transfer pathway in terrestrial ecosystems. Oikos 102 (2), 225–234.
Dickson, G.C., Poulter, R.T.M., Maas, E.W., Probert, P.K., Kieser, J.A., 2011. Marine bacterial succession as a potential indicator of postmortem submersion interval. Forensic Science International 209 (1), 1–10.
Dillon, L., 1995. Forensic Entomology: The Use of Insects in Death Investigations to Determine Elapsed Time since Death. Canadian Police Research Centre, Ottawa.
Donaldson, A.E., Lamont, I.L., 2013. Biochemistry changes that occur after death: potential markers for determining post-mortem interval. Plos One 8 (11), e82011.
Dymock, D., Weightman, A.J., Scully, C., Wade, W.G., 1996. Molecular analysis of microflora associated with dentoalveolar abscesses. Journal of Clinical Microbiology 34 (3), 537–542.
Elmas, I., Baslo, M.B., Ertas, M., Kaya, M., 2002. Compound muscle action potential analysis in different death models: significance for the estimation of early postmortem interval. Forensic Science International 127 (1), 75–81.
Finley, S.J., Benbow, M.E., Javan, G.T., 2015. Microbial communities associated with human decomposition and their potential use as postmortem clocks. International Journal of Legal Medicine 129 (3), 623–632.
Finley, S.J., Pechal, J.L., Benbow, M.E., Robertson, B.K., Javan, G.T., 2016. Microbial signatures of cadaver gravesoil during decomposition. Microbial Ecology 71 (3), 524–529.
Forbes, S.L., 2008. Decomposition chemistry in a burial environment. In: Tibbett, M., Carter, D.O. (Eds.), Soil Analysis in Forensic Taphonomy: Chemical and Biological Effects of Buried Human Remains. CRC Press, Boca Raton, pp. 203–224.
Forbes, S.L., Carter, D.O., 2016. Process and mechanisms of death and decomposition of vertebrate carrion. In: Benbow, M.E., Tomberlin, J.K., Tarone, A.M. (Eds.), Carrion Ecology, Evolution, and Rheir Applications. CRC Press, Boca Raton, pp. 13–30.
Forbes, S.L., Perrault, K.A., 2014. Decomposition odour profiling in the air and soil surrounding vertebrate carrion. PLoS One 9 (4), e95107.
Gibbs, J.P., Stanton, E.J., 2001. Habitat fragmentation and arthropod community change: carrion beetles, phoretic mites, and flies. Ecological Applications 11 (1), 79–85.

Guo, J., Fu, X., Liao, H., Hu, Z., Long, L., Yan, W., Ding, Y., Zha, L., Guo, Y., Yan, J., Chang, Y., 2016. Potential use of bacterial community succession for estimating post-mortem interval as revealed by high-throughput sequencing. Scientific Reports 6, 24197.
Haglund, W.D., 1997a. Dogs and coyotes: postmortem involvement with human remains. In: Haglund, W.D., Sorg, M.H. (Eds.), Forensic Taphonomy: The Post Mortem Fate of Human Remains. CRC Press, Boca Raton, pp. 367–379.
Haglund, W.D., 1997b. Rodents and human remains. In: Haglund, W.D., Sorg, M.H. (Eds.), Forensic Taphonomy: The Post Mortem Fate of Human Remains. CRC Press, Boca Raton, pp. 405–413.
Hansen, J., Lesnikova, I., Funder, A.M., Banner, J., 2014. DNA and RNA analysis of blood and muscle from bodies with variable postmortem intervals. Forensic Science, Medicine, and Pathology 10 (3), 322–328.
Hanski, I., Kuusela, S., 1977. An experiment on competition and diversity in the carrion fly community. Annales Entomologici Fennici 43, 108–115.
Hauther, K.A., Cobaugh, K.L., Jantz, L.M., Sparer, T.E., DeBruyn, J.M., 2015. Estimating time since death from postmortem human gut microbial communities. Journal of Forensic Sciences 60 (5), 1234–1240.
Hobischak, N.R., VanLaerhoven, S.L., Anderson, G.S., 2006. Successional patterns of diversity in insect fauna on carrion in sun and shade in the boreal forest region of Canada, near Edmonton, Alberta. The Canadian Entomologist 138 (3), 376–383.
Holmes, L.A., Vanlaerhoven, S.L., Tomberlin, J.K., 2012. Relative humidity effects on the life history of *Hermetia illucens* (Diptera: Stratiomyidae). Environmental Entomology 41 (4), 971–978.
Howard, G.T., Duos, B., Watson-Horzelski, E.J., 2010. Characterization of the soil microbial community associated with the decomposition of a swine carcass. International Biodeterioration & Biodegradation 64 (4), 300–304.
Human Microbiome Project Consortium, 2012. Structure, function and diversity of the healthy human microbiome. Nature 486 (7402), 207–214.
Hyde, E.R., Haarmann, D.P., Lynne, A.M., Bucheli, S.R., Petrosino, J.F., 2013. The living dead: bacterial community structure of a cadaver at the onset and end of the bloat stage of decomposition. PLoS One 8 (10), e77733.
Hyde, E.R., Haarmann, D.P., Petrosino, J.F., Lynne, A.M., Bucheli, S.R., 2015. Initial insights into bacterial succession during human decomposition. International Journal of Legal Medicine 129 (3), 661–671.
Janzen, D., 1977. Why fruits rot, seeds mold, and meat spoils. The American Naturalist 111 (980), 691–713.
Jenks, P.J., 1998. Sequencing microbial genomes—what will it do for microbiology? Journal of Medical Microbiology 47 (5), 375–382.
Kasper, J., Mumm, R., Ruther, J., 2012. The composition of carcass volatile profiles in relation to storage time and climate conditions. Forensic Science International 223 (1–3), 64–71 Ch7?.
Kelling, F.J., 2001. Olfaction in Houseflies: Morphology and Electrophysiology (PhD thesis). University of Groningen, Groningen.
Knipling, E.B., Sullivan, W.N., 1957. Insect mortality at low temperatures. Journal of Economic Entomology 50 (3), 368–369.
Kolbert, C.P., Persing, D.H., 1999. Ribosomal DNA sequencing as a tool for identification of bacterial pathogens. Current Opinion in Microbiology 2 (3), 299–305.
Lauber, C.L., Metcalf, J.L., Keepers, K., Ackermann, G., Carter, D.O., Knight, R., 2014. Vertebrate decomposition is accelerated by soil microbes. Applied and Environmental Microbiology 80 (16), 4920–4929.
LeBlanc, H.N., Logan, J.G., 2010. Exploiting insect olfaction in forensic entomology. In: Amendt, J., Goff, M.L., Campobasso, C.P., Grassberger, M. (Eds.), Current Concepts in Forensic Entomology. Springer, Dordrecht, pp. 205–221.
Ma, Q., Fonseca, A., Liu, W., Fields, A.T., Pimsler, M.L., Spindola, A.F., Tarone, A.M., Crippen, T.L., Tomberlin, J.K., Wood, T.K., 2012. *Proteus mirabilis* interkingdom swarming signals attract blow flies. The ISME Journal 6 (7), 1356–1366.
Mao, S., Fu, G., Seese, R.R., Wang, Z.Y., 2013. Estimation of PMI depends on the changes in ATP and its degradation products. Legal Medicine 15 (5), 235–238.
Melvin, J.R., Cronholm, L.S., Simson, L.R., Isaacs, A.M., 1984. Bacterial transmigration as an indicator of time of death. Journal of Forensic Science 29 (2), 412–417.

Metcalf, J.L., Parfrey, L.W., Gonzalez, A., Lauber, C.L., Knights, D., Ackermann, G., Humphrey, G.C., Gebert, M.J., Van Treuren, W., Berg-Lyons, D., Keepers, K., 2013. A microbial clock provides an accurate estimate of the postmortem interval in a mouse model system. Elife 2, e01104.

Metcalf, J.L., Xu, Z.Z., Weiss, S., Lax, S., Van Treuren, W., Hyde, E.R., Song, S.J., Amir, A., Larsen, P., Sangwan, N., Haarmann, D., 2016. Microbial community assembly and metabolic function during mammalian corpse decomposition. Science 351 (6269), 158–162.

Micozzi, M.S., 1997. Frozen environments and soft tissue preservation. In: Haglund, W.D., Sorg, M.H. (Eds.), Forensic Taphonomy: The Postmortem Fate of Human Remains. CRC Press, Boca Raton, pp. 171–180.

Mikami, H., Terazawa, K., Takatori, T., Tokudome, S., Tsukamoto, T., Haga, K., 1994. Estimation of time of death by quantification of melatonin in corpses. International Journal of Legal Medicine 107 (1), 42–51.

Mille-Lindblom, C., Fischer, H., Tranvik, L.J., 2006. Antagonism between bacteria and fungi: substrate competition and a possible tradeoff between fungal growth and tolerance towards bacteria. Oikos 113 (2), 233–242.

Mullens, B.A., Szijj, C.E., Hinkle, N.C., 2002. Oviposition and development of *Fannia* spp (Diptera: Muscidae) on poultry manure of low moisture levels. Environmental Entomology 31 (4), 588–593.

Mumcuoglu, K.Y., Miller, J., Mumcuoglu, M., Friger, M., Tarshis, M., 2001. Destruction of bacteria in the digestive tract of the maggot of *Lucilia sericata* (Diptera: Calliphoridae). Journal of Medical Entomology 38 (2), 161–166.

Muyzer, G., de Waal, E.C., Uitterlinden, A.G., 1993. Profiling of complex microbial populations by denaturing gradient gel electrophoresis analysis of polymerase chain reaction-amplified genes coding for 16S rRNA. Applied and Environmental Microbiology 59 (3), 695–700.

Norris, K.R., 1965. The bionomics of blow flies. Annual Review of Entomology 10, 47–68.

Olakanye, A.O., Nelson, A., Ralebitso-Senior, T.K., 2017. A comparative *in situ* decomposition study using still born piglets and leaf litter from a deciduous forest. Forensic Science International 276, 85–92.

Olakanye, A.O., Thompson, T., Ralebitso-Senior, T.K., 2014. Changes to soil bacterial profiles as a result of *Sus scrofa domesticus* decomposition. Forensic Science International 245, 101–106.

Olakanye, A.O., Thompson, T., Ralebitso-Senior, T.K., 2015. Shifts in soil biodiversity — a forensic comparison between *Sus scrofa domesticus* and vegetation decomposition. Science & Justice 55 (6), 402–407.

Paczkowski, S., Maibaum, F., Paczkowska, M., Schütz, S., 2012. Decaying mouse volatiles perceived by *Calliphora vicina* Rob.-Desv. Journal of Forensic Sciences 57 (6), 1497–1506.

Parkinson, R.A., Dias, K.R., Horswell, J., Greenwood, P., Banning, N., Tibbett, M., Vass, A.A., 2009. Microbial community analysis of human decomposition on soil. In: Ritz, K., Dawson, L.A., Miller, D. (Eds.), Criminal and Environmental Soil Forensics. Springer, New York, pp. 379–394.

Payne, J.A., 1965. A summer carrion study of the baby pig *Sus scrofa* Linnaeus. Ecology 46 (5), 592–602.

Pechal, J.L., Crippen, T.L., Benbow, M.E., Tarone, A.M., Dowd, S., Tomberlin, J.K., 2014. The potential use of bacterial community succession in forensics as described by high throughput metagenomic sequencing. International Journal of Legal Medicine 128 (1), 193–205.

Pechal, J.L., Crippen, T.L., Tarone, A.M., Lewis, A.J., Tomberlin, J.K., Benbow, M.E., 2013. Microbial community functional change during vertebrate carrion decomposition. Plos One 8 (11), e79035.

Petrosino, J.F., Highlander, S., Luna, R.A., Gibbs, R.A., Versalovic, J., 2009. Metagenomic pyrosequencing and microbial identification. Clinical Chemistry 55 (5), 856–866.

Reeves, M.A., 2009. Taphonomic effects of vulture scavenging. Journal of Forensic Sciences 54 (3), 523–528.

Rippley, A., Larison, N.C., Moss, K.E., Kelly, J.D., Bythermay, J.A., 2012. Scavenging behavior of *Lynx rufus* on human remains during the winter months of southeast Texas. Journal of Forensic Sciences 57 (3), 699–705.

Rochon, K., Lysyk, T.J., Selinger, L.B., 2004. Persistence of *Escherichia coli* in immature house fly and stable fly (Diptera: Muscidae) in relation to larval growth and survival. Journal of Medical Entomology 41 (6), 1082–1089.

Sampaio-Silva, F., Magalhães, T., Carvalho, F., Dinis-Oliveira, R.J., Silvestre, R., 2013. Profiling of RNA degradation for estimation of post morterm interval. PLoS One 8 (2), e56507.

Schabereiter-Gurtner, C., Maca, S., Rölleke, S., Nigl, K., Lukas, J., Hirschl, A., Lubitz, W., Barisani-Asenbauer, T., 2001. 16S rDNA-based identification of bacteria from conjunctival swabs by PCR and DGGE fingerprinting. Investigative Ophthalmology & Visual Science 42 (6), 1164–1171.

Schmidtmann, E.T., Martin, P.A., 1992. Relationship between selected bacteria and the growth of immature house flies, *Musca domestica*, in an axenic test system. Journal of Medical Entomology 29 (2), 232–235.

Sharanowski, B.J., Walker, E.G., Anderson, G.S., 2008. Insect succession and decomposition patterns on shaded and sunlit carrion in Saskatchewan in three different seasons. Forensic Science International 179 (2–3), 219–240.

Sherman, R.A., Hall, M.J.R., Thomas, S., 2000. Medicinal maggots: an ancient remedy for some contemporary afflictions. Annual Review of Entomology 45 (1), 55–81.

Shivik, J.A., 1999. Carrion, Context, and Lure Development: the Relative Importance of Sensory Modalities to Foraging Brown Treesnakes (*Bioga irregularis*) (PhD thesis). Colorado State University, Fort Collins.

Shivik, J.A., Clark, L., 1997. Carrion seeking in brown tree snakes: importance of olfactory and visual cues. Journal of Experimental Zoology 279 (6), 549–553.

Sigler, W.V., Crivii, S., Zeyer, J., 2002. Bacterial succession in glacial forefield soils characterized by community structure, activity and opportunistic growth dynamics. Microbial Ecology 44 (4), 306–316.

Sigler, W.V., Zeyer, J., 2002. Microbial diversity and activity along the forefields of two receding glaciers. Microbial Ecology 43 (4), 397–407.

Smith, K.G.V., 1986. A Manual of Forensic Entomology. Cornell University Press, New York.

Suau, A., Bonnet, R., Sutren, M., Godon, J.J., Gibson, G.R., Collins, M.D., Doré, J., 1999. Direct analysis of genes encoding 16S rRNA from complex communities reveals many novel molecular species within the human gut. Applied and Environmental Microbiology 65 (11), 4799–4807.

Spicka, A., Johnson, R., Bushing, J., Higley, L.G., Carter, D.O., 2011. Carcass mass can influence rate of decomposition and release of ninhydrin-reactive nitrogen. Forensic Science International 209 (1–3), 80–85.

Spradley, M.K., Hamilton, M.D., Giordano, A., 2012. Spatial patterning of vulture scavenged human remains. Forensic Science International 219 (1–3), 57–63.

Staley, J.T., Konopka, A., 1985. Measurement of *in situ* activities of nonphotosynthetic microorganisms in aquatic and terrestrial habitats. Annual Review of Microbiology 39 (1), 321–346.

Statheropoulos, M., Agapiou, A., Spiliopoulou, C., Pallis, G.C., Sianos, E., 2007. Environmental aspects of VOCs evolved in the early stages of human decomposition. Science of the Total Environment 385 (1), 221–227.

Statheropoulos, M., Spiliopoulou, C., Agapiou, A., 2005. A study of volatile organic compounds evolved from the decaying human body. Forensic Science International 153 (2), 147–155.

Suzuki, M.T., Taylor, L.T., DeLong, E.F., 2000. Quantitative analysis of small-subunit rRNA genes in mixed microbial populations via 5′-nuclease assays. Applied and Environmental Microbiology 66 (11), 4605–4614.

Tomberlin, J.K., Crippen, T.L., Tarone, A.M., Singh, B., Adams, K., Rezenom, Y.H., Benbow, M.E., Flores, M., Longnecker, M., Pechal, J.L., Russell, D.H., Beier, R.C., Wood, T.K., 2012. Interkingdom responses of flies to bacteria mediated by fly physiology and bacterial quorum sensing. Animal Behaviour 84 (6), 1449–1456.

Towne, E.G., 2000. Prairie vegetation and soil nutrient responses to ungulate carcasses. Oecologia 122 (2), 232–239.

Tuomisto, S., Karhunen, P.J., Pessi, T., 2013a. Time-dependent post mortem changes in the composition of intestinal bacteria using real-time quantitative PCR. Gut Pathogens 5 (1), 35.

Tuomisto, S., Karhunen, P.J., Vuento, R., Aittoniemi, J., Pessi, T., 2013b. Evaluation of postmortem bacterial migration using culturing and real-time quantitative PCR. Journal of Forensic Sciences 58 (4), 910–916.

Turnbaugh, P.J., Ley, R.E., Hamady, M., Fraser-Liggett, C.M., Knight, R., Gordon, J.I., 2007. The human microbiome project. Nature 449 (7164), 804–810.

Vass, A.A., 2001. Beyond the grave: understanding human decomposition. Microbiology Today 28, 190–192.

Vass, A.A., 2012. Odor mortis. Forensic Science International 222 (1), 234–241.

Vass, A.A., Eckenrode, B.A., Thompson, C.V., Wolf, D.A., Synstelien, J.A., Burnett, M.N., Dulgerian, N., Smith, R.R., 2004. Decompositional odor analysis database. Journal of Forensic Science 49 (4), 1–10.
Vass, A.A., Smith, R.R., Thompson, C.V., Burnett, M.N., Dulgerian, N., Eckenrode, B.A., 2008. Odor analysis of decomposing buried human remains. Journal of Forensic Sciences 53 (2), 384–391.
Watson, D.W., Martin, P.A., Schmidtmann, E.T., 1993. Egg yolk and bacteria growth medium for *Musca domestica* (Diptera: Muscidae). Journal of Medical Entomology 30, 820–823.
Weisburg, W.G., Barns, S.M., Pelletier, D.A., Lane, D.J., 1991. 16S ribosomal DNA amplification for phylogenetic study. Journal of Bacteriology 173 (2), 697–703.
Weiss, S., Carter, D.O., Metcalf, J.L., Knight, R., 2016. Carcass mass has little influence on the structure of gravesoil microbial communities. International Journal of Legal Medicine 130 (1), 253–263.
Wolff, M., Uribe, A., Ortiz, A., Duque, P., 2001. A preliminary study of forensic entomology in Medellin, Colombia. Forensic Science International 120 (1–2), 53–59.
Woese, C.R., Fox, G.E., 1977. Phylogenetic structure of the prokaryotic domain: the primary kingdoms. Proceedings of the National Academy of Sciences of the United States of America 74 (11), 5088–5090.
Zhang, L., Guo, J.J., Peng, Y.L., Xie, D., Guo, Y.D., Yan, J., Zha, L., Cai, J.F., 2016. Bacterial succession on rat carcasses and applications for PMI estimation. Fa Yi Xue Za Zhi 32 (1), 1–6.
Zhou, C., Byard, R.W., 2011. Factors and processes causing accelerated decomposition in human cadavers—an overview. Journal of Forensic and Legal Medicine 18 (1), 6–9.
Zurek, L., Schal, C., Watson, D.W., 2000. Diversity and contribution of the intestinal bacterial community to the development of *Musca domestica* (Diptera: Muscidae) larvae. Journal of Medical Entomology 37 (6), 924–928.

CHAPTER 6

What Is the "Thanatomicrobiome" and What Is Its Relevance to Forensic Investigations?

Gulnaz T. Javan, Sheree J. Finley
Alabama State University, Montgomery, AL, United States

THE HUMAN THANATOMICROBIOME

The human thanatomicrobiome is an original term introduced by Gulnaz Javan in 2014 at the 66th Annual Meeting of the American Academy of Forensic Sciences in Seattle, Washington. The thanatomicrobiome (*thanatos*—Greek for death) is characterized by a diverse assortment of microorganisms located in internal organs (brain, heart, liver, and spleen) and blood samples collected after a human dies. It is defined as the microbial community of internal body sites, created by a successional process whereby trillions of microorganisms populate, proliferate, and/or die within the dead body, resulting in temporal modifications in the community composition over time (Javan et al., 2016a, 2016b). Studies have reported that identifying and characterizing the fluctuations in the relative abundances of corpse microorganisms during decomposition has tremendous applicability for estimating postmortem interval (PMI) (Metcalf et al., 2013; Pechal et al., 2014; Damann et al., 2015). Conventional methods of determining PMI include concurrence methods (e.g., stomach contents) and rate (e.g., *algor*, *livor*, and *rigor mortis*). These methods often do not provide definitive answers, which consequently lead forensic investigators to subjective conclusions. In contrast, thanatomicrobiome studies assume that as a human body decays, time-dependent changes in the microbial communities within its internal organs are also predictive of the time of death (Can et al., 2014) (Table 6.1).

There is recent emphasis on elucidating the mechanisms of the thanatomicrobiome (microbiome of death), thanatotranscriptome (mRNA abundances of death), and thanatophagy (autophagy of death) in internal organs (brain, heart, liver, spleen) and blood from criminal and noncriminal cadavers. In the last century, forensic microbiology in criminal investigations emerged in postmortem studies with the potential to determine the correlation between ecological succession in an entire microbial community and cause of death. The ability to quantify the numbers and types of microbes within a human thanatomicrobiome is fundamental in understanding the structure and function of the macroecosystem of a dead body. Historically, there were considerable limitations

Forensic Ecogenomics
ISBN 978-0-12-809360-3
http://dx.doi.org/10.1016/B978-0-12-809360-3.00006-0

Table 6.1 Select thanatomicrobiome studies using human specimens

Cases	Specimen(s)	Detection/sequencing platform(s)	Microbiological finding(s)	References
27 criminal cadavers	Internal organs (brain, heart, liver, and spleen), buccal cavities, and/or blood	Illumina MiSeq	Cadaver thanatomicrobiomes demonstrated statistically significant succession related to time, organ, and sex	Javan et al. (2016b)
12 willed-donation cadavers	Proximal large intestine	qPCR	*Bacteroides* and *Lactobacillus* can be used as quantitative markers of PMI	Hauther et al. (2015)
12 willed-donation cadavers	Lower rib	Roche GS-FLX Titanium pyrosequencing	99.2% of sequences were from six bacterial phyla: Proteobacteria, Firmicutes, Bacteroidetes, Actinobacteria, Acidobacteria, and Chloroflexi	Damann et al. (2015)
11 criminal cadavers	Internal organs (brain, heart, liver, spleen) and blood	Roche 454-FLX-Titanium pyrosequencing	Anaerobic *Clostridium* spp. and *Lactobacillus* sp. were the predominant bacteria	Can et al. (2014)
2 willed-donation cadavers	Mouth, gastrointestinal tract, and general body cavity (2013); mouth, skin, and rectum (2015)	Roche 454-FLX-Titanium pyrosequencing	A significant percentage of Firmicutes, Bacteriodetes, and Actinobacteria were detected. A marked shift from aerobic to anaerobic bacteria in all tissues	Hyde et al. (2013) and Hyde et al. (2015)
33 criminal cadavers	Blood, liver, portal vein, mesenteric lymph node, and pericardial fluid	Bacterial culturing and RT-qPCR	21 bacteria genera were detected. The five most abundant species were: *Staphylococcus* sp., *Streptococcus* sp., *Clostridium* sp., *Enterococcus* sp., and *Escherichia* sp.	Tuomisto et al. (2013)

The cases, examined specimen(s), detection/sequencing platform(s), and microbiological finding(s) for selected postmortem microbiome studies. *PMI*, Postmortem interval; *qPCR*, quantitative polymerase chain reaction; *RT-qPCR*, real-time quantitative PCR.
Adapted from Javan, G.T., Finley, S.J., Can, I., Wilkinson, J.E., Hanson, J.D., Tarone, A.M., 2016b. Human Thanatomicrobiome succession and time since death. Scientific Reports 6.

in investigating the roles that microorganisms play in the decomposition of human remains because microbial populations are on an infinitesimal spatial scale far below human perception. Also previous sequencing technologies were limited to microbial taxa that could be recovered and studied using traditional cultivating techniques. Nevertheless, with the expanded use of high-throughput next-generation DNA sequencing, these limitations are steadily declining.

The human thanatomicrobiome consists of bacterial, eukaryotic, and fungal microorganisms (Fig. 6.1) and is supported by the genes and functional proteins of the associated microbiome. The same research techniques that enabled the study of the antemortem microbial communities in healthy adults can be used to characterize the signatures of the thanatomicrobiome of decaying bodies. Currently, the most common method for taxonomic evaluations of thanatomicrobiome community signatures is the use of microbial housekeeping genes. The prevailing paradigm of the current platforms involves cataloguing of the metagenomic inventory of the total number of operational taxonomic units (OTUs) of 16S (prokaryotic) and/or 18S (eukaryotic) rRNA genes (Wooley and Ye, 2010) and the internal transcribed spacer (fungal). These genes are amplified and sequenced separately using the appropriate universal primers and have produced reliable identification of microbes at the genus and species levels. For example, an analysis of the collective results of 16S rRNA gene sequencing data demonstrated a genus identification of greater than 90% in most cases and species identification as high as 83% (Janda and Abbott, 2007).

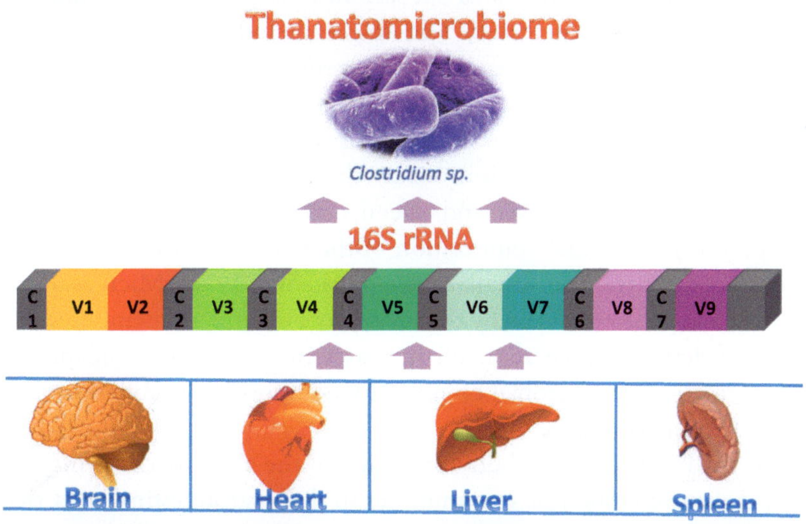

Figure 6.1 The components of the human thanatomicrobiome include the microbiomes of internal body sites (brain, heart, liver, and spleen) and blood of cadavers.

The 16S rRNA gene is the most widely used genetic marker for profiling prokaryotic communities (Woese et al., 1990; Baker et al., 2003; Tringe and Hugenholtz, 2008 Wang and Qian, 2009). Next-generation sequencing platforms include polymerase chain reaction (PCR)-based 454 GS FLX (Roche), HiSeq and MiSeq (Illumina), SOLiDv4 (Applied Biosystems), and Ion PGM (Life Technologies). Emerging "third"-generation sequencing technologies that read the 16S rRNA gene include single molecule, real-time (PacBio) (Schloss et al., 2016) and MinION (Oxford Nanopore) (Shin et al., 2016) platforms. The use of bacterial OTUs produced by the 16S rRNA gene from postmortem internal organ tissues is not always straightforward and has the potential to produce spurious reads that handicap efforts to ascertain microbial diversity. For example, OTU analysis is subject to sample clustering by sequencing depth. In such cases, the raw files are assembled, quality filtered, demultiplexed, and analyzed using the default settings in QIIME (Caporaso et al., 2010). The 16S rRNA gene sequencing techniques are not without limitations that are generally created by various sources of biases and errors (Janda and Abbott, 2007). Features such as the number of 16S rRNA copy variations (Klappenbach et al., 2000) and PCR primer selection and cycling artifacts potentially lead to exaggerated diversity estimates and reduce the strength of sequencing and bioinformatic analyses (Schloss et al., 2011). Nevertheless, innovative bioinformatics models have demonstrated the feasibility of sampling the microbiome of death (Javan et al., 2016b). Consequently, the aim of many thanatomicrobiomic decomposition studies is to document microbial successional patterns to produce very reliable means to estimate PMI (Maujean et al., 2013; Metcalf et al., 2013; Can et al., 2014; Pechal et al., 2014; Hauther et al., 2015; Javan et al., 2016b).

To understand the role of microbial succession during decomposition, the stages of decomposition should be elucidated. The stages include six different phases: fresh, bloated, active decay, advanced decay, dry, and remains (Payne, 1965). The fresh stage commences approximately 3–7 min after death (Gunn and Pitt, 2012). This stage is characterized by changes in the color of the tissues and continues until the remains begin to bloat. Microbial proliferation occurs throughout the body beginning in the ileocecal area, spreading to the liver and spleen, and continuing to the heart and brain (Akutsu et al., 2012). Microbial colonization of the ileocecal area occurs by invasion of capillaries of the lymphatic and vascular system (Noriko, 1995). Microbial proliferation also occurs in the respiratory system by the invasion of the mucus membranes (Giampaoli et al., 2012). Yet despite information on increases in microbial abundances, there is a paucity of information on microbial community composition in different organs of the human body after a person dies.

Bloating is the inflation of the body that starts in the abdomen. It is mediated by the multitude of thanatomicrobiomic communities in the gastrointestinal tract that ferment the cellular by-products by respiration, which produces hydrogen sulfide, methane, cadaverine, and putrescine. Active decay follows bloating and after 7–12 days postmortem, the active decay phase starts with a predominance of bacteria such as Proteobacteria and Firmicutes. Advanced decay is characterized by a decrease in entomological activity as the resource is consumed (Hewadikaram and Goff, 1991; Tomberlin et al., 2011). The remnant of the corpse includes bones, dry skin, and hair, and their decomposition constitutes the dry and remains stages.

Overall, the stages overlap because the decomposition process is a continuum rather than a series of discrete exclusive steps, and their determination is subject to the forensic investigator (Schoenly and Reid, 1987). Also, the stages are not relegated to a specific length of time due to several abiotic and biotic factors. The degree of decomposition varies from individual to individual and also differs in different body organs (Rodriguez, 1997). For example, the major difference in the rates of decay for aboveground versus belowground decomposition is the inaccessibility of the body to scavengers and arthropod decomposers and their microbes.

The microbial composition and abundance in internal organ tissues are dependent on temperature and time of death since bacteria have different growth optima (Ercolini et al., 2009) and different abilities to uptake and utilize nutrients (Deutscher, 2008). These components affect the succession of microbial species with time. For example, a cadaver of an aged adult human generally contains more microorganisms and decays more rapidly than a fetus or newborn, contingent upon the medications and disease state of the elderly adult (Campobasso et al., 2001). Discovering the trajectories and mechanisms regulating postmortem microbial succession is fundamental in hypothesizing the microbial responses to death and forecasting the microbes' future conditions. Microbial succession can vary between days to decades depending on variations in ecosystems, natural conditions, and perturbations. Putrefaction creates a nutrient-rich environment that generates perturbations to produce a domino effect through a microbial community that is hard to predict (Lemon et al., 2012).

THANATOMICROBIOME RESEARCH FINDINGS

Thanatomicrobiomic research involves cadavers obtained through donation (Hyde et al., 2013, 2015) or from autopsies (Tuomisto et al., 2013, 2014; Can et al., 2014; Javan et al., 2016b). Research has shown that the optimal sampling sites for studying the thanatomicrobiome are the liver (Tuomisto et al., 2013; Can et al., 2014; Javan et al., 2016b and pericardial fluids (Tuomisto et al., 2013). Specimens from both of these sites are predominantly microbe free for up to 5 day after death as reported by Tuomisto et al. (2013). This conclusion was determined from an investigation of 33 autopsied cadavers from criminal cases at the University of Tampere using bacterial culturing and real-time quantitative PCR (RT-qPCR). Overall, 21 bacterial genera were detected in different specimens that included blood, liver, portal vein, mesenteric lymph node, and pericardial fluid. The most abundant bacteria were *Staphylococcus* sp., *Streptococcus* sp., *Clostridium* sp., *Enterococcus* sp., and *Escherichia* sp.

Hyde et al. (2013) investigated thanatomicrobiomic signatures using corpses obtained through willed-body donations in outdoor research laboratory experiments performed at the Southeast Texas Applied Forensic Science Facility at Sam Houston State University. In this study, Roche 454 pyrosequencing of scrapings from the mouth, gastrointestinal tract, and general body cavity of two humans decomposing in a natural setting were analyzed. The cadavers were assessed using a point-based scoring method based on the presence of specific qualitative observations of decomposition in three portions of the body. A summation of the scores provided a total body score that correlated to an estimated postmortem stage. The results demonstrated that there was a marked shift from aerobic to anaerobic bacteria in the tissue samples. The studies also concluded that there were community signature variations within each individual cadaver and between different cadavers. Additionally, there were detectable variations between the microbial diversity at the start and ending of the bloat stage for specific cadaver sampling sites. The predominant bacteria detected in the samples were Firmicutes, Bacteriodetes, and Actinobacteria.

A noteworthy report provided significant findings using 16S rRNA gene amplicon sequencing to characterize the human thanatomicrobiome. The exploratory feasibility study, which was performed by Can et al. (2014) and used criminal cadavers, aimed to establish the best methodology for extracting and sequencing thanatomicrobiome DNA. The objectives of the Can et al. (2014) thanatomicrobiome study were to: (1) determine the best technique for extracting DNA from organ tissues (i.e., brain, heart, liver, and spleen) and blood, and (2) demonstrate the feasibility or efficacy of the technique to survey the thanatomicrobiome. Autopsies were performed within 20–240 h after death with thanatomicrobiome profiling conducted using Roche 454 pyrosequencing. The traditional phenol-chloroform method of extracting DNA proved to be superior to the heating-thawing approach. This study produced several other findings. First, the thanatomicrobiome was similar among organ tissues from the same cadaver but dissimilar between other cadavers. These differences across individuals were attributed to differentiation between time elapsed since death and/or various abiotic and biotic environmental factors. Secondly, the majority of the microbes present in the cadavers with different PMIs were the obligate anaerobe *Clostridium* sp. in those with the longest PMIs, while facultative anaerobes such as *Lactobacillus* spp. predominated in cadavers with short PMIs. A study by Hauther et al. (2015) showed that *Lactobacillus* was also prominent in an RT-qPCR thanatomicrobiome study of the proximal large intestines of 12 decaying human cadavers.

A study by Damann et al. (2015), which was conducted at the University of Texas Anthropological Research Facility and assessed the bones of 12 decaying corpses in the advanced to the dry skeletal remains stages, revealed that the diversity of the bone microbiome resembled that of related soil microbial communities at skeletonization. Similar to the results by Hyde et al. (2013), this study demonstrated that Firmicutes, Bacteriodetes,

Actinobacteria, Proteobacteria, Acidobacteria, and Chloroflexi were the most predominant bacteria in 99.2% of the sequences.

Another thanatomicrobiome study (Javan et al., 2016b) analyzed 27 human corpses involved in actual criminal investigations with PMIs ranging from 3.5 to 240 h. A total of 66 specimens including blood, buccal cavity, brain, heart, liver, and spleen were collected during autopsies. The PMIs were established from official daily crime logs generated and certified by local police departments in Alabama and Florida. A finding of particular interest was the incidence of a *Pseudomonas* sp. that was detected exclusively in female cadavers, which contrasted a *Rothia* sp. found only in a male cadaver. These results are expected to provide potentially substantial insight into the postmortem differentiation between sexes since *Rothia* sp. is one of most abundant metagenomically identified species in the buccal mucosa and tongue dorsum of the Human Microbiome Project (HMP) cohort of healthy adults (Human Microbiome Project Consortium, 2012).

APPLICATIONS OF MICROBIAL FORENSICS

Forensic microbiology is important because it incorporates knowledge from both theoretical and practical microbiology and forensic autopsy. Fundamentally, the following three issues are interrelated in the study of microbial forensics: (1) risks associated with infection of personnel conducting the forensic autopsies; (2) implications of an infectious pathogen as the underlying cause of death; and (3) investigations to determine causes of infant deaths. Although crime scene applications have yet to be fully implemented, recent human postmortem microbiome studies have provided exciting and highly promising potential for the determination of time and cause of death.

The HMP created an unparalleled data set that demonstrated that humans and their commensal microorganisms have coevolved to produce a microbiome that, upon death, is converted to the microbiome of death. It is important to note that before humans are born, they are essentially "microbial cell free" (Ford, 1901). Using traditional culture methods, Fredette (1916) discovered that 65% of dissected internal organs were sterile. As the PMIs extended, the proportion of cases that were positive for the presence of microorganisms increased. HMP data resulted in a paradigm shift in our comprehension of the number and types of cells in humans. Researchers now estimate that a healthy adult body contains approximately 10 trillion human cells, but as many as 10–100 trillion microbial cells depending on the body location (Turnbaugh et al., 2007; Sender et al., 2016). Moreover, humans are born with more than 20,000 genes (Clamp et al., 2007) that increase during life to a putative 1 million at death (Human Microbiome Project Consortium, 2012), which are attributable to the integration and proliferation of microorganisms as part of the normal flora.

Upon death, the percentage of microbial cells in a human body upsurges as microorganisms proliferate in the internal organs due to the cessation of the immune system and a massive release of nutrients from human cells that lose membrane integrity. After death, the environment changes in the host due to the autolysis of cells and release of cellular components to the peripheral tissues (Gevers, 1975; Proskuryakov et al., 2003; Paczkowski and Schütz, 2011). Comprehensively, these changes lead to substantial proliferation of various types of microorganisms and the inactivity and/or death of others. The microbes discovered in internal organs conceivably originated from communities directly associated with putrefaction. Morris et al. (2006) asserted that postmortem translocation of microorganisms does not affect results if specimens are collected shortly after death (i.e., 15–48 h) or if the body is promptly stored at 4°C prior to autopsy. The thanatomicrobiome signatures in the largest and most diverse internal organ, which is the liver, will significantly contribute to practical forensic applications. The diversity of the liver is potentially caused by: (1) nearby stomach acids, pancreatic enzymes, and gallbladder fluids that initiate putrefaction and produce immediate autolysis that extends to the liver; (2) the liver receives blood high in nutrients from the hepatic portal venous system; and (3) the liver is the largest internal organ in the human body (1.4–1.8 kg) and all metabolism occurs in this vital organ (Sibulesky, 2013).

HUMAN POSTMORTEM MICROBIOME PROJECT

The Human Postmortem Microbiome Project (HPMP), which is analogous to the HMP, is an initiative with the goal of identifying and characterizing the thanatomicrobiome (internal body sites), epinecrotic communities (i.e., epithelial tissues, body cavities, and the alimentary canal), necrobiome (all micro- and macroorganisms involved in decomposition), and soil microbial communities found in association with decomposing humans (Javan et al., 2016a,b) (Fig. 6.2). The HPMP will facilitate the development of experimental modus operandi used to empower data comparisons obtained from different international laboratories and thousands of cadavers. To unify the global research communities, the HPMP will aid in extending existing data, which will encompass sampling, processing, sequencing, and bioinformatics analysis. Consequently, it will potentially establish a universal standard for postmortem microbial signature analysis. The HPMP will provide awareness within the broader scientific community of the opportunity to have existing and future decomposition samples processed using standard protocols developed by HPMP collaborators and contributors. The realization of the HPMP will provide a scientific forum for information and knowledge exchange between individual postmortem microbiology studies. Ultimately, concerted efforts toward standardized methods and protocols such as suggested by the Earth Microbiome Project (Gilbert et al., 2010) and HMP can be executed. Through collaborative efforts from forensic researchers and investigators to improve, validate, and standardize protocols, a framework for applicable tools for human postmortem microbiomic studies will advance the comprehension of the roles that microorganisms play in human decomposition.

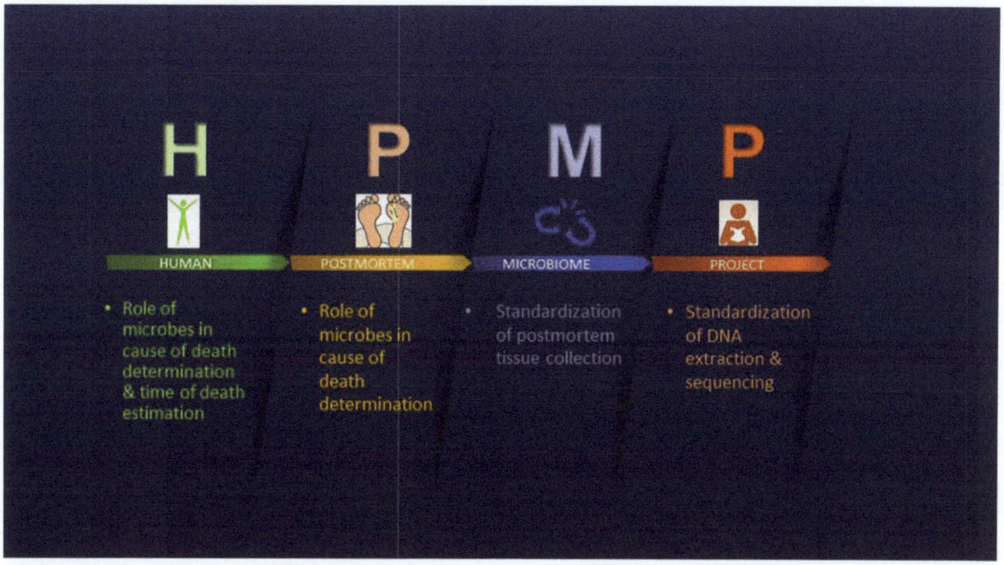

Figure 6.2 The Human Postmortem Microbiome Project (HPMP) will cultivate forensic and criminal investigative tools and databases for the law enforcement and forensic research communities. The HPMP will be the largest catalogue of sequencing and bioinformatics data of relevant microorganisms associated with internal organs, blood, skin, etc. and cadaver soil associated with human decomposition.

ACKNOWLEDGMENTS

This work was supported by the National Science Foundation (NSF) grant HRD 1401075 and Forensic Sciences Foundation Lucas Research Grant.

REFERENCES

Akutsu, T., Motani, H., Watanabe, K., Iwase, H., Sakurada, K., 2012. Detection of bacterial 16S ribosomal RNA genes for forensic identification of vaginal fluid. Legal Medicine 14 (3), 160–162.

Baker, G.C., Smith, J.J., Cowan, D.A., 2003. Review and re-analysis of domain-specific 16S primers. Journal of Microbiological Methods 55 (3), 541–555.

Campobasso, C.P., Di Vella, G., Introna, F., 2001. Factors affecting decomposition and Diptera colonization. Forensic Science International 120 (1), 18–27.

Can, I., Javan, G.T., Pozhitkov, A.E., Noble, P.A., 2014. Distinctive thanatomicrobiome signatures found in the blood and internal organs of humans. Journal of Microbiological Methods 106, 1–7.

Caporaso, J.G., Kuczynski, J., Stombaugh, J., Bittinger, K., Bushman, F.D., Costello, E.K., Fierer, N., Pena, A.G., Goodrich, J.K., Gordon, J.I., Huttley, G.A., 2010. QIIME allows analysis of high-throughput community sequencing data. Nature Methods 7 (5), 335–336.

Clamp, M., Fry, B., Kamal, M., Xie, X., Cuff, J., Lin, M.F., Kellis, M., Lindblad-Toh, K., Lander, E.S., 2007. Distinguishing protein-coding and noncoding genes in the human genome. Proceedings of the National Academy of Sciences 104 (49), 19428–19433.

Damann, F.E., Williams, D.E., Layton, A.C., 2015. Potential use of bacterial community succession in decaying human bone for estimating postmortem interval. Journal of Forensic Sciences 60 (4), 844–850.

Deutscher, J., 2008. The mechanisms of carbon catabolite repression in bacteria. Current Opinion in Microbiology 11 (2), 87–93.

Ercolini, D., Russo, F., Nasi, A., Ferranti, P., Villani, F., 2009. Mesophilic and psychrotrophic bacteria from meat and their spoilage potential *in vitro* and in beef. Applied and Environmental Microbiology 75 (7), 1990–2001.

Ford, W.W., 1901. On the bacteriology of normal organs. Parasitology 1 (02), 277–284.

Fredette, J.W., 1916. Bacteriemias in the agonal period. The Journal of Laboratory and Clinical Medicine 2 (3), 180–188.

Gevers, W., 1975. Biochemical aspects of cell death. Forensic Science 6 (1), 25–29.

Giampaoli, S., Berti, A., Valeriani, F., Gianfranceschi, G., Piccolella, A., Buggiotti, L., Rapone, C., Valentini, A., Ripani, L., Spica, V.R., 2012. Molecular identification of vaginal fluid by microbial signature. Forensic Science International: Genetics 6 (5), 559–564.

Gilbert, J.A., Meyer, F., Antonopoulos, D., Balaji, P., Brown, C.T., Brown, C.T., Desai, N., Eisen, J.A., Evers, D., Field, D., Feng, W., 2010. Meeting report: the terabase metagenomics workshop and the vision of an Earth microbiome project. Standards in Genomic 3 (3), 243.

Gunn, A., Pitt, S.J., 2012. Microbes as forensic indicators. Tropical Biomedicine 29, 311–330.

Hauther, K.A., Cobaugh, K.L., Jantz, L.M., Sparer, T.E., DeBruyn, J.M., 2015. Estimating time since death from postmortem human gut microbial communities. Journal of Forensic Sciences 60 (5), 1234–1240.

Hewadikaram, K.A., Goff, M.L., 1991. Effect of carcass size on rate of decomposition and arthropod succession patterns. The American Journal of Forensic Medicine and Pathology 12 (3), 235–240.

Human Microbiome Project Consortium, 2012. A framework for human microbiome research. Nature 486 (7402), 215–221.

Hyde, E.R., Haarmann, D.P., Lynne, A.M., Bucheli, S.R., Petrosino, J.F., 2013. The living dead: bacterial community structure of a cadaver at the onset and end of the bloat stage of decomposition. PLoS One 8 (10), e77733.

Hyde, E.R., Haarmann, D.P., Petrosino, J.F., Lynne, A.M., Bucheli, S.R., 2015. Initial insights into bacterial succession during human decomposition. International Journal of Legal Medicine 129 (3), 661–671.

Janda, J.M., Abbott, S.L., 2007. 16S rRNA gene sequencing for bacterial identification in the diagnostic laboratory: pluses, perils, and pitfalls. Journal of Clinical Microbiology 45 (9), 2761–2764.

Javan, G.T., Finley, S.J., Abidin, Z., Mulle, J.G., 2016a. The thanatomicrobiome: a missing piece of the microbial puzzle of death. Frontiers in Microbiology 7.

Javan, G.T., Finley, S.J., Can, I., Wilkinson, J.E., Hanson, J.D., Tarone, A.M., 2016b. Human Thanatomicrobiome succession and time since death. Scientific Reports 6.

Klappenbach, J.A., Dunbar, J.M., Schmidt, T.M., 2000. rRNA operon copy number reflects ecological strategies of bacteria. Applied and Environmental Microbiology 66 (4), 1328–1333.

Lemon, K.P., Armitage, G.C., Relman, D.A., Fischbach, M.A., 2012. Microbiota-targeted therapies: an ecological perspective. Science Translational Medicine 4 (137), 137rv5.

Maujean, G., Guinet, T., Fanton, L., Malicier, D., 2013. The interest of postmortem bacteriology in putrefied bodies. Journal of Forensic Sciences 58 (4), 1069–1070.

Metcalf, J.L., Parfrey, L.W., Gonzalez, A., Lauber, C.L., Knights, D., Ackermann, G., Humphrey, G.C., Gebert, M.J., Van Treuren, W., Berg-Lyons, D., Keepers, K., 2013. A microbial clock provides an accurate estimate of the postmortem interval in a mouse model system. Elife 2, e01104.

Morris, J.A., Harrison, L.M., Partridge, S.M., 2006. Postmortem bacteriology: a re-evaluation. Journal of Clinical Pathology 59 (1), 1–9.

Noriko, T., 1995. Immunohistochemical studies on postmortem lividity. Forensic Science International 72 (3), 179–189.

Paczkowski, S., Schütz, S., 2011. Post-mortem volatiles of vertebrate tissue. Applied Microbiology and Biotechnology 91 (4), 917–935.

Payne, J.A., 1965. A summer carrion study of the baby pig *Sus scrofa* Linnaeus. Ecology 46 (5), 592–602.

Pechal, J.L., Crippen, T.L., Benbow, M.E., Tarone, A.M., Dowd, S., Tomberlin, J.K., 2014. The potential use of bacterial community succession in forensics as described by high throughput metagenomic sequencing. International Journal of Legal Medicine 128 (1), 193–205.

Proskuryakov, S.Y., Konoplyannikov, A.G., Gabai, V.L., 2003. Necrosis: a specific form of programmed cell death? Experimental Cell Research 283 (1), 1–16.

Rodriguez, W.C., 1997. Decomposition of buried and submerged bodies. In: Haglund, W.D., Sorg, M.H. (Eds.), Forensic Taphonomy: The Postmortem Fate of Human Remains. CRC Press, Boca Raton, USA, pp. 459–468.

Sender, R., Fuchs, S., Milo, R., 2016. Are we really vastly outnumbered? Revisiting the ratio of bacterial to host cells in humans. Cell 164 (3), 337–340.

Schloss, P.D., Gevers, D., Westcott, S.L., 2011. Reducing the effects of PCR amplification and sequencing artifacts on 16S rRNA-based studies. PLoS One 6 (12), e27310.

Schloss, P.D., Jenior, M.L., Koumpouras, C.C., Westcott, S.L., Highlander, S.K., 2016. Sequencing 16S rRNA gene fragments using the PacBio SMRT DNA sequencing system. PeerJ 4, e1869.

Schoenly, K., Reid, W., 1987. Dynamics of heterotrophic succession in carrion arthropod assemblages: discrete seres or a continuum of change? Oecologia 73 (2), 192–202.

Sibulesky, L., 2013. Normal liver anatomy. Clinical Liver Disease 2 (S1).

Shin, J., Lee, S., Go, M.J., Lee, S.Y., Kim, S.C., Lee, C.H., Cho, B.K., 2016. Analysis of the mouse gut microbiome using full-length 16S rRNA amplicon sequencing. Scientific Reports 6 ahead-of-print.

Tomberlin, J.K., Mohr, R., Benbow, M.E., Tarone, A.M., VanLaerhoven, S., 2011. A roadmap for bridging basic and applied research in forensic entomology. Annual Review of Entomology 56, 401–421.

Tringe, S.G., Hugenholtz, P., 2008. A renaissance for the pioneering 16S rRNA gene. Current Opinion in Microbiology 11 (5), 442–446.

Tuomisto, S., Karhunen, P.J., Vuento, R., Aittoniemi, J., Pessi, T., 2013. Evaluation of postmortem bacterial migration using culturing and realtime quantitative PCR. Journal of Forensic Sciences 58 (4), 910–916.

Tuomisto, S., Pessi, T., Collin, P., Vuento, R., Aittoniemi, J., Karhunen, P.J., 2014. Changes in gut bacterial populations and their translocation into liver and ascites in alcoholic liver cirrhotics. BMC Gastroenterology 14 (1), 1.

Turnbaugh, P.J., Ley, R.E., Hamady, M., Fraser-Liggett, C., Knight, R., Gordon, J.I., 2007. The human microbiome project: exploring the microbial part of ourselves in a changing world. Nature 449 (7164), 804.

Wang, Y., Qian, P.Y., 2009. Conservative fragments in bacterial 16S rRNA genes and primer design for 16S ribosomal DNA amplicons in metagenomic studies. PLoS One 4 (10), e7401. http://dx.doi.org/10.1371/journal.pone.0007401.

Woese, C.R., Kandler, O., Wheelis, M.L., 1990. Towards a natural system of organisms: proposal for the domains Archaea, Bacteria, and Eucarya. National Academy of Sciences of the United States of America 87 (12), 4576–4579.

Wooley, J.C., Ye, Y., 2010. Metagenomics: facts and artifacts, and computational challenges. Journal of Computer Science and Technology 25 (1), 71–81.

FURTHER READING

Benninger, L.A., Carter, D.O., Forbes, S.L., 2008. The biochemical alteration of soil beneath a decomposing carcass. Forensic Science International 180 (2), 70–75.

Carter, D.O., Yellowlees, D., Tibbett, M., 2008. Temperature affects microbial decomposition of cadavers (*Rattus rattus*) in contrasting soils. Applied Soil Ecology 40, 129–137.

Carter, D.O., Yellowlees, D., Tibbett, M., 2010. Moisture can be the dominant environmental parameter governing cadaver decomposition in soil. Forensic Science International 200, 60–66.

Carter, D.O., Metcalf, J.L., Bibat, A., Knight, R., 2015. Seasonal variation of postmortem microbial communities. Forensic Science, Medicine, and Pathology 11 (2), 202–207.

Howard, G.T., Duos, B., Watson-Horzelski, E.J., 2010. Characterization of the soil microbial community associated with the decomposition of a swine carcass. International Biodeterioration & Biodegradation 64 (4), 300–304.

McFall-Ngai, M., Hadfield, M.G., Bosch, T.C., Carey, H.V., Domazet-Lošo, T., Douglas, A.E., Dubilier, N., Eberl, G., Fukami, T., Gilbert, S.F., Hentschel, U., 2013. Animals in a bacterial world, a new imperative for the life sciences. National Academy of Sciences of the United States of America 110 (9), 3229–3236.

Metcalf, J.L., Xu, Z.Z., Weiss, S., Lax, S., Van Treuren, W., Hyde, E.R., Song, S.J., Amir, A., Larsen, P., Sangwan, N., Haarmann, D., 2016. Microbial community assembly and metabolic function during mammalian corpse decomposition. Science 351 (6269), 158–162.

Vass, A.A., 2011. The elusive universal post-mortem interval formula. Forensic Science International 204 (1), 34–40.

CHAPTER 7

Assessing Subsurface Decomposition and Potential Impacts on Forensic Investigations

Ayodeji O. Olakanye, T. Komang Ralebitso-Senior
Teesside University, Tees Valley, United Kingdom

SOIL, DECOMPOSITION, AND FORENSICS

Forensically, soil is regarded as important crime scene evidence (Petraco et al., 2008; Woods et al., 2014) and is subjected typically to physicochemical analyses such as carbon dioxide emission, ninhydrin analysis, and organic matter determination (Carter and Tibbett, 2006; Damann et al., 2012; van Belle et al., 2009). In contrast, the efficacies of biochemical and microbiological profiling, particularly in decomposition/burial soils, have been investigated more closely only recently (Hyde et al., 2015; Metcalf et al., 2013). Various factors, including soil horizon and/or depth, electron donor/acceptor occurrence, nutrient availability, temperature, moisture content, and redox potential, determine soil heterogeneity and hence the physiological, phenotypic, and phylogenetic diversities of its microbial communities. As in other microbial ecology contexts, understanding the roles of microbial community parameter changes during decomposition is essential for subsequent application in real crime scenes.

Cadaver decomposition is a complex process that is influenced directly by the metabolic activities of vertebrate and invertebrate scavengers and microorganisms. These processes introduce numerous compounds, such as amino acids, acetic acid, and propionic acid, into the surrounding soil (Cobaugh et al., 2015; Metcalf et al., 2016), making a cadaver an energy resource with key roles in nutrient cycling. The decomposition and influx of nutrients have specific impacts on the surrounding environmental microbiota (Metcalf et al., 2016; Pechal and Benbow, 2015) and ecology, hence Carter et al. (2007) designated this unique and dynamic area as a cadaver decomposition island (CDI). As a consequence, several cross-disciplinary topics have emerged that recognize the potential value of studying the microbial community shifts on the decomposing cadaver and the CDI to estimate postmortem interval (PMI) and/or locate areas of (clandestine) burials. Specifically, advances in molecular microbial ecology tools have ensured that researchers can explore the epinecrotic and necrobiome communities in these complex interactions within the novel topic that we have designated "forensic ecogenomics" (Ralebitso-Senior et al., 2016; Chapter 1).

Forensic Ecogenomics
ISBN 978-0-12-809360-3
http://dx.doi.org/10.1016/B978-0-12-809360-3.00007-2

Factors Affecting Decomposition

Although several factors, including temperature, moisture, trauma, and associated material such as clothing and body mass, have been reported to affect cadaver decomposition rate, they vary between aboveground and underground situations (Carter and Tibbett, 2008; Mann et al., 1990; Zhou and Byard, 2011). Hence, as reported by workers such as Mann et al. (1990) and Carter and Tibbett (2008), cadaver decomposition rate often slows in underground environments. Notwithstanding this, the individual parameters are considered as follows:

1. Temperature: Ambient temperature increase has the largest effect on body decomposition rate as reported by Carter and Tibbett (2008), Gill-King (1997), and Mann et al. (1990). According to Carter and Tibbett (2008), an increase in biological activity during decomposition was due to temperature increase. Zhou and Byard (2011) reported that microorganisms use the body as a growth medium after death and the most favorable temperature for putrefactive bacteria (anaerobic catabolic bacteria) occurs between 21 and 38°C, while their activities are inhibited at temperatures below 4°C. As observed by both Micozzi (1986) and Stokes et al. (2009), the rate of aerobic decomposition was enhanced in a frozen cadaver compared with a fresh cadaver where putrefaction occurred due to anaerobic activity. In an underground environment, as observed by Carter and Tibbett (2006), microbial activity rates increase as the temperature rises up to 38°C, while at −5°C both enzymatic and microbial activity stop.
2. Water activity: A cadaver consists of 60%–80% (w/w) water, which, according to Carter et al. (2010), affects soil microbial activity. Cadaver breakdown is usually described in terms of decomposition and desiccation, where rapid desiccation can inhibit decomposition and lead to mummification (Carter and Tibbett, 2008). Extreme dry conditions dehydrate cadavers rapidly, which results in preservation, whereas extreme wet conditions promote waterlogging and adipocere formation. Both situations slow the decomposition rate (Campobasso et al., 2001; Carter and Tibbett, 2008; Zhou and Byard, 2011).
3. Trauma: Open wounds or cuts in a cadaver have been reported to promote its decomposition rate (Campobasso et al., 2001; Carter and Tibbett, 2008; Mann et al., 1990) since they serve as entry points for external microorganisms and insects.
4. Associated material: The presence of clothing on a cadaver has been reported to aid the rate of decomposition. For example, maggots tend to avoid sunlight by gathering under clothing (Mann et al., 1990; Campobasso et al., 2001; Zhou and Byard, 2011).

Microbial Ecology in the Forensic Context

Earth burial to honor the dead has been practiced for thousands of years. Although soil is viewed as important crime scene evidence in a forensic context (Bull et al., 2006;

Petraco et al., 2008; Woods et al., 2014), its use in accurate PMI and time-since-burial (TSB) estimations can be very challenging. Nevertheless, much research has been made to gain a better understanding of this. For example, forensic entomologists have used insect life cycles successfully in minimum PMI estimations in aboveground studies (Al-Mesbah et al., 2012; Dadour and Harvey, 2008; Rodriguez and Bass, 1983; see also Chapter 4). Similarly, Vass et al. (1992, 2002) reported the use of cadaver decomposition volatile organic compounds from a gravesoil in PMI estimation. Furthermore, Benninger et al. (2008) studied the biochemical changes below a cadaver by recording shifts in pH and nitrogen and phosphorus contents of a gravesoil at different postmortem time intervals. Also Metcalf et al. (2013) observed microbial community changes in a mouse cadaver model and suggested the potential of the microbial community as a "postmortem microbial clock."

Billions of microorganisms inhabit terrestrial ecosystems with bacteria the most predominant (Maier and Pepper, 2009). As reported by McGuire and Treseder (2010), 90% of organic matter catabolism can be attributed to bacterial and fungal activities coupled with their important roles in the carbon and nitrogen cycles. Numerically, less than 1% of microorganisms have been characterized by culture-based techniques (Madigan et al., 2012a; Maier and Pepper, 2009), so the use of culture-independent tools to analyze microbial communities structures, compositions, and diversities has proven to be very successful (Elsas and Rutgers, 2006). For the forensic context specifically, the use of both culture-based and culture-independent tools to study the relationships/interactions between soil microbiomes and cadaver necrobiomes (e.g., Chun et al., 2015; Howard et al., 2010; Hyde et al., 2013; Lerner et al., 2006; Moreno et al., 2011; Pechal et al., 2014) has identified their potential to estimate PMI. The most frequently used techniques for microbial community characterization are based on macro cell components such as whole-cell fatty acids and nucleic acids that can be extracted directly from soil.

Whole-Cell Fatty Acid Community Profiling

Microbial cell membranes contain lipids where they also act as storage products. Different cytoplasmic lipids that include free fatty acids, fatty alcohols, glycolipids, and phospholipids have been identified and used as signature molecules to characterize microbial community structures (Dunfield, 2007; Kandeler, 2007; Madigan et al., 2012a). This application can be based on two analyses: phospholipid fatty acid (PLFA) and fatty acid methyl ester (FAME). The former are good signature molecules since they are found in the cytoplasmic membranes of viable microorganisms but not as storage products. Although the extraction of PLFAs from soil samples is a lengthy process, it has been used to characterize different microbial environmental adaptation strategies in a range of soil types (Dunfield, 2007; Kandeler, 2007; Marschner, 2007). According to Kandeler (2007), Gram-positive bacteria produce odd number and branched-chain fatty acids, whereas Gram-negative bacteria produce even number, straight-chain, and cyclopropane fatty acids. While there are up to 15 bacterial fatty acid signatures, few are found to be characteristic of fungi, which may lead to an underestimation of the fungal biomass (Marschner, 2007). The fatty acids 18:2ω6 account numerically for about 43% of the total fatty acids of 47 soil fungal species (Kandeler, 2007).

Fatty acid methyl ester analysis is a rapid method used in community profiling for viable and nonviable microorganisms, and animal and plant biomass (Dunfield, 2007; Marschner, 2007). The method has been used to detect reliably changes in soil community profiles following agricultural management (Dunfield, 2007). Although the common fatty acids of animals, microorganisms, and plants question the reliability of FAME in microbial community profiling, animal and plant fatty acids tend to be longer chained ($C > 20$) than those of microorganisms (Dunfield, 2007; Marschner, 2007).

The successful application of PLFA and FAME (Hedrick et al., 2000; Marschner, 2007) in soil microbial profiling has prompted their adaptation as forensic tools. This was demonstrated, for example, by Parkinson et al. (2009) where PLFA profiling of human cadaver gravesoil showed successional changes in the bacterial and fungal communities. Breton et al. (2016) used FAME to reveal that shifts in the fatty acid methyl esters profiles aligned with the start of the active decay and continued until the dry period. Both seasonal and annual differences in the FAME profiles were recorded during the study, thus necessitating proper documentation for this technique to become an effective PMI estimation tool.

Nucleic Acid-Based Community Profiling

The development of culture-independent techniques and their applications in polymerase chain reaction (PCR) amplification and hybridization experiments have enabled researchers to identify and characterize numerous previously unidentified microorganisms (Muyzer et al., 1993; Thies, 2007). The use of nucleic acid extracts, as described by Thies (2007), falls into three categories:

1. Direct analysis of extracted nucleic acids;
2. Analysis of PCR amplicons; and
3. In situ analysis of extracted nucleic acids.

Various techniques have been developed to monitor community DNA profile changes but the results are often simplified in comparison to the actual populations. Thus, according to Felske and Osborn (2004), community DNA profiling is defined by the specificity of the primers used for the amplification and the preferential DNA fragments. Commonly used techniques include denaturing- or temperature-gradient gel electrophoresis (DGGE, TGGE), terminal restriction fragment length polymorphism (T-RFLP), and single strand conformation polymorphism (SSCP). While both DGGE and TGGE are based on DNA melting behavior, T-RFLP generates DNA fragments due to the presence of restriction sites, and SSCP separates microbial community members based on the melting behavior of the secondary structure of single-stranded DNA (Felske and Osborn, 2004; Madigan et al., 2012b; Marschner, 2007).

As one of the commonly used soil ecology profiling tools, DGGE is based on the electrophoretic mobility of PCR amplicons of similar size but different base sequences that are denatured partially through a polyacrylamide gel of increasing concentrations of denaturants (usually formamide and urea) (Green et al., 2009; Madigan et al., 2012b; Muyzer et al., 1993). The application of DGGE as a possible forensic tool was demonstrated by Lerner et al. (2006) where the profiling of crime scene and alibi soils showed large bacterial diversity, which clustered according to soil type and location. Likewise, Parkinson et al. (2009) used T-RFLP and phospholipid fatty acid analysis and showed soil bacterial and fungal community successional changes beneath a human cadaver that could be linked to the decomposition timeline. According to Pasternak et al. (2012), both DGGE and T-RFLP were powerful techniques that successfully distinguished between soils and treatments with potential usage as forensic tools. Furthermore, the use of amplicon length heterogeneity-PCR, according to Moreno et al. (2011), produced distinct amplicons of anaerobic bacteria and variations in nitrogen-fixing bacteria that could be used to differentiate between control and gravesoils.

More recently, advances in molecular profiling with the use of next-generation sequencing (NGS) platforms such as 454-pyrosequencing, Illumina, and Ion Torrent have identified likely microbial taxa that are involved in and/or affected by cadaver decomposition. Consequently, terms such as "microbiome," "necrobiome," and "thanatomicrobiome" have been applied to describe microbial communities associated with decomposition. According to Metcalf et al. (2013) and Pechal et al. (2014), successional changes in microbial community structure and composition can be used as a potential "postmortem microbial clock." Similarly, the work of Lauber et al. (2014) showed changes in the necrobiome of mice (*Mus musculus*) during active and advanced decay, while Carter et al. (2015) studied the ecological succession of soil microorganisms affected by decomposing swine carcasses and emphasized the importance of seasonality during PMI estimation. Also Finley et al. (2016) observed changes in bacterial community composition, with the dominance of the Proteobacteria phylum for human cadaver grave site.

Aboveground Versus Subsurface Investigations

As discussed earlier, the importance of cadaver decomposition knowledge is reflected further by emergent studies that have analyzed changes in the postmortem microbiomes or necrobiomes of the abdominal, interior anal, and buccal cavities and skin of decomposing carcasses (Hyde et al., 2013; Metcalf et al., 2013; Pechal et al., 2014). Similarly, the thanatomicrobiomes of different body organs and tissues are being used for potentially enhanced PMI estimations (see Chapter 6). Nonetheless, as reported in Chapter 1 (Table 1.1), the majority of research in these novel forensic disciplines has focused on aboveground decomposition. As a result, considerable knowledge gaps remain of soil microbial community changes following subsurface cadaver decomposition (Carter et al., 2010; Carter and Tibbett, 2006, 2008; Olakanye et al., 2017; van Belle et al., 2009).

AN ILLUSTRATIVE CASE STUDY

Determining the relationship between soil ecology and cadaver decomposition as a tool for accurate PMI and TSB estimation can be very challenging. As a consequence, we have established and reported on different lysimeters to gain a better understanding of this relationship (Bergmann et al., 2014; Chimutsa et al., 2015; Olakanye et al., 2014, 2015, 2017). Key analyses by PCR-DGGE and NGS were used with the principal objective of assessing soil community changes with the burial of *Sus scrofa domesticus* and relative to depth. A microcosm is a small experimental medium that is used to study ecological processes in a controlled or monitored environment. Microcosm-based study is a well-established procedure that has been used in high-impact forensic research for decomposition knowledge development (Bergmann et al., 2014; Carter et al., 2010). For example, Carter and Tibbett (2006) observed decomposition rate changes at different temperatures (2, 12, and 22°C), and Stokes et al. (2009) reported that freezing had no significant effect on decomposition rate when compared to unfrozen skeletal muscle in controlled microcosm studies.

The current illustrative study was made with outdoor lysimeters containing whole stillborn piglets (*S. scrofa domesticus*), plant litter (grass; *Agrostis/Festuca* spp.) cuttings, and a mixture of both to address overarching questions as follows:

1. What are the ecological indices and taxa trends observed with a whole piglet carcass?;
2. How does the mixture of the carbon sources affect the necrobiome community compared to sole application?; and
3. Will seasonal variations influence microbial community structures and compositions as measured by 16S/18S ecological indices trends and taxa distributions?

Experimental Design and Method Overview

To explore further the trends for 16S bacterial and 18S fungal genes observed in previous studies for an *S. scrofa domesticus* leg (Bergmann et al., 2014; Chimutsa et al., 2015; Olakanye et al., 2014) and muscle tissue cubes (Olakanye et al., 2015), a mesocosm study was made with whole stillborn piglets and plant litter from a domestic garden.

Study Soil and Mesocosm Design

Soil from a well-secured site at Framwellgate Moor, County Durham, UK (lat. 53.15°N, long. 1.59°W) was homogenized, sieved, and characterized (Forestry Commission, Surrey, UK; Derwentside Environmental Testing Services Ltd., Durham, UK). The sandy clay loam was constituted by (w/w) 26% clay, 21% silt, and 53% sand and physicochemical characteristics of Al (13 g/kg), Ca (2.2 g/kg), K (1.8 g/kg), Mg (1.1 g/kg), Na (0.25 g/kg), nitrate aqueous extract as NO_3 (4.6 mg/L), total organic carbon (4.1%), total S (0.03%), pH (6.3), P (1.2 mg/kg), calorific value (2.5 MJ/kg), and electrical conductivity (1400 μS/cm).

Prior to burial, the piglets were defrosted at ambient temperature and lysimeters established as follows: 20 kg soil (control); piglet (1.64 kg) buried in soil (32.8 kg); plant litter (1.5 kg) buried in soil (30 kg); and piglet (1.32 kg) plus plant litter (1.2 kg) buried in soil (50.4 kg).

As published in a previous study (Olakanye et al., 2014), the carbon source-to-soil ratio was 1:20 (w/w). Soil samples (1 g) were collected from multiple mesocosm positions on weeks 2 and 4 and then monthly for 10 months from November 2014 to September 2015. The homogenized (10 g) samples were stored (25 mL sterile universal bottles; Sarstedt, Germany) at −20°C until required for both pH measurement and DNA extraction. Ecological indices and normal distribution, statistical, and multivariate determinations were used to analyze the DGGE community fingerprints and NGS taxa profiles.

Overview of Sample, Data, and Statistical Analyses

The study methods were all as published in Olakanye et al. (2014, 2015). Briefly, soil pH measurements were made according to the method described by Stokes et al. (2009) where the soil samples were mixed thoroughly with sterile deionized water in a ratio of 1:5 (w/v) and measured with a pH probe (Fisher Scientific, Loughborough, UK) and 213 microprocessor (Hanna Instruments, Bedfordshire, UK)

Total microbial soil DNA was extracted using the FastSPIN DNA kit (MP Biomedicals, UK) from mesocosm samples that were taken once every month between November 2014 (day 0) and September 2015 (day 300). The extracted DNA samples were purified with PowerClean DNA Clean-Up Kit (Mo Bio Laboratories, Inc., USA) according to the manufacturer's instructions before NGS. PCR-DGGE of the 16S and 18S rRNA genes consisted of amplifications using GC388F/530R (16S) and NS1/NS8/NS10 (18S) primers followed by separation on 40%–70% and 20%–45% denaturing gradients for the bacterial and fungal communities, respectively. The DGGE data were analyzed further with key ecological measurements including the Shannon–Wiener and Simpson diversity indices, taxa richness and evenness.

The Illumina Miseq platform (NU-OMICS, Northumbria University, Newcastle upon Tyne, UK) was used to sequence the V4 region of the bacterial community 16S rRNA gene as described previously by Kozich et al. (2013). The FASTQ format was used to process the raw sequencing reads with subsequent analysis using the Mothur software package (version 1.36.1) (University of Michigan, USA). Quality checking and filtering of the FASTA formatted sequences were made with UCHIME. The sequences were then aligned to the SILVA reference and taxonomic identification of the reads assessed by assigning sequences to operational taxonomic units (OTUs) with Ribosomal Database Project classifier. PCR negative controls were run and sequenced in parallel to the samples with OTUs present in negative controls and samples excluded from any further analysis. Nonbacterial sequences (e.g., archaea) were discarded and reads rarified at 14,300 sequences per sample. OTUs less than 3% were classified as rare taxa. Both the rare taxa and the unclassified OTUs were omitted from the plots.

Alpha diversity indices, which measure taxa diversity within samples (Gonzalez et al., 2011; Pylro et al., 2014), were estimated with Shannon–Wiener diversity. The phylogenetic distance matrices were analyzed using Bray–Curtis dissimilarity with nonmetric dimensional scaling (NMDS) by the paleontological statistics software package for education and data analysis (PAST 3.10, 2015). Relationships between soil pH, temperature, and phyla relative abundance were analyzed using Spearman's rank correlation coefficient (xlstats 2016.02.27313, New York, USA).

Case Study Findings and Discussion

Postmortem microbial changes are gaining considerable attention with studies of cadaver decomposition epinecrotic communities (e.g., Hyde et al., 2015; Metcalf et al., 2013; Weiss et al., 2016). In the absence of the appropriate ethical and legal framework, accepted mammalian surrogates, including species of pigs, rats, and mice, are used for investigative purposes (see also Chapter 4). Although the use of piglets in this study may not have effected decomposition and associated microbial metabolic/activity rates of adult pigs, Benbow et al. (2015) stated that they are good models for research purposes. A report by Weiss et al. (2016) identified a marginal difference in the epinecrotic community of a 1 kg swine when compared with 20–50 kg carcasses and recommended the use of the latter weight range as human surrogates in postmortem microbial investigations. Also, since research initiatives must aim to replicate real crime scenes whenever feasible, this study included plant litter decomposition to mimic clandestine graves where human remains may be buried with domestic plant litter.

Environmental Parameters Trends

The pH values of the control and treatments soils were compared between days 0 (November 2014) and 300 (September 2015) and showed an increase for the piglet mesocosm on day 14 to reach 7.25 compared to the control (6.69), plant litter (6.75), and piglet + plant litter (6.75) mesocosms (Fig. 7.1). The piglet mesocosm recorded a slightly alkaline pH of 7.83 on day 60, while the piglet + plant litter treatment similarly recorded an alkaline value of 7.95 on day 90 in contrast to the control (6.98) and plant litter mesocosms (6.88). For the piglet and piglet + plant litter mesocosms, subsequent pH decreases resulted between days 120 and 270 to reach values of 6.09 and 5.57, respectively. Although temporal changes in trends were recorded, the pH values of the control and treatments mesocosms showed no statistically significant differences ($P = .075$) during the study.

An increase in piglet gravesoil pH between days 14 and 60 was in agreement with earlier reports by Haslam and Tibbett (2009) and Meyer et al. (2013) where the initial increase was attributed to mineralization of base-forming cations (Ca^{2+}, K^{+}, and Mg^{2+})

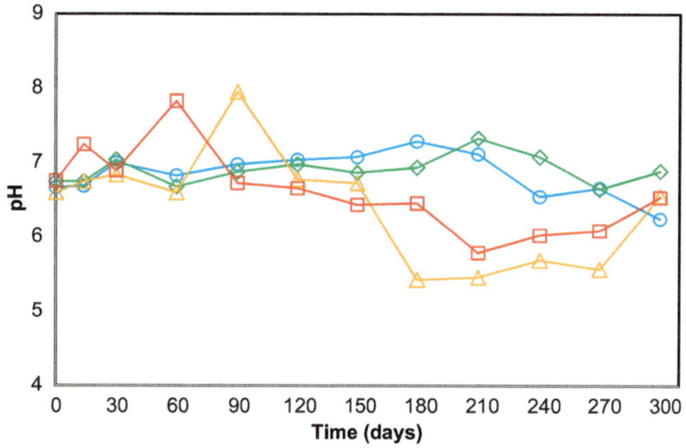

Figure 7.1 Changes in pH values of the control (○), piglet (□), plant litter (◊), and piglet + plant litter (△) mesocosms during 300 days of study.

and ammonification of organic nitrogen (proteins and peptides). The subsequent decrease was possibly due to nitrate accumulation (Meyer et al., 2013). The differences in pH recorded for the piglet + plant litter mesocosm, when compared to both the piglet and plant litter only mesocosms, can be attributed to changes in soil microbial metabolic and activity rates in relation to catabolic products where the *S. scrofa domesticus* contributed proteins, lipids, and carbohydrates (Janaway et al., 2009), while plant litter largely contributed cellulose and lignin (Tagliavini et al., 2007).

The average ambient and mesocosm soil temperatures were recorded on each sampling day and expressed further as accumulated degree days (ADD) (Table 7.1). Similar trends were recorded for the control and the treatments with temperature increases from day 14 (average ADD 91.5) to day 30 (average ADD 194.1) when the average mesocosm temperature was 10.7°C. Decreases were then recorded between day 60 (average ADD 310.6) and day 90 (average ADD 382.2) (late autumn to winter) when the average temperature was 5.6°C. A change in season from spring (day 120, average ADD 564.4) to summer (day 240, average ADD 1929) resulted in an increase in temperature to reach an average of 16.7°C and was followed by falls (day 270, average ADD 2411.8; day 300, average ADD 2848.3) to reach an average of 13.6°C. The one-way ANOVA showed no statistically significant temporal differences ($P = .99$) between the control and treatments lysimeters, which suggested that any exothermic microbial catabolism temperature increases were negated by the ambient temperature.

Differences in ambient and mesocosm temperature can be attributed directly to seasonal weather changes and exothermic microbial catabolism. For this study, the seasonal shifts occurred for autumn 2014 (day 0–30), winter 2014 (day 30–90), spring 2015 (day 120–180), summer 2015 (day 210–270), and autumn 2015 (day 300). As reported by

Table 7.1 Decomposition temperature timeline as expressed by ADD

Day	Control	Plant litter	Piglet + plant litter	Piglet
0	6.3	6.5	6	6.1
14	91.6	92	91	91.2
30	194.1	194.6	193.7	194.1
60	310.7	310.9	310.3	310.4
90	382.6	382.4	381.9	381.9
120	564.8	564.5	564.2	564
150	808.6	807.9	807.6	806.5
180	1066.6	1063.2	1063.8	1061.6
210	1466.9	1462.1	1463.5	1460.9
240	1932.8	1927.8	1929	1926.4
270	2415.4	2410.6	2411.9	2409.1
300	2852.4	2847.2	2848.3	2845.3

Meyer et al. (2013), seasonal differences between winter and summer have considerable impacts on microbial catabolic rates, with reduced and increased rates resulting in winter and summer, respectively.

Mesocosm Soil Ecological Analysis

The soil microbial community structures of the four lysimeter types were studied with culture-independent techniques where changes in species diversity were expressed as OTUs. The alpha microbial diversity, defined as the number of species present and the evenness of species distribution within a particular area (Gerber, 2011), was determined using ecological measures of richness, Shannon–Wiener diversity, and Simpson diversity indices. The Shannon–Wiener index is an informative index that reflects evenness and species relative abundance, while the Simpson's index is a dominance parameter that reflects richness and relative abundance (Bandeira et al., 2013; Barry et al., 2013; Hill et al., 2003). According to Bandeira et al. (2013), the use of a single ecological index to define a microbial community oversimplifies the biodiversity of that community, hence three were used simultaneously.

Richness

For the 16S rRNA gene richness profiles, similar trends were recorded for the control and experimental lysimeters between days 0 and 90 (Fig. 7.2A). Specifically, periods of increasing richness resulted between days 0 and 30, to values of 27 (control), 28 (plant litter), 25 (plant litter + piglet), and 29 (piglet), while those for days 90–120 reached 18 (control), 23 (plant litter), and 29 (piglet). These were separated by a phase of decreased richness between days 30 and 90 to reach 16 (control), 15 (plant litter), 16 (piglet + plant litter), and 17 (piglet). Decreases in richness were recorded for the treatment mesocosms

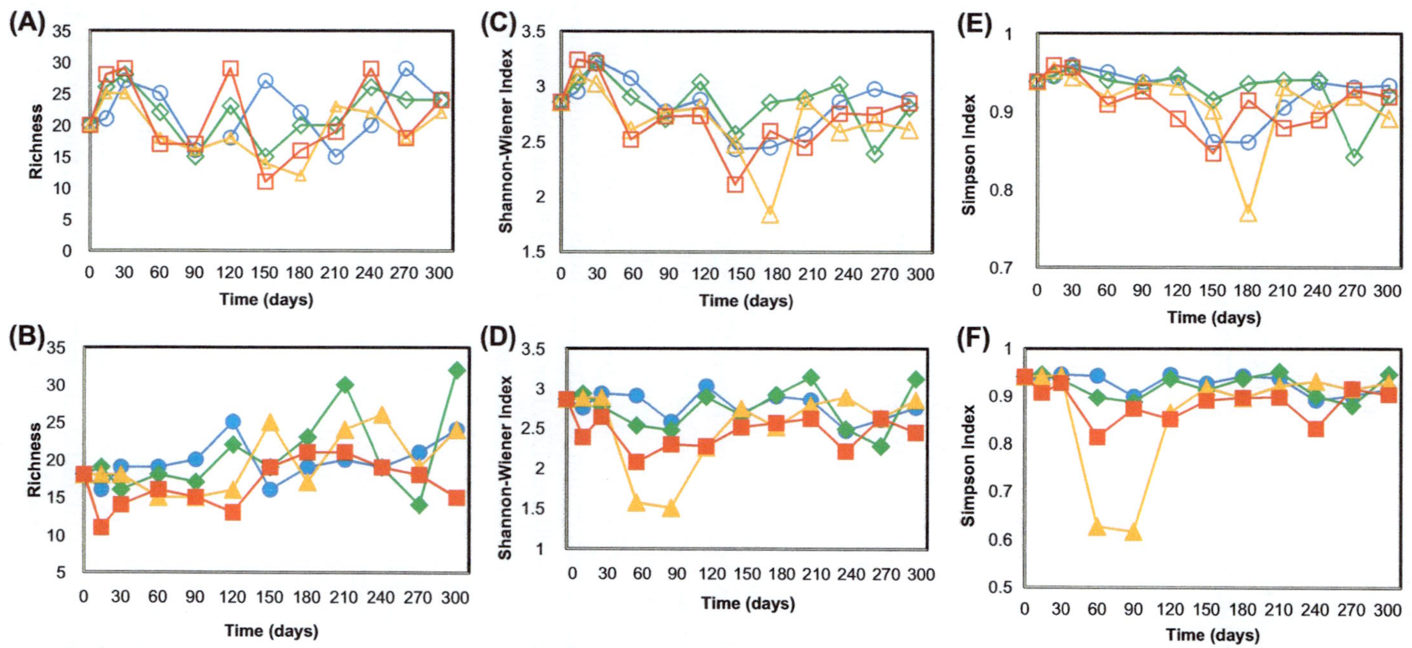

Figure 7.2 Richness (A, B), Shannon–Wiener (C, D), and Simpson (E, F) indices for 16S bacterial (*open symbols*) and 18S fungal communities (*closed symbols*) of the control (○), piglet (□), plant litter (◊), and piglet + plant litter (△) mesocosms during 300 days of study.

from day 120 to day 150 to reach 15 (plant litter), 14 (piglet + plant litter), and 11 (piglet), which contrasted the control where an increase to 27 was observed between days 120 and 150. Richness increases were then recorded from day 180 to day 240 when values of 26 (plant litter) and 29 (piglet) were observed in contrast with the control, which reached 15 on day 210. Nonetheless, the one-way ANOVA for the 16S bacterial richness trends showed no statistically significant temporal differences ($P = .52$) between the control and treatment mesocosms.

The 18S rRNA gene richness profiles also revealed differences between the control and treatments with contrasting trends first recorded on day 14. Decreases in the control (16) and piglet (11) mesocosms differed from an increase to 19 for the plant litter mesocosm. Increases in richness then resulted from day 30 to day 120 to reach 25 (control) and 22 (plant litter). The piglet mesocosm decreased in richness to 15 from day 180 to day 300, which contrasted an increasing trend from day 270 to day 300 to 32 OTUs for the plant litter mesocosm (Fig. 7.2B). Despite the observed changes in trends, the one-way ANOVA revealed no statistically significant differences ($P = .10$) between the control and treatment mesocosms.

Shannon–Wiener Diversity

The bacterial 16S rRNA gene Shannon–Wiener index profiles showed differences in diversity between the control and treatments (Fig. 7.2C). Initially, increasing trends were recorded with values of 2.95 (control), 3.04 (plant litter), 3.11 (piglet + plant litter), and 3.24 (piglet) recorded on day 14. Between days 30 and 150, decreases in the Shannon–Wiener indices were observed with 2.44 (control), 2.48 (piglet + plant litter), and 2.11 (piglet) reached. The one exception was the plant litter mesocosm where an increase to 3.04 resulted between days 90 and 120. For days 150–240, the Shannon–Wiener indices of the control and piglet mesocosms increased to 2.86 and 2.76, respectively, while an increase to 3.02 in the same period was followed by a decrease to 2.39 on day 270 in the plant litter mesocosm.

For the piglet + plant litter mesocosm, a decrease to 1.84 between days 150 and 180 was followed by an increase to 2.88 on day 210 after which a decrease was again apparent to 2.59 on day 240. In general, and despite temporal fluctuations, the piglet mesocosm recorded similar bacterial Shannon–Wiener indices at the beginning (day 0, 2.86) and end (day 300, 2.85) of the study. Also, there were no statistically significant differences ($P = .41$) between the control and treatment mesocosms despite temporal changes in trends.

In contrast to the 16S bacterial dynamics, the 18S fungal Shannon–Wiener indices profiles revealed unique trends and showed statistically significant temporal differences ($P = .038$) between the control and treatments. Specifically, there was a decrease in the fungal Shannon–Wiener index (Fig. 7.2D) for the piglet mesocosm from day 0 (2.86) to day 60 (2.08), after which a progressive increase was recorded until day 210 (2.62) before a further increase resulted between days 240 and 270 to reach 2.62. For the plant litter mesocosm, a Shannon–Wiener index increase resulted between days 0 and 14 (2.93) and was followed by subsequent decreases until day 90 (2.47). Further increases were then recorded between days 150 and 210 to reach 3.14, before falling to 2.28 on day 270. A plateau at approximately $H' = 2.88$ was recorded for the piglet + plant litter mesocosm during the first 30 days of incubation. This was followed by a marked decrease in the Shannon–Wiener index between days 30 and 90 (1.51) and increases between days 120 and 150 (2.74) and days 180 and 240 (2.89). For the control a different trend was recorded with decreases from day 30 to day 90 (2.57) and 180 to 240 (2.47), while increases resulted between days 90 and 120 (3.03) and 240 and 300 (2.76).

Simpson Diversity

As recorded for the Shannon–Wiener indices, the 16S bacterial Simpson indices also revealed diversity trend differences between the control and treatments (Fig. 7.2E). Increases were recorded for all four mesocosm types during the first 14 days with the control and treatments then showing different decreasing rates for the Simpson index between days 30 and 60 (piglet + plant litter, 0.92; piglet, 0.91) and day 90 to day 150 (control, 0.86; pig, 0.85). A further marked decrease resulted for the piglet + plant litter mesocosm from day 120 to day 180 to reach 0.77, which was followed by a steep increase to 0.93 on day 210. An increase in the Simpson index was recorded for the control from day 180 to day 240 to reach 0.94, while a decrease to 0.89 resulted between days 210 and 300 for the piglet + plant litter mesocosm. Notwithstanding these apparent shifts, the Simpson index did not identify statistically significant differences ($P = .55$) between the control and treatments.

The 18S Simpson indices showed similar trends for fungal community diversity (Fig. 7.2F) as the Shannon–Wiener indices (Fig. 7.2D). For example, the piglet + plant litter treatment recorded a plateau during the first 30 days of the study and was followed by marked decreases to day 90 (0.62) and subsequent increases by day 150 (0.92) (Fig. 7.2F). Also the control and plant litter mesocosms recorded similar temporal trends with indices higher than the piglet mesocosm. Both the control and plant litter lysimeters indices fell between days 210 and 270 to reach 0.90 and 0.88, respectively, in contrast with the piglet mesocosm, which rose between days 240 and 270 to 0.92. Similar to the 16S Simpson index, a one-way ANOVA for the 18S index revealed no statistically significant temporal differences ($P = .10$) between the control and treatments although unique temporal trends were recorded.

Principal Component Analysis for Ecological Measures

Multivariate analyses are recommended for robust interpretations of multiple sources of data in several disciplines, including (molecular) microbial ecology. Since microbial ecology is being adapted in the present study and similar initiatives for a forensic context, we applied principal component analysis of data for the three ecological indices determinations reported earlier.

The 16S rRNA gene principal component analysis biplot of the Shannon–Wiener (*H′*), Simpson (*D*), and Richness (*S*) ecological measures (Fig. 7.3A) showed that PC1 accounted for 53.59% of the variations in the bacterial community dynamics, while PC2 accounted for 17.33%. The location of ecological parameters along the right axis

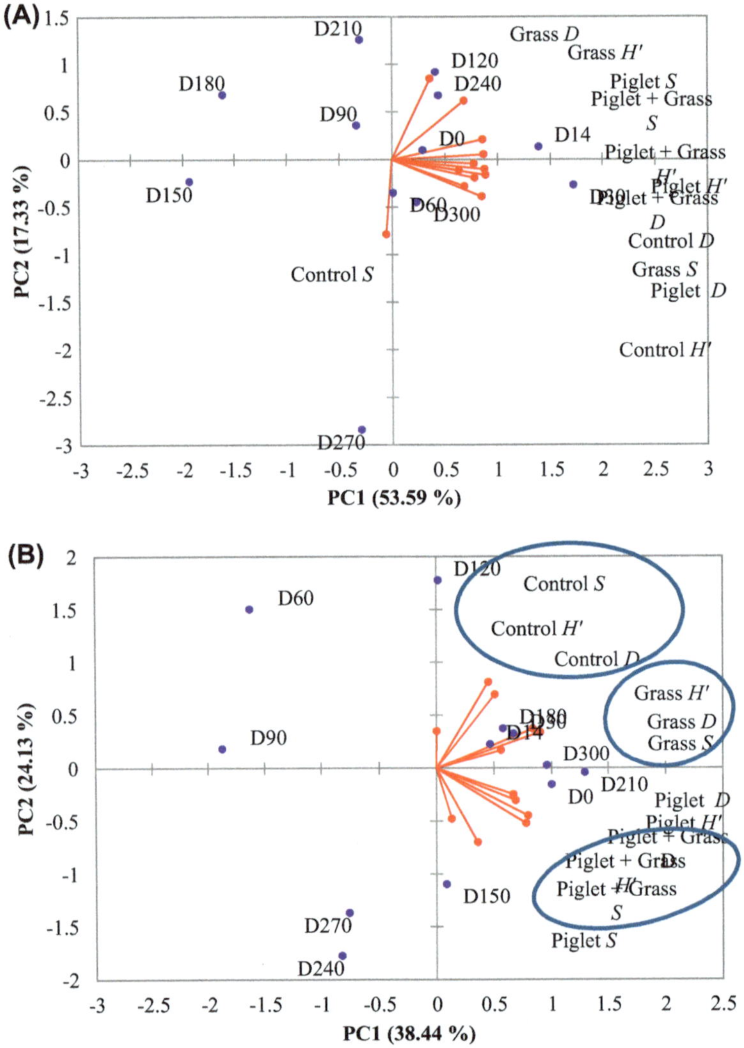

Figure 7.3 16S bacterial (A) and 18S bacterial (B) principal component analysis biplot for ecological measures (Shannon–Wiener, *H′*; Simpson, *D*; Richness, *S*) at specific sampling times of the control, piglet, plant litter (grass), and piglet+plant litter (Piglet+grass) mesocosms.

showed high measures of diversity at the sampling times with no distinct divergences for the control and treatment mesocosms. For the 18S fungal ecological measures, PC1 accounted for 38.44% of the variations, while PC2 accounted for 24.13% (Fig. 7.3B). Also, in contrast to the 16S bacterial ecological measures, the 18S fungal community dynamics clusters for the control and treatments mesocosms correlated more strongly with each mesocosm type and corresponding ecological measures. This is highlighted by the delineations for the control, plant litter, and pig + plant litter treatments.

Overall, the ecological measures of richness, Shannon–Wiener index, and Simpson index were highly correlated throughout the study. The linear regressions for both the 16S bacterial and 18S fungal genes were $R^2 < 0.7$ and judged to be statistically insignificant. Nevertheless, the clustering of the indices according to the mesocosm type for the 18S gene suggested that DGGE-based fungal community profiling may be a potentially useful tool to differentiate between control, piglet, and plant litter soils, which necessitates further investigation consisting also of replicated lysimeters.

Generally, the ecological measures revealed trends that fluctuated with the decomposition timeline in the control and treatments mesocosms, which were linked to seasonal temperature shifts during the study. For example, both 16S and 18S ecological trends for the control, plant litter, and piglet mesocosms showed decreased microbial diversity between days 14 and 90 (autumn to mid-winter, 2014) while those of the piglet + plant litter mesocosm plateaued between days 0 and 30 (autumn 2014). Overall, there was no clear and consistent differentiation between the control and treatments, or between the piglet and plant litter, for the current soil type. The exceptions were for the mixed carbon source treatment where both the bacterial 16S and fungal 18S rRNA genes recorded decreased diversities on day 180 (16S) and days 60 and 90 (18S).

Community profiling tools such as DGGE continue to have a role to play in microbial ecology investigations, provided that their caveats are recognized and mitigated for. Also the relevance of attendant richness, diversity, and evenness measurements has been well established. Therefore more replicated subsurface studies, with whole cadavers or human surrogates, should be used to investigate the applicability and utility of ecological indices analyses in enhanced PMI and TSB determinations. Naturally, these can be augmented with high-throughput analyses where accessible.

Taxonomic Resolution With Next-Generation Sequencing

Phylum-Level Resolution

The taxonomic resolution at phylum level revealed general dominances in decreasing order of Proteobacteria (18.03%–55.95%), Acidobacteria (5.99%–41.77%), Bacteroidetes (3.39%–27.24%), Verrucomicrobia (3.81%–18.96%), Actinobacteria (5.16%–12.86%), and Planctomycetes (2.53%–11.89%) in the control and experimental mesocosms (Fig. 7.4). Also Acidobacteria, Planctomycetes, Firmicutes, and Verrucomicrobia were found

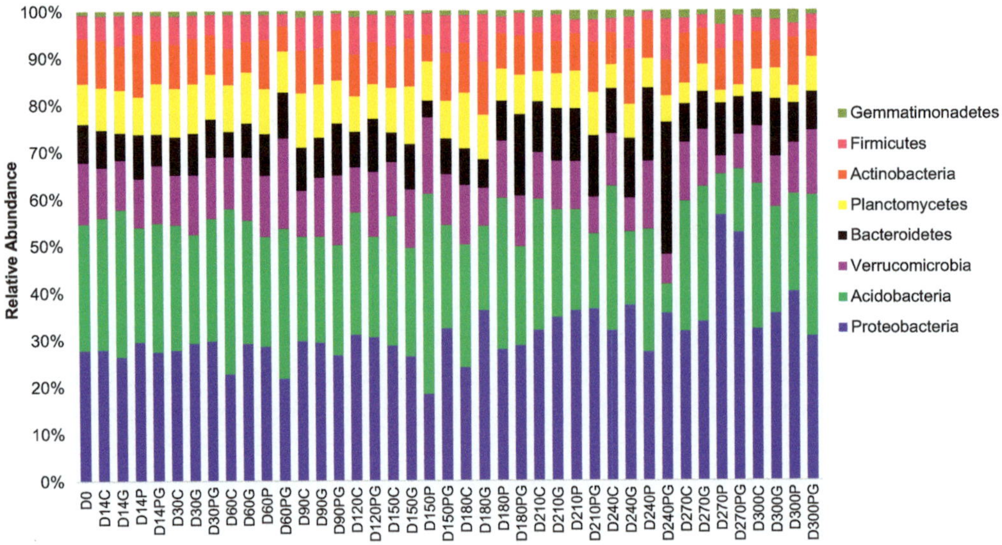

Figure 7.4 Phylum-level bacterial resolution of extracted DNA samples of the control (C), piglet (P), plant litter (G), and piglet + plant litter (PG) mesocosms.

to correlate negatively with temperature, while Bacteroidetes, Gemmatimonadetes, and Proteobacteria correlated positively (Table 7.2).

While characteristically predominant in soils (Arroyo et al., 2015; Ligi et al., 2014; Peralta et al., 2013; Roesch et al., 2007), the numerical abundances of Proteobacteria, Acidobacteria, and Actinobacteria specifically in cadaver/taphonomic proxy decomposition-impacted soils have been reported by various researchers (Carter et al., 2015; Damann et al., 2015; Finley et al., 2016). Furthermore, the dominance of Verrucomicrobia (Spartobacteria_family and Subdivision3_family) has been reported by Bergmann et al. (2011) who also observed its underestimation in soil metagenomics due to primer bias. The dominances of Acidobacteria and Verrucomicrobia observed in this study aligned the investigation to the work of Finley et al. (2016) who also reported their numerical abundances in an underground decomposition study when compared to its aboveground equivalent.

The Bray–Curtis dissimilarity with NMDS for the samples showed that the control soils were similar, while differences were observed for the plant litter, piglet, and piglet + plant litter mesocosms (Fig. 7.5). These differences in the experimental mesocosms could possibly be attributed to seasonal temperature change as observed from day 210 to day 270 (summer). In summary, the phylum-level resolution could potentially identify season-based differences for this study soil. Nevertheless, the recorded phylum-level dominances did not generally provide sufficient composition-based community clustering or differentiation between the mammalian proxy decomposition and the control or plant litter soils.

Table 7.2 Operational taxonomic units (OTUs) recording statistically significant correlations ($P<.05$) with soil temperature and pH

Temperature					
Positive			**Negative**		
OTUs (phylum)	**R**	***P***	**OTUs (phylum)**	**R**	***P***
Bacteroidetes	0.342	0.029	Acidobacteria	−0.386	0.013
Gemmatimonadetes	0.518	0.001	Planctomycetes	−0.678	<0.0001
Proteobacteria	0.449	0.004	Verrucomicrobia	−0.498	0.001
			Firmicutes	−0.339	0.031
pH					
Chloroflexi (rare taxon)	0.460	0.003			

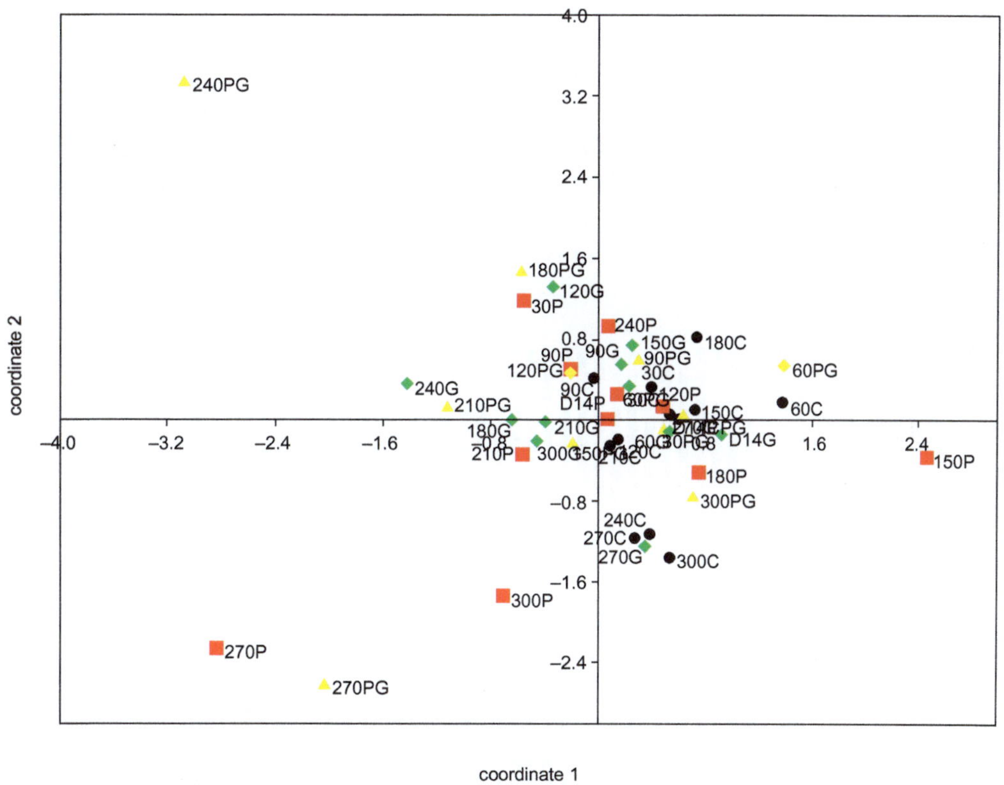

Figure 7.5 Nonmetric dimensional scaling (NMDS) plot ($R^2=0.87$; stress = 0.12) of phylum-level analysis of extracted DNA samples of the control (C, ●), piglet (P, ■), plant litter (G, ♦), and piglet + plant litter (PG, ▲) mesocosms.

Order-Level Resolution

16S bacterial community resolution at the order level (Fig. 7.6) revealed some temporal changes between the control and treatment lysimeters. Between days 0 and 60 (autumn to spring 2014), the dominant orders for all mesocosms were Acidobacteria_Gp6_order, Spartobacteria, and Planctomycetales. However, some taxa differences were observed at group level such as the relative abundance increase of Actinomycetales to 8.49% that was recorded on day 14 for the piglet mesocosm. Similarly, relative abundance increases of Spartobacteria_order (16.13%) and Flavobacteriales (4.31%), accompanied by a decrease of Rhizobiales (5.71%), were recorded on day 60 for the piglet + plant litter mesocosm. Therefore taxonomic resolution at order level would not necessarily be conclusive in differentiating burial from nonburial samples during the first 2 months for the current soil type. The potential for improved order-level differentiation during this decomposition timeline would require further investigation, possibly at family and genus levels.

For the control, an increase in the relative abundance of Xanthomonadales to 6.37% was apparent on day 120. From day 150 (April 2015), a seasonal change to spring effected a shift in the community taxa composition with increases in the relative abundances of Xanthomonadales (8.71%) and Bacillales (8.09%) for the piglet + plant litter treatment compared to the other mesocosms, which for the piglet mesocosm was characterized by increases in Acidobacteria_Gp6_order (29.90%), Spartobacteria_order (14.92%), and Acidobacteria_Gp4_order (7.60%). On day 180, taxa differences were again recorded with predominance of Xanthomonadales (13.57%) (plant litter), Acidobacteria_Gp4_order (8.37%), and Acidobacteria_Gp3_order (2.79%) (piglet), and increases in the relative abundances of Flavobacteriales (6.66%) and Bacteriodales (4.07%) (piglet + plant litter).

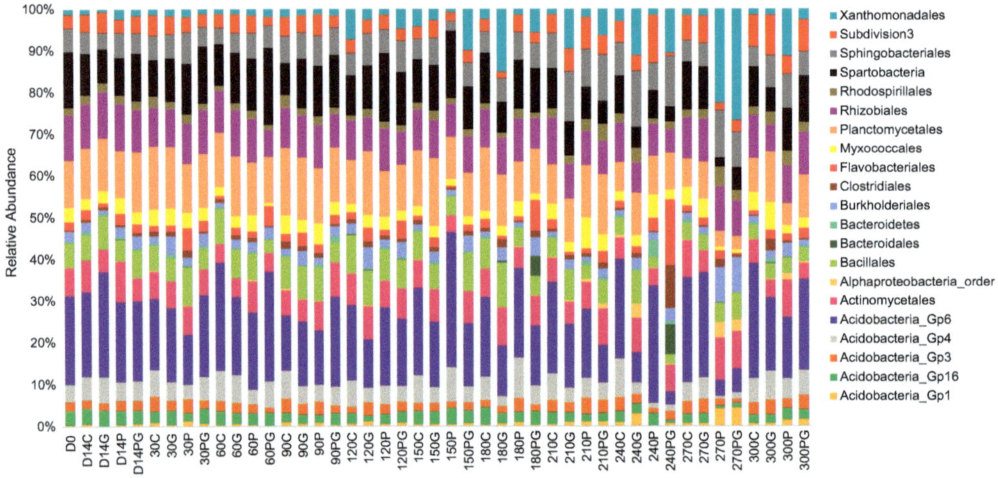

Figure 7.6 Order-level bacterial resolution of extracted DNA samples of the control (C), piglet (P), plant litter (G), and piglet + plant litter (PG) mesocosms.

Further changes were observed on day 210 with decreases of Xanthomonadales (8.06%) and Acidobacteria_Gp6 (7.12%) in the plant litter and piglet + plant litter mesocosms, respectively. In contrast, an increase of Sphingobacteriales was recorded for all mesocosms (7.04%, control; 10.25%, plant litter; 7.04%, piglet; 8.90%, piglet + plant litter) with an additional increase of Myxococcales (5.75%) in the presence of the piglet, while Planctomycetales (11.48%) was the dominant order of the piglet + plant litter mesocosm. Despite obvious shifts in community structure, no obvious taxa candidates were identified at order level as distinct microbial clock indicators in spring for subsurface PMI estimation. Also none were ideal for differentiating between the decomposition of plant organic matter and *S. scrofa domesticus*.

Changes in the epinecrotic microbial communities structures were seen on day 240 with increases in taxa abundances of Flavobacteriales (12.69%), Sphingobacteriales (9.69%), Clostridiales (8.12%), Bacteroidales (5.65%), and Xanthomonadales (8.45%) in the piglet + plant litter mesocosm, where they became the dominant orders. The marked increase in Clostridiales, which tended to be absent or occur in relative abundances less than 0.1%, identified this order as a potential summer microbial clock indicator for the mixed carbon sources. Likewise, the differential presence and absence of Bacteriodales in the four mesocosm types identified it as a potential microbial clock and TSB indicator due to its occurrence and abundance on days 180 (late spring) and 240 (mid-summer) for the mixed treatment.

On day 270, both the piglet and piglet + plant litter treatments recorded similar taxa trends with increases in the relative abundances of Xanthomonadales (P, 20.54%; PG, 24.65%), Burkholderiales (P, 7.63%; PG, 7.88%), and Acidobacteria_Gp1_order (P, 3.93%; PG, 4.18%) and decreases in Planctomycetales (P, 3.43%; PG, 2.99%). In contrast, Acidobacteria_Gp6 was predominant for the control (20.73%) and plant litter (20.89%) mesocosms. Finally, Xanthomonadales decreases (P, 9.74%; PG, 2.20%) and increases of Acidobacteria_Gp6_order (P, 12.61%; PG, 18.57%) and Spartobacteria_order (P, 8.90%; PG, 9.44%) were recorded on day 300. Increased relative abundances of Subdivision3_order resulted for the control (6.48%) and plant litter (7.29%) mesocosms.

The numerical dominances on day 270 of Alphaproteobacteria_order (P, 3.30%; PG, 2.65%) and Acidobacteria_Gp1_order (P, 3.93%; PG, 4.18%), above "background" occurrences in the other sampling times, identified them as potential indicators for piglet and piglet + plant litter decomposition with community structure as the target variable. The differential dominance of Xanthamonadales seemed to distinguish the early (day 0–90), mid (day 120–210), and late (day 270) TSB intervals for the pig + plant litter treatment in particular. Nevertheless, this order was not necessarily useful for differentiating between soil containing a decomposing mammalian taphonomic proxy and its control. Also it seemed suboptimum for distinguishing between the two different organic materials.

Family-Level Resolution

It was anticipated for the current study that the mixture of the carbon sources would effect differences in the epinecrotic communities when compared to the individual carbon sources. Days 240–270 (summer, July–August 2015) were, however, the only period when considerable differences were recorded in structure, and composition to a lesser extent, with increases of Gram-negative nonmotile rod-shaped Porphyromonadaceae (Krieg et al., 2010), often described as fecal bacteria (Newton et al., 2013), and obligate anaerobic rod-shaped Gram-positive Clostridiaceae_1 (De-Vos et al., 2009) for the piglet + plant litter mesocosm observed on day 240 (Fig. 7.7). Further shifts with the dominance of Gram-positive Microbacteriaceae (Goodfellow et al., 2012) and Alcaligenaceae, aerobic Gram-negative rod or coccobacilli chemoorganotrophic bacteria (Whiteson et al., 2014), were recorded for the piglet and piglet + plant litter mesocosms on day 270. Likewise, Metcalf et al. (2013) associated Alcaligenaceae with advanced stages of decomposition.

Some family-level resolutions identified more detailed phylogenetic variations between the mesocosm soils relative to the decomposition timelines. For example, resolution of the order Sphingobacteriales revealed two dominant families, Sphingobacteriaceae and Chitinophagaceae, with the latter consisting of aerobic or facultative anaerobic rod-shaped bacteria (Krieg et al., 2010), whose functions include limited fermentative capabilities of carbohydrates and the possession of menaquinones MK-7. While the dominance of Chitinophagaceae was observed for all of the mesocosms from day 0 to day 300, Sphingobacteriaceae predominated in the piglet + plant litter mesocosm on days 60, 120, and 240. This contrasted the piglet mesocosm in particular, where

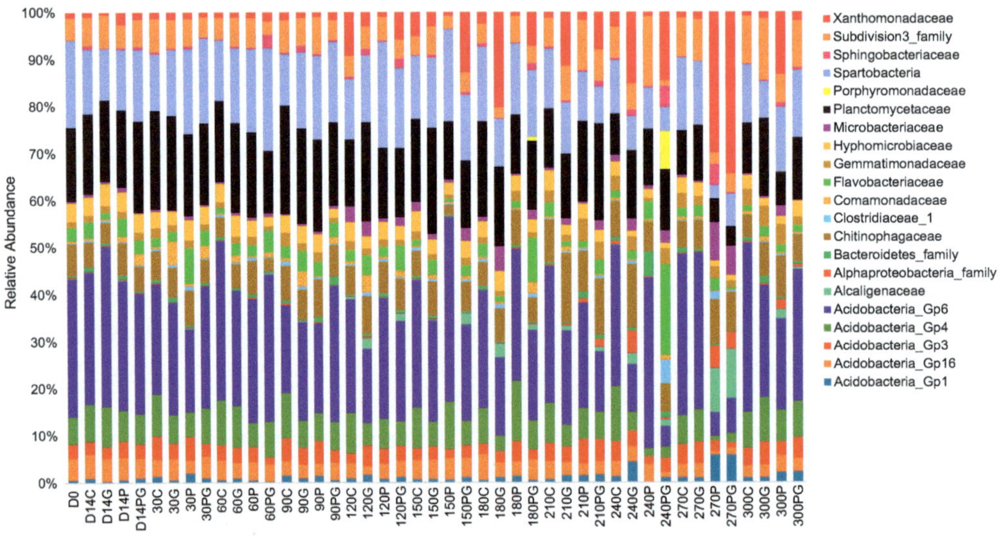

Figure 7.7 Family-level bacterial resolution of extracted DNA samples of the control (C), piglet (P), plant litter (G), and piglet + plant litter (PG) mesocosms.

increased abundance was observed only on day 270 (late summer 2015). Therefore the family could be used as a potential summer microbial clock indicator for pig (human) burials for this soil type. The Alphaproteobacteria_family recorded presences and increased abundances in particular for the piglet (3.81%) and piglet + plant litter (3.08%) treatments on day 270. Although recorded on day 240 (3.43%), the family was just above the detection limit on day 270 in the plant litter lysimeter, thus becoming another likely target indicator group for mammalian proxy decomposition, singly and when mixed with a (highly lignocellulosic) plant-derived substrate.

Carter et al. (2015) and Metcalf et al. (2013) identified Sphingobacteriaceae as a potential microbial indicator, while the former researchers aligned this bacterial group with advanced stages of decomposition. Also the predominance of Chitinophagaceae from day 0 to day 300 (November 2014–September 2015) contrasted the work of Carter et al. (2015) who observed flushes of *Psychrobacter* spp. and Chitinophagaceae in winter and summer months, respectively. Therefore the differences between the findings of the current study and those reported in the literature may be in part due to the carbon mixture in the piglet + plant litter mesocosm.

Overall, some unique taxa were observed at family level in the piglet and piglet + plant litter mesocosms possibly due to the seasonal temperature change. During the middle of summer 2015, increased dominances of Flavobacteriaceae (12.31%), Clostridiaceae_1 (3.22%), and Sphingobacteriaceae (2.87%), and the presence of Porphyromonadaceae (5.20%), were recorded in the piglet + plant litter mesocosm on day 240. Therefore the first three members were possible indicators for abundance- and community structure-based PMI/TSB estimations, while the last was a potential presence/absence and community composition-based indicator.

Microbacteriaceae (P, 6.34%; PG, 5.09%) and Alcaligenaceae (P, 7.23%; PG, 8.61%) were recorded on day 270 (late summer, August 2015) with Xanthomonadaceae (*Rhodanobacter* sp.), a Gram-negative denitrifying bacterium (Green et al., 2012), observed to be the most abundant taxon for both the piglet (23.16%) and piglet + plant litter (28.46%) mesocosms. Therefore these six family members, particularly Xanthomonadaceae (*Rhodanobacter* sp.), were potential seasonal and TSB indicators, regarding microbial community structure and composition, for the human taphonomic proxy, either individually or in combination with plant litter.

Case Study Conclusions

Abiotic factors such as temperature and pH are key variables that must be used parallel to microbial community profiles to establish and validate robust PMI (Lauber et al., 2014; Weiss et al., 2016) and TSB estimation tools. Temperature-mediated microbial activity was discussed by Mann et al. (1990) and Zhou and Byard (2011) where an optimum temperature range of 21–38°C was reported to enhance microbial activity, while limited activity was recorded at temperatures below 4°C. As observed in this study, seasonal temperature shifts resulted in microbial community structure changes as expressed by ecological indices measurements of richness, Shannon–Wiener, and Simpson indices of both 16S bacterial and 18S fungal rRNA gene profiles in the control and experimental lysimeters. For example, 16S bacterial ecological measures revealed distinct changes between spring and summer, while 18S fungal ecological measures changes were more pronounced in winter and summer.

Distinguishing between the gravesoils of the individual carbon sources and the control based on microbial community profiling remains a challenge due to the presence of several common dominant taxa such as Proteobacteria, Acidobacteria, Verrucomicrobia, Bacteroidetes, Planctomycetes, and Actinobacteria. Overall, occurrences of the same taxa indicated that the community composition at phylum level did not show distinct differences due to treatment but the structure changed as evidenced by the different numerical abundances of some components.

Although taxa resolution at this level would probably not be ideal to identify specific PMI indicators, shifts in some predominant phyla were recorded especially in the summer. Since a similar trend was observed at family level, there was potential to suggest that some community members could be used as seasonal microbial clock indicators in the subsurface for this soil with whole piglet as human surrogates. For example, some unique taxa, such as Sphingobacteriaceae and Alcaligenaceae, at family-level resolution were identified during the summer season in the piglet and piglet + plant litter mesocosms. Furthermore, the mixture of carbon sources altered the pH when compared to the individual substrates and revealed Porphyromonadaceae and Clostridiaceae_1 as potential taxa indicators to differentiate between the two.

Correlation of ecological measures with NGS taxonomic resolution remains a challenge because of the limitations of the DGGE technique (Crippen et al., 2015; Green et al., 2009). Notwithstanding this, some temporal differences recorded with the DGGE-dependent ecological measures between the control and treatments mesocosms were also observed in the NGS-based taxonomic classification during the summer period. Caution was, however, taken not to align these differences directly since the DGGE bands were not excised and subjected to sequencing.

It was hypothesized that: (1) individual *S. scrofa domesticus* and plant matter decompositions would result in distinct temporal shifts in soil microbial community composition; (2) individual *S. scrofa domesticus* and plant matter decompositions would result in distinct temporal shifts in soil microbial community structure; and (3) specific taxa would be identified as potential microbial clock indicators for subsequent use in subsurface PMI and TSB estimations. Hypotheses (1) and (3) were rejected at phylum-level resolution since only the abundance of specific phyla (structure) changed temporally and in response to decomposition.

A Shannon–Wiener diversity box plot (data not shown) revealed no statistically significant differences ($P = .06$) between the control and treatments when using order-level taxonomic resolution. Notwithstanding this, the presence and absence of Bacteroidales, as well as the shifts in the numerical dominances of this and Clostridiales, identified them as possible order-level TSB indicators for the mixed carbon sources. Therefore hypotheses (1), (2), and (3) regarding community composition, structure, and unique taxa, respectively, were accepted for this study soil and treatment at this level of resolution. Similarly, all three hypotheses were accepted at family-level profiling where some community composition delineation existed between the control and piglet + plant litter mesocosms due to the occurrence and increased abundance of Porphyromonadaceae. Also the numerical abundances of several members such as Microbacteriaceae, Flavobacteriaceae, Alcaligenaceae, and Xanthomonadaceae identified them as potential community structure-based indicators for differentiation between the control/plant litter and piglet/piglet + plant litter treatments on days 240 and 270 (summer 2015).

Overall, the presence, absence, and relative abundance of taxa, as parameters that could then be used to identify potential microbial clock and TSB indicators, depended on the level of resolution. Although differences for most taxa within and between mesocosms seemed to be less dependent on the presence of any decomposing material or the presence of piglet as the human taphonomic proxy in particular, some members could be targeted potentially relative to seasonal temperature changes especially for mid- to late summer 2015 (days 240–270).

Charneca et al. (2010) reported a higher protein-to-lipid ratio in newborn piglets, which countered our assumption that the stillborn piglet carcasses used in this study would consist of relatively high lipid contents. Therefore future studies should investigate the effects of age and nutrient composition of the animal model on the environmental/soil microbial community dynamics (see also Chapter 4). These comparative studies would not only facilitate experimental database development but also provide information with potential relevance to investigations of suspected clandestine child burials in contrast to those of adults. In summary, additional, multiple, and replicated subsurface investigations should resolve further the decomposition-specific taxa occurrences/dominances and changes in microbial community profiles as recorded in the current mesocosm study and similar future initiatives. Also these future studies should consider different soil types, climatic conditions, and geographical regions.

The value of replicated and repeat studies is recognized widely in molecular microbial ecology, from where tools are being adopted and adapted increasingly for forensic ecogenomics, forensic microbiology, environmental forensics, and geoforensics. Consequently, replication has been used in the experimental designs of several decomposition studies, which are intended to illustrate the applicability of microbial ecology techniques in forensic contexts. Similarly, this good scientific and experimental practice must be matched with the use of relevant mathematical and statistical tools. The relevance of robust statistical analyses in novel forensic contexts was recognized and illustrated, for example, by Pasternak et al. (2012) who investigated two commercial soil DNA extraction kits, two widely used microbial community profiling techniques, and the efficacy of different restriction enzymes for T-RFLP. Furthermore, the new forensic disciplines are defined by simultaneous measurements of multiple parameters spatiotemporally and therefore necessitate the application of multivariate analyses.

For the current illustrative study, we applied NMDS and principal component analysis, which facilitated closer data interrogation to then determine whether the decomposition of infant *S. scrofa domesticus*, plant litter, and a mixture of the two carbon sources effected measurable differences on the gravesoils. While justified as earlier, researchers and practitioners in the new disciplines of forensic ecogenomics, microbial forensics, forensic microbiology, environmental forensics, and geoforensics must decide when and where mathematical and statistical analyses are critical, seminal, informative, or superfluous for application in, and knowledge transfer to, real crime scenes and cases.

KEY CONCLUSIONS FROM OUR SUBSURFACE STUDIES

Cadaver decomposition is a complex process with microbial activity playing an important role. Nevertheless, the complex interactions of the cadaveric and environmental microbial communities in both surface and subsurface decompositions still remain a "black box" for forensic researchers and practitioners. Studies are beginning to address the knowledge gap regarding cadaver decomposition with a view to using microbial community profiles as potential tools in PMI and TSB estimations. To address this paucity, four different studies were made by our team. Thus we: (1) explored temporal changes in total (DNA) and functional (RNA) soil microbial communities during *S. scrofa domesticus* decomposition relative to burial depth (Bergmann et al., 2014; Chimutsa et al., 2015; Olakanye et al., 2014); (2) compared shifts in microbial biodiversity in response to animal tissue and plant-based carbon sources with links made also to key environmental variables (Olakanye et al., 2015); (3) compared changes in microbial community structure and composition in the presence of whole piglets and plant litter, individually and together (this chapter); and (4) used an in situ underground decomposition investigation with whole piglets and leaf litter where the environmental variables of soil pH and temperature were also monitored (Olakanye et al., 2017).

In general, we designed studies to address a key knowledge gap by testing the overarching hypothesis that forensic ecogenomics can be applied in subsurface decomposition studies for potential PMI and TSB estimations, identification of potential microbial clock indicators, and clandestine grave location. This was made by addressing specific research questions through four separate studies with different soil types, plant litter, and amounts of *S. scrofa domesticus*. Furthermore, three geophysical techniques were used in the in situ study as a preliminary investigation of the applicability of forensic ecogenomics parallel with analyses that are used typically in crime scenes.

Overall, the results of our investigations reflected other published reports and highlighted that abiotic factors such as temperature and pH are important variables that must be considered in PMI/TSB estimations. Experimental designs and subsequent data interpretations must then take into account that ambient conditions in outdoor studies reflect real cases more closely, while lysimeters under monitored/controlled environmental (e.g., temperature, pH, moisture) conditions do not indicate real scenarios but afford specific analysis of the impact of decomposition alone. As observed from the DGGE-derived ecological trends for diversity, richness, and evenness and NGS data, microbial community dynamics were related to soil temperature differences and seasonal changes. Consequently, the impacts of differences in weather, climate, soil type, and geographical location on the necrobiome must be studied further to assess the effective, relevant, and appropriate use of postmortem microbial clock indicators in PMI/TSB estimations. Protracted future studies in different geographical locations should then consider the long-term implications of global climate change where monthly climatic conditions vary between years, which will invariably affect rates of decomposition and related microbial community dynamics.

All four studies recorded increased pH trends for the *S. scrofa domesticus* soils in the early phases of decomposition, which may be indicative of the added substrate composition in comparison with plant litter, as nonpig carbon sources, and the controls. Also the dual carbon sources altered the pH trends in comparison with individual substrates. This could be useful potentially when considering the possibility of cadaver and plant litter mixtures in clandestine grave crime scenes.

While no statistically significant differences were recorded, except for some of the 18S profiling, analysis and interpretation of the PCR-DGGE fingerprints by Shannon–Wiener, Simpson, richness, and evenness ecological indices, trends revealed changes in the microbial community structure relative to the subsurface decomposition timelines. One of the key findings from these analyses was that profiling of the 16S rRNA bacterial gene seemed to be the most suitable for *S. scrofa domesticus* PMI estimation, while ecological indices of the fungal 18S rRNA gene were better indicators of plant litter decomposition. Due to its limitations, the microbial community profiles may be underestimated by denaturing gradient gel electrophoresis and so commend use of NGS.

The metagenomic profiles revealed some decomposition-mediated changes within the different soil microbiota, but with seasonal changes seemingly having a bigger impact for some soil types. This program is one of the first comprising subsurface investigations and certainly the first research where belowground epinecrotic communities of two carbon sources were compared in a forensic ecogenomics context. The results highlighted the potential of using these communities for PMI and/or TSB estimation. Some unique taxa, such as *Arthrobacter* and *Rhodococcus* spp. and *Lindia* and *Sporobolomyces* spp., were bacterial and eukaryote members, respectively, that could be tracked for *S. scrofa domesticus* decomposition relative to soil type. Sphingobacteriaceae and Streptomycetaceae provided preliminary indicators to differentiate between pig and plant (leaf) litter soils during late belowground decomposition. Likewise, taxa such as Microbacteriaceae, Alcaligenaceae. and Xanthomonodaceae were identified during the summer season as potential indicators for piglet and piglet+plant litter (grass) mesocosms, whereas Porphyromonadaceae was a likely indicator to differentiate between the two carbon sources. Therefore these taxa could be targeted potentially to distinguish between cadaveric (with pig as the taphonomic proxy) and plant matter decompositions in the subsurface. Finally, the in situ necrobiome metagenomic profiles also identified Methylococcaceae as potential seasonal bacterial indicators, from winter to summer with Anaerolineaceae and Methylophilaceae as microbial clock indicators for leaf litter and piglet, respectively, for decomposition locations in similar soil types.

Generally, taxanomic resolution was achieved to different degrees in the different study soils. Direct comparisons were, however, not possible due to different experimental designs. The complementary application of relevant ecological, statistical, and mathematical analyses, with subsurface decomposition intended to reflect real forensic contexts, was also illustrated. In particular, principal component analysis of DGGE-based data often allowed clearer differentiation between control and treatment soils than the ecological indices alone.

RESEARCH QUESTIONS FOR FUTURE WORK

The potential use of forensic ecogenomics as a novel suite of techniques for crime scene investigation is gaining momentum. Most of the studies reported between 2006 and March 2017 have focused on microbial ecology dynamics of the cadaver or human taphonomic proxy and surface soils impacted directly by the decomposing material. Further and more detailed investigations are essential to elucidate fully the interactions between the surrounding ecology, particularly of the subsurface gravesoil and cadaver decomposition. Consequently, the successional soil ecology changes that are effected by cadaver decomposition can have increased applicability in PMI estimations, TSB determinations, and location of clandestine graves. Although new knowledge has resulted from our research program and other similar initiatives, further research questions have emerged and key paucities still remain. These can be summarized as follows:

1. To what extent do abiotic factors affect the necrobiome dynamics?
2. What are the effects of seasonal differences on the postmortem microbial community?
3. What role does the cadaver/carcass size play in accurate PMI estimation?
4. What effects does the age of the study animal model have on the necrobiome dynamics and therefore postmortem and TSB estimations?
5. What are the implications of depth of burial for PMI and TSB determinations?
6. How should the impacts of global climate change be investigated with regards to PMI estimation?

Therefore future decomposition investigations should include comprehensive study designs and analyses and consider: various animal models of different sizes and ages (see also Chapter 4); study animals of similar age and size in different in situ soils and local climates; same mammalian taphonomic proxies buried in the same soil but at different depths; soil nutrient analysis; gaseous and volatile organic carbon emissions; and volatile fatty acid profiling relative to soil pH. All of these must be implemented parallel to both affordable microbial community profiling techniques and more high-throughput platforms such as NGS. In the long term, a better understanding of global climate change on decomposition activities and dynamics would also be useful in PMI and TSB estimations.

Earth electrical resistance survey can be an effective method for detecting cut features, and its efficacy in locating covered and uncovered cadavers was illustrated in field tests by Pringle et al. (2012a). Ground-penetrating radar (GPR) is recommendable since previous studies have demonstrated its efficacy in locating graves (Pringle et al., 2012b; Schultz and Martin, 2012). Differences in results and the efficacy of GPR must then be interpreted relative to the antenna used, e.g., 500 versus 800 MHz, and depth of burials per study. In an attempt to test their applicability, several relevant geophysical analysis tools, including geomagnetic detection, earth electrical resistance measurement and GPR, were applied in parallel with molecular microbial ecological analysis of burial pits in our in situ study (Olakanye et al., 2017). The principal aim was to investigate the potential of forensic ecogenomics to complement and expand the current crime scene investigative toolkit where geophysical techniques are used to locate clandestine graves or areas of mass burials.

Although geophysical survey of our in situ study did not provide conclusive results regarding the efficacy of the various techniques for the piglet burials at the research site, it afforded useful preliminary information and insight for the way forward. For example, a greenfield site in a nonigneous geological environment would probably be a more appropriate test area for a geomagnetic survey. Also trial surveys could confirm the suitability of a study site location prior to burial for research, investigative, and proof-of-concept purposes. The burial of larger carcasses and/or cadavers, subject to appropriate ethical clearance, would facilitate more pertinent detection of any decomposition-associated geophysical effects, a limitation that ecogenomics does not necessarily have. Additionally, spatial and temporal survey intervals should be appropriate to the size and depth of the buried targets. For our study, for example, it is considered that a sampling interval of at least half the minimum target size would have been appropriate for both the electrical resistance determination and geomagnetic survey. Also depending on both the target size and burial, it may be useful to increase the density of radar profiles across a test site, particularly for higher frequency antennae and shallower targets.

The case study and related investigations as reported in this chapter were made mostly with pigs/piglets as surrogates for human cadavers. Therefore the use of human cadavers would provide more robust and conclusive data sets for forensic practitioners in understanding the complex relationships between cadaver and soil microbial community dynamics. Finally, the use of the geophysical techniques as crime scene investigative tools should be applied and tested more rigorously to determine how forensic ecogenomics complements and/or mitigates the limitations of existing forensic investigations.

ACKNOWLEDGMENTS

Henny Folorunso and Professor Tim Thompson are acknowledged gratefully for their contributions to the experimental design of the study used in this chapter.

REFERENCES

Al-Mesbah, H., Moffatt, C., El-Azazy, O.M., Majeed, Q.A., 2012. The decomposition of rabbit carcass and associated necrophagous Diptera in Kuwait. Forensic Science International 217 (1–3), 27–31.

Arroyo, P., Saenz de Miera, L.E., Ansola, G., 2015. Influence of environmental variables on the structure and composition of soil bacterial communities in natural and constructed wetlands. Science of the Total Environment 506–507, 380–390.

Bandeira, B., Jamet, J.-L., Jamet, D., Ginoux, J.-M., 2013. Mathematical convergences of biodiversity indices. Ecological Indicators 29, 522–528.

Barry, J., Birchenough, S., Norris, B., Ware, S., 2013. On the use of sample indices to reflect changes in benthic fauna biodiversity. Ecological Indicators 26, 154–162.

Benbow, M.E., Pechal, J.L., Lang, J.M., Erb, R., Wallace, J.R., 2015. The potential of high-throughput metagenomic sequencing of aquatic bacterial communities to estimate the postmortem submersion interval. Journal of Forensic Sciences 60 (6), 1500–1510.

Benninger, L.A., Carter, D.O., Forbes, S.L., 2008. The biochemical alteration of soil beneath a decomposing carcass. Forensic Science International 180 (2–3), 70–75.

Bergmann, G.T., Bates, S.T., Eilers, K.G., Lauber, C.L., Caporaso, J.G., Walters, W.A., Knight, R., Fierer, N., 2011. The under-recognized dominance ofVerrucomicrobia in soil bacterial communities. Soil Biology & Biochemistry 43 (7), 1450–1455.

Bergmann, R.C., Ralebitso-Senior, T.K., Thompson, T.J., 2014. An RNA-based analysis of changes in biodiversity indices in response to *Sus scrofa domesticus* decomposition. Forensic Science International 241, 190–194.

Breton, H., Kirkwood, A.E., Carter, D.O., Forbes, S.L., 2016. The impact of carrion decomposition on the fatty acid methyl ester (FAME) profiles of soil microbial communities in southern Canada. Canadian Society of Forensic Science Journal 49 (1), 1–18.

Bull, P.A., Parker, A., Morgan, R.M., 2006. The forensic analysis of soils and sediment taken from the cast of a footprint. Forensic Science International 162 (1–3), 6–12.

Campobasso, C.P., Della, G.D., Introna, F., 2001. Factors affecting decomposition and Diptera colonization. Forensic Science International 120, 18–27.

Carter, D.O., Metcalf, J.L., Bibat, A., Knight, R., 2015. Seasonal variation of postmortem microbial communities. Forensic Science, Medicine and Pathology 11 (2), 202–207.

Carter, D.O., Tibbett, M., 2006. Microbial decomposition of skeletal muscle tissue (*Ovis aries*) in a sandy loam soil at different temperatures. Soil Biology & Biochemistry 38, 1139–1145.

Carter, D.O., Tibbett, M., 2008. Cadaver decomposition and soil: processes. In: Tibbett, M., Carter, D.O. (Eds.), Soil Analysis in Forensic Taphonomy: Chemical and Biological Effects of Buried Human Remains. CRC Press, Roca Baton, pp. 29–51.

Carter, D.O., Yellowlees, D., Tibbett, M., 2007. Cadaver decomposition in terrestrial ecosystems. Naturwissenschaften 94 (1), 12–24.

Carter, D.O., Yellowlees, D., Tibbett, M., 2010. Moisture can be the dominant parameter governing cadaver decomposition in soil. Forensic Science International 200 (1–3), 60–66.

Charneca, R., Nunes, J.L.T., Dividich, J.L., 2010. Body composition and blood parameters of newborn piglets from Alentejano and conventional (Large White × Landrace) genotype. Spanish Journal of Agricultural Research 8 (2), 317–325.

Chimutsa, M., Olakanye, A.O., Thompson, T.J.U., Ralebitso-Senior, T.K., 2015. Soil fungal community shift evaluation as a potential cadaver decomposition indicator. Forensic Science International 257, 155–159.

Chun, L.P., Miguel, M.J., Junkins, E.N., Forbes, S.L., Carter, D.O., 2015. An initial investigation into the ecology of culturable aerobic postmortem bacteria. Science and Justice 55 (6), 394–401.

Cobaugh, K.L., Schaeffer, S.M., DeBruyn, J.M., 2015. Functional and structural succession of soil microbial communities below decomposing human cadavers. PLoS One 10 (6), e0130201.

Crippen, T.L., Benbow, E.M., Pechal, J.L., 2015. Microbial interactions during carrion decomposition. In: Benbow, E.M., Tomberlin, J.K., Tarone, A.M. (Eds.), Carrion Ecology, Evolution, and Their Applications. CRC Press, Boca Raton, pp. 31–63.

Dadour, I.R., Harvey, M.L., 2008. The role of invertebrates in terrestrial decomposition: forensic applications. In: Tibbett, M., Carter, D.O. (Eds.), Soil Analysis in Forensic Taphonomy: Chemical and Biological Effects of Buried Human Remains. CRC Press, Boca Raton, pp. 109–122.

Damann, F.E., Williams, D.E., Layton, A.C., 2015. Potential use of bacterial community succession in decaying human bone for estimating post-mortem interval. Journal of Forensic Sciences 60 (4), 844–850.

Damann, F.E., Tanittaisong, A., Carter, D.O., 2012. Potential carcass enrichment of the University of Tennessee Anthropology Research Facility: a baseline survey of edaphic feature. Forensic Science International 222 (1–3), 4–10.

De-Vos, P., Garrity, G.M., Jones, D., Krieg, N.R., Ludwig, W., Rainey, F.A., Schleifer, K.-H., Whitman, W.B. (Eds.), 2009. Bergey's manual of systematic bacteriology. In: The Firmicutes, vol. 3. second ed. Springer, New York, pp. 764–766.

Dunfield, K.E., 2007. Lipid-based community analysis. In: Carter, M.R., Gregorich, E.G. (Eds.), Soil Sampling and Methods of Analysis, second ed. CRC Press, Boca Raton, pp. 557–566.

Elsas, J.D., Rutgers, M., 2006. Soil microbial diversity and community composition. In: Bloem, J., Hopkins, D.W., Benedetti, A. (Eds.), Microbiological Methods for Assessing Soil Quality. CABI Publishing, Wallingford, Oxfordshire, pp. 183–185.

Felske, A., Osborn, M.A., 2004. DNA fingerprinting of microbial communities. In: Osborn, M., Smith, C. (Eds.), Molecular Microbial Ecology. Taylor and Francis, New York, pp. 59–87.

Finley, S.J., Pechal, J.L., Benbow, M.E., Robertson, B.K., Javan, G.T., 2016. Microbial signatures of cadaver gravesoil during decomposition. Microbial Ecology 71 (3), 524–529.

Gerber, N., 2011. Biodiversity measures based on species-level dissimilarities: a methodology for assessment. Ecological Economics 70, 2275–2281.

Gill-King, H., 1997. Chemical and ultrastructural aspects of decomposition. In: Haglund, W.D., Sorg, M.H. (Eds.), Forensic Taphonomy: The Postmortem Fate of Human Remains. CRC Press, Boca Raton, pp. 93–108.

Gonzalez, A., Clemente, J.C., Shade, A., Metcalf, J.L., Song, S., Prithiviraj, B., Palmer, B.E., Knight, R., 2011. Our microbial selves: what ecology can teach us. EMBO Reports 12 (8), 775–784.

Goodfellow, M., Kampfer, P., Busse, H.-J., Trujilo, M.E., Suzuki, K.-I., Ludwig, W., Whitman, W.B. (Eds.), 2012. Bergey's manual of systematic bacteriology. In: The Actinobacteria, Part A, vol. 5. second ed. Springer, New York.

Green, S.J., Leigh, M.B., Neufeld, J.D., 2009. Denaturing gradient gel electrophoresis (DGGE) for microbial community analysis. In: Timmis, K.N. (Ed.), Microbiology of Hydrocarbons, Oils, Lipids, and Derived Compounds. Springer, Heidelberg, pp. 4137–4158.

Green, S.J., Prakash, O., Jasrotia, P., Overholt, W.A., Cardenas, E., Hubbard, D., Tiedje, J.M., Watson, D.B., Schadt, C.W., Brooks, S.C., Kostka, J.E., 2012. Denitrifying bacteria from the genus *Rhodanobacter* dominate bacterial communities in the highly contaminated subsurface of a nuclear legacy waste site. Applied and Environmental Microbiology 78 (4), 1039–1047.

Haslam, T.C., Tibbett, M., 2009. Soils of contrasting pH affect the decomposition of buried mammalian (*Ovis aries*) skeletal muscle tissue. Journal of Forensic Sciences 54 (4), 900–904.

Hedrick, D.B., Peacock, A., Stephen, J.R., Macnaughton, S.J., Bruggemann, J., White, D.C., 2000. Measuring soil microbial community diversity using polar lipid fatty acid and denaturing gradient gel electrophoresis data. Journal of Microbiological Methods 41, 235–248.

Hill, T.C.J., Walsh, K.A., Harris, J.A., Moffett, B.F., 2003. Using ecological diversity measures with bacterial communities. FEMS Microbiology Ecology 43 (1), 1–11.

Howard, G.T., Duos, B., Watson-Horzelski, E.J., 2010. Characterization of the soil microbial community associated with the decomposition of swine carcass. International Biodeterioration and Biodegradation 64 (4), 300–304.

Hyde, E.R., Haarmann, D.P., Lynne, A.M., Bucheli, S.R., Petrosino, J.F., 2013. The living dead: bacterial community structure of a cadaver at the onset and end of the bloat stage of decompostion. PLoS One 8 (10), e77733.

Hyde, E.R., Haarmann, D.P., Petrosino, J.F., Lynne, A.M., Bucheli, S.R., 2015. Initial insights into bacterial succession during human decomposition. International Journal of Legal Medicine 129 (3), 661–671.

Janaway, R.C., Percival, S.L., Wilson, A.S., 2009. Decomposition of human remains. In: Percival, S.L. (Ed.), Microbiology and Aging: Clinical Manifestations. Springer, New York, pp. 313–334.

Kandeler, E., 2007. Physiological and biochemical methods for studying soil biota and their function. In: Paul, E.A. (Ed.), Soil Microbiology, Ecology and Biochemistry, third ed. Academic Press, Burlington, pp. 53–83.

Kozich, J.J., Westcott, S.L., Baxter, N.T., Highlander, S.K., Schloss, P.D., 2013. Development of a dual-index sequencing strategy and curation pipeline for analyzing amplicon sequence data on the MiSeq Illumina sequencing platform. Applied and Environmental Microbiology 79 (17), 5112–5120.

Bergey's manual of systematic bacteriology. In: Krieg, N.R., Staley, J.T., Brown, D.R., Hedlund, B.P., Paster, B.J., Ward, N.L., Wolfgang, L., Whitman, W.B. (Eds.), 2010. The Bacteroidetes, Spirochaetes, Tenericutes (Mollicutes), Acidobacteria, Fibrobacteres, Fusobacteria, Dictyoglomi, Gemmatimonadetes, Lentisphaerae, Verrucomicrobia, Clamydiae, and Planctomycetes, vol. 4. second ed. Springer, New York.

Lauber, C.L., Metcalf, J.L., Keepers, K., Ackermann, G., Carter, D.O., Knight, R., 2014. Vertebrate decomposition is accelerated by soil microbes. Applied and Environmental Microbiology 80 (16), 4920–4929.

Lerner, A., Shor, Y., Vinokurov, A., Okon, Y., Jurkevitch, E., 2006. Can denaturing gradient gel electrophoresis (DGGE) analysis of amplified 16S rDNA of soil bacterial population be used in forensic investigation? Soil Biology & Biochemistry 38, 1188–1192.

Ligi, T., Oopkaup, K., Truu, M., Preem, J.-K., Nõlvak, H., Mitsch, W.J., Mander, U., Truu, J., 2014. Characterization of bacterial communities in soil and sediment of a created riverine wetland complex using high-throughput 16S rRNA amplicon sequencing. Ecological Engineering 72, 56–66.

Madigan, M.T., Martinko, J.M., Stahl, D.A., Clark, D.P., 2012a. Microbial evolution and diversity. In: Madigan, M.T., Martinko, J.M., Stahl, D.A., Clark, D.P. (Eds.), Brock Biology of Microorganisms, thirteenth ed. Pearson Education, San Francisco, pp. 446–474.

Madigan, M.T., Martinko, J.M., Stahl, D.A., Clark, D.P., 2012b. Methods in microbial ecology. In: Madigan, M.T., Martinko, J.M., Stahl, D.A., Clark, D.P. (Eds.), Brock Biology of Microorganisms, thirteenth ed. Pearson Education, San Francisco, pp. 641–668.

Maier, R.M., Pepper, I.L., 2009. Bacterial communities in natural ecosystems. In: Maier, R.M., Pepper, I.L., Gerba, C.P. (Eds.), Environmental Microbiology, second ed. Academic Press, London, pp. 347–356.

Mann, R.W., Bass, W.M., Meadows, L., 1990. Time since death and decomposition of the human body: variables and observations in case and experimental field studies. Journal of Forensic Sciences 35, 103–111.

Marschner, P., 2007. Soil microbial community structure and function assessed by FAME, PLFA and DGGE - advantages and limitations. In: Varma, A., Oelmüller, R. (Eds.), Advanced Techniques in Soil Microbiology. Springer, Heidelberg, pp. 181–196.

McGuire, K.L., Treseder, K.K., 2010. Microbial communities and their relevance for ecosystem models: decomposition as a case study. Soil Biology & Biochemistry 42, 529–535.

Metcalf, J.L., Parfrey, L.W., Gonzalez, A., Lauber, C.L., Knights, D., Ackermann, G., Humphrey, G.C., Gebert, M.J., Treuren, W.V., Berg-Lyons, D., Keepers, K., Guo, Y., Bullard, J., Fierer, N., Carter, D.O., Knight, R., 2013. A microbial clock provides an accurate estimate of the postmortem interval in a mouse model system. eLIFE 2, e01104.

Metcalf, J.L., Xu, Z.Z., Weiss, S., Lax, S., Treuren, W.V., Hyde, E.R., Song, S.J., Amir, A., Larsen, P., Sangwan, N., Haarmann, D., Humphrey, G.C., Ackermann, G., Thompson, L.R., Lauber, C., Bibat, A., Nicholas, C., Gebert, M.J., Petrosino, J.F., Reed, S.C., Gilbert, J.A., Lynne, A.M., Bucheli, S.R., Carter, D.O., Knight, R., 2016. Microbial community assembly and metabolic function during mammalian corpse decomposition. Science 351 (6269), 158–162.

Meyer, J., Anderson, B., Carter, D.O., 2013. Seasonal variation of carcass decomposition and gravesoil chemistry in a cold (Dfa) climate. Journal of Forensic Sciences 58 (5), 1175–1182.
Micozzi, M., 1986. Experimental study of postmortem change under field conditions: effects of freezing, thawing and mechanical injury. Journal of Forensic Sciences 31, 953–961.
Moreno, L.I., Mills, D., Fetscher, J., John-Williams, K., Meadows-Jantz, L., McCord, B., 2011. The application of amplicon length heterogeneity PCR (LH-PCR) for monitoring the dynamics of soil microbial communities associated with cadaver decomposition. Journal of Microbiological Methods 84, 388–393.
Muyzer, G., Waal, E.C., Uitterlinden, A.G., 1993. Profiling of complex microbial populations by denaturing gradient gel electrophoresis analysis of polymerase chain reaction-amplified genes coding for 16S rRNA. Applied and Environmental Microbiology 59 (3), 695–700.
Newton, R.J., Bootsma, M.J., Morrison, H.G., Sogin, M.L., McLellan, S.L., 2013. A microbial signature approach to identify fecal pollution in the waters off an urbanized coast of Lake Michigan. Microbial Ecology 65 (4), 1011–1023.
Olakanye, A.O., Thompson, T., Ralebitso-Senior, T.K., 2014. Changes to soil bacterial profiles as a result of *Sus scrofa domesticus* decomposition. Forensic Science International 245, 101–106.
Olakanye, A.O., Nelson, A., Ralebitso-Senior, T.K., 2017. A comparative *in situ* decomposition study using still born piglets and leaf litter from a deciduous forest. Forensic Science International 276, 85–92.
Olakanye, A.O., Thompson, T., Ralebitso-Senior, T.K., 2015. Shifts in soil biodiversity – a forensic comparison between *Sus scrofa domesticus* and vegetation decomposition. Science & Justice 55 (6), 402–407.
Parkinson, R.A., Dias, K.-R., Horswell, J., Greenwood, P., Bannin, N., Tibbett, M., Vass, A.A., 2009. Microbial community analysis of human decomposition on soil. In: Ritz, K., Dawson, L., Miller, D. (Eds.), Criminal and Environmental Soil Forensics. Springer, New York, pp. 379–394.
Pasternak, Z., Al-Ashhab, A., Gatica, J., Gafny, R., Avraham, S., Frenk, S., Minz, D., Gillor, O., Jurkevitch, E., 2012. Optimization of molecular methods and statistical procedures for forensic fingerprinting of microbial soil communities. International Research Journal of Microbiology 3 (11), 363–372.
Pechal, J.L., Benbow, E.M., 2015. Community ecology. In: Tomberlin, J.K., Benbow, E.M. (Eds.), Forensic Entomology: International Dimensions and Frontiers. CRC Press, Boca Raton, pp. 347–360.
Pechal, J.L., Crippen, T.L., Benbow, M.E., Tarone, A.M., Dowd, S., Tomberlin, J.K., 2014. The potential use of bacterial community succession in forensics as described by high throughput metagenomic sequencing. International Journal of Legal Medicine 128 (1), 193–205.
Peralta, R.M., Ahn, C., Gillevet, P.M., 2013. Characterization of soil bacterial community structure and physicochemical properties in created and natural wetlands. Science of the Total Environment 443, 725–732.
Petraco, N., Kubic, T.A., Petraco, N.D., 2008. Case studies in forensic soil examinations. Forensic Science International 178 (2–3), e23–e27.
Pringle, J.K., Ruffell, A., Jervis, J.R., Donnelly, J., McKinley, J., Hansen, J., Morgan, R., Pirrie, D., Harrison, M., 2012a. The use of geoscience methods for terrestrial forensic searches. Earth Science Reviews 114 (1–2), 108–123.
Pringle, J.K., Jervis, J.R., Hansen, J.D., Jones, G.M., Cassidy, N.J., Cassella, J.P., 2012b. Geophysical monitoring of simulated clandestine graves using electrical and ground-penetrating radar methods: 0–3 years after burial. Journal of Forensic Sciences 57 (6), 1467–1486.
Pylro, V.S., Roesch, L.F., Morais, D.K., Clark, I.M., Hirsch, P.R., Tótola, M.R., 2014. Data analysis for 16S microbial profiling from different benchtop sequencing platforms. Journal of Microbiological Methods 107, 30–37.
Ralebitso-Senior, T.K., Thompson, T.J.U., Carney, H.E., 2016. Microbial ecogenomics and forensic science: new methods for investigating clandestine grave sites. Human Remains & Violence 2 (1), 41–57.
Rodriguez, W.C., Bass, W.M., 1983. Insect activity and its relationship to decay rates of human cadavers in east Tennessee. Journal of Forensic Sciences 28 (2), 423–432.
Roesch, L.F., Fulthorpe, R.R., Riva, A., Casella, G., Hadwin, A.K., Kent, A.D., Daroub, S.H., Farmerie, W.G., Triplett, E.W., 2007. Pyrosequencing enumerates and contrasts soil microbial diversity. The ISME Journal 1 (14), 283–290.
Schultz, J.J., Martin, M.M., 2012. Monitoring controlled graves representing common burial scenarios with ground penetrating radar. Journal of Applied Geophysics 83, 74–89.

Stokes, K.L., Forbes, S.L., Tibbett, M., 2009. Freezing skeletal muscle tissue does not affect its decomposition in soil: evidence from temporal changes in tissue mass, microbial activity and soil chemistry based on excised samples. Forensic Science International 183, 6–13.

Tagliavini, M., Tonon, G., Scandellari, F., Quinones, A., Palmieri, S., Menarbin, G., Gioacchini, P., Masia, A., 2007. Nutrient recycling during decomposition of apple leaves (*Malus domestica*) and mowed grasses in orchard. Agriculture, Ecosystems & Environment 118 (1–4), 191–200.

Thies, J.E., 2007. Molecular methods for studying soil ecology. In: Paul, E.A. (Ed.), Soil Microbiology, Ecology, and Biochemistry, third ed. Academic Press, Oxford, pp. 86–118.

van Belle, L.E., Carter, D.O., Forbes, S.L., 2009. Measurement of ninhydrin reactive nitrogen influx into gravesoil during aboveground and belowground carcass (*Sus domesticus*) decomposition. Forensic Science International 193 (1–3), 37–41.

Vass, A.A., Barshick, S.A., Sega, G., Caton, J., Skeen, J.T., Love, J.C., Synstelien, J.A., 2002. Decomposition chemistry of human remains: a new methodology for determining the postmortem interval. Journal of Forensic Sciences 47 (3), 542–553.

Vass, A.A., Bass, W.M., Wolt, J.D., Foss, J.E., Ammons, J.T., 1992. Time since death determinations of human cadavers using soil solution. Journal of Forensic Sciences 37 (5), 1236–1253.

Weiss, S., Carter, D.O., Metcalf, J.L., Knight, R., 2016. Carcass mass has little influence on the structure of gravesoil microbial communities. International Journal of Legal Medicine 130 (1), 253–263.

Whiteson, K.L., Hernandez, D., Lazarevic, V., Gaia, N., Farinelli, L., François, P., Pilo, P., Frey, J., Schrenzel, J., 2014. A genomic perspective on a new bacterial genus and species from the Alcaligenaceae family, *Basilea psittacipulmonis*. BMC Genomics 15, 169.

Woods, B., Lennard, C., Kirkbride, P.K., Robertson, J., 2014. Soil examination for a forensic trace evidence laboratory-part 1: spectroscopic techniques. Forensic Science International 245, 187–194.

Zhou, C., Byard, R.W., 2011. Factors and processes causing accelerated decomposition in human cadavers – an overview. Journal of Forensic and Legal Medicine 18 (1), 6–9.

CHAPTER 8

From Experimental Work to Real Crime Scenes and the Courts

Jifeng Cai[1], Lorna Dawson[2], Gulnaz T. Javan[3], Sait Özsoy[4], Frederike C.A. Quaak[5], T. Komang Ralebitso-Senior[6]
[1]Central South University, Changsha, PR China; [2]The James Hutton Institute, Aberdeen, United Kingdom; [3]Alabama State University, Montgomery, AL, United States; [4]University of Health Sciences, Ankara, Turkey; [5]Netherlands Forensic Institute, The Hague, The Netherlands; [6]Teesside University, Tees Valley, United Kingdom

RATIONALE

Intelligence gathered from crime investigations often informs deliberations in court proceedings. Therefore the applicability of emergent forensic techniques and disciplines, including the forensic ecogenomics approach, must be proposed from informed perspectives, tested using appropriately comprehensive experimental designs, i.e., asking the right experimental questions, and adopted, incrementally, in relevant crime cases. This pathway can potentially then be used in subsequent legal proceedings.

The significance of laboratory experiments and case studies that investigate the complete necrobiome, i.e., both macrobial (insects, plants, small animals) and microbial (bacteria, fungi, nematodes, protozoa) communities, cannot be underestimated or overemphasized. Therefore research programs can be designed with crime scene investigators to explore how time-since-death or postmortem interval (PMI) and time-since-burial (TSB) determinations can be improved by studying shifts in the cadaver or mammalian proxy microbiome, cadaver decomposition island (CDI) communities, subsurface decompositional soil microbiota, and postmortem submersion microbiome. Ideally, researchers can promote their skill sets to police departments so that they can be invited to collect, examine, and analyze samples from existing crime scenes to illustrate the applicability of research data in real cases. Irrespective of how the collaborations are instigated, the potential of these undertakings would be more realizable where the (micro)biological analyses are underpinned by complementary chemical, biogeochemical, geophysical, physicochemical, botanical, and entomological examinations of the atmospheric, terrestrial, and aquatic environments around and under the cadaver or taphonomic surrogate. Table 8.1 provides some examples of peer-reviewed literature, which illustrate the potential for different forensic analyses in real cases or crime scenes, including ecogenomics-based profiling.

Deliberations on the value of knowledge exchange and application between researchers and real crimes are also exemplified by reports in scientific magazines and news articles for mixed audiences including researchers, practitioners, and the general public

Forensic Ecogenomics
ISBN 978-0-12-809360-3
http://dx.doi.org/10.1016/B978-0-12-809360-3.00008-4

Table 8.1 Some examples of published collaborative forensic casework between researchers, practitioners, and court proceedings

Context	Analytical techniques or approaches	Findings	Forensic discipline	References
1. Entomological comparisons between experimental findings and analysis of forensic case materials that corresponded to seven judicial inquiries **2.** The seven cases included male and female bodies found in different locales, environments, seasons, months and states of burial.	**1.** Collection and classification of sarcosaprophagous insects **2.** Appraisals by researchers **3.** Decomposition stage assessment **4.** Assessment of postmortem interval (PMI) estimations provided during judiciary proceedings	**1.** Arthropod succession, distribution, and abundance were related also to season **2.** Abundance and life cycle stages of some were also related to phases of decomposition **3.** Links established between experimental data or model and judiciary inquiries	Forensic entomology	Arnaldos et al. (2005)
1. Feasibility study analyzing the microbial community profiles of soils from a crime scene, an alibi scene, and locations not related to the crime **2.** Blind testing with origins of samples not known to researcher or operator	Denaturing gradient gel electrophoresis	**1.** Relatively high clustering between soil type and location, i.e., the crime scene, its vicinity, and the suspect's home **2.** Apparent need to test and standardize soil DNA extraction protocols **3.** Suggested use of complementary methods for increased statistical confidence and method reliability/validation	Forensic ecogenomics	Lerner et al. (2006)

1. Application of a modified Graves (1979) mineralogical soil classification method on samples from four cases **2.** Comparisons of known samples and questioned samples from construction site, crime scenes, and suspects' clothing, van, or home	**1.** Modified Graves method **2.** Munsell Soil Color system	**1.** Similarities and dissimilarities between known and questioned samples allowed sufficient differentiation for the findings to be used in real court cases **2.** Levels of similarities or dissimilarities were relevant to support an environmental laboratory that was consulted in a civil action case and trials for use by the jury or as testimony by the relevant author	Geoforensics	Petraco et al. (2008)
Skeletonized cadaver discovered in a forest in northern Portugal	**1.** Recovered bryophytes and vascular plants growing in, around, and through the cadaver remains **2.** Measured the growth of bryophytes **3.** Analyzed clothing from the remains **4.** Accounted for stage of decomposition	**1.** Estimated minimum postmortem interval ($_{min}$PMI) **2.** The $_{min}$PMI was consistent with the time of disappearance of the presumptive individual	Forensic botany	Cardoso et al. (2010)

Continued

Table 8.1 Some examples of published collaborative forensic casework between researchers, practitioners, and court proceedings—cont'd

Context	Analytical techniques or approaches	Findings	Forensic discipline	References
1. Access to autopsy reports held by Australia's National Coronial Information System 2. Used only cases where individuals were found between 0 and 14 days following death indoors.	1. Time-since-death (TSD) estimations 2. Total body decomposition (time-since-burial) score calculations 3. Systematic and quantitative analyses	1. Developed models for accurate TSD estimations from the determined total body scores 2. Tested and confirmed the models as accurate within several hours to half a day for the study region	–	Hayman and Oxenham (2017)
1. Access to 19 indoor death scenes with known PMIs 2. Nine scenes in Nebraska and 10 in Hawaii, USA	1. Development of a new PMI equation by modifying that published by Madea (2016) 2. Testing and optimization of PMI estimations	1. Accuracy achieved for 79% of the indoor deaths scenes 2. Decreased accuracy resulted relative to body mass loss and PMI greater than 4 days 3. Effect of climate inferred on the accuracy of the attained PMIs	–	Maile et al. (2017)
1. Attempted rape 2. Soil-stained clothing from suspect and victim, and suspect's shoes supplied by the police	1. Soil stains inspected visually and sampled for bacterial profiling using terminal restriction fragment length polymorphism and pollen analysis 2. Results from different techniques were combined	1. Findings reported in Bayesian framework 2. Combined results much more likely when soil samples on victim's clothing and suspect's shoes originated from same location	Forensic ecogenomics, forensic palynology, geoforensics	Uitdehaag et al. (2016)

(Hopper, 2011; Parry, 2011; Wald, 2015; Williams, 2015). Parallel discussions on the need for investigations, guidelines, and policy that are increasingly informed by scientific research, hence the role of different disciplines within forensic science, are also illustrated in governmental contexts, with the UK Parliamentary Committee meeting of 2016 one of several examples. In summary, these exchanges identify and emphasize the wide scope of opportunities where research areas such as forensic ecogenomics can be developed for knowledge pursuance, not simply for the sake of it but specifically for the advancement of intelligence gathering in real crime scenes and subsequently attribution in relevant court cases. Concomitant with these are debates on the potentials and limitations of different geographical, ecosystem, and legal contexts, as well as the availability of human taphonomic facilities (e.g., Williams, 2015; Witt et al., 2015).

Overall, the aforementioned findings, preliminary deliberations, and reports highlight the importance of capturing existing exemplar experimental work, simulations, and real cases, which can then be expanded and used to illustrate the potential for forensic ecogenomics beyond the laboratory. In full cognizance that real crime scene investigations adopt multiple, complementary, and cross-/interdisciplinary techniques and/or protocols, the discussions in the rest of the chapter reflect cases where forensic entomology, forensic microbiology, environmental forensics, soil forensics, forensic geoscience, etc. have been applied singly and/or in combination. Where relevant, key deliberations in preceding chapters have been extended to appraise succinctly the potential and limitations of implementing experimental findings in real crime scenes. Some of these discussions reflect the unique challenges and opportunities that are likely to arise from different investigative protocols and, to a lesser extent, different legal systems. The discussions consist of some country-specific historical perspectives, case studies, and/or trends for adopting new forensic approaches within specific national policing and legal structures. Although not all-inclusive, the range of cases is presented from different parts of the world and therefore start to suggest a global perspective.

We recognize that some country-specific, regional, and global initiatives, which aim to consolidate research, study findings, and real crime scenes, are already under way in parts of the world. Some of these include: the Australian Facility for Taphonomic Experimental Research (Australia); the summation by Archer and Wallman (2016) on forensic entomology achievements in Australia and New Zealand; the combination of computed tomography scanning and entomology (Johnson et al., 2012); the publications by Cockle and Bell (2015, 2017) where 42 Canadian cases with known PMIs, and 96 cases that had already been investigated by the Canadian police, were analyzed retrospectively for decomposition progression using PMI and accumulated degree days (ADD) determinations; the comparison of experimental and case study data in the Iberian Peninsula, Spain (Arnaldos et al., 2005); the Institute of Forensic Medicine (Switzerland); the University of Tennessee Anthropological Research Facility (USA; Mann et al., 1990);

and the Academic Medical Centre Cemetery due to be established in Amsterdam, the Netherlands (Enserink, 2017).

EXAMPLES OF COUNTRY-/REGION-SPECIFIC CASES AND PERSPECTIVES

From Experimental Work to Forensic Application at the Crime Scene: Developments in Forensic Medicine and Forensic Biology in China Over Time

Dr. Jifeng Cai, Central South University, Changsha, PR China

Ancient Chinese forensic development dates far earlier than in the West to c. 1000 BC, where China utilized the inspection procedure in the judicial activity. China's ancient history of forensic medicine can be divided into six stages (Yan, 2008): budding stage (Pre-Qin period), development period (Han Dynasty), peak period (Song Dynasty), low tide period (Yuan and Ming Dynasties), new high tide period (Qing Dynasty, before the Opium War), and the transition Period (Qing Dynasty, after the Opium War). The book *Xi Yuan Lu*, written by Song Ci during the Southern Song Dynasty, was completed in 1247 and is the world's first complete forensic monograph. It was translated into its English version *Washing Away of Wrongs* by Name McKnight in 1981 and it records the formation, mechanism, and distribution of *livor mortis*, the relationship between postmortem phenomena and time of death, mechanical asphyxia, mechanical injury, and lightning death, some of which are the fundamentals of modern forensic science. For a long time, a number of other important ancient Chinese forensic treatises have been written and utilized in practice. From the 1860s to the 1890s, the Westernization Movement in China set off a long history of reform and innovation, which was intended to utilize advanced technology developed in Western countries. As a result, *Legal Medicine*, the earliest modern forensic translation in China, was published in 1899 by the Jiangnan Manufacturing General Administration. Western modern forensic science then spread throughout China and the ancient forensic inspection methods have been replaced gradually by the Western practices.

In the first half of the 20th century, Chinese society was changing from a very traditional rural society to a modern generally urban one, and the forensic industry has also experienced the evolution from the ancient inspection by Wu Zuo (forensic examiner in ancient China) to modern forensic medicine. Lin Ji (1897–1951) is one of the earliest practitioners to introduce Western forensic practices to China and is therefore considered the founder of modern Chinese forensic medicine (Huang and Gu, 2014). After studying forensic medicine at the University of Würzburg, Germany, he returned to China in 1931 and established the Forensic Medicine Department in Beijing University (Huang and Chen, 2005). The pathological examination room, anatomical room, photography room, toxic laboratory, witness examination room, psychological identification room, eye otolaryngology darkroom, and animal room were built.

One of the first cases to be investigated in the department was that of a 16-year-old man who died after eating red shrimp pork, with his wife suspected of poisoning him. Lin examined the pork in the toxicity laboratory where the initial and retesting laboratory reports confirmed that the pork was nontoxic. Subsequent analysis by the Shanghai Commodity Inspection Bureau only found a single bacillus in the pork sample without any botulism. They questioned whether the strain was virulent with the potential to lead to animal poisoning resulting in death. As a result, Lin cultured the bacterium for 72 h and injected 1 mL of its growth medium extract into the abdominal cavity of a guinea pig. The guinea pig was still alive 5 days after the injection. Lin repeated the experiments twice with the same outcome. These experimental guinea pigs were killed and pathologic examinations on them recorded no pathogenic changes. The experiments, analyses, and findings were confirmed independently by the Shanghai Commodity Inspection Bureau. Therefore Lin reached the conclusion that the red pork meat did not have any toxin or botulism and hence surmised that there was likely another reason for that death. This case is an example where toxin inspections, bacterial culture, animal experiments, and pathological examinations were utilized systematically and most probably represents the earliest forensic case experimentation in China.

After the founding of the People's Republic of China in 1949, the Chinese government began training forensic examiners with the help of former Soviet experts. Chinese medical colleges and universities have since introduced systematic forensic education using, initially, teaching materials that were translations of the former Soviet Union (Zhang, 2013). Now, forensic medicine is a target discipline of study in numerous universities in the country and many established technologies such as DNA typing, immunohistochemistry, electron microscopy, gas chromatography, and gas chromatography–mass spectrometry are applied extensively in forensic research and investigations. For example, DNA typing, especially the short tandem repeat (STR) typing, is used widely for the identification and paternity testing of individuals in China. Specifically, the PowerPlex 16 System Kit (Promega, Madison, WI) and AmpF/STR Identifier Kit (Applied Biosystems, Foster City, CA) are the earliest kits that were used commonly for forensic casework in China, while Applied Biosystems invented the AmpF/STR Sinofiler PCR Amplification Kit especially for the Chinese population. Also several STR multiplex amplification kits such as the STRtyper-10 F/G Kit (Condon, Zhuhai, China), Goldeneye16 A Kit (Peoplespot, Beijing, China), DNATyper15 Kit (China's National Ministry of Public Security, Beijing, China), AGCU 21+1 STR Fluorescence Assay Kit (AGCU ScienTech Incorporation, Wuxi, Jiangsu, China), and AGCU EX22 STR Fluorescence Assay Kit (AGCU ScienTech Incorporation, Wuxi, Jiangsu, China) have been invented by Chinese companies for use in various forensic casework and research initiatives.

Since the 1990s, the forensic DNA database in China has been built at three levels: central DNA database, province DNA database, and city DNA database, which includes the convicted offender DNA database, forensic casework sample DNA database, missing people DNA database, and the basic DNA database. In 2002, the National Ministry of Public Security promulgated two documents to standardize the laboratory practice of forensic DNA collection and handling. In 2003, two specification standards, which selected the loci D16S539, Vwa, D3S1358, D18S51, D21S11, D8S1179, FGA, TH01, D7S820, D5S818, D13S317, CSF1PO, TPOX, F13A01, FESPES, PENTAD, PENTAE, D1S80, D2S1388, D19S433, and amelogenin, were developed to establish the forensic DNA database. Nowadays, the China national DNA database includes more than 30 million STR profiles (Liu, 2015).

Many Chinese forensic scientists pursue different areas of research and have published peer-reviewed papers in many international journals. Among these studies is the use of PMI estimation, which has become topical and entails the application of a wide range of analytical methods. These include, but are not limited to, DNA degradation (Chen and Cheng, 2002), RNA degradation (Liu et al., 2007), protein degradation (Xiao and Chen, 2005), ATP degradation (Mao et al., 2013), chemical changes in the vitreous humor (Chen et al., 2009), entomological methods (Tang, 1994; Zhou et al., 1997; Wang et al., 2000, 2001, 2002a,b), and microbiological methods (Guo et al., 2016; Zhang et al., 2016). Nevertheless, the application of these research results in actual forensic practices and crime scene work will still require considerably more work, at least in their use as evidence. In contrast, forensic entomology has been studied to estimate the PMI of human remains and determine the cause of death for more than 20 years in China (Tang, 1994). Wang (2015) summarized recent (1997–2011) Chinese forensic entomology investigations and listed the dominant insect taxa found during field experiments, and these included Diptera and Coleptera. Chinese police and other forensic departments are making a conscious effort to use forensic entomology as part of their investigations, and several cases that employed this subdiscipline to estimate PMI have been published (Basangciren, 2001; Lu, 2001; Chen, 2006; Jia, 2009; Lv et al., 2010; Li et al., 2003; Wei and Huang, 2016, Table 8.2).

Initially, PMI estimation using insects was crude and heavily dependent on temperature. When the temperature is between 21 and 27°C, fly eggs will hatch into maggots within 12–24 h, and within 8–14 h at about 30°C. In contrast, fly eggs will hatch into maggots quickly and maggots can migrate after a few minutes to several hours at temperatures above 35°C.

The implications of PMI estimation using entomology were exemplified in a case where a large number of fly eggs and some 0.1 cm-long larvae occurred in the mouth, nasal cavity, vulva, and multiple superficial scars on the neck and two upper limbs of a female corpse found in Shanghai. Although the practical PMI after the crime was solved was estimated at approximately 9 h, Lu (2001) used the general development information of the fly and estimated the PMI at about 10 h, since the temperature around the incident was 31°C. In the same year, two male corpses were found in Shigatse City on

Table 8.2 Summary of published cases conducted in China between 2001 and 2016 where forensic entomology was used

Citation	Case context	Discovery time and date (where known)	Discovery site	Insects species found on the crime scene	Estimated PMI based on entomological analyses	Actual crime time
Basangciren (2001)	Two male bodies	August 10	Outdoor, Shigatse, Tibet	Fly larvae and pupa	60 days	June 10
Lu (2001)	Female body	7 a.m.	Outdoor, Shanghai	Fly eggs and larvae	10 h	9 p.m. on previous day
Chen (2006)	Female body	April 5	Indoor, Guizhou	*Aldrichina grahami* larvae and pupa	28 days	March 8
Jia (2009)	Male body	6 p.m. on July 20	Indoor, Xinji, Hebei	*Lucilia sericata* larvae	60.7–66.7 h	4 a.m. on July 17
Lv et al. (2010)	Three dismembered bodies	March 9		Fly larvae	3–5 days	March 5
		March 24	Outdoor, Wuhan, Hubei	Fly larvae	7–10 days	March 10
		May 4		*L. sericata* larvae and pupa	10–14 days	March 28
Li et al. (2003)	Female body	July 28	Outdoor, Chongqing	*A. grahami* and *Chrysomya pinguis* larvae and pupa	>35 days	February 28
Wei and Huang (2016)	Male body	9 a.m. on June 10	Outdoor, Zhongshan, Guangdong	*Chrysomya megacephala* larvae	4.2/4.57 days	5 p.m. on June 5

the Tibet Plateau. Although no young maggots were present, a few thick, dark brown, 1.5 cm-long maggots were found on the bodies along with a few brown pupae, and a large number of rupture residues of the pupae shells. Following comprehensive consideration of the degree of tissue decay, low temperature (19°C), and developmental stages of four generations of insects, Basangciren (2001) inferred that the PMI was about 60 days, which was proven by subsequent detection.

Numerous entomological studies in relation to the development cycle of insects and accumulative temperature models (ADD or hours) have been conducted by other researchers such as Marchenko (2001) and Amendt et al. (2007). These have similarly been applied in China. For example, Chen (2006) first used ADD to estimate the PMI of a female corpse found in the Guizhou Province. Many fly maggots were found on and around the body, and some of the larvae had become pupae. The maggots were allowed to feed to the adult stages and identified subsequently as *Aldrichina grahami*. The PMI was estimated as 21 days based on the developmental data of *A. grahami* and ADD. Considering the low temperature (<10°C) before insect colonization, the PMI was estimated as 28 days, which matched the real PMI after solving the crime. As reported by Jia (2009), a male body that had begun to decay was discovered at 6 p.m. on July 20 in Xinji, Hebei Province, with maggots found in the victim's mouth and nasal cavity. The preliminary PMI was inferred to be 3–4 days due to the observed late postmortem phenomena. To obtain a more accurate PMI range and delineate the suspect, the maggots from the corpse's mouth were collected and identified morphologically as *Lucilia sericata*. The average length from 30 of the longest larvae within the population of maggots was 12.7 mm, hence the PMI that was inferred by a previous formula (Niu et al., 2000) ranged from 60.7 to 66.7 h. The crime time was estimated to be between 1 and 6 a.m. on July 17 with the victim determined to have been killed about 4 a.m. on July 17 after the crime was solved.

Some criminals dispose of their victims by burying the bodies or hiding them in remote areas such as dry wells or abandoned buildings where few people visit. As a result, the dead bodies are often discovered much later relative to the time of the crimes, with some severely corrupted. Because the postmortem estimation phenomenon was no longer being used as a forensic tool and no other valuable evidence was found on the scene, Wei and Huang (2016) utilized fly larvae to infer the PMI of a male corpse found in Zhongshan, Guangdong Province. Some red flies of different sizes and a great amount of white smooth fly larvae without protuberance or cilia were found on the body, while no pupae were recorded. The morphological characterization of the fly larvae identified them as *Chrysomya megacephala*. The average length of larvae was 12 mm and the PMIs inferred by previous formulae were 4.57 days (Tang, 1994) and 4.2 days (Wang et al., 2012), respectively. The suspects were finally arrested and the actual PMI was ascertained to be 4.2 days.

Despite these illustrative case studies, estimation of PMI using insects in practical casework could result in considerable uncertainties due to the complex environmental and climatic conditions. In particular, the deviations of PMI estimation from the true value will be greater when the time after death is longer. For example, Lv et al. (2010) reported on the PMI estimation process of three dismembered corpses that were discovered from different sites in Wuhan, Hubei Province, between March and May. The PMI of a corpse that possessed first instar larvae only was estimated as 3–5 days, which included the actual PMI of 4 days. The longest maggots found on the other two corpses were 1.2 and 1.3 cm long, respectively. Their estimated PMIs were 7–10 days and 10–14 days, while the real PMIs were established to be 14 days and 38 days. Li et al. (2003) assisted the police to estimate the PMI of a female corpse found in Chongqing. Few fly larvae, many adult flies, and some pupa shells were found on the corpse. The adult flies were designated as *A. grahami* and *C. pinguis* after morphological identifications. The estimated PMI was greater than 35 days and the real-time interval was determined to be about 2 months.

Numerous factors may cause deviations in PMI estimation based on forensic entomology and limit its wider application in real cases. Tomberlin et al. (2011) divided the PMI into two principal parts: the precolonization interval (pre-CI), which spans the period between the time of death and the arrival of sarcosaphagous insects, and the post-colonization interval, which is applied to the broad timeframe between initial insect colonization and body infestation. The pre-CI is not fixed, ranging from a few minutes to many days. The addition of clothing and/or wrapping around a corpse could inhibit egg laying by the adult flies on the body. Furthermore, environmental factors such as temperature and humidity may interfere with maggot growth and the development cycle. Insects may occur on a corpse in many waves during a protracted postmortem period. It is difficult to determine the species of immature insects by morphological identification and the wave to which the different larvae belong. This can complicate PMI calculation further if the first insects to arrive at and colonize the body have pupated due to the lack of information about pupae.

Although several shortfalls and limitations still remain in the entomological application to PMI estimation, it is exciting to see the emerging use of forensic entomology from experiments to real cases. Since the growth and development rates of different species of larvae are quite different, species identification should be conducted with care and rigor and PMI should be estimated according to the corresponding insect developmental data. Also PMI estimation must consider key determinants such as the immediate case-specific environmental factors, maggot growth and development conditions, and the clothes or covering of the corpse. Ultimately, the practical application in real crime scenes and cases still requires more detailed and systematic research initiatives.

In summary, there is a long history of forensic medicine development from ancient to modern China with increased developments in forensic medicine particularly during the last 20 years. Although established, simpler, and easy-to-standardize technologies have been utilized in forensic caseworks to date, numerous Chinese forensic scientists are now focusing on and adopting different research strategies and aim ultimately to further improve the accuracy or predictions from the discipline. In particular, forensic entomological methods have been used in several challenging real crime scene investigations from experimental work in China. Further studies should be carried out in this and other emerging disciplines, such as forensic ecogenomics/forensic microbiology, to provide more useful data and to help reduce the limitations of applying experimental findings in real cases. However, such methods can be applied currently as intelligence to assist investigators decipher when a body may have been deposited at a crime scene. Its use as evidence, with the necessary stringency and scrutiny of degrees of uncertainty in the time estimations, will require much more experimentation.

The Netherlands: From Scientific Developments to Application in Forensic Investigations

Ir. Frederike Quaak, MSc, Netherlands Forensic Institute, The Hague, The Netherlands

Shortly after the Second World War on July 30, 1945, the Judicial Laboratory of the Netherlands was founded by Professor W. Froentjes, with only three researchers employed. Six years later the Laboratory for Judicial Pathology was founded by Dr. J. Zeldenrust, where he and his assistant were also the only employees. Prior to the establishment of these laboratories, the majority of forensic research in the Netherlands was performed by hospital staff or pharmacists. One of the most well-known Dutch pharmacists was C.J. van Ledden Hulsebosch (1877–1952) (van Ledden Hulsebosch, 1945), who started performing forensic research in the early 1900s, just before finishing his degree in pharmacy. His father, also a pharmacist, had undertaken forensic research and supported police investigations since 1885. In March 1902, C.J. van Ledden Hulsebosch was coopted by the prosecutor to assist the police and provide expertise on a sexual assault case in his father's absence. His investigation was successful and marked the start of his career as a forensic scientist. In 1910 he resigned from his post as a pharmacist and focused solely on forensic science and assisting with police investigations until his retirement in 1950. In 1914 he founded the first school for scientific police research and was the first to use UV light in criminal investigations.

In 1999 the Judicial Laboratory and the Laboratory for Judicial Pathology merged to become the Netherlands Forensic Institute (NFI). The NFI, a broadly oriented research institute, hosts several areas of expertise, hence a wide range of technical and scientific techniques are applied. As with most global forensic institutes, a large number of cases investigated by the NFI include biological traces such as nonhuman biological traces. The first case investigations using nonhuman biological traces were performed in 2003 where the preliminary focus was mainly on (morphological) determination of plant material and comparison of pollen profiles in soil samples.

The field of forensic science has changed over the past decades not only in the Netherlands but worldwide. For example, criminal investigations in the 19th and 20th centuries largely focused on evidence that was connected directly and unequivocally to the crime, e.g., a dead body, fire arms, or damaged items. The majority of cases were solved using eye witness reports and, to a lesser extent, expert witness accounts. Also the expertise of a forensic scientist was typically never questioned. Today, advances in both chemical and biological scientific techniques, parallel with the growing interest of the general public, have catalyzed the many developments in forensic science. Anecdotal examples include TV series such as *CSI*, which have made the general public and scientists increasingly aware of the possibilities for applying a wide range of scientific techniques to forensic investigations. There is a growing awareness among scientists from other fields of expertise (i.e., nonforensic) that their techniques have potential relevance in forensic investigations. However, appropriately robust research and validation is necessary before a method can be applied reliably in real scenes of crime and become acceptable in court.

The evidential value of scientific evidence has increased tremendously over the past 20 years with random match probabilities of one in one billion being reported in human DNA analysis, for instance. Although legal systems around the world require different standards of evidence, one generally accepted criterion for scientific evidence is the "Daubert standard": the technique should be validated, peer reviewed, and generally accepted by the relevant community (Kuiper, 2016). Therefore in Europe, the European Network of Forensic Science Institutes plays an important role in the development, illustration, and application of new techniques in forensic investigations by European laboratories (ensfi.eu).

There is a growing interest within the forensic community to apply microbial DNA analyses in forensic investigations. Microorganisms are the smallest and ubiquitous living organisms known, hence they are present in almost every habitat on earth. Even the smallest traces of environmental samples can contain large amounts of microorganisms. Furthermore, both the abundance and diversity of microorganisms present within different habitats make them particularly interesting for forensic analyses. Concomitant with the advances in DNA or molecular techniques is an increasing demand for determining their potential applicability in forensic casework. An example of the application of scientific methods and tools from other fields in a forensic investigation is the analysis of the 2001 anthrax attacks in the United States. Analyses performed by clinical microbiologists were used to provide evidence in the investigation of the attacks. Following these investigations, guidelines and validation criteria for using microbiological techniques in court were developed and the field of forensic microbiology or microbial forensics emerged (Budowle et al., 2005, 2008).

Both specific organisms and diverse communities can be of interest in forensics. Identification of specific strains can be used to determine the cause of (sudden unexpected) death. More detailed analyses such as strain typing can be used to determine the source of an (intentional) infection. Apart from the investigations of the anthrax attacks, strain typing has since been reported in intentional infections with pathogens like HIV (Abecasis et al., 2011; Leitner and Albert, 2000; Lemey et al., 2005). Specific organisms have also been reported as indicators for determining the origin of human samples (Donaldson et al., 2010; Fleming and Harbison, 2010; Power et al., 2010). Nonetheless, studies on human-associated microbial communities have shown that using specific organisms as indicators can sometimes lead to erroneous results (Benschop et al., 2012).

Enormous progress has been made within the field of environmental microbiology since the application of denaturing gradient gel electrophoresis (Muyzer et al., 1993). Many microbial ecology studies have been performed to characterize communities in diverse (extreme) habitats, determine the effects of perturbations or chemicals on the indigenous consortia, and assess the seasonal and temporal stability of the communities (e.g., Pasternak et al., 2013; Prevost-Boure et al., 2011). Although seasonal and temporal changes create possibilities to apply soil microbial community analyses to establish a link between a soil trace and a crime scene, uncertainties still exist on the influence of wetting and drying, for example, on the resultant microbial profiles (Habtom et al., 2017). Additionally, soil microbial communities can be used to verify proposed scenarios. For example, the impact of the burial of pig muscle tissue resulted in a shift in soil microbial communities (Olakanye et al., 2015), which may be used to detect clandestine graves or determine the TSB. Similarly, Pechal et al. (2014) reported changes in bacterial communities associated with decomposing pig carcasses, suggesting that changes in human-associated microbial communities may also be used to determine a PMI.

With the advanced DNA (sequencing) techniques, microbial communities have started to play even more important roles in medicine and the food industry. In recent decades, studies have been performed to characterize microbial communities in the gut, for instance. From a medical point of view, this community is interesting in determining the difference between healthy and diseased states (e.g., Bergström et al., 2012; Donovan, 2017). Similarly, the principal focus in the food industry is on the effects of pre- or probiotics on the gut communities. Overall, these studies showed that the gut communities are generally stable over time and differ to a certain extent between individuals (Lozupone et al., 2012; Rajilic-Stojanovic et al., 2013), indicating some potential for forensic application (Quaak et al., 2017). In most studies, community profiling has been performed using techniques such as terminal restriction fragment length polymorphism (T-RFLP) profiling, next-generation sequencing, and mRNA/marker amplification followed by fragment analysis using capillary electrophoresis or microarray analysis.

Techniques used in other scientific fields can have forensic potential when applied correctly. As a consequence, technical validation through determining detection limit, repeatability, and robustness is essential in forensic science just as it is necessary for "regular" science. Furthermore, biological and/or forensic validation of any given method needs to be performed specifically to make its forensic application possible (Kuiper, 2016). For example, the application of T-RFLP in a forensic setting was first described by Horswell et al. (2002). The method described in this paper was subsequently optimized, validated, and implemented at the NFI (Quaak and Kuiper, 2011), and has since become a standard tool for bacterial community profiling of soils in forensic investigations by the Institute where questioned samples are recovered at the same time as the crime scene samples are collected. Following the technical validation, mock cases were analyzed as part of the forensic validation. The mock cases, where a shoe had to be used to make a shoeprint in soil, were prepared by students of the Police Academy of the Netherlands. The shoe sole, the shoeprint, and at least one other location from which they thought the soil would be different were sampled. By having different individuals prepare mock cases, various methods of evidence collection were intentionally and inherently introduced, as no one will sample shoes and soil in the same manner. Although this variability could influence the analysis, it is also realistic and representative of real crime scene investigations. In summary, different individuals will not perform sampling in the exact same manner but the validated analytical method used should not be affected by this variability.

Another important parameter when comparing soil samples is spatial variation where soil microbial communities can be highly similar or very different at short and large distances. Several factors can contribute to these (dis)similarities with soil type or soil usage known to have a large influence on the occurring microbial community. Within a garden, for instance, the microbial community in a flowerbed may differ considerably from that in the lawn despite a separating distance that can be less than 1 m. On the other hand, when two soil samples are taken from two gardens that are over 20 m apart, but with similar history and usage, high similarities can still be expected. Overall, it is important in forensic casework to determine the variability of the relevant reference location. Therefore it may be a requirement to collect a sample not only from a shoeprint, for instance, but also from multiple other reference samples from the crime scene.

Apart from spatial variation, the influence of different environmental exposure of the trace evidence and reference sample should be examined. Soil underneath a shoe will be subject to a cascade of events that are different to a reference sample from a crime scene, with a direct impact on the microbial community. These events can include mixing with additional soil types while walking around, and differences in "storage" conditions. The shoe could, for instance, be kept in the suspect's home under relatively constant environmental conditions, while the outdoor weather at the crime scene could be highly variable with implications for the microbial communities of this same soil. Additionally, there can be a considerable time interval between committing the crime and retrieving a reference sample. It can take weeks or months before trace evidence is discovered, potentially leading to divergence of the microbial community in these samples. Shifts in the microbial population can also be introduced by the crime itself. Comparing the microbial community in a soil sample taken from beneath a (decomposing) dead body to that collected from a shovel could result in a large difference between these samples. Body decomposition will probably result in a shift in gravesoil microbial communities, as was described by Olakanye et al. (2015) for buried pig muscle tissue. The soil on a suspect's shovel will not be subject to this change caused by decomposition, resulting in differences between soil communities from the crime scene and the shovel.

Overall, it is highly unlikely that a perfect "match" will result when comparing microbial communities in trace evidence and its respective references. As can be inferred from the foregoing deliberations, one of the main difficulties when comparing microbial communities in soil is that not finding a match does not necessarily mean that the samples originated from different locations. Therefore it is important in forensic microbiology/ecogenomics to statistically assess how much of a difference can be accepted to report a common origin or a "match" between two communities or samples. As a result, the NFI uses a database of Bray–Curtis similarities between samples of known origin to assess the similarity of questioned samples (Quaak and Kuiper, 2011; Quaak et al., 2017). The soil microbial community database consists of comparisons between T-RFLP profiles of samples from the same sampling point and/or replicate analyses of the same soil sample, and comparisons between T-RFLP profiles from samples from different sampling points. This results in a histogram of Bray–Curtis distances, which can be used as a decision support model. When unknown samples are compared, the histogram is used to assess the probability of the samples originating from the same sampling point. Next to this assessment, the Institute also takes into account other factors before a "match" or "nonmatch" is reported to the police. For instance, the time between the crime and collection of reference samples, as well as pollen analysis, is often determined as part of the metadata (Uitdehaag et al., 2016).

Several peer-reviewed papers have been published demonstrating the potential use of microbial communities in identifying suspects. Microbial communities on hands have, for instance, been used to link keyboards and computer mice to their users (Fierer et al., 2010), link objects to the person who touched them (Aaspõllu et al., 2011; Nishi et al., 2015), or link shoes to their users (Goga, 2012). Although most of these studies were performed under controlled conditions where objects were sterilized before they were touched or used only by one person, the methods applied could in theory make considerable contributions to forensic investigations. Nevertheless, and as described earlier, the outcome of these investigations could be very different under uncontrolled and less than "ideal" conditions as in real crime scenarios. Consequently, several key questions then arise, which should be addressed in the forensic validation of a method in particular. These include, but are not limited to:

1. If two individuals touched an object, is it possible to unravel their respective microbial profiles from the mixed deposited communities?;

2. When profiling a microbial community on a questioned item, will it be possible to determine if the retrieved profile could be a mixed or single donor profile (comparable to mixed or single donor human short tandem repeat profiles)?;
3. What happens if an item is cleaned or washed?;
4. Will it be possible to link a microbial trace to a donor when the suspect has been on a course of antibiotics in the time between committing the crime and collecting the reference sample?

In summary, the theoretical applicability of a new method or technique, whether developed *de novo* or coopted from other disciplines, should always be examined under ideal (laboratory) conditions and then assessed under (true) forensic conditions before it can be used in casework. The forensic validation process can also be used to identify the limitations of each individual technique. Naturally, this could mean that the use of one technique may not be appropriate or ideal for a specific situation. As described earlier, comparing the microbial community in a soil sample taken from under a dead body to that collected from a shovel could result in a large difference between these samples. In such specific cases, microbial community profiling may not be the recommended analytical technique. Therefore determining which technique to use in analyzing a specific case requires consultation with the relevant forensic experts. Many scientific techniques can be used in casework as long as their limitations or restrictions are known and reported. Hence forensic validation is a valuable tool in determining the applicability of novel protocols/techniques. New knowledge and findings, ever advancing scientific techniques, and growing creativity in supplying alternative hypotheses inevitably mean that the validation of techniques used in forensic investigations is a dynamic and ongoing process, which must therefore be reevaluated and revised accordingly.

Forensic Medicine and Criminal Investigation in Turkey

Dr. Gulnaz T. Javan, Alabama State University, Montgomery, AL, USA
Dr. Sait Özsoy, University of Health Sciences, Ankara, Turkey

History of Forensic Medicine in Turkey

In the early years of the 20th century, Dr. Edmond Locard (1877–1966) proposed that during the commission of any crime, there is a physical exchange of information between the perpetrator and the crime scene. Based on Locard's Exchange Principle, all criminals leave something behind whenever they come into physical contact with any object at the crime scene just as they acquire some materials on themselves from the surrounding crime environments. Therefore, regardless of what criminals do, they leave a plethora of evidence, which can include fingerprints, footprints, DNA, skin cells, blood, hair, bodily fluids, fibers, and articles of clothing. He also coined the phrase "the physical evidence is never wrong and never lies." On the contrary, evidence may just be misinterpreted. Also Locard postulated that "mishandling and mistakes in collecting evidences by CSI personnel can reduce or eliminate their values." This statement sums up the importance of thorough and methodical crime scene investigation.

Locard's principle has since been accepted and advanced by different nations globally. Parallel to this advancement have been many medical developments in Turkish-Islamic civilizations. In particular are the contributions of the renowned scholar and philosopher Ibn-Sinâ or Avicenna's (980–1037). His book titled *Al Qanun Fi Al-Tibb* (*The Canon of Medicine*) was translated into Latin and used as the seminal medical textbook at Montpellier and Louvain Universities until the end of the 17th century. The most important feature of this globally important text is Ibn-Sinâ's inclusion of, albeit just a few, real anatomical findings of autopsies (Shoja and Tubbs, 2007).

The teaching of modern medicine in Turkey started on March 14, 1827 when Sultan Mahmud II of the Ottoman Empire established the Tiphane and the Cerrahane-i Amire (Medical and Surgery Learning Center), which now operates as the Marmara University Haydarpasha Campus in Istanbul. The importance of this day in the history of modern medicine in Turkey is still recognized through annual celebrations of Medicine Day. In 1841, Dr. Charles Ambroise from Vienna, Austria, became the first academic to teach forensic science in Turkey. In 1843, the Ottoman Empire Sultan Abdulmejid II authorized dissection and autopsy of Christian cadavers, whereas autopsies on Muslim cadavers were not permitted for religious reasons. This law allowed the first autopsy in Turkey to be performed by Dr. Ambroise on a laborer who had passed away after being struck by a pole.

By the order of Sultan Abdulmejid II in 1857, The Forensic Medical Commission was established and was the first step toward the organization of forensic medicine in the country. In 1879, the official rules for forensic autopsies were written with forensic science defined and recognized as a medical expertise. Sultan Abdulhamid II subsequently combined all medical disciplines within one institution by establishing the Mekteb-i Tibbiye-i Sahane Medical School in 1903. In reality, forensic science education in Turkey began with the establishment of this school and its name then changed to Istanbul Medical University during the final years of the Ottoman Empire. Similarly, the first morgue and chemistry offices in Turkey were established in 1908 (Gok and Ozen, 1982). In general, the restructuring of forensic science departments in the last period of the Ottoman Empire in 1917 established the Board of Forensic Science, with the morgue, chemistry, and psychiatry observation departments under the management of the Ministry of Justice. The Ministry of Health no longer oversees operations of the forensic science department.

To provide dedicated education and training on scientific and technical aspects of forensic science, the Ministry of Justice established the Council of Forensic Medicine of Turkey in 1982 in Istanbul. The Council of Forensic Medicine consists of central and provincial divisions (Fig. 8.1). The Central Division is located in Istanbul and includes the following organizations: general board; specialty boards; branch offices; and specialty

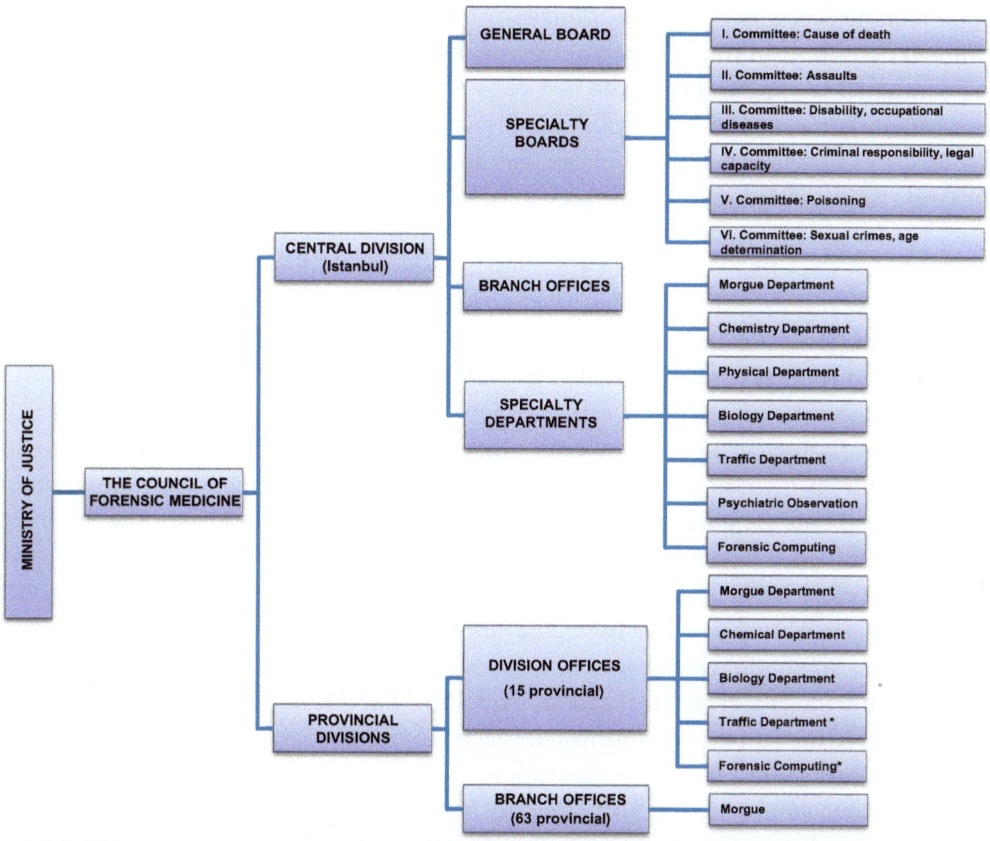

Figure 8.1 Organization chart of the Council of Forensic Medicine in Turkey. * These departments only exist in Ankara.

departments. The specialty departments encompass the morgue, psychiatric observation, chemistry, biology, physics, traffic, and forensic computing departments. All of these departments conduct investigations and provide official reports on the incident when there is an official request by the Prosecutor's Office or the court. Since they have different scopes of responsibility, each of these departments provides unique expert opinion on unsolved or mysterious cases. The Provincial Divisions consist of 15 cities (Adana, Ankara, Antalya, Bursa, Diyarbakir, Erzurum, İzmir, Malatya, Trabzon, Denizli, Edirne, Gaziantep, Kayseri, Kocaeli, Samsun) each with division offices, and 63 cities with branch offices (Gok, 1998; Koc, 1999; Soysal and Eke, 1999).

In addition to the Institute of Forensic Sciences, forensic science departments in different universities and forensic science experts based in the Ministry of Health's hospitals perform a range of forensic duties in Turkey. Also there are two institutes of forensics with one located at Ankara University and the other at Istanbul University (Gok, 1998; Koc, 1999; Soysal and Eke, 1999).

Modern Crime Scene Investigation in Turkey

Important advances in the field of forensic medicine began during the Ottoman Empire and continued to expand during the first years of the Republic of Turkey. One of the first laws passed by the Grand National Assembly of Turkey was the Forensic Law Act (Law No. 38) of 1920, which is still one of the laws governing forensic medicine. This law stipulates that the examination of a corpse, establishment of the cause of death, and preparation of reports should be conducted by a medical specialist. It also addresses compensation for these experts (The Official Gazette, 1921). Furthermore, according to Turkey's Constitution, "*findings obtained through illegal methods shall not be considered evidence*" (The Turkish Republic Constitution, 1982). In general, any evidence with an unknown source or is collected unlawfully constitutes "unlawful evidence" and is not permissible in any trial.

The crime scene is where a criminal act starts, but it continues to wherever the criminal travels and whatever they come into contact with. As a result, it can provide clues as to the manner and time of the crime. An accepted understanding among forensic scientists is that the lack of complete crime scene investigations makes the solving of cases very difficult, if not impossible. Consequently, the crime scene investigation process has a special place in intelligence gathering where all evidence leads to the criminal. Any tangible or verbal information whose legal importance has not been evaluated is a "finding," whereas any finding that has been collected and obtained legally that can help solve a crime and convict a criminal is called "evidence." For a finding to be used and valued as evidence, it has to be obtained in compliance with the law (Erdag, 2010; Gultekin, 2011; Karaburun, 2001).

As in other countries, the Turkish legal system identifies a person who uses their technical knowledge and expertise to give written or oral opinions, and examine or interpret evidence, as an expert witness. The authority to investigate a criminal event rests with the prosecutor. In response to an order from the prosecutor, the crime scene investigation unit from the police or rural security forces examines and collects evidence from the scene of the crime (Gultekin, 2011). Opinions of medical experts about a criminal case are crucial. In particular, mutilation, rape, and death cases require the presence of a forensic examiner on the scene of the crime to examine the victim(s) and the evidence. As a result, a forensic scientist is always a member of an investigative team (Demirci and Dogan, 2011; Inanici et al., 2004; Koc, 1999). According to Horswell (2004) and Prahlow (2010), a forensic investigator has to examine the crime scene and evaluate evidence in a range of cases. These cases include, but are not limited to, accidental death that occurred under various environmental conditions, suicide, homicide, suspicious sudden death, and mummification, and saponification cases where identification of the victim is essential, mass murder and any suspicious cases requiring an expert opinion.

Overall, the ideal crime scene investigation includes preservation of evidence that can help prosecute the suspect while protecting his or her rights. In most cases, crime scene investigation is more important than the autopsy, hence it is essential to preserve the crime scene. A comprehensive and thorough investigation can also elucidate the manner of death (Avis, 1993; Dix and Ernst, 1999). Finally, the role of an investigation is more than just answering the two primary questions of how and why the death occurred. Even though the dead may not benefit from a criminal investigation, the real value of a correct and thorough investigation is also in the benefits that these findings can provide for future cases (Demirci and Dogan, 2011; Wagner, 2009) and for the victim's family.

Similar to other countries, the crime scene investigation procedure in Turkey consists of: (1) notification of authorities about the crime; (2) first intervention team, preservation of the crime scene, and evidence; (3) investigative team work; (4) examination of the crime scene; (5) examination of the laboratory evidence; and (6) bringing charges and prosecution (Gultekin, 2011). In cases of offenses against a person, such as homicide, crime scene investigations in Turkey consist of physical examination of the body and the environment, collection of evidence, and implementation of relevant laboratory and diagnostic tests. The goal is to provide the legal system with solid, indisputable, and objective evidence that can prove the cause of death, time of death, manner of death, and perhaps most importantly withstand the scrutiny of a defense lawyer (Demirci and Dogan, 2011).

Overall, it is essential that crime scene investigative teams include members with relevant educational backgrounds, established experience, renowned expertise, recognized capability to protect the crime scene from contamination, and proven ability to collect evidence according to the law. The presence of people at the crime scene can disturb the evidence and leave traces behind that contaminate the crime scene. If paramedics or fire fighters arrive at the scene before the police, then they should, if possible, perform their duties without altering the scene or handling any evidence. If conducting their duties requires altering the crime scene or handling evidence, then all changes made at the crime scene should be documented. Furthermore, all key information including the address, date and time of the crime, and names of all the investigators present should be recorded. Trained, licensed, and experienced investigators should handle video recording, photography, sketch drawing, and developing fingerprints of the crime scene. Using the relevant tools, they must also collect any crime weapons and ballistic evidence, as well as evidence for subsequent biological and toxicological analyses (Cubuk, 2011).

It is critical that a forensic investigator is present in any investigation involving homicide, murder, and when the body was moved from the scene. England and Wales rely on Home Office pathologists for investigations of crime scenes. This responsibility rests with medical examiners in the United States, and with the European state and the Institute of Forensic Medicine in Europe (Saukko and Knight, 2004). In Turkey, a forensic examiner will accompany the prosecutor to the scene of the crime if a body was moved. If the body was moved from the crime scene to a morgue, then the presence of a forensic examiner along with the prosecutor for investigation is required.

It is important to investigate and examine all vehicles at the crime scene and talk to all persons who were present or have possible connections to the crime. Therefore no vehicle or person should leave the crime scene. The investigator should scan the entire area carefully to determine the possibility of a secondary crime scene (Cubuk, 2011). When the crime scene is spread over a wide geographical area, as in cases of plane crashes or explosions, then the area should be divided into smaller sections to ensure thorough and methodical investigative processing (Caymaz, 2001; Cihangiroglu et al., 2011).

Although a suicide note is an important clue in solving each suicide case, the presence of such evidence does not automatically confirm that the death is a result of suicide. Therefore the note and the cause of death should be investigated thoroughly and verified forensically. Typically, a suicide note reflects the emotional state or frame of mind of the individual at the time of the incident. It can start to elucidate the reasons for committing the suicide (Karbeyaz et al., 2014) and hence help direct the examiner of the crime scene (Bhatia et al., 2006; Ho et al., 1998; Salib et al., 2002). Due to its development and increasing popularity, the internet, especially social media sites, has become another platform and repository for suicide notes. As a consequence, a victim's record on social media can offer a key opportunity to interrogate their mind set (Barak and Miran, 2005; Lester, 1994; O'Connor et al., 1999; Ruder et al., 2011).

When attending an examination and/or autopsy, forensic examiners typically carry a "murder bag," which holds all the necessary tools to perform the examination. Also, in developed countries, there are well-equipped facilities and expert teams that can conduct a thorough investigation of the crime scene, which ensures the implementation of proper autopsies and preparation of complete reports of the crime. As observed by Saukko and Knight (2004) and Demirci and Dogan (2011), the situation can differ considerably for developing countries.

Concluding Remarks

Despite the robust legal infrastructure and recommended protocols in Turkey, there are some shortcomings in evidence collection and crime scene investigation. Reports have stated that sometimes judges and prosecutors do not go to crime scenes and that they only examine bodies of victims at the morgue (Asirdizer et al., 2001). As a result, perpetrators are sometimes acquitted due to the lack of, or the improper collection of, evidence. Solving a criminal incident depends on the correct evaluation of information collected by the officials at the site, the methods and techniques used in examining the scene, and results from laboratory tests. Errors or limitations in any of these stages can result in incorrect final reports, which can subsequently lead to the release of a criminal or punishment of the innocent (Bulut et al., 2013; Ceker, 2016; Stanojevich, 2012). Therefore it is prudent to increase the number of qualified professional investigators, with diverse expertise, for potentially more comprehensive crime scene investigation.

For example, the future of crime scene investigation in Turkey will most likely include digital forensics. Computer and digital forensics are bridged into analytical and investigative techniques used to extract, preserve, identify, document, analyze, and interpret computer media, which are stored or encoded and can be included with evidence. As a result, new forensic frameworks developed by technology experts are needed to clarify the complexity of computer evidence collected at crime scenes. Naturally, the use of digital evidence must comply with all established legal requirements of Turkish laws (Bulbul et al., 2013).

Forensic Geoscience Provision in the United Kingdom, Ireland and the Irish Republic, 2017

Professor Lorna Dawson, James Hutton Institute, Aberdeen, United Kingdom

Forensic geoscience (known also as forensic geology or geoforensics) provision in the United Kingdom falls into two main areas: intelligence gathering and evidence evaluation (Dawson and Hillier, 2010). The majority of intelligence work is carried out directly for police forces predominantly assisting with ground search operations for missing people, unmarked homicide graves, and buried or concealed objects. The other area of assistance is in the analysis of natural soil/superficial deposits in addition to artificial products derived from materials (e.g., glass, bricks, tiles). Such analyses can then be included in the provision of evidence in court or in determining the geographical provenance (source location) of a questioned (unknown) sample found on an item of interest associated with a crime (questioned item). Increasingly, a combination complementary approach is used to provide the most robust evidence, including both inorganic and organic soil characteristics in comparisons of a questioned soil with a crime scene soil (Dawson and Mayes, 2014).

Since the closure of the Forensic Science Service in 2010, all forensic science (with the exception of Northern Ireland and Scotland), including forensic geoscience, is carried out by private forensic companies, consultants, individual practitioners, and experts often in university departments. Forensic geoscience is a niche discipline, not provided in-house within the larger forensic service providers, but normally subcontracted to individual experts with relevant experience and qualifications, and smaller specialist forensic service suppliers. Some of the larger forensic service providers such as Cellmark and LGC subcontract the expert services of individual geoscientists to work alongside their mainstream forensic scientists.

In Scotland, the Scottish Police Authority (SPA) is responsible for providing forensic services to support operational policing. These forensic services are managed and delivered as part of the SPA, ensuring a suitable degree of independence and impartiality, while also supporting the strong crime scene to court partnership that forensic services has with both operational policing and the wider criminal justice system in Scotland. The SPA's forensic services provide a service to policing that brings together forensic and fingerprint capability and scene of crime officers, placing forensic services in Scotland at the forefront of evidence capture and analysis. Forensic geoscience is contracted out to specialists to work alongside the core forensic discipline experts at SPA.

Intelligence work is generally carried out directly for the police forces. In Scotland, there is one police force, Police Scotland. In England there are currently 38 individual police forces, while in Wales there are four police forces and in Northern Ireland there is the Police Service of Northern Ireland (PSNI). There are also special police forces that geoscientists in the United Kingdom can work with, such as the British Transport Police, the Civil Nuclear Constabulary, and the Ministry of Defence Police. The environment agencies of these areas of the United Kingdom also investigate specific crimes: in Northern Ireland the Northern Ireland Environment Agency Environmental Crime Unit have power of arrest, as do officers of the Royal Society for the Prevention of Cruelty to Animals and Birds. In Scotland the Scottish Environment Protection Agency and in England and Wales the Environment Agency fulfill this role. The UK military also use forensic geology, mainly through the various divisions of the Royal Engineers, in remote sensing for the Royal Air Force, for searches of water via the Royal Navy, and also through the Centre of Applied Science and Technology (CAST).

The United Kingdom is divided into several legal entities, which oversee forensic casework on behalf of the prosecution. England and Wales have the Crown Prosecution Service, Northern Ireland has the Public Prosecution Service, and Scotland has the Crown Office and the Procurator Fiscal Services. The Irish Republic (*Poblacht na hÉireann* or *Saorstát Éireann*) was a state that declared its independence from Britain in January 1919. An Garda Síochána (meaning "the Guardian of the Peace"), commonly referred to as the Gardaí or "the guards," is the police force of the Irish Republic. The service is headed by the Garda Commissioner who is appointed by the Irish government.

In the United Kingdom, expert witnesses may also be appointed by defense counsel to challenge the expert opinions provided on behalf of the prosecution. Expert work carried out for the court either on behalf of the prosecution or defense, and the role of the expert is to assist the court in understanding the evidence that they present.

When providing evidence it is important that authoritative guidance, protocols, and approved standards are adhered to. Many forensic methods are accredited by the United Kingdom Accreditation Service (UKAS) to the international laboratory ISO17025 quality control standard. This accreditation ensures that forensic laboratories follow standard procedures and encourage the delivery of precise, accurate test data. All other methods followed in forensic geoscience laboratories follow similar quality control procedures and are in general covered by ISO9001. The Codes of Practice and Conduct for Forensic Science Providers and Practitioners (the Codes), which have been in place since 2011, have consistently emphasized the importance of scientific validation. Validity of methods is a factor for courts to take into account in determining the reliability of expert opinion (Criminal Practice Directions, England and Wales, part 19A.5(a)). Validation includes characterizing the performance of a method for its intended purpose, and ensuring that its limitations and the uncertainties associated with it are explicitly understood. This is an element that UK forensic geoscience practitioners are trying to ensure and that the methods reported within their forensic statements meet these criteria. If they do not, as can be the case in some aspects of intelligence giving and for aspects of search advice, then this should be stated on the accompanying report. Currently, there is no approved standard for conducting ground searches, although some general guidance does exist in publications (e.g., Donnelly, 2013; Harrison et al., 2016; Ruffell and McAllister, 2015).

The Forensic Science Regulator (FSR), UK, works with the UK Home Office and ensures that the provision of forensic science services across the criminal justice system is subject to an appropriate regime of scientific quality standards (Tully, 2017). Although sponsored by the Home Office, the regulator is a public appointee and operates independently of the Home Office, on behalf of the criminal justice system as a whole to formulate unbiased recommendations and decisions. The role of the FSR is to identify the requirement for new or improved quality standards, lead on the development of new standards where necessary, and provide advice and guidance so that providers of forensic science services can demonstrate compliance with common standards. Furthermore, the FSR collaborates with the authorities in Scotland and Northern Ireland who have expressed their willingness to be partners in the setting of quality standards that will be adopted within their justice systems.

Practicing forensic geoscientists may become chartered scientists, or register through their own professional societies, such as through membership of their professional organizations including the Geological Society of London, the European Federation of Geologists, or the British Society of Soil Science. Laboratories carrying out case investigations are encouraged to have UKAS accreditation, which ensures that a minimal acceptable and regulated standard is met. In addition, individual scientists have the option to register with the National Crime Agency if they have relevant casework experience and are invited to apply.

Forensic geoscience is used predominantly in cases of serious crime such as murder, rape, and ground searches associated with organized crime and counterterrorism. Geoscience has also been applied in several high-profile cases. For example, microfossil analysis was used in the R. vs. Ian Huntley double murder case (2003). Soil and rock evidence was used to show that Ian Huntley had driven his car on the remote track where the bodies of his child victims Holly Wells and Jessica Chapman were found. More recent case examples in England include: the murder of Pamela Jackson (R. vs. Adrian Muir, 2013) where soil on the suspect's gloves helped identify the geographical location of the deposition site; and the murder of Rebecca Godden (R. vs. Christopher Halliwell, 2016) where soils recovered from tools at Halliwell's address were virtually indistinguishable from those at the grave site. In both cases, relevant organic and inorganic analyses were coupled and results were used in the subsequent search, recovery, and trace evidence analysis. In Scotland, in the investigation of the World's End murders (HMV vs. Angus Sinclair, 2014), soil samples on the feet of one of the victims were shown to contain wheat grains and characteristics of the grass verge and the wheat soil where the victim was found, even though the samples had been collected in 1977 but analyzed subsequently in 2014.

Forensic geology has also been used in investigations in Northern Ireland, from the search for a murder victim (R. vs. Trevor Hamilton, 2006), through the sampling of crime scenes and the evaluation of soil trace evidence (e.g., R. vs. Henryck Gorski, 2009). An example from the Irish Republic concerning trace evidence is one where sand, paint, and explosives residues were used by the An Garda Síochána Technical Bureau (Phoenix Park, Dublin) in the investigation into the murder of Lord Mountbatten offshore of County Sligo in 1979. The case brought against the IRA volunteer Thomas McMahon was ultimately successful.

Geoscientists have assisted many police forces in crime reconstruction and in the search for persons or objects. Of note is the successful find in 2014, with the assistance of geophysics, in locating a grave in the Pennines where victim Gemma Simpson's body had previously lain undiscovered for at least 10 years. Martin Bell was subsequently found guilty of killing Gemma Simpson. The geomorphological analysis of air photos have also assisted with locating graves in several locations. Furthermore, geoscientists have assisted the police with several defensive and evidential searches across the United Kingdom to locate buried physical items associated with serious crimes.

Ground searches are carried out by the Irish Police Force, the An Garda Síochána, for buried objects and also by the Independent Commission for the Location and Recovery of Human Remains (ICLVR) for buried victims of the period known as "The Troubles" (1969–98). An example of the work of the An Garda Síochána is that conducted in conjunction with UK police and scientists on several missing persons (mainly young women) in the Wicklow Mountains, south of Dublin, through the 1980s and 1990s. The ICLVR were set up by the governments of the United Kingdom and Ireland as part of the Good Friday Agreement that marked the end of The Troubles. Of the 16 missing people thought to have been abducted by paramilitary organizations, the ICLVR have recovered nine.

Forensic geoscience practice in the United Kingdom delivers to aspects of intelligence, investigation, crime reconstruction, trace evidence, and expert witness provision. Standards are high but are continually developing and improving. Networks of experts such as the International Union of Geological Sciences (IUGS) Initiative on Forensic Geology (IFG) and the European Network of Forensic Science Institutes (with the specialist Animal, Plant, Soil Traces working group; focusing on animal, soil, and vegetation) were established to enable good collaboration globally and share good practice. As a consequence, complementary skills of value are offered in assisting police, forensic, and legal practitioners across Britain and abroad. In addition, UK geoscientists have provided formal and informal advice, training, and operations support for law enforcement-led searches throughout Europe, Asia, Africa, Australia, Canada, the United States, and Latin America, mainly through the IUGS-IFG international network. At the time of writing, UK forensic geoscientists were assisting the police with a few long-term search operations such as for: Moira Anderson with Police Scotland; Arlene Atkinson with PSNI; and the last remaining victim of the "Moors Murders," and continue to support police forces and agencies in evidence gathering and crime reconstruction.

SUMMARY

This chapter has presented some historical overviews of the use of forensic analyses generally and in real life cases in particular in China, Turkey, the Netherlands, and the United Kingdom. Although not by design, the discourse is not exhaustive, hence the obvious gaps with the absence of perspectives from Africa, Australia, North America, and South America. Notwithstanding this, the examples included here highlight further exciting opportunities for scientific research in the new forensic subdisciplines to inform crime scene investigations and demonstrate how forensic science can be built on a strong foundation of research and peer-reviewed publications. Naturally, scientific method validation necessitates robust mathematical and statistical scrutiny as illustrated by Quaak and Kuiper (2011), Pasternak et al. (2012), and Moffatt et al. (2016), for example. In acknowledgment of the paucities and restrictions in the current chapter and context, the reader is referred to other publications such as Gunn (2009), Haglund and Sord (1996), and Tilley and Ford (1996) for relevant discourse on the importance of forensic knowledge and expertise exchange between researchers and police/real crime scene investigators. Other contexts where forensic ecogenomics in particular can potentially be applied are considered in Chapter 9.

Overall, opportunities for researchers, practitioners, and investigators of crime scenes to collaborate should continue to be sought actively whenever possible, and then published/publicized widely thereafter. Testing and proving both the successes and limitations of these endeavors should subsequently suggest their potential application and relevance in scenes of crime and to ultimately inform future court cases/hearings. For example, protocol optimization, standardization, and validation, particularly for forensic ecogenomics, will be an essential if admittedly demanding/ambitious requirement.

Finally, the range of perspectives presented here start to highlight, both implicitly and explicitly, the opportunities and challenges that researchers and practitioners will face in different parts of the world in relation to: (1) expanding existing crime scene toolkits and practices with forensic ecogenomics; (2) introducing forensic ecogenomics and related emergent forensic subdisciplines *de novo* to current crime scene investigation protocols; (3) accessibility and affordability of these new disciplines; and in the long term (4) having these novel suites of techniques recognized and accepted by different legal/court systems. We hope that our discourse contributes to ongoing efforts for improvements across the wide range of forensic contexts, while also identifying new areas of transdisciplinary and cross-national collaborative work between the research, practitioner, police, crime scene, and legal fraternities.

ACKNOWLEDGMENTS

Professor Dawson would like to acknowledge: all police forces in the United Kingdom and Ireland for their professionalism and care, with particular thanks for comments received from DCI Patrick Campbell (Police Scotland), Chris Ganniclifte (SPA), Amanda Pirie (SPA), and Gillian Tully (FSR); and Laurance Donnelly, Alastair Ruffell, and Duncan Pirrie (IUGS-IFG) for informal discussions about forensic geoscience in the United Kingdom.

Dr. Javan acknowledges the National Science Foundation (NSF) Grant HRD 1401075 for partially supporting her contribution.

REFERENCES

Aaspõllu, A., Lillsaar, T., Tummeleht, L., Simm, J., Metsis, M., 2011. Can microbes on skin help linking persons and crimes? Forensic Science International: Genetics Supplement Series 3 (1), e269–270.

Abecasis, A.B., Geretti, A.M., Albert, J., Power, L., Weait, M., Vandamme, A.M., 2011. Science in court: the myth of HIV fingerprinting. The Lancet Infectious Diseases 11 (2), 78–79.

Amendt, J., Campobasso, C.P., Gaudry, E., Reiter, C., LeBlanc, H.N., Hall, M.J., 2007. Best practice in forensic entomology—standards and guidelines. International Journal of Legal Medicine 121 (2), 90–104.

Archer, M., Wallman, J., 2016. The development of forensic entomology in Australia and New Zealand: an overview of casework practice, quality control and standards. Australian Journal of Forensic Sciences 1–9. http://dx.doi.org/10.1080/00450618.2015.1137972.

Arnaldos, M.I., García, M.D., Romera, E., Presa, J.J., Luna, A., 2005. Estimation of postmortem interval in real cases based on experimentally obtained entomological evidence. Forensic Science International 149 (1), 57–65.

Asirdizer, M., Canturk, G., Sarı, H., Buken, B., Isler, H., 2001. Problems in the investigation of the crime scene in death cases and proposals for the solution of these problems. Adli Tıp Dergisi. Fa Yi Xue Za Zhi 5 (1), 45–54.

Avis, S.P., 1993. An unusual suicide. The importance of the scene investigation. American Journal Forensic Medicine Pathology 14 (2), 148–150.

Barak, A., Miran, O., 2005. Writing characteristics of suicidal people on the internet: a psychological investigation of emerging social environments. Suicide Life-threatining Behavior 35, 507–524.

Basangciren, 2001. Estimation of the death time of corpse in the plateau by entomological analysis. Fa Yi Xue Za Zhi 17 (3), 185.

Benschop, C.C.G., Quaak, F.C.A., Boon, M.E., Sijen, T., Kuiper, I., 2012. Vaginal microbial flora analysis by next generation sequencing and microarrays; can microbes indicate vaginal origin in a forensic context? International Journal of Legal Medicine 126, 303–310.

Bergström, A., Licht, T.R., Wilcks, A., Andersen, J.B., Schmidt, L.R., Grønlund, H.A., Vigsnaes, L.K., Michaelsen, K.F., Bahl, M.I., 2012. Introducing GUt low-density array (GULDA): a validated approach for qPCR-based intestinal microbial community analysis. FEMS Microbiology Letters 337 (1), 38–47.

Bhatia, M.S., Verma, S.K., Murty, O.P., 2006. Suicide notes: psychological and clinical profile. International Journal of Psychiatry in Medicine 36, 163–170.

Budowle, B., Schutzer, S.E., Breeze, R.G., Keim, P.S., Morse, S.A., 2005. Microbial Forensics. Academic Press. ISBN: 9780120884834.

Budowle, B., Schutzer, S.E., Morse, S.A., Martinez, K.F., Chakraborty, R., Marrone, B.L., Messenger, S.L., Murch, R.S., Jackson, P.J., Williamson, P., Harmon, R., Velsko, S.P., 2008. Criteria for validation of methods in microbial forensics. Applied and Environmental Microbiology 74 (18), 5599–5607.

Bulbul, H.I., Yavuzcan, H.G., Ozel, M., 2013. Digital Forensics: an analytical crime scene procedure model (ACSPM). Forensic Science International 233 (1–3), 244–256.

Bulut, Ö., Bol, S., Karakus, O., 2013. Adli vakalara ait iskelet buluntuları icin saha prosedürü ve standartları. Polis Bilimleri Dergisi 15 (3), 1–22.

Cardoso, H.F.V., Santos, A., Dias, R., Garcia, C., Pinto, M., Sérgio, C., Magalhães, T., 2010. Establishing a minimum postmortem interval of human remains in an advanced state of skeletonization using the growth rate of bryophytes and plant roots. International Journal of Legal Medicine 124 (5), 451–456.

Centre for Applied Science and Technology (CAST). https://www.gov.uk/government/collections/centre-for-applied-science-and-technology-information.

Caymaz, A., 2001. The importance of crime scene investigation in fire and arson cases. Fa Yi Xue Za Zhi 15 (1), 73–83.

Ceker, D., 2016. The role of forensic archaeologists and forensic anthropologists in crime scene investigations: current status in North Cyprus and Turkey. Ankara University, Faculty of Language, History and Geography. Journal of Anthropology 32, 13–21.

Chen, L.S., 2006. Using the accumulated temperature method to predict postmortem interval in a case. Forensic Science and Technology 5, 54–56.

Chen, Y.C., Cheng, J.D., 2002. The relationship between postmortem degradation of marrow DNA in bosom bone and late postmortem interval estimation. Fa Yi Xue Za Zhi 18 (3), 114–115.

Chen, Y.Q., Cai, J.F., Wen, J.F., 2009. Advances in the studies of postmortem interval estimation by the levels of chemical components in human vitreous humor after death. Fa Yi Xue Za Zhi 25 (1), 53–56.

Cockle, D.L., Bell, L.S., 2015. Human decomposition and the reliability of a 'Universal' model for post mortem interval estimations. Forensic Science International 253, 136.e1-9.

Cockle, D.L., Bell, L.S., 2017. The environmental variables that impact human decomposition in terrestrially exposed contexts within Canada. Science & Justice 57 (2), 107–117.

Cihangiroglu, B., Çubuk, M.C., Yildiz, O., Kilic, N., 2011. Felaket kurbanlarının kimliklendirilmesi. In: Cihangiroglu, B. Adli Bilimler, Cilt II. Jandarma Kriminal Daire Başkanlığı Yayinlari, Ankara, pp. 239–279.

Criminal Practice Directions, England and Wales, part 19A.5(a). https://www.justice.gov.uk/courts/procedure-rules/criminal/docs/criminal-procedure-rules-practice-directions-2015-February-2017.pdf.

Cubuk, M., 2011. Biyolojik incelemeler. In: Cihangiroglu B. Adli Bilimler, Cilt II. Jandarma Kriminal Daire Başkanlığı Yayınları, Ankara, pp. 103–143.

Dawson, L.A., Hillier, S., 2010. Measurement of soil characteristics for forensic applications. Surface and Interface Analysis 42, 363e377.

Dawson, L.A., Mayes, R.W., 2014. Criminal and environmental soil forensics: soil as physical evidence in forensic investigations. In: Murphy, B.L., Morrison, R.D. (Eds.), Introduction to Environmental Forensics, third ed. Academic Press, Oxford, pp. 457–486 (Chapter 12).

Demirci, S., Dogan, K.H., 2011. Death scene investigation from the viewpoint of forensic medicine expert, forensic medicine – from old problems to new challenges. In: Prof. Duarte Nuno Vieira. ISBN: 978-953-307-262-3.

Dix, J., Ernst, M.F., 1999. Handbook for Death Scene Investigators. CRC Press, Boca Raton, Florida.

Donaldson, A.E., Taylor, M.C., Cordiner, S.J., Lamont, I.L., 2010. Using oral microbial DNA analysis to identify expirated bloodspatter. International Journal of Legal Medicine 124 (6), 569–576.

Donnelly, L., 2013. Use of quaternary proxies in forensic science. Use of geology in forensic science: search to locate burials. Reference Module in Earth Systems and Environmental Sciences? Encyclopaedia of Quaternary Science 521–534. http://dx.doi.org/10.1016/B978-0-444-53643-3.00364-2.

Donovan, S.M., 2017. Introduction to the special focus issue on the impact of diet on gut microbiota composition and function and future opportunities for nutritional modulation of the gut microbiome to improve human health. Gut Microbes. http://dx.doi.org/10.1080/19490976.2017.1299309.

Enserink, M., 2017. Amsterdam to host Europe's first 'forensic cemetery'. Science. http://dx.doi.org/10.1126/science.aal0637.

Erdag, A.I., 2010. The power of law-enforcement officers to stop and ask identity (ID) card (Article 4/A of the Law on Duties and Powers of Police. Ankara Barosu Dergisi 68 (4), 37–60.

European Network of Forensic Science Institutes. http://enfsi.eu/about-enfsi/structure/working-groups/animal-plant-and-soil-traces/.

Fierer, N., Lauber, C.L., Zhou, N., McDonald, D., Costello, E.K., Knight, R., 2010. Forensic identification using skin microbial communities. Proceedings of the National Academy of Sciences USA 107 (14), 6477–6481.

Fleming, R.I., Harbison, S., 2010. The use of bacteria for the identification of vaginal secretions. Forensic Science International Genetics 4 (5), 311–315.

Goga, H., 2012. Comparison of bacterial DNA profiles of footwear insoles and soles of feet for the forensic discrimination of footwear owners. International Journal of Legal Medicine 126, 815–823.

Gok, S., 1998. Adli Tıbbın Türkiye'de Geçirdiği Evreler. Temel Matbaacılık Ambalaj Sanayi Ltd, Sti. Istanbul.

Gok, S., Ozen, C., 1982. History and Organization of Forensic, first ed. Istanbul University Cerrahpasa Medical School Publications, Istanbul.

Graves, W., 1979. A mineralogical soil classification technique for the forensic scientist. Journal of Forensic Science 24, 323–338.

Gultekin, O., 2011. Olay yeri incelemesinde karşılaşılan sorunlar ve çözüm önerileri. Türkiye Adalet Akademisi Dergisi 2 (4), 473–508.

Gunn, A., 2009. Essential Forensic Biology, second ed. Wiley-Blackwell, West Sussex.

Guo, J., Fu, X., Liao, H., Hu, Z., Long, L., Yan, W., Ding, Y., Zha, L., Guo, Y., Yan, J., Chang, Y., 2016. Potential use of bacterial community succession for estimating post-mortem interval as revealed by high-throughput sequencing. Scientific Reports 6, 24197.

Habtom, H., Demaneche, S., Dawson, L.A., Azulay, C., Matan, O., Robe, P., Gafny, R., Simonet, P., Jurkevitch, E., Pasternak, Z., 2017. Soil characterisation by bacterial community analysis for forensic applications: a quantitative comparison of environmental technologies. Forensic Science International 26, 21–29.

Haglund, W.D., Sord, M.H., 1996. Forensic Taphonomy: The Postmortem Fate of Human Remains. CRC Press, Boca Raton.

Harrison, K., Dawson, L., Mackinnon, G., 2016. Interdisciplinary approaches to the search and location of buried bodies: a United Kingdom context. In: Kars, H., van den Eijkel, L. (Eds.), Soil in Criminal and Environmental Forensics: Proceedings of the Soil Forensics Special, 6th European Academy of Forensic Science Conference. Springer, The Hague, pp. 201–239.

Hayman, J., Oxenham, M., 2017. Estimation of the time since death in decomposed bodies found in Australian conditions. Australian Journal of Forensic Sciences 49 (1), 31–44.

Ho, T.P., Yip, P.S., Chiu, C.W., Halliday, P., 1998. Suicide notes: what do they tell us? Acta Psychiatrica Scandinavica 98, 467–473.

Hopper, J., June 2011. Casey Anthony trial: witness rebuts human decomposition in car's trunk. ABC News. abcnews.go.com.

Horswell, J., 2004. The Practice of Crime Scene Investigation. CRC Press, Boca Raton.

Horswell, J., Cordiner, S.J., Maas, E.W., Martin, T.M., Sutherland, K.B., Speir, T.W., Nogales, B., Osborn, A.M., 2002. Forensic comparison of soils by bacterial community DNA profiling. Journal of Forensic Science 47 (2), 350–353.

Huang, R.T., Gu, Z., 2014. The founder of modern forensic science in China – Lin Ji. Mindu Culture 5, 45–51.

Huang, R.T., Chen, X.S., 2005. Hundred Chinese forensic medicine. Chinese Journal of Forensic Medicine 20 (5), 318–319.

Inanici, M.A., Colak, B., Ozaslan, A., 2004. Olay yeri İncelemesi ve Adli Tıp Uzmanının yeri, Türkiye Klinikleri. Fa Yi Xue Za Zhi 2, 97.

International Union of Geological Sciences – Initiative on Forensic Geology (IUGS-IFG). http://forensic-geologyinternational.com.

Jia, B.Q., 2009. A case that utilized the effective accumulated temperature of the development of *Lucilia sericata* for postmortem interval estimation. Peertechz Journal of Forensic Science and Technology 5, 42.

Johnson, A., Archer, M., Leigh-Shaw, L., Pais, M., O'Donnell, C., Wallman, J., 2012. Examination of forensic entomology evidence using computed tomography scanning: case studies and refinement of techniques for estimating maggot mass volumes in bodies. International Journal of Legal Medicine 126 (5), 693–702.

Karaburun, G., 2001. Adlî Tıp Açısından AIHM Kararları ve Ic Hukukumuz Cercevesinde Olay yeri İncelemesi ve Otopsi. Adalet Dergisi 92 (8), 112.
Karbeyaz, K., Akkaya, H., Balci, Y., Urazel, B., 2014. Analysis of suicide notes: an experience in Eskişehir City. Archives of Neuropsychiatry 51, 275–279.
Koc, S., 1999. Keşif [Discovery]. In: Soysal, Z., Cakalir, C. (Eds.), Adli Tıp, Cilt I. Istanbul University. Cerrahpaşa Tıp Fakültesi Yayınları, Rek. No: 4165, Fak. No: 224, pp. 153–161.
Kuiper, I., 2016. Microbial forensics: next-generation sequencing as catalyst. EMBO Reports 17 (8), 1085–1087.
Leitner, T., Albert, J., 2000. Reconstruction of HIV-1 transmission chains for forensic purposes. AIDS Reviews 2, 241–251.
Lemey, P., Van Dooren, S., Van Laethem, K., Schrooten, Y., Derdelinckx, I., Goubau, P., Brun-Vézinet, F., Vaira, D., Vandamme, A.M., 2005. Molecular testing of multiple HIV-1 transmissions in a criminal case. AIDS 19, 1649–1658.
Lerner, A., Shor, Y., Vinokurov, A., Okon, Y., Jurkevitch, E., 2006. Can denaturing gradient gel electrophoresis (DGGE) analysis of amplified 16S rDNA of soil bacterial populations be used in forensic investigations? Soil Biology & Biochemistry 38, 1188–1192.
Lester, D., 1994. A comparison of fifteen theories of suicide. Suicide and Life Threatening Behaviour 24, 80–88.
Li, X.B., Gong, Q., Wan, L.H., Jiang, D., Jiao, Y.G., 2003. A case that utilized sarcosaphagous flies for postmortem interval estimation. Chinese Journal of Forensic Medicine 28 (3), 248–249.
Liu, B., 2015. Several key issues for China national DNA database development. Forensic Science and Technology 40 (4), 318–323.
Liu, J., Song, Z.Z., Xie, R.H., Ren, G.M., Wang, Y.Y., 2007. A pilot study on cerebral RNA degradation and its applicability to estimation of postmortem interval in rats. Chinese Journal of Forensic Medicine 22 (4), 226–228.
Lozupone, C.A., Stombaugh, J.I., Gordon, J.I., Jansson, J.K., Knight, R., 2012. Diversity, stability and resilience of the human gut microbiota. Nature 220–230.
Lu, J.P., 2001. Application of forensic entomology in a case inspection. Fa Yi Xue Za Zhi 17 (3), 184–185.
Lv, Z., Li, X.B., Liu, J., Mo, Y.N., 2010. Deviation analysis of postmortem interval estimation of decomposed corpses according to insect development cycle in 3 Cases. Chinese Journal of Forensic Medicine 25 (1), 51–52.
Maile, A.E., Inoue, C.G., Barksdale, L.E., Carter, D.O., 2017. Toward a universal equation to estimate postmortem interval. Forensic Science International 272, 150–153.
Mann, R.W., Bass, W.M., Meadows, L., 1990. Time since death and decomposition of the human body: variables and observations in case and experimental field studies. Journal of Forensic Sciences 35, 103–111.
Mao, S., Fu, G., Seese, R.R., Wang, Z.Y., 2013. Estimation of PMI depends on the changes in ATP and its degradation products. Legal Medicine 15 (5), 235–238.
Marchenko, M.I., 2001. Medicolegal relevance of cadaver entomofauna for the determination of the time of death. Forensic Science International 120 (1), 89–109.
Moffatt, C., Simmons, T., Lynch-Aird, J., 2016. An improved equation for TSB and ADD: establishing a reliable postmortem interval framework for casework and experimental studies. Journal of Forensic Sciences 61, S201–S207.
Muyzer, G., de Waal, E.C., Uitterlinden, A.G., 1993. Profiling of complex microbial populations by denaturing gel electrophoresis analysis of polymerase chain reaction-amplified genes coding for 16S rRNA. Applied and Environmental Microbiology 59 (3), 695–700.
Nishi, E., Tashiro, Y., Sakai, K., 2015. Discrimination among individuals using terminal restriction fragment length polymorphism profiling of bacteria derived from forensic evidence. International Journal of Legal Medicine 129, 425–433.
Niu, Q.S., Li, J., Zhang, X.M., 2000. The experimental observation and forensic application of *Lucilia sericata*'s developmental rate and effective accumulated temperature. Chinese Journal of Forensic Medicine 15 (4), 214.
O'Connor, R., Sheeby, N., O'Connor, D., 1999. A thematic analysis of suicide notes. Crisis 20, 106–114.
Olakanye, A.O., Thompson, T., Ralebitso-Senior, T.K., 2015. Shifts in soil biodiversity – a forensic comparison between *Sus scrofa domesticus* and vegetation decomposition. Science & Justice: Journal of the Forensic Science Society 55, 402–407.

Parry, W., June 7, 2011. Goo of death helps solve mystery of headless corpse. Life Science.

Pasternak, Z., Al-Ashhab, A., Gatica, J., Gafny, R., Avraham, S., Frenk, S., Minz, D., Gillor, O., Jurkevitch, E., 2012. Optimization of molecular methods and statistical procedures for forensic fingerprinting of microbial soil communities. International Research Journal of Microbiology 3 (11), 363–372.

Pasternak, Z., Al-Ashhab, A., Gatica, J., Gafny, R., Avraham, S., Minz, D., Gillor, O., Jurkevitch, E., 2013. Spatial and temporal biogeography of soil microbial communities in arid and semiarid regions. PLoS One 8 (7), e69705.

Pechal, J.L., Crippen, T.L., Benbow, M.E., Tarone, A.M., Dows, S., Tomberlin, J.K., 2014. The potential use of bacterial community succession in forensics as described by high throughput metagenomic sequencing. International Journal of Legal Medicine 128, 193–205.

Petraco, N., Kubic, T.A., Petraco, N.D., 2008. Case studies in forensic soil examinations. Forensic Science International 178 (2–3), e23–e27.

Power, D.A., Cordiner, S.J., Kieser, J.A., Tompkins, G.R., Horswell, J., 2010. PCR-based detection of salivary bacteria as a marker of expirated blood. Science & Justice: Journal of the Forensic Science Society 50 (2), 59–63.

Prahlow, J., 2010. Forensic Pathology for Police, Death Investigators, Attorneys, and Forensic Scientists. Humana Press.

Prevost-Boure, N.C., Maron, P.A., Ranjard, L., Nowak, V., Dufrene, E., Damesin, C., Soudani, K., Lata, J.C., 2011. Seasonal dynamics of the bacterial community in forest soils under different quantities of leaf litter. Applied Soil Ecology 47, 14–23.

Quaak, F.C.A., Kuiper, I., 2011. Statistical data analysis of bacterial t-RFLP profiles in forensic soil comparisons. Forensic Science International 210 (1–3), 96–101.

Quaak, F.C.A., de Graaf, M.M., Weterings, R., Kuiper, I., 2017. Microbial population analysis improves the evidential value of faecal traces in forensic investigations. International Journal of Legal Medicine 131 (1), 45–51.

Rajilic-Stojanovic, M., Heilig, H.G.H.J., Tims, S., Zoetendal, E.G., de Vos, W.M., 2013. Long-term monitoring of the human intestinal microbiota composition. Environmental Microbiology 15 (4), 1146–1159.

Ruder, T.D., Hatch, G.M., Ampanozi, G., Thali, M.J., Fischer, N., 2011. Suicide announcement on Facebook. Crisis 32, 280–282.

Ruffell, A., McAllister, S., 2015. A RAG system for the management of forensic and archaeological searches of burial grounds. International Journal of Archaeology 3 (1–1), 1–8. http://dx.doi.org/10.11648/j.ija.s.20150301.11.

Salib, E., Cawley, S., Healy, R., 2002. The significance of suicide notes in the elderly. Aging & Mental Health 6, 186–190.

Saukko, P., Knight, B., 2004. Knight's Forensic Pathology, third ed. Arnold, London.

Shoja, M.M., Tubbs, R.S., 2007. The history of anatomy in Persia. Journal of Anatomy 210 (4), 359–378. http://dx.doi.org/10.1111/j.1469-7580.2007.00711.x.

Soysal, Z., Eke, M., 1999. Dünyada Adli Tıbbın Tarihçesi ve Gelişimi/Gök Ş. Adli Tıbbın Türkiye'de Geçirdiği Tarihi Evreler. Adli Tıp, Cilt I. İstanbul Üniversitesi Basımevi ve Film Merkezi, Istanbul, pp. 1–44.

Stanojevich, V., 2012. The role of a forensic anthropologist in death investigation. Journal of Forensic Research 3 (6), 154.

Tang, Z.Z., 1994. The regression equation for postmortem interval estimation according to maggot length. Fa Yi Xue Za Zhi 10 (3), 113–121.

The Official Gazette, 1921. http://www.kanuntr.net/tababeti-adiye-kanunu/.

The Turkish Republic Constitution 1982. Law No: 2709; November 7, 1982.

Tilley, N., Ford, A., 1996. Forensic science and crime investigation. In: Webb, B. (Ed.), Crime Detection and Prevention Series Paper 73. Home Office Police Department, London.

Tomberlin, J.K., Mohr, R., Benbow, M.E., Tarone, A.M., VanLaerhoven, S., 2011. A roadmap for bridging basic and applied research in forensic entomology. Annual Review of Entomology 56, 401–421.

Tully, G., 2017. Forensic Science Regulator: Annual Report. http://www.forensic-access.co.uk/wp-content/uploads/2017/01/25802-FSR_Annual_Report_2015_16_125033.pdf.

Uitdehaag, S.C.A., Quaak, F.C.A., Kuiper, I., 2016. Soil comparisons using small soil traces, a case report. In: Kars, H., van den Eijkel, L. (Eds.), Soil in Criminal and Environmental Forensics; Proceedings of the Soil Forensics Special 6th European Academy of Forensic Science Conference. Editors, The Hague. ISBN: 978-3-319-33113-3, pp. 61–69.

van Ledden Hulsebosch, C.J., 1945. Veertig Jaren Speurderswerk. Kemink en Zonen.

Wagner, S.A., 2009. Death scene investigation: a field guide. CRC Press, Boca Raton, Florida.

Wald, C., 2015. The soil sleuth. Nature 520, 422–424.

Wang, J.F., 2015. China. In: Tomberlin, J.K., Benbow, M.E. (Eds.), Forensic Entomology International Dimensions and Frontiers. CRC Press, Boca Raton, pp. 7–18.

Wang, J.F., Chang, P., Liao, M.Q., Li, Z.G., Ma, T., Gui, L.F., Yu, L.C., 2012. On the application of forensic entomology to the investigation of indoor, outdoor and poisoning death cases in Guangdong Province. Journal of Political Science and Law 29 (1), 116–121.

Wang, J.F., Chen, Y.C., Hu, C., Min, J.X., Li, J.T., 2000. Chronology of development within puparium of *Lucilia sericata* in different constant temperature and its application in the determination of post-mortem interval. Acta Scientiarum Naturalium Universitatis Sunyatseni 39 (6(A)), 250–254.

Wang, J.F., Chen, Y.C., Hu, C., Min, J.X., Li, J.T., 2001. Chronology of development within puparium of *Chrysomya megacephala* in different constant temperature and its application in the determination of postmortem interval. Acta Parasitologica et Medica Entomologica Sinica 8 (4), 232–236.

Wang, J.F., Hu, C., Chen, Y.C., Min, J.X., Li, J.T., 2002a. Chronometrical morphology of *Aldrichina graham* and its application in the determination of postmortem interval. Acta Entomologica Sinica 45 (2), 265–270.

Wang, J.F., Hu, C., Chen, Y.C., Min, J.X., Li, J.T., 2002b. Chronometrical morphology of *Chrysomya megacephala* and its application on the determination of postmortem interval. Acta Parasitology et Medica Entomologica Sinica 9 (1), 33–38.

Wei, Z.W., Huang, A.H., 2016. The application of postmortem interval estimation regression equation based on maggot length in a decomposed corpse identification case. Chinese Journal of Forensic Medicine 31 (3), 316–317.

Williams, A., November 13, 2015. Would YOU leave your body to medical science if it meant going to a 'body farm'? Human remains left to decompose in the open air in the name of research. Daily Mail.

Witt, I., Casella, J., Brown, R., 2015. The Feasibility of a United Kingdom Human Taphonomic Research Centre (UKHTRC). Blurb Books, pp. 1–88. http://www.blurb.co.uk/b/6632826-the-feasibility-of-a-united-kingdom-human-taphonom.

Xiao, J.X., Chen, Y.C., 2005. A study on the relationship between the degradation of protein and the post-mortem interval. Fa Yi Xue Za Zhi 21 (2), 110–112.

Yan, H., 2008. Research on Forensic Medicine Literature Reorganization of the Qing Dynasty (Master thesis). Guiyang College of Traditional Chinese Medicine, Guiyang.

Zhang, J.Z., 2013. Research of forensic anthropology for 30 years in China. Acta Anthropological Sinica 32 (3), 256–263.

Zhang, L., Guo, J.J., Peng, Y.L., Xie, D., Guo, Y.D., Yan, J., Zha, L., Cai, J.F., 2016. Bacterial succession on rat carcasses and applications for PMI estimation. Fa Yi Xue Za Zhi 32 (1), 1–6.

Zhou, H.Z., Yang, Y.P., Ren, J.C., Liu, L., Wang, S.Y., Yan, R., Li, Y.W., 1997. Studies on forensic entomology in Beijing District. Chinese Journal of Forensic Medicine 12 (2), 79–83.

CHAPTER 9

Summary: An Assessment of Achievements, Limitations, and Potential of Forensic Ecogenomics

T. Komang Ralebitso-Senior
Teesside University, Tees Valley, United Kingdom

"FORENSIC ECOGENOMICS" AND DISCIPLINE MILESTONES

Several names are used for related novel interface disciplines where microbiological and molecular micro-/macrobial ecology techniques are being considered for use forensically in crime scene investigations. These include "microbial forensics," "microbioforensics," "environmental forensics," "forensic microbiology," and "forensic ecogenomics". A succinct discussion of when the terms first appeared in published literature, the lead researcher and/or team who identified and used the designation, and examples of critical reviews/books that have been used to define or encapsulate each term as of April 2017 is presented in Chapter 1. Irrespective of the specific terminologies and contexts, it is indisputable that the crime scene investigative toolkit is expanding with increasing applications of established culture-based and cutting-edge molecular microbiological techniques.

"Forensic ecogenomics" was defined (Ralebitso-Senior et al., 2016; Chapter 1) as an all-encompassing term with explicit and implicit applications to study ecological succession in microbial and microbial communities for a wide range of forensic contexts, both ante- and postmortem. These include, but are not limited to, profiling the human microbial fingerprint, necrobiome, and thanatomicrobiome. Also since forensic ecogenomics can be applied in decomposition analysis above- and belowground, it is relevant directly for characterizing the total microbiomes of all animals and plants found on or linked to a suspected crime scene. Additionally, the discipline has direct links to: (1) microbial forensics where environmental and food samples can be analyzed in biocrime and bioterrorism cases, and (2) environmental forensics with ecogenomic tools used to study or investigate deliberate environmental contamination.

In its strictest definition and application, forensic ecogenomics is synonymous with "microbioforensics," which was not used beyond its description by Ruffell (2010), and "microbial forensics" as used by different research teams including Carter et al. (2017) in their compilation *Forensic Microbiology*. The state of the art for forensic ecogenomics is

Forensic Ecogenomics
ISBN 978-0-12-809360-3
http://dx.doi.org/10.1016/B978-0-12-809360-3.00009-6

illustrated in the current manuscript with research questions, as identified in its chapters and/or understood from existing publications, also stated in relevant sections that follow. Overall, the methods and research questions as summarized herein must be underpinned by essential parameters such as method validation with attendant mathematical and statistical analyses.

METHOD VALIDATION

Several statements have been made on the many advances in microbial ecology as a direct result of the emerging application of "multi-meta-omics" to study and address key knowledge gaps in diverse ecosystems (e.g., Jansson et al., 2012; Yilmaz et al., 2011). While proven in other disciplines, the advantages and limitations of ecogenomic tools need to be considered specifically for application in forensic contexts and crime scenes. A comprehensive review was presented by Budowle et al. (2008) on the key criteria for validating methods in microbial forensics. Although their discourse focused on biocrimes and bioterrorism, many of the points raised are transferable to forensic ecogenomics, and are applicable subject to the relevant contextual modifications. That process and deliberation are outwith the context of this chapter but must be pursued parallel to research and case studies that aim to develop forensic ecogenomic methods as components of the real crime scene toolkit. For example, Young et al. (2014) presented a critical review of microbial DNA extraction from forensic soil samples, which is an essential step in all soil-related forensic ecogenomic protocols. The authors considered 11 commercial soil DNA extraction kits and highlighted: the recognized strengths and limitations of each approach; implications of soil sample storage conditions; the absence of protocol standardization/choice between laboratories, hence the difficulty for cross-comparisons; differences in sample sizes; and, most importantly, differences in soil types. Consequently, they recommended that physicochemical characterization of forensic soil samples must be made to then decide which extraction kit and protocol to use. Naturally, a similar comprehensive critique of each protocol upstream (e.g., MacDonald et al., 2008) and downstream of DNA extraction (e.g., Krakat et al., 2016) must be made with the final decision most probably dependent on the specific case and site conditions, or the investigative context (e.g., Camarinha-Silva et al., 2011).

Multivariate Analysis in Forensic Ecogenomics

The use of multivariate analysis in microbial ecology has increased to allow (statistical) comparisons of several and complementary data sets from the same study. According to Ng and Cavagnaro (2016), multidimensional data can be explored and visualized with several multivariate analysis approaches such as: correspondence analysis; cluster analysis; principal coordinate analysis; principal component analysis; and nonmetric multidimensional scaling (NMDS). Further scrutiny to elucidate the relationship between specific environmental parameters and recorded patterns, for example, can then be achieved with: variation partitioning; redundancy analysis; linear discriminant analysis; and constrained canonical analysis. The authors concluded that the use of different methods to corroborate results increases the robustness of the observed trends, while similar ordination plots from constrained and unconstrained analyses provide further evidence that the observed patterns were explained largely by the environmental variables factored into the constrained analysis.

Inevitably, the use of microbial ecology tools and attendant statistical analyses in forensic science has, and will, generate multiple and often large data sets. Their comprehensive analysis and subsequent detailed appreciation of their potential to enhance the crime scene toolkit may be ensured by the use of multivariate analytical tools. This strategy has been highlighted and/or illustrated by, for example, Cobaugh et al. (2015), Macdonald et al. (2011), Olakanye et al. (2017), and Pasternak et al. (2012) who applied ranked mixed model ANOVA, Tukey–Kramer post hoc test, Spearman ranking, analysis of similarity *R*-statistic, multiresponse permutation procedure on Bray–Curtis distance matrices, and NMDS. Specifically, Quaak and Kuiper (2011) and Uitedehaag et al. (2016) presented deliberations on different bacterial profile comparison platforms and statistics before the subsequent application of Bray–Curtis analysis of data derived from terminal restriction fragment length polymorphism (T-RFLP) analyses of soil traces at the Netherlands Forensic Institute.

The subsurface soil necrobiome was assessed (Olakanye et al., 2014, 2015, 2017; Olakanye and Ralebitso-Senior, 2017) during *Sus scrofa domesticus* and plant litter (*Agrostis/Festuca* spp. and *Quercus robur*) decomposition by applying denaturing gradient gel electrophoresis (DGGE)-derived ecological index measurements, next-generation sequencing-based analysis of community structure and composition, and different statistical analytical tools (two-way ANOVA with repeated measure, Tukey and Bonferroni post hoc tests, principal component analysis, Bray–Curtis distance unweighted pair-group using the arithmetic average clustering, Bray–Curtis dissimilarity with NMDS, and Spearman's rank correlation coefficient). The approaches facilitated comparisons of findings and trends on the basis of addressing key questions such as: which constraint revealed distinct changes for each experimental parameter?; which constraint(s) and parameter revealed the most statistical/clearest differentiation of the impact of *S. scrofa domesticus* decomposition?; and which constraint(s) and parameter afforded distinction between burial and nonburial soils. Corroboration of specific trends by the various tools and approaches emphasized the robustness of the actual findings and relevance of the multivariate analyses.

In summary, the findings of these and other studies demonstrate and highlight the relevance and potential of the following for furtherance of ecogenomic tools in forensics: (1) the need for experimental and mathematical replicates; (2) the application of different statistical analysis tools to interrogate comprehensively the study or case data;

and (3) the necessity for caution when interpreting data, with and without further statistical/multivariate analyses. All will be critical for conclusive evidence in real crime scenes and for court cases in particular. For the wider context, questions remain on the applicability and relevance of the chosen approach for different needs and users, i.e., researchers, practitioners, registered laboratories, and law enforcers. So, are data of shifts in microbial community structure, composition, diversity, and richness enough to differentiate between burial and nonburial soils from real crime scenes or do these always need to be analyzed further with multivariate and statistical tools? These questions should be posed and answered with mindfulness that the forensic ecogenomics data and analyses, for example, would be used as part of a bigger set of intelligence metadata to then address key questions such as: what/who is buried where and for how long. Therefore the tools applied and the degree of scrutiny required will depend on the specific crime scenario and the intended or likely use of the gathered intelligence where greater inspection would be essential for court proceedings and convictions.

PROSPECTING: FUTURE POTENTIALS AND LIMITATIONS

Although the focus of this book is the ecology of cadaver decomposition, the definition of "forensic ecogenomics" as indicated in Chapter 1 encapsulates the application of different microbial ecology techniques to environmental samples for forensic diagnostics as a whole. Therefore Table 9.1, which should be considered in conjunction with Table 1.1, presents a summary of the techniques, including their strengths and limitations, that have been applied to date and a forward-looking perspective of other methods with potential within and outwith decomposition-related forensic ecogenomics. As posited in a critical review (Ralebitso-Senior et al., 2016), the future projections in particular consider: environmental degradation; stable isotope probing and analysis; microarrays or genechips; and lab-on-a-chip or solid phase polymerase chain reaction (PCR).

As discussed in Chapters 1 and 3, taphonomic investigations have established that changes in available substrates, including ammonia, volatile fatty acids, phenolics, alcohols, etc., occur with the decomposition process. These, combined with soil-specific physicochemical characteristics, should serve as the basis for techniques that probe changes in microbial community structure and function. Further studies could also be made specifically to identify which microbial taxa provide stronger indication of decomposition "history" and hence potentially more accurate determinations of time since burial. Stable isotope labeling and bespoke microarrays, for example, could be exploited to this end.

Microbiomes and Evidence of Sources of Environmental Degradation

Increasingly, data from molecular microbial ecology studies of human (gut) microbiomes (Bergström et al., 2012; Li et al., 2009; Quaak et al., 2017; Zoetendal et al., 2008) and several animals (Kim and Mundt, 2011; Shepherd et al., 2011; Sundset et al., 2009)

Table 9.1 Published and potential applications of (molecular) microbial ecology methods in forensic ecogenomics

Target biomolecule and protocol	Significance	Potential shortfalls	Current and potential applications/observations	References/studies
DNA/RNA	Extraction and subsequent amplification steps are often rapid and successful. A range of extraction protocols is available including commercial kits for quality control. Downstream (semi-) quantitative analyses can also be facilitated with concentration measurement kits. RNA can be targeted for quantitative detection of specific catabolic genes	Variable cell lysis efficiencies may lead to biased community profiling. Sample pretreatment is sometimes required to ensure the successful extraction of high-quality, high-quantity DNA/RNA. Subject to polymerase chain reaction (PCR) bias	Most investigations in crime scene science and forensic ecogenomics rely on DNA-based protocols. RNA-based forensic analysis may be required generally for functional community profiling	
Denaturing/temperature gradient gel electrophoresis	Rapid and cost-effective community structure profiling. Can target bacterial (16S) and fungal (18S) rRNA genes	Subject to DNA/RNA extraction and amplification biases. Primer specificity and sensitivity become increasingly important. One band does not necessarily represent one operational taxonomic unit. Detection limits of less abundant members in complex communities	Denaturing gradient gel electrophoresis and other profiling techniques have relevance in forensics. The reliability of the data as part of a robust intelligence is probably dependent on the establishment and adoption of specific protocols. Capacity to differentiate between control and gravesoils	Bergmann et al. (2014), Chimutsa et al. (2015), Lerner et al. (2006), Olakanye et al. (2015), and Pasternak et al. (2012)

Continued

Table 9.1 Published and potential applications of (molecular) microbial ecology methods in forensic ecogenomics—cont'd

Target biomolecule and protocol	Significance	Potential shortfalls	Current and potential applications/observations	References/studies
Quantitative-polymerase chain reaction (qPCR)	Quantitative analysis of communities in forensic ecogenomics	Subject to PCR bias	Traced sources of environmental degradation. Quantified the expression of catabolic enzymes or functional communities for specific substrates in decomposing materials, e.g., proteolytic and lipolytic microorganisms	Cobaugh et al. (2015), Howard et al. (2010), and Lamendella et al. (2009)
Length heterogeneity - PCR	Rapid and cost-effective. Community profiling using amplicons of small subunit rRNA gene variable regions potentially from individual species. Highly reproducible results	Individual peaks may monitor the dynamics of more than one species or genus. No indication of function	Composition of specific functional microbial clades/genes identified for an individual. Potential for body identification in criminal or missing person cases	Moreno et al. (2011)
Homologous 16S rRNA gene analysis	Cost-effective identification of bacterial species from specific forensic contexts	Comparison and subsequent identification are dependent directly on the makeup of the reference database, hence it is limited to known strains	Established the occurrence and dominance of different genera in victims drowned in saline and fresh water	Kakizaki et al. (2008)

Terminal restriction fragment length polymorphism	Rapid and cost-effective community structure or composition profiling. May allow predictions of microorganisms that might be present. Multiple restriction enzymes increase specificity	Subject to database restrictions and PCR bias. Fluorescent labels can retard fragment migration	Potential use of soils from clothing or shoe sole as associative evidence. Established changes in fugal community structure that could be linked to early and late phases of decomposition. Identified that air drying altered microbial taxa resolution with fungi affected less than bacteria	Camarinha-Silva et al. (2011), Horswell et al. (2002), MacDonald et al. (2008), Macdonald et al. (2011), Parkinson et al. (2009), and Pasternak et al. (2012)
FISH-based, e.g., MAR-FISH, STAR-FISH	Shifts in numbers within bacterial communities. Spatial scaling and quantitative analysis of specific communities	Probe design, availability, and specificity. Novel probe design can be labor intensive. Successful detection, analysis, and elimination of false-positive and false-negative mismatches. Number of target versus hybridized probes. Limited application for phylogenetically diverse/versatile groups, e.g., sulfide-oxidizing bacteria. Limited permeability of some functional glades to oligonucleotide probes. Feasibility of radiolabeling study material	Potential application especially in identifying cadaver decomposition island. Potential to estimate the size and/or weight of the original buried material	[a]

Continued

Table 9.1 Published and potential applications of (molecular) microbial ecology methods in forensic ecogenomics—cont'd

Target biomolecule and protocol	Significance	Potential shortfalls	Current and potential applications/observations	References/studies
Stable isotope probing	Tracks the dynamics of specific microbial communities to changes in response to key parameters (which are deemed relevant to forensics)	Cost of stable isotope-labeled substrates. Decision on labeling C, N, or H dependent on the target substrate. Incubation periods for labeling efficacy, which require optimization studies. Cross-feeding. Subject to recovery of high biomass and high-quantity biomolecules	Current application of gas chromatography/mass spectrometry-based lipids for fatty acid methyl ester (FAME) analysis. Can be combined with DNA-/RNA-/protein-/amino acid-based profiling to track specific microbial communities and expression of specific enzymes in response to decomposition	Bull et al. (2009)
Hierarchical oligonucleotide primer extension	Potential for high-throughput analysis of group/genus/species dynamics	Can have detection biases relative to the predominance and persistence of the target group/genus/species	Afford activity-specific comparisons between microbial communities from pristine and contaminated ecosystems (e.g., *Bacteroidales-Prevotella* distribution/predominance due to farming activities). Quantitative data may allow estimates of contaminant migration relative to source	Hong et al. (2009a,b) and Lamendella et al. (2009)
Metagenomic analysis	High-throughput analysis of environmental microbial communities	Potentially labor intensive	Can be used: (1) before, during, and after cadaver deposition/decomposition; (2) above, around, below, and away from cadaver decomposition island; and (3) upstream, within, and downstream of a pollution source	[a]

Microarrays	High-throughput, quantitative, and simultaneous analysis	Array specificity, sensitivity. and reliability. Data analysis	Potential for bespoke platforms targeting common members of the human microbiome ante- and postmortem. Apply existing arrays, e.g., GeoChip 2.0/3.0 and PhyloChip, for phylogenetic structure and composition analyses of ecosystem necrobiome	Quaak et al. (2017)
Clone libraries	Used widely in molecular microbial ecology. Afford subsequent identification of specific/important microbial community members via sequencing	Potentially labor intensive. Subject to bias due to DNA extraction, PCR, choice of cloning system, chimeras, etc.	Highly applicable for defined or specialized microhabitats such as bone cavity of decomposing animals and "microbial fingerprinting" with relatively simple human/individual microbiome	Reeb et al. (2011)
Sequencing	Different platforms (Sanger, 454-/pyrosequencing, BIPES) are available relative to cost and high-throughput considerations	Cost. Sequence error detection and management. Methodical analysis is required for the large data sets generated	Identify indicator members/communities, e.g., those that are indicative of decomposition or provide definitions of resident "microbial fingerprints." Provide sequencing data to design new primers/probes including for application in genechips, solid-phase PCR, and lab on a chip	Howard et al. (2010), Kong (2011), Lamendella et al. (2009), and Shepherd et al. (2011)

Continued

Table 9.1 Published and potential applications of (molecular) microbial ecology methods in forensic ecogenomics—cont'd

Target biomolecule and protocol	Significance	Potential shortfalls	Current and potential applications/observations	References/studies
Reverse transcription PCR	Quantitative detection of specific catabolic genes	Subject to recovery of high-quality, high-quantity RNA and PCR bias		[a]
Protein				
SDS-PAGE	Well-established, rapid and cost-effective determinations of changes in protein dynamics in response to decomposition	Subject to high biomass recovery	Applicable for rapid analysis of protein-based response to decomposition, for example	[a]
Fatty Acids				
FAME	Cost-effective analysis and profiling of community physiology	Conclusive interpretation of changes in community physiology is dependent on a reference database	Lipid analysis of gravesoil to confirm location of disinterred grave. Can be augmented with microbial community profiling relative to decomposition, e.g., identify active decay to dry periods	Breton et al. (2016) and Bull et al. (2009)

Phospholipid fatty acid analysis	High labeling of characteristic fatty acids facilitates correct catabolic taxon identification. Availability of large fatty acid data ensures constitutive lipid marker identification independent of environmental physicochemical parameters	Dependent on database and large data set of lipid profiles	Provided robust evidence of changes in soil microbial community structure due to cadaver decomposition	Parkinson et al. (2009)
Microbial Community Metabolic Profiling				
CLPP	Identifies physiological and metabolic changes in culturable microbial communities	Subject to the bias and limitations of culture-based techniques	Biolog EcoPlates used to profile epinecrotic bacteria to estimate minimum decomposition interval. Potential applicability in environmental necrobiome profiling to compare and contrast physiological/metabolic profiles between crime and noncrime scene samples	Pechal et al. (2014)

BIPES, barcoded Illumina paired-end (PE) sequencing; *CLPP*, Community-level physiological profiling; *FISH*, fluorescent in situ hybridization; *MAR-FISH*, microautoradiography-fluoresence in situ hybridization; *SDS-PAGE*, sodium dodecyl sulfate polyacrylamide gel electrophoresis; *STAR-FISH*, substrate-tracking autoradiography-FISH.

[a]Identifies the microbial ecology methods that are not used yet in forensic ecogenomics/microbiology.

Adapted from Ralebitso-Senior, T.K., Senior, E., Di Felice, R., Jarvis, K., 2012. Waste gas biofiltration: advances and limitations of current approaches in microbiology. Environmental Science & Technology 46 (16), 8542–8573; Ralebitso-Senior, T.K., Thompson, T.J.U., Carney, H.E., 2016. Microbial ecogenomics and forensic archaeology: new methods for investigating clandestine grave sites. Human Remains & Violence 2 (1), 41–57; see also Table 1.1.

continue to indicate that these communities can be unique to specific hosts. Therefore it is unsurprising that suggestions have subsequently been made of both the potential and need to link environmental degradation to specific pollution sources such as human- or animal-type fecal matter in surface water (Newton et al., 2013), which aligns with the "environmental forensics" (Ruffell, 2010) subdiscipline. For example, Li et al. (2009) used *Bacteroides* spp. group-specific 16S rRNA gene sequencing to characterize human fecal microbiota with a seven-member four-generation family as a model. While most of the sequences revealed a high biodiversity across the samples, distinctive interindividual differences in *Bacteroides* spp. compositions were also recorded.

Investigations by Lamendella et al. (2009) used *Prevotella* PCR-based analyses to track sources of pig fecal matter from geographically diverse ecosystems including waste lagoons, manure pits, and surface waters adjacent to swine-farming activities/operations. Although some specific links were made, the results highlighted the importance of improving these assays for more accurate detection. Consequently, Hong et al. (2009a,b) developed and patented hierarchical oligonucleotide primer extension as a quantitative and high-throughput technique that targeted the Bacteroidales-*Prevotella* 16S rRNA gene to indicate single and multiple sources of contamination from cows, pigs, dogs, and humans. The tool's main benefits are its ability to differentiate environmental samples on the basis of the origin of fecal contamination and its capability for time- and cost-effective detection of PCR assay false negatives and false positives. It does, however, also have limitations including detection bias due to differences in the abundance and persistence of host-specific Bacteroidales in the environment.

These deliberations highlight how molecular microbial ecology assays could be used to make potentially stronger, more conclusive links between farming activities as sources of environmental degradation and a farm as a crime scene where conventional intelligence gathering such as soil on a suspect's/victim's body, shoes, and clothes would be tested for some of the microbial strains/communities above. Overall, the methods considered here, especially within the context of environmental forensics, could also have long-term implications for policy development and/or revision by bodies such as the Department for Environment, Food and Rural Affairs and the Environment Agency in the United Kingdom, and the US Environmental Protection Agency.

Stable Isotope Probing and Analysis

A number of workers (e.g., Blaser, 2010; Bull et al., 2009; Fraser et al., 2006; Meier-Augenstein, 2002, 2010; Meier-Augenstein et al., 2012) have demonstrated the application and potential of stable isotope analysis in forensic science including human body analysis. Therefore a prospective use of its two elements could entail investigations of whether the fractionation detected in mummies (Finucane, 2007), for example, is transferred to and traceable in the surrounding soils and thus their constituent microbial communities. Robust contemporary experimental designs could then determine whether carbon and nitrogen isotopic fractionation can be used to identify locations of crime-related graves, even if these have been disinterred and/or the buried material has long decomposed and/or mineralized.

This is still a very hypothetical discourse, but if stable isotopes can be detected in mummies, then research questions can be posed on their half-lives in soils and their respective microbial populations, and the potential to use this knowledge in the modern crime scene toolkit. Specifically, laboratory-scale and pilot studies can establish proof-of-concept for the relevance of this ecogenomic approach. For example, stable isotope-labeled substrates and/or gases (amino acids, carbohydrates, N_2, H_2, H_2O, etc.) could be injected into materials prior to decomposition studies. The soil, sediment, and aquatic microbial communities that are responsible for and/or affected by the decay process could then be tracked by DNA-, RNA-, and phospholipid fatty acid-based stable isotope profiling (Neufeld et al., 2007). A combination of this approach with sequencing in particular would then provide evidence of the typical environmental populations or core microbiota (Astudillo-García et al., 2017) for targeting as indicators of decomposition in subsequent investigations. Adoption of the latter would be dependent on numerous, comprehensive, and parallel replication of the protocol in different ecosystems and/or sites across multiple geographical regions.

Microarrays/Genechips

The potential for microarrays or genechips was deliberated within the context of studying the human microbiome in relation to age, health, diet, environment, geographical origin (e.g., Paliy and Agans, 2012), and by extrapolation to ante- and post-mortem knowledge application in crime scenes. This was expanded with links to platforms such as the gut low density array as designed by Bergström et al. (2012). Specifically, Paliy and Agans (2012) presented a comprehensive list of arrays, together with their defining characteristics or analytical capabilities and their applications and limitations. Therefore their detailed discourse could be used to identify the most appropriate design or strategies for adopting microarray analyses in forensic ecogenomics. Some potential applications for decomposition-based contexts were explored briefly also in Chapter 4.

In recognition of their potential in human microbiome-based forensic analysis and as proposed previously (Ralebitso-Senior et al., 2016), Quaak et al. (2017) used a 616-probe microarray, which they had applied for profiling vaginal microbial communities (Benschop et al., 2012), to assay the microbiome of human fecal traces. The researchers used fecal matter from 35 volunteers and showed that targeting the 16S rRNA, GroEL, and 18S rRNA genes from known microbial species, genera, and families, with attendant Bray–Curtis analysis for robust statistical analysis, increased forensic evidential value particularly where no or partial human short tandem repeat profiles could be derived from fecal samples.

Lab-on-a-Chip/Solid-Phase PCR Platforms

Developments that combine the principles of microarrays, real-time (quantitative) PCR, microfluidics, and nanotechnology have led to the immobilization of PCR/molecular reagents on solid substrates such as glass and plastic polymers to create portable solid-phase PCR and lab-on-a-chip (LOC) platforms (Liu et al., 2004; Wang and Li, 2011). Research is ongoing toward their state-of-the-art exploitation globally in a wide spectrum of applications including the tracking of genetically modified organisms and foods/feed, and comparisons between genuine and counterfeit products. These techniques and platforms are being developed increasingly with the recognition that they will be applied by potentially untrained end-users for rapid analyses on site. Thus they must be robust, disposable (single use), easy to use, fit for purpose, consistent, and reliable with high sensitivities and specificities to obviate false (negative and positive) results.

The final criterion is vital in particular, where the findings of in situ investigations are intended to support subsequent court cases. Furthermore, the LOCs should ideally be flexible for timely updates. Thus while a first-generation platform will often be designed with primers or probes that target a specific gene or molecular biomarker (Chen et al., 2010; Sun et al., 2012), its capacity should be amenable to improvements to then analyze new or modified strains/genes. High-throughput and next-generation sequencing platforms as discussed earlier can provide high-quantity and high-quality data on the sequences of new strains and/or variants. These can then be used to design primers/probes de novo for immobilization and detection on upgraded second-generation lab-on-a-chip platforms, and so ensure that law enforcers are proactive/preemptive or reactive to (micro)biology-based crimes (e.g., Budowle et al., 2005). Although not high throughput, other molecular techniques have been adopted in the food industry as exemplified by Congiu et al. (2000) who used random amplified polymorphic DNA as part of evidence in a court case involving patented strawberries.

Overall, some of the techniques discussed are characterized by their ease of use, high resolution, and potential for high sensitivity and specificity, resulting in large data sets of high quantity and quality. Admittedly, the multiplex and high-throughput platforms are less readily available due to cost. Nevertheless, their potential to extend the crime scene investigative toolkit, to match the exploitation of the globally growing DNA databases, for example, justifies their application and the requisite investments, as made in other research areas. For example, sequencing affords comprehensive analyses of the microbiota of different animals and humans from diverse geographical regions, which are essential to establish the requisite databases for effective application in cutting-edge forensic science. Several studies have already been made (e.g., Howard et al., 2010; Kong, 2011; Lamendella et al., 2009; Reeb et al., 2011; Shepherd et al., 2011) and have established that novel and high-throughput techniques will play a key role in increasing rapidly the requisite comparative libraries.

The Human Microbiota

The potential for other human contexts and method application in forensic science and crime scene investigation have been deliberated and illustrated by several researchers such as Benschop et al. (2012), Djuric et al. (2008), Kuiper (2016), and Quaak et al. (2017). For example, reviews and primary research (Fierer et al., 2008, 2010; Grice et al., 2009; Krause et al., 2017; Ottman et al., 2012; Zhou et al., 2013) have demonstrated that the human microbiome is unique and can be used potentially for identification in health, disease, and forensic contexts. Specifically, Ottman et al. (2012) highlighted the application of meta-omics in understanding the genome sequences of more than 1000 microorganisms associated with the human body. It seems obvious therefore that these should serve as platforms, models, and databases for application and exploitation in contemporary forensic investigations.

Fig. 9.1 illustrates some methods and the potential strategy that could be used to create knowledge, establish or contribute to existing databases, and develop platforms that can then be used to analyze the human microbiome ante- and postmortem in research programs and crime scenes. Despite their known limitations, profiling techniques such as DGGE, T-RFLP, fatty acid methyl ester/phospholipid fatty acid analysis remain popular in general microbial ecology and hence in forensic ecogenomics. Similarly, next-generation sequencing has surpassed the other tools with its many platforms used to characterize the epinecrobiome, the total necrobiome, and the thanatomicrobiome. These analyses are revealing microbial strains, genera, orders, and families that are associated with the human microbiome both ante- and postmortem, including the associated soil/water for the latter context. Consequently, the sequencing data are being, or can be, used progressively to generate national and international databases. These should, in turn,

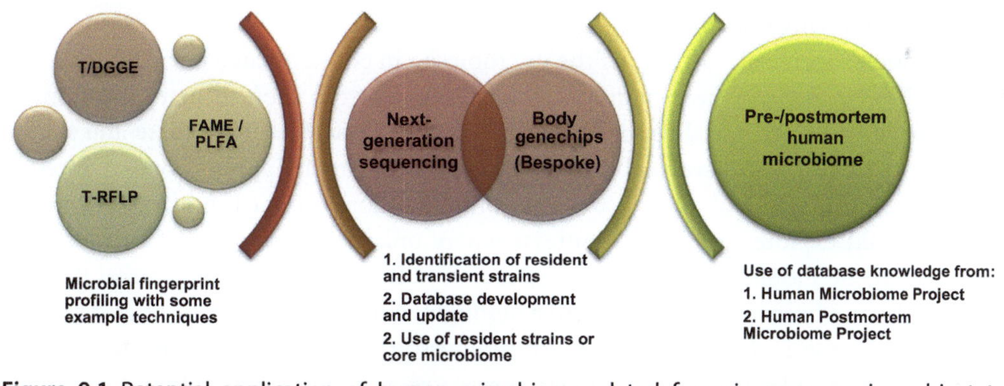

Figure 9.1 Potential application of human microbiome-related forensic ecogenomics subject to method validation with attendant statistical robustness. *FAME*, Fatty acid methyl ester; *PLFA*, phospholipid fatty acid analysis; *T/DGGE*, temperature/denaturing gradient gel electrophoresis; *T-RFLP*, terminal restriction fragment length polymorphism.

be interrogated to identify likely core microbiomes and microbial targets that can be used in generic and bespoke microarrays or as references for the profiling tools.

Before the human microbiome can be considered as a viable marker, however, it needs to be tested rigorously and verified for use within the forensic field. This should entail large sample sizes, significant numbers of individuals, multiple areas of the human body, and exploitation of global initiatives such as the Human Microbiome Project (Blaser, 2010; The NIH HMP Working Group et al., 2009). Cross-comparisons of profiles and/or metadata of one person under different conditions, such as personal hygiene regime, environmental exposure, and work, and between multiple individuals would ensure a comprehensive and robust database. Also requisite rigorous ethical scrutiny should precede these investigations.

PAUCITIES AND OTHER CONTEXTS

The deliberations presented in Chapters 1–8 have highlighted the knowledge development that is required to build informed and consistent databases to validate/adopt forensic ecogenomics, and related forensic subdisciplines, in real crime scene toolkits. While not intended, some paucities exist including the analysis of decomposition in aquatic ecosystems to then differentiate between postmortem interval and postmortem submergence interval estimation, and recognize the value of the latter. Although a relatively new area, emergent decomposition-related forensic ecogenomic studies have focused on aboveground terrestrial environments. Different challenges arise for aquatic ecosystems and these have been illustrated by researchers such as Dickson et al. (2011), Kakizaki et al. (2008), Lang et al. (2016), and Ueland et al. (2014), and explored in chapters as exemplified by Stuart and Ueland (2017) and Wallace (2015). Therefore there is considerable scope for further research to ensure that knowledge development for fresh and saline environments is made in tandem with that for soils.

Forensic ecogenomic analyses of the microbiome in contaminated environments will be useful for scenarios where bodies have been moved from their primary locations to secondary clandestine burials in polluted sites, or vice versa. Naturally, these and similar research initiatives will have to be complemented by parallel applications of forensic chemistry (e.g., Bull et al., 2009) and environmental forensics at the least. Also future studies should explore agronomic contexts where unlawful deposition of farm animals may need to be monitored in its own right, or to differentiate between animal disposal and clandestine human burials. The latter highlights further the discussions and recommendations made in Chapter 4 for requisite investigations that compare the necrobiomes of human cadavers and mammalian surrogates, and their surrounding ecosystems.

As proposed in several critical reviews (e.g., Finley et al., 2015a,b; Ralebitso-Senior et al., 2016), culture-based and molecular microbiological analyses have been adopted as additional tools for postmortem, postmortem submersion, and postburial interval determinations, albeit mostly in research. Chapter 8 presented some example case studies where different forensic subdisciplines, including forensic ecogenomics, were applied in real cases with analysis of the likely potential and their limitations also stated where relevant. It is envisaged therefore that more collaborations between researchers and scene of crime officers in the first instance will be pursued and published widely with the ultimate goal of methods adoption in real crime scenes and court cases.

Finally, initiatives and institutions such as the Human Postmortem Microbiome Project, Anthropological Research Facility at the University of Tennessee, Australian Facility for Taphonomic Experimental Research, Institute of Forensic Medicine of the University of Zurich, Netherlands Forensic Institute, and Academic Medical Center Cemetery, Amsterdam (see also Chapters 2, 4, and 6), demonstrate the potential and goals for harmonized and concerted efforts to: (1) facilitate cross-comparisons within and across studies; (2) ensure knowledge sharing and exchange; (3) develop standard protocols as much as is achievable; and ultimately (4) establish global baselines. As illustrated by Metcalf et al. (2016), Morriën et al. (2016), and Stone et al. (2016), for example, efforts by large interdisciplinary teams of researchers from different institutions, regions, and countries may be more effective in addressing core questions collectively. If implemented by teams with relatively global representation whenever feasible, then the outcomes of these initiatives would have inherent applicability, significance, and relevance for researchers, practitioners, and registered forensic laboratories internationally.

A PROPOSED APPROACH

Parallel to efforts in forensic entomology as proposed by Tomberlin et al. (2011), concerted global initiatives are essential to ensure that fundamental forensic ecogenomics research can translate ultimately to applications in real crime scenes and in the longer term become part of crime scene intelligence that informs court cases. This probably necessitates a protocol for subsequent use by all forensic ecogenomists both in ante- and postmortem micro-/macrobial community profiling as proposed in Fig. 9.2. Naturally, adoption of a standardized protocol would be subject to wide and comprehensive tests relative to the strengths and limitations of the different techniques (see also Tables 1.2 and 9.1) and their accessibility.

These highlight an obvious underpinning of site specificity in how this protocol is applied by different researchers and practitioners for a wide range of study questions and ultimately real scenes of crime. In the first instance, parameters such as climatic conditions (temperature and moisture), soil type (clay, sand, and silt ratio; pH), indigenous flora and fauna (scavengers, vegetation presence and absence, and species) and deposition conditions (aboveground or belowground; open or sheltered area) will have different degrees of importance. Further to these will be accessibility to the various methods/protocols in different geographical regions regarding affordability, particularly of the high-throughput techniques such as next-generation sequencing.

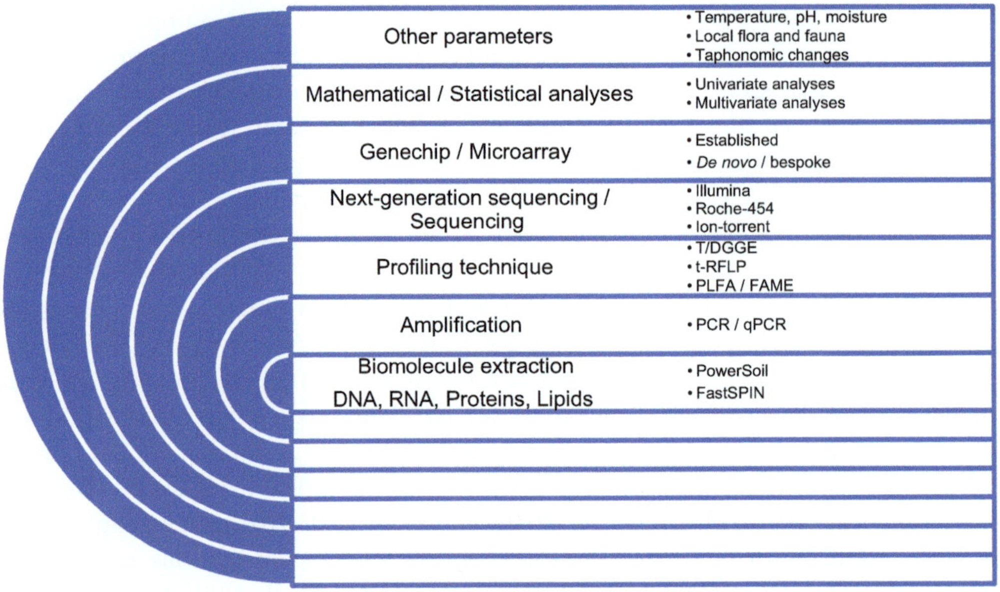

Figure 9.2 Proposed structure for method application in forensic ecogenomics with some example techniques/kits. The schematic takes cognizance that different biomolecules can be targeted but reflects the current practice where analyses are largely DNA based. *FAME*, Fatty acid methyl ester; *PCR*, polymerase chain reaction; *PLFA*, phospholipid fatty acid analysis; *q-PCR*, quantitative PCR; *T/DGGE*, temperature/denaturing gradient gel electrophoresis; *T-RFLP*, terminal restriction fragment length polymorphism.

Ultimately, functional microbial communities can be targeted to identify the stage of decomposition, especially in subsurface scenarios where body mass loss analysis would be less straightforward, and therefore deduce the time since deposition. Further to this would be potential analyses for the duration of the cadaver decomposition island (CDI). For example, and although considered in different soil ecology contexts (Morriën et al., 2016; Shi et al., 2015), assessing the CDI longevity regarding measurable impact on the surrounding micro-/macrobial community structure and ecosystem function would have the attendant value of locating clandestine burials even after the decomposing material has been removed, degraded, or mineralized. This would naturally take into account site-specific defining parameters such as: local climatic conditions; soil type, pH, temperature, and moisture content; and the local flora and fauna in relation to cover and scavenger activity, for example. It is highly unlikely that a consensus will be reached; instead decisions will most certainly be made on a site-specific or case-by-case basis. These deliberations will then inform decisions on which forensic subdisciplines must be applied in parallel to generate the requisite robustness of intelligence gathering for enhanced postmortem interval/postburial interval/postmortem submergence interval estimations generally and for subsequent court proceedings in particular.

SUMMARY

Captive and emotive news headlines such as "Casey Anthony trial: witness rebuts human decomposition in car's trunk" by J. Hopper (ABC News, 2011), "Goo of death helps solve mystery of headless corpse" by W. Parry (Life Science, 2011), and "Would YOU leave your body to medical science if it meant going to a 'body farm'? Human remains left to decompose in the open air in the name of research" by A. Williams (Daily Mail, 2015) continue to attract and highlight the need for collaborative and concerted efforts by key stakeholders such as researchers, practitioners, police forces, and the courts. This is exemplified further and captured appropriately in Stuff.co.nz News (https://twitter.com/NZStuff, 2017) where New Zealand police deputy chief executive for strategy Mr. M. Evans stated that "Being able to work alongside academia will enable us to not only improve our research capability, but also influence future policing decisions using evidence and insights gained from research." Similarly, scientific and scientifically informed reports in magazines such as by Wald (2015) and Ash (2016) in *Nature* and *Science*, respectively, should ensure a greater appreciation of the potential and existing knowledge gaps to practitioners and the wider public, i.e., beyond the microbial ecology, forensic, and crime scene science research community. Furthermore, deliberations and exchanges such as by the USNRC Committee on Identifying the Needs of the Forensic Sciences Community (2009), Silverman (2011), and UK House of Commons Science and Technology Committee (2016), even if others such as the US National Commission on Forensic Science are being closed (Grant, 2017), could ensure that the relevant balance is achieved between how research informs policy and the courts, and vice versa.

Increases in the number of peer-reviewed articles, book chapters, and books reflect the recognized value, adoption, and application of methods from microbial and macrobial ecology to develop and expand the crime scene investigation toolkit. Discussions in these outputs highlight the utility, strengths, and limitations of the different techniques including for the cross-, multi-, and transdisciplinary forensic ecogenomics topic. Toward standardization in forensic ecogenomics, a protocol is proposed but with full cognizance that there may never be a consensus on which specific methods are used by different researchers and practitioners. Ultimately, the requirements for specific crime scenes and subsequent court proceedings where relevant and the involved (registered) analytical laboratory will dictate which components of the approach are adopted. Finally, the research and application questions that need to be addressed by concerted multidisciplinary approaches have been considered and it is anticipated that they will continue to drive exciting new developments and applications in cutting-edge forensic and crime scene science.

The actual value of the novel and/or updated suite of crime scene investigative techniques lies in their adoption in real scenes of crime, including to inform subsequent court proceedings. This will be realized fully and only through an underpinning of relevantly robust discourse on, and development of, requisite policy statements at local/regional, national, and international levels. Embedded in research initiatives underpinned by forensic ecogenomics are ethical considerations, hence the requirements for more human taphonomic facilities in other countries beyond the United States, Australia, and latterly the Netherlands. Therefore, and as considered for the biological sciences (Casadevall et al., 2016), a clear roadmap or framework will be required among researchers initially, and in collaboration with practitioners in the long term, toward the adoption of forensic ecogenomics and the other forensic subdisciplines in real scenes of crime (e.g., Arnaldos et al., 2005) and the courts. Critical analysis will be necessary for any existing policy statements, those likely to be drawn and those that need to be made, together with their differences and their relevance to different police forces, countries, societies, and possibly geopolitical regions. The framework and underpinning discourse must still be pursued despite the full cognizance/acknowledgment of the inevitable challenges of reconciling the needs of different stakeholders, i.e., researchers, practitioners, policy developers, and legal fraternities.

REFERENCES

Arnaldos, M.I., García, M.D., Romera, E., Presa, J.J., Luna, A., 2005. Estimation of postmortem interval in real cases based on experimentally obtained entomological evidence. Forensic Science International 149, 57–65.

Ash, C., 2016. Decomposition spawns a microbial zoo. Science 351 (6269), 134–136.

Astudillo-García, C., Bell, J.J., Webster, N.S., Glasi, B., Jompa, J., Montoya, J.M., Taylor, M.W., 2017. Evaluating the core microbiota in complex communities: a systematic investigation. Environmental Microbiology 19 (4), 1450–1462.

Benschop, C.C.G., Quaak, F.C.A., Boon, M.E., Sijen, T., Kuiper, I., 2012. Vaginal microbial flora analysis by next generation sequencing and microarrays; can microbes indicate vaginal origin in a forensic context? International Journal of Legal Medicine 126, 303–310.

Bergmann, R.C., Ralebitso-Senior, T.K., Thompson, T.J.U., 2014. An RNA-based analysis of changes in biodiversity indices in response to *Sus scrofa domesticus* decomposition. Forensic Science International 241, 190–194.

Bergström, A., Licht, T.R., Wilcks, A., Andersen, J.B., Schmidt, L.R., Grønlund, H.A., Vigsnaes, L.K., Michaelsen, K.F., Bahl, M.I., 2012. Introducing gut low-density array (GULDA) – a validated approach for qPCR-based intestinal microbial community analysis. FEMS Microbiology Letters 337 (1), 38–47.

Blaser, M.J., 2010. Harnessing the power of the human microbiome. Proceedings of the National Academy of Sciences of the United States of America 107, 6125–6126.

Breton, H., Kirkwood, A.E., Carter, D.O., Forbes, S.L., 2016. The impact of carrion decomposition on the fatty acid methyl ester (FAME) profiles of soil microbial communities in southern Canada. Canadian Society of Forensic Science Journal 49 (1), 1–18.

Budowle, B., Murch, R., Chakraborty, R., 2005. Microbial forensics: the next forensic challenge. International Journal for Legal Medicine 119, 317–330.

Budowle, B., Schutzer, S.E., Morse, S.A., Martinez, K.F., Chakraborty, R., Marrone, B.L., Messenger, S.L., Murch, R.S., Jackson, P.J., Williamson, P., Harmon, R., Velsko, S.P., 2008. Criteria for validation of methods in microbial forensics. Applied and Environmental Microbiology 74 (18), 5599–5607.

Bull, I.D., Berstan, R., Vass, A., Evershed, R.P., 2009. Identification of a disinterred grave by molecular and stable isotope analysis. Science and Justice 49, 142–149.

Camarinha-Silva, A., Wos-Oxley, M.L., Jáuregui, R., Becker, K., Pieper, D.H., 2011. Validating T-RFLP as a sensitive and high-throughput approach to assess bacterial diversity patterns in human anterior nares. FEMS Microbiology Ecology 79, 98–108.

Carter, D.O., Tomberlin, J.K., Benbow, M.E., Metcalf, J.L. (Eds.), 2017. Forensic Microbiology. Wiley, West Sussex.

Casadevall, A., Ellis, L.M., Davies, E.W., McFall-Ngai, M., Fang, F.C., 2016. A framework for improving the quality of research in the biological sciences. mBio 7 (4). http://dx.doi.org/10.1128/mBio.01256-16. e01256-16.

Chen, D., Mauk, M., Qiu, X., Liu, C., Kim, J., Ramprasad, S., Ongagna, S., Abrams, W., Malamud, D., Corstjens, P., Bau, H.H., 2010. An integrated, self-contained microfluidic cassette for isolation, amplification, and detection of nucleic acids. Biomedical Microdevices 12 (4), 705–719.

Chimutsa, M., Olakanye, A.O., Thompson, T.J., Ralebitso-Senior, T.K., 2015. Soil fungal community shift evaluation as a potential cadaver decomposition indicator. Forensic Science International 17, 155–159.

Cobaugh, K.L., Schaeffer, S.M., DeBruyn, J.M., 2015. Functional and structural succession of soil microbial communities below decomposing human cadavers. PLoS One 10 (6), e0130201.

Congiu, L., Chicca, M., Cella, R., Rossi, R., Bernacchia, G., 2000. The use of random amplified polymorphic DNA (RAPD) markers to identify strawberry varieties: a forensic application. Molecular Ecology 9 (2), 229–232.

Dickson, G.C., Poulter, R.T., Mass, E.W., Probert, P.K., Keiser, J.A., 2011. Marine bacterial succession as a potential indicator of postmortem submersion interval. Forensic Science International 209 (1–3), 1–10.

Djuric, M., Varljen, T., Stanojevic, A., Stojkovic, O., 2008. DNA typing from handled items. Forensic Science International: Genetics Supplement Series 1, 411–412.

Fierer, N., Hamady, M., Lauber, C.L., Knight, R., 2008. The influence of sex, handedness, and washing on the diversity of hand surface bacteria. Proceedings of the National Academy of Sciences of the United States of America 105, 17994–17999.

Fierer, N., Lauber, C., Zhou, N., McDonald, D., Costello, E., Knight, R., 2010. Forensic identification using skin bacterial communities. Proceedings of the National Academy of Sciences of the United States of America 107, 6477–6481.

Finley, S.J., Benbow, M.E., Javan, G.T., 2015a. Potential applications of soil microbial ecology and next-generation sequencing in criminal investigations. Applied Soil Ecology 88, 69–78.

Finley, S.J., Benbow, M.E., Javan, G.T., 2015b. Microbial communities associated with human decomposition and their potential use as postmortem clocks. International Journal of Legal Medicine 129 (3), 623–632.

Finucane, B.C., 2007. Mummies, maize, and manure: multi-tissue stable isotope analysis of late prehistoric human remains from the Ayacucho Valley, Peru. Journal of Archaeological Science 34, 2115–2124.

Fraser, I., Meier-Augenstein, W., Kalin, R.M., 2006. The role of stable isotopes in human identification: a longitudinal study into the variability of isotopic signals in human hair and nails. Rapid Communications in Mass Spectrometry 20, 1109–1116.

Grant, B., 2017. Forensics left in lurch by sessions. The Scientist. www.the-scientist.com.

Grice, E.A., Kong, H.H., Conlan, S., Deming, C.B., Davis, J., Young, A.C., NISC Comparative Sequencing Program, Bouffard, G.G., Blakesley, R.W., Murray, P.R., Green, E.D., Turner, M.L., Seger, J.A., 2009. Topographical and temporal diversity of the human skin microbiome. Science 324, 1190–1192.

Hong, P.Y., Yap, G.C., Lee, B.W., Chua, K.Y., Liu, W.T., 2009a. Hierarchical oligonucleotide primer extension (HOPE) as a time- and cost effective approach for the quantitative determination of *Bifidobacterium* spp in infant feces. Applied and Environmental Microbiology 75, 2573–2576.

Hong, P.Y., Wu, J.H., Liu, W.T., 2009b. A high-throughput and quantitative hierarchical oligonucleotide primer extension (HOPE)-based approach to identify sources of faecal contamination in water bodies. Environmental Microbiology 11, 1672–1681.

Hopper, J., June 2011. Casey Anthony trial: witness rebuts human decomposition in car's trunk. ABC News. abcnews.go.com.

Horswell, J., Cordiner, S.J., Maas, E.W., Martin, T.M., Sutherland, K.B.W., Spier, T.W., Nogales, B., Osborn, A.M., 2002. Forensic comparison of soils by bacterial community DNA profiling. Journal of Forensic Sciences 47 (2), 350–353.

House of Commons Science and Technology Committee, 2016. Forensic Science Strategy: Fourth Report of Session 2016-2017. House of Commons, UK.

Howard, G.T., Duos, B., Watson-Horzelski, E.J., 2010. Characterization of the soil microbial community associated with the decomposition of swine carcass. International Biodeterioration and Biodegradation 64 (4), 300–304.

Jansson, J.K., Neufeld, J.D., Moran, M.A., Gilbert, J.A., 2012. Omics for understanding microbial functional dynamics. Environmental Microbiology 14 (1), 1–3.

Kakizaki, E., Takahama, K., Seo, Y., Kozawa, S., Sakai, M., Yukawa, N., 2008. Marine bacteria comprise a possible indicator of drowning in seawater. Forensic Science International 176, 236–247.

Kim, T., Mundt, E., 2011. Metagenomic analysis of intestinal microbiomes in chickens. Methods in Molecular Biology 733, 185–194.
Kong, H.H., 2011. Skin microbiome: genomics-based insights into the diversity and role of skin microbes. Trends in Molecular Medicine 17 (6), 320–328.
Krakat, N., Anjum, R., Demirel, B., Schröder, P., 2016. Methodological flaws introduce strong bias into molecular analysis of microbial populations. Journal of Applied Microbiology 122, 364–377.
Krause, R., Moissl-Eichinger, C., Halwachs, B., Gorkiewicz, G., Berg, G., Valentin, T., Prattes, J., Högenauer, C., Zollner-Schwetz, I., 2017. Mycobiome in the lower respiratory tract – a clinical perspective. Frontiers in Microbiology 7, 2169. http://dx.doi.org/10.3389/fmicb.2016.02169.
Kuiper, I., 2016. Microbial forensics: next-generation sequencing as catalyst. EMBO Reports 17 (8), 1085–1087.
Lamendella, R., Santo Domingo, J.W., Yannarell, A.C., Ghosh, S., Di Giovanni, G., Mackie, R., Oerther, D.B., 2009. Evaluation of swine-specific PCR assays used for fecal source tracking and analysis of molecular diversity of swine-specific "Bacteroidales" populations. Applied and Environmental Microbiology 75, 5787–5796.
Lang, J.M., Erb, R.E., Pechal, J.L., Wallace, J.R., McEwan, R.W., Benbow, M.E., 2016. Microbial biofilm community variation in flowing habitats: potential utility as bioindicators of postmortem submersion intervals. Microoganisms 4, 1. http://dx.doi.org/10.3390/microorganisms4010001.
Lerner, A., Shor, Y., Vinokurov, A., Okon, Y., Jurkevitch, E., 2006. Can denaturing gradient gel electrophoresis (DGGE) analysis of amplified 16S rDNA of soil bacterial populations be used in forensic investigations? Soil Biology & Biochemistry 38, 1188–1192.
Li, M., Zhou, H., Hua, W., Wang, B., Wang, S., Zhao, G., Li, L., Zhao, L., Pang, X., 2009. Molecular diversity of *Bacteroides* spp in human fecal microbiota as determined by group-specific 16S rRNA gene clone library analysis. Systematic and Applied Microbiology 32 (3), 193–200.
Liu, R.H., Yang, J., Lenigk, R., Bonanno, J., Grodzinski, P., 2004. Self-contained, fully integrated biochip for sample preparation, polymerase chain reaction, amplification, and DNA microarray detection. Analytical Chemistry 76, 1824–1831.
Macdonald, C.A., Ang, R., Cordiner, S.J., Horswell, J., 2011. Discrimination of soils at regional and local levels using bacterial and fungal T-RFLP profiling. Journal of Forensic Sciences 56 (1), 61–69.
MacDonald, L.M., Singh, B.K., Thomas, N., Brewer, M.J., Campbell, C.D., Dawson, L.A., 2008. Microbial DNA profiling by multiplex terminal restriction fragment length polymorphism for forensic comparison of soil and the influence of sample condition. Journal of Applied Microbiology 105 (3), 813–821.
Meier-Augenstein, W., 2002. Stable isotope analysis of fatty acids by gas chromatography–isotope ratio mass spectrometry. Analytica Chimica Acta 465, 63–79.
Meier-Augenstein, W., 2010. Stable Isotope Forensics: An Introduction to the Forensic Application of Stable Isotope Analysis. John Wiley & Sons Ltd, West Sussex.
Meier-Augenstein, W., Kemp, H.F., Hardie, S.M.L., 2012. Detection of counterfeit scotch whisky by ^{2}H and ^{18}O stable isotope analysis. Food Chemistry 133 (3), 1070–1074.
Metcalf, J.L., Xu, Z.Z., Weiss, S., Lax, S., Van Treuren, W., Hyde, E.R., Song, S.J., Amir, A., Larsen, P., Sangwan, N., Haarmann, D., Humphrey, G.C., Ackermann, G., Thompson, L.R., Lauber, C., Bibat, A., Nicholas, C., Gebert, M.J., Petrosino, J.F., Reed, S.C., Gilbert, J.A., Lynne, A.M., Bucheli, S.R., Carter, D.O., Knight, R., 2016. Microbial community assembly and metabolic function during mammalian corpse decomposition. Science 351 (6269), 158–162.
Moreno, L.I., Mill, D., Fetscher, J., John-Williams, K., Meadows-Jantz, L., McCord, B., 2011. The application of amplicon length heterogeneity PCR (LH-PCR) for monitoring the dynamics of soil microbial communities associated with cadaver decomposition. Journal of Microbiological Methods 84, 388–393.
Morriën, E., Hannula, S.E., Snoek, L.B., Helmsing, N.R., Zweers, H., de Hollander, M., Soto, R.L., Bouffaud, M.-L., Buée, M., Dimmers, W., Duyts, H., Geisen, S., Girlanda, M., Griffiths, R.I., Jørgensen, H.-B., Jensen, J., Plassart, P., Redecker, D., Schmelz, R.M., Schmidt, O., Thomson, B.C., Tisserant, E., Uroz, S., Winding, A., Bailey, M.J., Bonkowski, M., Faber, J.H., Martin, F., Lemanceau, P., de Boer, W., van Veen, J.A., van der Putten, W.H., 2016. Soil networks become more connected and take up more carbon as nature restoration progresses. Nature Communications 8, 14349. http://dx.doi.org/10.1038/ncomms14349.
Neufeld, J.D., Wagner, M., Murrell, J.C., 2007. Who eats what, where and when? Isotope-labelling experiments are coming of age. The ISME Journal 1, 103–110.

Newton, R.J., Bootsma, M.J., Morrison, H.G., Sogin, M.L., McLellan, S.L., 2013. A microbial signature approach to identify fecal pollution in the waters off an urbanized coast of Lake Michigan. Microbial Ecology 65 (4), 1011–1023.

Ng, E.-L., Cavagnaro, T.R., 2016. Biochar effects on ecosystems: insights from lipid-based analysis. In: Ralebitso-Senior, T.K., Orr, C.H. (Eds.), Biochar Application: Essential Soil Microbial Ecology. Elsevier, Amsterdam, pp. 55–77.

NRC Committee on Identifying the Needs of the Forensic Sciences Community, 2009. Strengthening Forensic Science in the United States: A Path Forward. The National Academies Press.

Olakanye, A.O., Nelson, A., Ralebitso-Senior, T.K., 2017. A comparative *in situ* decomposition study using still born piglets and leaf litter from a deciduous forest. Forensic Science International 276, 85–92.

Olakanye, A.O., Ralebitso-Senior, T.K., 2017. Subsurface decomposition analysis reveals shifts in soil necrobiome community structure. Forensic Science International (Submitted).

Olakanye, A.O., Thompson, T.J.U., Ralebitso-Senior, T.K., 2014. Changes to soil bacterial profiles as a result of *Sus scrofa domesticus* decomposition. Forensic Science International 245, 101–106.

Olakanye, A.O., Thompson, T., Ralebitso-Senior, T.K., 2015. Shifts in soil biodiversity – a forensic comparison between *Sus scrofa domesticus* and vegetation decomposition. Science and Justice 55 (6), 402–407.

Ottman, N., Smidt, H., de Vos, W.M., Belzer, C., 2012. The function of our microbiota: who is out there and what do they do? Frontiers in Cellular and Infection Microbiology 2 (104), 1–11.

Paliy, O., Agans, R., 2012. Application of phylogenetic microarrays to interrogation of human microbiota. FEMS Microbiology Ecology 79 (1), 2–11.

Parkinson, R.A., Dias, K.R., Horswell, J., Greenwood, P., Banning, N., Tibbett, M., Vass, A.A., 2009. Microbial community analysis of human decomposition on soil. In: Ritz, K., Dawson, L.A., Miller, D. (Eds.), Criminal and Environmental Soil Forensics. Springer, New York, pp. 379–394.

Parry, W., June 7, 2011. Goo of death helps solve mystery of headless corpse. Life Science.

Pasternak, Z., Al-Ashhab, A., Gatica, J., Gafny, R., Avraham, S., Frenk, S., Minz, D., Gillor, O., Jurkevitch, E., 2012. Optimization of molecular methods and statistical procedures for forensic fingerprinting of microbial soil communities. International Research Journal of Microbiology 3 (11), 363–372.

Pechal, J.L., Crippen, T.L., Benbow, M.E., Tarone, A.M., Dowd, S., Tomberlin, J.K., 2014. The potential use of bacterial community succession in forensics as described by high throughput metagenomic sequencing. International Journal of Legal Medicine 128 (1), 193–205.

Quaak, F.C.A., de Graaf, M.M., Weterings, R., Kuiper, I., 2017. Microbial population analysis improves the evidential value of faecal traces in forensic investigations. International Journal of Legal Medicine 131 (1), 45–51.

Quaak, F.C.A., Kuiper, I., 2011. Statistical analysis of bacterial t-RFLP profiles in forensic soil comparisons. Forensic Science International 210 (1–3), 96–101.

Ralebitso-Senior, T.K., Senior, E., Di Felice, R., Jarvis, K., 2012. Waste gas biofiltration: advances and limitations of current approaches in microbiology. Environmental Science and Technology 46 (16), 8542–8573.

Ralebitso-Senior, T.K., Thompson, T.J.U., Carney, H.E., 2016. Microbial ecogenomics and forensic archaeology: new methods for investigating clandestine grave sites. Human Remains & Violence 2 (1), 41–57.

Reeb, V., Kolel, A., McDermott, T.R., Bhattacharya, D., 2011. Good to the bone: microbial community thrives within bone cavities of a bison carcass at Yellowstone National Park. Environmental Microbiology 13, 2403–2415.

Ruffell, A., 2010. Forensic pedology, forensic geology, forensic geoscience, geoforensics and soil forensics. Forensic Science International 202, 9–12.

Shepherd, M.L., Swecker Jr., W.S., Jensen, R.V., Ponder, M.A., 2011. Characterization of the fecal bacteria communities of forage-fed horses by pyrosequencing of 16S rRNA V4 gene amplicons. FEMS Microbiology Letters 326 (1), 62–68.

Shi, S., Nuccio, E., Herman, D.J., Rijkers, R., Estera, K., Li, J., da Rocha, U.N., He, Z., Pett-Ridge, J., Brodie, E.L., Zhou, J., Firestone, M., 2015. Successional trajectories of rhizosphere bacterial communities over consecutive seasons. mBio 6 (4). http://dx.doi.org/10.1128/mBio.00746-15. e00746-15.

Silverman, B., 2011. Research and Development in Forensic Science: A Review. The U.K. Home Office, pp. 1–24.

Stone, D., Blomkvist, P., Hendriksen, N.B., Bonkowski, M., Jørgensen, H.B., Carvalho, F., Dunbar, M.B., Gardi, C., Geisen, S., Griffiths, R., Hug, A.S., Jensen, J., Laudon, H., Mendes, S., Morais, P.V., Orgiazzi, A., Plassart, P., Römbke, J., Rutgers, M., Schmelz, R.M., Sousa, J.P., Steenbergen, E., Suhadolc, M., Winding, A., Zupan, M., Lemanceau, P., Creamer, R.E., 2016. A method of establishing a transect for biodiversity and ecosystem function monitoring across Europe. Applied Soil Ecology 97, 3–11.

Stuart, B.H., Ueland, M., 2017. Decomposition in aquatic environments. In: Schotsmans, E.M.J., Márquez-Grant, N., Forbes, S.L. (Eds.), Taphonomy of Human Remains: Forensic Analysis of the Dead and the Depositional Environment. Wiley & Sons, West Sussex, pp. 235–250.

Stuff.co.nz News @NZStuff, 2017. Police and University of Waikato Form Research Partnership to Tackle Crime. http://dlvr.it/N59W71.

Sun, Y., Perch-Nielsen, I., Dufva, M., Sabourin, D., Bang, D.D., Høgberg, J., Wolff, A., 2012. Direct immobilization of DNA probes on non-modified plastics by UV irradiation and integration in microfluidic devices for rapid bioassay. Analytical and Bioanalytical Chemistry 402 (2), 741–748.

Sundset, M.A., Edwards, J.E., Cheng, Y.F., Senosiain, R.S., Fraile, M.N., Northwood, K.S., Præsteng, K.E., Glad, T., Mathiesen, S.D., Wright, A.-D.G., 2009. Molecular diversity of the rumen microbiome of Norwegian reindeer on natural summer pasture. Microbial Ecology 57 (2), 335–348.

The NIH HMP Working Group, Peterson, J., Garges, S., Giovanni, M., McInnes, P., Wang, L., Schloss, J.A., Bonazzi, V., McEwen, J.E., et al., 2009. Genome Research 19, 2317–2323.

Tomberlin, J.K., Mohr, R., Benbow, M.E., Tarone, A.M., VanLaerhoven, S., 2011. A roadmap for bridging basic and applied research in forensic entomology. Annual Review of Entomology 56, 401–421.

Ueland, M., Breton, H.A., Forbes, S.L., 2014. Bacterial populations associated with early-stage adipocere formation in lacustrine waters. International Journal of Legal Medicine 128 (2), 379–387.

Uitedehaag, S.C.A., Quaak, F.C.A., Kuiper, I., 2016. Soil comparisons using small soil traces, a case report. In: Kars, H., van den Eijkel, L. (Eds.), Soil in Criminal and Environmental Forensics; Proceedings of the Soil Forensics Special 6th European Academy of Forensic Science Conference, The Hague. ISBN: 978-3-319-33113-3, pp. 61–69.

Wald, C., 2015. The soil sleuth. Nature 520, 422–424.

Wallace, J.R., 2015. Aquatic vertebrate carrion decomposition. In: Benbow, M.E., Tomberlin, J.K., Tarone, A.M. (Eds.), Carrion Ecology, Evolution, and Their Applications. CRC Press, Boca Raton, pp. 247–272.

Wang, L., Li, P.C., 2011. Microfluidic DNA microarray analysis: a review. Analytica Chimica Acta 687 (1), 12–27.

Williams, A., November 13, 2015. Would you leave your body to medical science if it meant going to a 'body farm'? Human remains left to decompose in the open air in the name of research. Daily Mail.

Yilmaz, P., Gilbert, J.A., Knight, R., Amaral-Zettler, L., Karsch-Mizrachi, I., Cochrane, G., Nakamura, Y., Sansone, S.A., Glöckner, F.O., Field, D., 2011. The genomic standards consortium: bringing standards to life for microbial ecology. The ISME Journal 5, 1565–2567.

Young, J.M., Rawlence, N.J., Weyrich, L.S., Cooper, A., 2014. Limitations and recommendations for successful DNA extraction from forensic soil samples: a review. Science and Justice 54, 238–244.

Zhou, Y., Gao, H., Mihindukulasuriya, K.A., La Rosa, P.S., Wlie, K.M., Vishnivetskaya, T., Podar, M., Warner, B., Tarr, P.I., Nelson, D.E., Fortenberry, J.D., Holland, M.J., Burr, S.E., Shannon, W.D., Sodergren, E., Weinstock, G.M., 2013. Biogeography of the ecosystems of the healthy human body. Genome Biology 14, R1. http://dx.doi.org/10.1186/gb-2013-14-1-r1.

Zoetendal, E.G., Rajilić-Stojanović, M., de Vos, W.M., 2008. High-throughput diversity and functionality analysis of the gastrointestinal tract microbiota. Gut 57, 1605–1615.

INDEX

"*Note*: Page numbers followed by "f" indicate figures, "t" indicate tables."

G

H

I

Kolibri 360 GmbH
Ferdinand-Jühlke-Straße 7
99095 Erfurt, Deutschland
produktsicherheit@kolibri360.de